Beethoven and the Voice of God

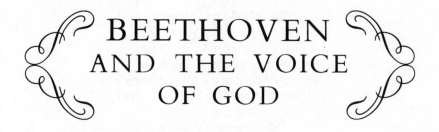

BEETHOVEN
AND THE VOICE
OF GOD

Wilfrid Mellers

New York

OXFORD UNIVERSITY PRESS

1983

First published in Great Britain
by Faber and Faber Limited, 1983
First published in the United States
by Oxford University Press, Inc., 1983

ISBN 0–19–520402–6

Library of Congress Catalog Number: 82–60914

Printed in Great Britain

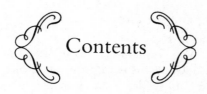

Contents

Preface

This book and its companion volume, *Bach and the Dance of God*, have been thirty years in the writing and are a distillation of analysis classes given throughout my career as university teacher. Originally the analyses were presented orally, at a piano, the spoken word being intimately related to the sound of music. Though this method has obvious advantages over presentation in written form, there's something to be said for a written script which can be reread and an analytical-interpretive comment which can be checked by reference to both text and score—and, if desired, to recording. In the published books the music examples are no more than pointers or momentary alleviations; the analysis can be *fully* intelligible only if read with a score at one's elbow.

As a writer about music I have learned, as have most of us, from Schenker, Tovey and Réti, among others. I suppose I take more risks than they did in that, starting from a fairly—sometimes very—detailed description of what happens in musical terms, I proceed to relate these musical events to their physiological and psychological consequences. Nowadays any attempt to talk about music's 'meanings' in other than technical terms is often deplored; yet it seems to me self-evident that description that goes no further than musical facts can never be more than a trivial occupation. Since music is made by human beings, any musical judgement, however technical, is also psychological: it is not merely improbable, but totally impossible, that musical events could be separable from human experience—thoughts, feelings, actions—conceptualized in other than musical terms. Verbal comment and comparison is entirely valid so long as it stems from a careful delineation of the musical facts; and such subjective elements as enter into one's commentary on music are neither more nor less damaging than those that occur in reference to any human activity. I cannot prove that my account of a problematical work like Beethoven's op. 101 is unequivocally *right*. I can however demonstrate that it is a possible, even probable, deduction from a given sequence of musical events; and I could point to other accounts which would be demonstrably *wrong* in that they did not take account of those musical facts. In any case, if it is worth while to write about music at all—and clearly I believe it is—one has no choice but to have the courage of one's musical and human convictions. Musical analysis cannot and shouldn't be a science, since music itself isn't. Responsibly carried out it may, however, be an aid to human understanding; and is perhaps most fully justified in approaching, with humility, the greatest music so far created by Western man.

Being detailed, the analysis in these studies doesn't make for easy reading, but if it weren't detailed it couldn't be an adequate basis for philosophical and theological extension; and if it weren't thus extended it would be pitifully inadequate to Bach and Beethoven, neither of whom doubted that their music had 'meanings' discussable in terms simultaneously musical, theological and philosophical. Since some reviewers of *Bach and the Dance of God* accused me of distorting Bach's music in order to preach a sermon in support of the True Faith, I should perhaps state unequivocally that I am not and never have been a Christian, and that I subscribe to no creed religious or political. I have tried to understand, on the evidence of their music, what Bach and Beethoven believed, but to respect their beliefs is not necessarily to share them. Like most modern men I'm closer to embryonically and evolutionarily religious Beethoven than I am to Bach, though this is not to make a value judgement between the two composers. Certainly teaching, and therefore verbalizing about, the music of Bach and Beethoven over thirty years has helped me to respond to and enjoy their art and their collateral beliefs more deeply; and I've some evidence to lead me to believe that I've helped my students in helping myself.

W.M.
Highbury Fields, London   *May 1982*

And the eternal voice does, indeed, speak today, just as it did in times immemorial. But just as then, now too, one requires preparation to be able to hear it. As it is written: 'Now, therefore, if ye will hearken, hearken to my voice'. The word 'now' means at whatever moment we hear it.

The Ten Rungs of Hasidic Lore trans. MARTIN BUBER

I heard a murmur, something gone wrong with the silence.

SAMUEL BECKETT

In the midst of the silence there was spoken in me a secret word.

MEISTER ECKHART

Through the hush of air a voice sang to them, low, not rain, not leaves in murmur, like no voice of strings or reeds or whatdoyoucallthem dulcimers ... Good, good to hear: sorrow from each seemed to from both depart when first they heard ... first merciful lovesoft word.

JAMES JOYCE

That was her song, for she was the maker. Then we,
As we beheld her striding there alone,
Knew that there never was a world for her
Except the one she sang and, singing, made.

WALLACE STEVENS

PRELUDE

The world is a King and would be flattered if it is to show favour; but true art is self-willed and cannot take the forms of flattery.

BEETHOVEN: Conversation Book, March 1820

It might seem strange that opinions of weight are found in the work of artists rather than of philosophers. The reason is that artists create through enthusiasm and imagination; there are in us seeds of knowledge, as of fires in a flint; philosophers extract them by way of reason, but artists strike them out by imagination, and then they shine more bright.
The Lord has made three marvels:
things out of nothing (*res ex nihilo*)
free will (*liberum arbitrium*)
and the Man who is God (*Hominem Deum*)

DESCARTES: *Cogitationes privatæ*, 1619

Religion may have been the peculiar means for enabling individual men to enjoy but once the entire self-satisfaction of a God and all his self-redeeming power. Indeed—one may ask—would man have learned at all to get on the tracks of hunger and thirst for *himself*, or to extract satiety and fullness out of *himself*, without that religious schooling and preliminary history? Had Prometheus first to *fancy* that he had stolen the light, and that he did penance for the theft—in order finally to discover that he had created the light, *in that he had longed for the light*, and that not only man, but also God, had been the work of *his* hands and the clay in his hands?

NIETZSCHE: *The Joyful Wisdom*

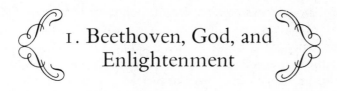

1. Beethoven, God, and Enlightenment

In *The Dance of God* we saw how Bach was a man of faith, both in the sense that he belonged to a society that knew or thought it knew what it believed in, and also in that his mind was of its nature theologically orientated. In another sense, however, both he and his society were marooned in a past era, for his Christianity inherited much from traditions that were already outmoded. Now Beethoven was born into precisely the world that had superseded Bach's; and though this world was politically buoyant, in religious matters its inhabitants were animated by doubt rather than by hope, and by reason rather than by conviction. All the major composers of the nineteenth century except Bruckner were to tend to agnosticism; and even Bruckner's single-hearted though not simple-minded faith was compromised by the fact that, revering Bach and Beethoven equally, he expressed himself most consummately through the divisiveness of sonata rather than through Bachian formal absolutes.

Beethoven was, of course, pre-eminently a composer of sonata strife. Though the last sacraments were administered to him on his death-bed and he remained formally a Roman Catholic, he had little use for institutionalized religion, was suspicious of the feudal hier-archy of the Church, and was spiritually subversive enough to be described by Haydn as an atheist. He didn't so describe himself; and his library contained a number of fashionable devotional and pietistic works by J. S. Sailer, Fenter and Christian Sturm, as well as such a 'personalized' Catholic classic as Thomas à Kempis's *Imitation of Christ*. He was also aware of the work of deeply emotive religious leaders such as Hofbauer and F. L. Z. Werner, who fostered a humanely 'common' belief founded on the penance and person of Christ, in response to the anti-superstitious system of education intro-duced in 1781 by the Patent of Toleration of the 'enlightened' despot, Joseph II. On the other hand the young Beethoven composed an impressive cantata in honour of Joseph as progressive politician; and often referred to the activities of religious zealots in derisive, even dismissive, terms. In the long run it doesn't matter how much or how little Beethoven was affected by the religious ferments of his time; what is of consequence is that by the end of his not very long but spiritually eventful life he had become a religious composer of a kind without precedent. Whether one thinks of him politically or religiously, Beethoven was a part of history, and history in the making. It's true that one cannot fully understand him in humanitarian and social terms if one knows nothing of the impulses that went to make the French Revolution; it's equally true that one cannot fully understand the French Revolution if one has no awareness of Beethoven's music. Similarly in philosophical terms there is a deep affinity between Beethoven and Kant, Schlegel and Hegel, who were his near-contemporaries. But one cannot say that his music 'reflects' their thought, or even the *Zeitgeist* they represent. His music rather renders incarnate some truths that philosophers discuss abstractly, revealing the 'reality' of his age at a level of which it couldn't be intellectually conscious. Only in a superficial sense is Beethoven exceptional in his age, as was Bach in his. The artist is, in I. A. Richards's phrase, the 'point at which the growth of the mind shows itself'; the greater the mind, the more universal the verities revealed will be.

Legend has it that Beethoven was born, in squalid circumstances, of a drunkard and a serving maid. The story is untrue. His father, who was of Flemish extraction, from the province of Brabant, was a professional court musician (albeit a tenor) who took to drink in the face of fairly dire misfortune. His mother, whom Beethoven dearly loved, was admittedly the daughter of a chief cook; the family, however, was of quite cultured Moselle stock, and she, though 'a gentle, serious woman who seldom smiled', was more than the mouse she's commonly depicted as. Yet the legend, like most legends, contains a proportion of allegorical truth: for the temperaments of Beethoven's parents, their relationship or lack of it, and his mother's early death all predestined him to be a loner. Given that background, his exceptional gifts would of themselves make adjustment to the external world precarious, if not impossible. When Beethoven was at the height of his powers, in 1811, Schnyder von Wartensee wrote to Hans Nägeli that, while 'great thoughts drift through Beethoven's mind, he cannot express them in any form but music; he has no command over words. His whole education has been neglected and, apart from his art, he is coarse, but honest and unaffected; he says quite bluntly whatever he may be thinking.' It's too simple to blame this, if blameworthy it be, on lack of formal education, of which Beethoven had virtually none after the age of ten. Bach received, by the standards of his time, an all-round education because in the society in which he was nurtured the purpose of education, and music's part in it, was clearly understood. The society Beethoven was reared in, at Bonn, was not so sure of its values and destiny, being a world in transition. Within this society Beethoven, who unlike Bach was not intellectually precocious except in one direction, learned to read and write with facility, because he needed to. Other academic skills, however, left him cold, and to the end of his days he was unable to cope adequately with arithmetical calculation. As a schoolboy he was 'shy and taciturn, observing and pondering more than he spoke'; even as a grown young man, Ferdinand Ries tells us, he was 'awkward and helpless; his uncouth movements were often destitute of all grace. He seldom took anything into his hands without dropping or breaking it. Thus he frequently knocked his inkwell into the pianoforte, which stood by the side of his writing table. No piece of furniture was safe from him, least of all a costly piece. Everything was overturned, soiled, and destroyed. It is hard to comprehend how he accomplished so much as to be able to shave himself, even leaving out of consideration the number of cuts on his cheeks.' During his maturity Anton Schmith, a physician in Vienna, called him 'as freakish as he is unserviceable'; while even Goethe, in paying respect to his total dedication and commitment to his art, described him as an 'unlicked bear, who found the world despicable but did not thereby render it any the pleasanter either for himself or for other people' (letter to Zelter, 1812).

Yet despite his lack of social graces and shortage of formal schooling, it would be misleading to call Beethoven an uneducated or even an ill-educated man. He read widely, so long as he was following his inclinations rather than a curriculum; and Bonn was a good place for a musician of genius to have been born in. By contemporary standards it was a neat, clean town of about nine thousand inhabitants, ruled by an ecclesiastical Electoral Court that, from the seventeenth century onwards, had proved less oppressive than a political and military tyranny. Men of the Church were devoted to music and theatre, and lavished largesse on both. Even as a schoolboy Beethoven would have heard, since his father was a court musician, a variety of fashionable music, including the operas of Mozart and Gluck, as well as the small-change of Rococo music-theatre, German, French and Italian. By Beethoven's adolescence the city was ruled by the Elector Max Franz, an amiably decent man who cared about education and the arts, and was intelligent enough to delegate authority to men of talent. It was the new Elector who established a university in Bonn, and thus attracted to the town many intellectually distinguished and cultivated people. The young Beethoven became an intimate friend of the brilliant Von Breuning family, initially because he taught the piano to the daughters. That he was accepted as part of the family, staying with them for extended periods, testifies to the magnetic charm that must always have accompanied his boorishness.

Through the Breunings Beethoven gained acquaintance with modern (German Romantic) poetry, and laid the foundations of his knowledge of classical antiquity. His copies of the *Iliad* and the *Odyssey* and of Virgil and Plutarch were as well-thumbed as his copies of Goethe and Schiller; other classical authors later included in his library were Euripides, Ovid, Quintillian, Tacitus, Lucius, Xenophon, Plato and Aristotle. Almost certainly the Breunings encouraged him to extend his philosophical interest to writers of his own day, notably Kant and Hegel. Though we have no evidence that he knew the writings of Rousseau and Voltaire, he talked of them with his aristocratic friends; and discussed politics passionately though without definite commitment. He also acquired Bibles in French and Latin as well as German; and although his devotion to Shakespeare was based on translation, he occasionally quoted the English original with apparent relish. The seeds of all this were sown by the Breunings—and to a lesser degree by Count Waldstein, the earliest and, except for the Archduke Rudolf, the most distinguished of Beethoven's patrons; but they were planted in fertile soil. Though Beethoven was not a disciplined thinker, he certainly thought. His thought was also feeling; both were ultimately realized in musical sound. Since music was his life, it could not possibly be estranged from other human preoccupations.

So although it is not valid to suggest that Beethoven was in any sense a dunderhead, there may be some basis to the conventional notion that the only education that ultimately mattered to him was musical. He wasn't an infant prodigy like Mozart (who was established as pianist and as opera composer by the age of twelve), nor like Schubert (who had created songs of supreme genius by the age of sixteen); but he was precocious enough to give a public recital at the age of seven (his father pretended he was six), and to be appointed assistant court organist at the age of thirteen. Such unusual abilities in youth, fostered by his tyrannical (because vicariously ambitious) father, were probably no asset to Beethoven as a social being; his later distrust of child prodigies, including Liszt, suggests that his own experience was more painful than rewarding. None the less, exceptional natural abilities helped Beethoven to musical self-discovery, with the assistance of one of those surrogate fathers that men of genius often alight on at precisely the right moment in their developing lives. Christian Gottlob Neefe was a prolific and competent, but now forgotten, composer of music in most current forms, especially successful in the field of comic opera. That he was less competent as court organist was all to the good, since Beethoven may have got the job as second organist because Neefe wasn't proficient. He doesn't seem to have been reluctant to relinquish the post; court administrators were delighted, since Beethoven's services were relatively cheap. Neefe was also musical director of the opera house, which had been efficiently reorganized by the new Elector. He helped Beethoven, at the age of seventeen, to a desk in the orchestral violas, where he played in Mozart's operas, as well as in more ephemeral works. Such practical experience within the orchestral pit—especially since the band consisted of extremely able young musicians, recently appointed on tolerable but not lavish salaries—was invaluable training for the young composer. Performance experience ran in harness with the pedagogic training that Neefe offered privately.

Neefe didn't attempt to teach Beethoven the fashionable Rococo styles he himself practised, but introduced him to C. P. E. Bach's famous pedagogic work, and also to the *Well-tempered Clavier* of J. S. Bach. At least, that is what Neefe tells us, though the publisher, Simrock, claimed to have presented the Forty-eight to Beethoven much earlier, and to have heard him play them as a *Wunderkind*. The question of precedence is unimportant; what matters is that under Neefe's guidance the young virtuoso earned fame for his performances of them. It seems clear that Neefe, a mild man who 'hated bad rulers more than pirates', must have had remarkable acumen and an awareness of Beethoven's deepest needs. Relevant to this is the fact that, although Neefe lived in a Catholic community and brought up his children in the Old Faith, he was himself a Calvinist and Freemason. If that seems emotionally and intellectually fuddled, we can recognize the ambiguity as significant in relation to Beethoven. Not surprisingly, Neefe fostered Beethoven's literary and philosophical as well as musical explorations. With the Breunings, he was the most formative influence on Beethoven in youth, and the composer was sensible of his debt to him. In 1793, shortly after he'd settled in Vienna, he wrote to Neefe: 'Thank you for the counsel you have given me in my God-given art. Should I ever become a great man, you will have contributed to it.'

Contributed to it, perhaps; but we note that in Beethoven's view his art is attributable to no man, but to God. He made this evident when he went to Vienna in 1787, ostensibly in pursuit of his musical education. This first visit proved abortive. He had intended to have lessons with Mozart, possibly at the Elector's expense. He certainly played to Mozart, whose response doesn't seem to have been rapturous, though he was impressed with Beethoven's improvisation. Nothing came of any projected studies, as Beethoven was recalled to Bonn by his mother's fatal illness. In any case it is doubtful if Mozart would have been the right teacher for the fiery young Beethoven, whose early music was to start from a rejection of Mozart's civilized equilibrium between lyrical grace and tonal drama. Beethoven's early music was a discovery of his freedom: which is probably why his attempt, after he'd arrived in Vienna in 1792, to take lessons with Haydn also proved unfruitful. By this time Mozart was dead; Haydn, who was thirty-eight when Beethoven was born in 1770, was now sixty, at the pinnacle of his European fame. Yet Haydn advised Beethoven not to publish the C minor trio from his opus 1, the work which Beethoven justifiably thought the most distinguished and original of the set. Beethoven in his turn refused Haydn's invitation to describe himself on the title page as 'pupil of Haydn', on the grounds that he'd learned nothing from his tuition. The two men preserved a mutual respect, for Beethoven didn't deny his roots in the tradition that Haydn supremely embodied, while Haydn recognized a genius that, though more subversively turbulent, was closer to his own than it was to Mozart's. In a general sense Beethoven could profit from the music he heard in Vienna, which included Bach and Handel as well as Haydn, Mozart, Gluck and Italian opera. In particular terms, however, he rejected Haydn as teacher in favour of Johann Schenk, a modest man, a minor composer of comic operas, and a competent pedagogue who at least paid Beethoven the compliment of correcting his exercises. Beethoven was kind enough not to tell Haydn of his defection. He had no need of help from creative genius, having more than enough of his own.

It was Schenk who put Beethoven on to Fux's famous *Gradus ad Parnassum*, which J. S. Bach knew of through J. P. Kirnberger, and on which most of the great composers of the late eighteenth century had been trained. Published in 1725, it purported to teach the rules of counterpoint as practised by Palestrina and his school. But it was not what we would call 'style study', for it reinterpreted both modality and rhythm in the light of Fux's eighteenth-century experience. The isolation of Strict Species Counterpoint from 'real' music became its virtue, since it made no pretence of teaching anything other than a craft. Many teachers, even in our own day, still believe that it has value in the training of a professional composer, whatever kind of music he may ultimately create; although other teachers and especially pupils have resented its 'artificial' discipline, Beethoven didn't. When in 1794 he embarked on more strenuous studies with the celebrated contrapuntist, J. G. Albrechtsberger, he used that teacher's own textbook, which was based on Fux. In the course of a year he worked many exercises in species counterpoint, and wrote a considerable number of fugues to Albrechtsberger's prescription. He also worked exercises in double and triple counterpoint, devoting himself assiduously to this somewhat mechanical task. Albrechtsberger corrected the exercises with a care commensurate with Beethoven's labour. Though it would seem from the sketchbooks that Beethoven never acquired the facility that was Mozart's by birthright, this was the only tuition from which Beethoven, on his own admission, profited. He is even reported to have said (but only on the authority of a newspaper) that he wished he'd studied counterpoint between the ages of seven and eleven, since the time he spent during those years on Thoroughbass was wasted, his harmonic sense being intuitive. However this may be, by the end of his year with Albrechtsberger he had learned what he needed, and was ready to challenge the rules if they conflicted with the truth of his experience. Increasingly they did so; for, as he remarked to Karl Holz, 'To make a fugue requires no particular skill; in my student days I made dozens of them. But the fancy also wishes to assert its privileges, and today a new and really poetical element must be introduced into the traditional form.' Czerny tells us that when Beethoven played, with phenomenal skill, the full scores of Handel or Gluck, he put as much 'polyphony and spirit' into them as he did into his performance of a Bach fugue. His harmonic sense implied 'horizontalization'. By his 'third period' he was not only a natural polyphonist but also one of the greatest contrapuntists in music.

But on his own terms: Beethoven would never allow his daemon to be curbed by precedents, even when he respected them. There is further evidence of this when, later in life, he took lessons in vocal composition, which some said he needed, from Mozart's rival, Salieri.

Contemporary opinion, including Salieri's, admitted that Beethoven handled voices with 'thorough understanding of their specific characteristics as to vowel sounds and so on, but called for a range and endurance far beyond normal requirements'. The chequered history of *Fidelio* is inseparable from the fact that singers trained according to Salieri's standards found it 'the most troublesome thing in the world'. Beethoven refused to alter a note; nor was he more amenable when, in 1823, the soprano soloist in the Missa Solemnis pronounced her part unsingable. Ultimately she capitulated, with the words—deeper and wiser than she realized—'Well then, I suppose we must go on torturing ourselves in the name of God.' In fact, according to Schindler, she didn't, for contemporary singers made their own simplifications in the obvious way: when they could not negotiate a note they remained silent. If they mimed, deaf Beethoven-Christ wouldn't notice, or if he did, might forgive their human frailty. But Beethoven-Yahveh did not forgive, and time has proved that he was right. Though the Mass will never sound in any way easy, because it isn't, all the parts can be sung and played, given total commitment. With spiritual and emotional fortitude, technical problems take their place as means to an end.

This is to anticipate. When Beethoven arrived in Vienna he behaved and was received like a young lion, but made no claim to divine infallibility. He came under favourable auspices, as court organist and pianist to the Emperor's uncle, as a pupil of the esteemed Haydn, and as a protégé of Count Waldstein, through whom he had access to the highest circles of society. Not for long, however, did he need such crutches; within a few years he was on his own, without Church appointment like Bach, or State appointment like Handel or Haydn. A man of the New Age, he was to live on his own superabundant gifts, about which he fortunately had no doubts. Ries tells us that a reverential friend, examining the C minor string quartet of opus 18, timidly pointed out that in one bar parallel fifths seemed to have crept in. Beethoven truculently demanded what was wrong about that: to which the friend stuttered that the 'rules' did not permit them. Beethoven retorted: 'Then *I* permit them'; for despite his respect for vital tradition, he knew that he was the instrument through which tradition must be remade. The avoidance of parallel fifths, or any musical technique, has meaning only in relation to an end. Only man himself can arbitrate as to the validity of these ends, so every musical judgement is also moral. When Ignaz Moscheles wrote at the conclusion of his laboriously copied score of *Fidelio*: 'Finished, with the help of God', Beethoven angrily obliterated the words with the counter-comment, 'Man, help thyself!' There is no fundamental distinction between this plea for self-reliance in artistic matters and Beethoven's incredulous or wry rebuke to Goethe, who accepted the bowing and scraping of the nobility as properly due to a titular Lord, whereas in Beethoven's view it should have been addressed to the poet and the composer.

Such self-reliance is reconcilable with true humility, which is that due to God and to Art. In social and political terms, however, Beethoven was a revolutionary in a revolutionary era. He believed, theoretically, in liberty and fraternity; and in the equality of people spiritually and intellectually distinguished—without reference to social status, since he had no doubt that he was the peer of, if not superior to, the aristocratic patrons whom he counted among his friends. In effect this qualified his belief in liberty and fraternity: some unequal people didn't deserve liberty because they wouldn't know what to do with it, while with many others fraternity was impossible, since their restricted and restrictive values would also limit the liberty of Beethoven. He mistrusted 'Establishment' and believed in minorities, because ultimately he believed in a minority of one—himself. Certainly in the Austria of his day, especially after the Carlsbad Decrees of 1822, it was evident that the society Beethoven lived in was savagely repressive; Frida Knight has even argued that Beethoven's nonproductive period in the immediately preceding years may have been attributable to economic and political causes as well as to a psychological crisis from which they were inseparable. When the new Emperor Francis I addressed a congress of teachers at Laibach he spoke in terms as unequivocally philistine as any Nazi: 'I do not need savants but good honest citizens. Your task is to teach young men to be this. He who serves me must teach what I order him. If anyone cannot do this, or comes with new ideas, he can go, or I will remove him.' Small wonder that Franz Grillparzer wrote in Beethoven's Conversation Books: 'Musicians are lucky, they don't have to bother about the censors. But if only the censors knew what the musicians are thinking about as they compose!' Grillparzer, who was to speak the oration at Beethoven's funeral, found his position as civil servant jeopardized because of supposedly subversive politics in his play *König Ottakars Glück*. Anton Schindler, Beethoven's student, disciple and secretary, had spent a year in prison for political activity, and repeatedly expressed anxiety about the composer's reckless public pronouncements. Metternich himself thought Beethoven, though not dangerous, sufficiently suspect to have him spied on; but this may have been more because dictators are mistrustful of any oddity of appearance or eccentricity in behaviour than because Beethoven had given evidence of subversion. Beethoven was indeed arrested and briefly imprisoned late in life (1821), having been mistaken for a vagrant while wandering the streets drunk on composition. '*Ein Lump sind Sie: so sieht der Beethoven nicht aus*', grunted the policeman. He was released as soon as his identity was proved: politicians and police were then, as now, ill-equipped to appreciate the sense in which Beethoven's music, unlike his actions and opinions, was and is subversive. Revolutionary though he was, Beethoven made some (unjustified) pretensions to nobility of rank; what the supporters of Establishment could not understand, and therefore feared, was Beethoven's deeper (justified) claim when, pointing to his head and heart, he said: 'My nobility is here, and here'.

For the revolution with which Beethoven was concerned was not at bottom political, but psychological: the destiny of Europe was being decided not on the battlefield of Waterloo, but in Beethoven's mind. Superficially the era into which Beethoven was born, though fraught with religious doubt, was optimistic: post-Renaissance man's confidence in his intellectual and sensuous powers reached an apex in the Enlightenment's belief that human life could be governed by reason or by intuition, or by a mixture of both. Voltaire was the arch-priest of sceptical intelligence and of Reason. Rousseau, would-be child of Nature, was the saint of sensuous spontaneity. Beethoven, communing with Nature as a refuge from human intractabilities, had more in common with Rousseau than he had with Voltaire, but he had no truck with half-baked libertarianism, and revered Nature moralisticly in that it could be a 'school for the heart'. (This phrase was heavily underscored in Beethoven's dog-eared copy of Sturm's book, which proclaimed that 'Nature teaches us in a very enlightened manner the obligations to God, to ourselves, and to our fellow men that it is our duty to fulfil. . . . Here shall I learn to know God and in this knowledge of Him to find a foretaste of Heaven.') To apprehend the limitations of Reason was one thing; to abdicate from intellectual control was another, to which Beethoven could hardly subscribe, since he had the most formidable intellect ever to manifest itself in musical terms.

Nature, for men of the Enlightenment, whether they were self-

conscious intellectuals such as Diderot, Voltaire and the Encycloped-
ists, or confessional instinctives such as Rousseau, was never merely
the phenomena of the material world outside human institutions; it
was rather the whole field of man's response to and experience of his
environment. In this context it is therefore useful to consider the
relationship between Beethoven and the German philosophers,
notably Kant and Hegel, who were his contemporaries. Kant's major
writings all appeared during Beethoven's lifetime, and we know that
the composer owned some of them, even though he refused to attend
Kant's public lectures. As the philosopher put it in *Religion within the
limits of Reason alone* (1793), he, as the apostle of Reason, believed that
'there are mysteries which are hidden things in nature (*arcana*) and
there can be mysteries (secrecies, secrets) in politics which *ought* not to
be known publicly; but both *can*, after all, be known to us, in as much
as they rest on empirical causes. There can be no mystery with respect
to what all men are in duty bound to know (i.e. what is moral). Only
with respect to that which God alone can do and the performance of
which exceeds our capacity, and therefore our duty, can there be a
genuine, that is a holy mystery (*mysterium*) of religion; and it may well
be expedient merely for us to know and understand that there is such a
mystery, not to comprehend it.'

Kant thus admits the possibility of a numinal reality that cannot be
grasped either through reason or through intuition, but points out that
'although physical teleology impels us to seek a theology, it cannot
produce one, however far we may investigate nature through experience. The most we can hope is to give 'sufficient ground of proof to
our theoretical reflective judgement to *assume* the being of an intelligent World-Cause'. What we can analyse, through reason, is the nature
of the physical world, 'the forms of space and time'; what we may
acquire, from that analysis, is the sense of an ethically moral law and of
a duty to obey it. A moral quality may be thought of as a transcendent
idea because it may exist independently of the man who conceives
it, since it belongs to a numinal man whose 'life is in Heaven'. This is
what is meant by 'The kingdom of God cometh not with obser-
vation: Neither shall they say Lo here! or, lo there! for, behold, the
kingdom of God is within you' (Luke 17: 20–1). A rational religion
presupposes an Invisible Church to which all 'right-thinking' men
belong by virtue of their capacity for thought. These men are subject
to the Invisible Church's moral law, while at the same time being
freely responsible agents in relation to it. 'There are only two cardinal

principles', according to Kant, 'in all metaphysics: the ideality of space and time and the reality of the concept of freedom. . . . The idea of freedom is the *only* concept of the supersensible that proves its reality in nature.'

Given this philosophical basis for the concept of freedom and duty in Beethoven's day, we can appreciate that the composer's frequent references to such concepts may not be the pious platitudes they appear to be: in being Kant rather than cant, they have another dimension, which accords with that manifest in Beethoven's music. We may deplore Beethoven's disapproval (reported by Seyfried) of Mozart's *Don Giovanni* on the grounds of its salacious subject; but when he approves of *The Magic Flute* we know, from the evidence of the *Missa Solemnis*, that it is not the surface morality he is concerned with but, in the profoundest sense, a way of life and death. As early as 1793 Beethoven had written in a friend's autograph album:

> I am not wicked, fiery blood
> is all my malice, and my crime is youth.
>
> Wicked I am not, truly I am not wicked:
> though wild upsurgings often plead against my heart,
> my heart is good.
>
> To help wherever one can,
> love liberty above all things,
> never deny the truth
> even at the foot of the throne.

There is evidence that, as he grew older, Beethoven tried to live up to that exhortation, and succeeded better, for all his paranoid delusions, than most of us would have done. It is an achievement that calls for no apology.

There is, however, a deeper dimension to the relation between Beethoven and Kant than a concern with humanitarian ethics. It lies in the fact that Kant's view that perceptions without conceptions are inoperative implies that man is of his nature an *active* being. Freedom is 'supersensible', but freedom of choice is a human activity, and of all men Beethoven is supremely the activist. He owned, and seems to have valued, Kant's *Natural History and Theory of the Firmament*: a comprehensive cosmology which provides a link with Hegel, whose relationship to Beethoven is both more potent and more direct. Hegel was born in 1770, the same year as Beethoven, and his most crucial book, *The Phenomenology of Spirit*, published in 1806, was gestated during the very years in which Beethoven was working through the first of his two spiritual crises. Hegel had been trained as a theologian as well as philosopher. Not surprisingly, his theology was permeated by rationalistic deism and Kantian ethics; indeed in his early years he seems to have regarded Jesus as exclusively a moral teacher, almost as a precursor of Kant! But Hegel came to feel, and then to think, that the Kantian concept of Law and Duty was inadequate; and to believe that, in substituting love for law, Christ did not abrogate morality, but merely freed it from legal content. The germ of this re-formation was in Luther, though Hegel gave it philosophical validity in demonstrating that Christ, through love, could overcome the otherwise unbridgeable gulf between man and God, finite and infinite. The Absolute is infinite life, and love is the consciousness of the unity of this life with itself, with nature, with mankind and with history. This creative life, which bears the Many within its Oneness, is called God or Spirit.

So the Absolute is not an impenetrable reality existing above or beyond its manifestations; it *is* its self-manifestation. Reality comes to know itself in the human spirit, since the human mind, though finite, is also more than finite. In this process Hegel traces three main stages. The first he calls *Bewusstsein*, by which he means consciousness of the object as existing independently of the subject. The second stage he names *Selbstbewusstsein*, by which he means the consciousness of self in relation to other selves (i.e. social consciousness). The third stage he calls *Vernunft*, by which he implies a synthesis of the two previous stages. This is of course a gross oversimplification, almost to the point of parody, of Hegel's argument; it serves, however, to isolate the elements in Hegelian thought that are peculiarly relevant to Beethoven. For in attempting to understand the functioning of his own mind, Hegel came to see that, as soon as consciousness introspects on itself, it inevitably separates the internal world from external reality. The more this duality is encouraged, the wider will the breach grow, until there are two separate realities: the one an order ideally envisaged within the mind, the other a chaos of sense impressions and un-coordinated or ill-coordinated actions. Hegel called this state *das unglückliche Bewusstsein*, the unhappy consciousness; and knew that it is a perennial human condition, though one comparatively easy to deal with when people live in communities dominated by shared

assumptions, and by the acceptance of a Law which they imagine to
be superhuman. Such conditions did not obtain in a society dominated, as was Hegel's and Beethoven's, by that freedom of moral
choice which was a legacy of Protestant ethics. This must engender
alarm, but is no cause for despair: on the contrary it offers man his
greatest challenge, since the three phases of consciousness may
become a resolution of 'Faustian' man's pilgrimage. In the first stage
the subject sees the object as external to itself; in the second stage the
subject turns back on itself as a finite self; in the third stage it sees
nature as the objective expression of infinite spirit (God), with which
it is itself united. To discover God becomes a discovery of the Self;
the divided spirit seeks, and finds, the Whole. 'God cannot be equated
with man. For God is Being, the Totality, and man is not. But the
Totality comes actually to know itself in and through the spirit of
man. Ultimately this cannot be achieved by thinking about it, only
by living it.' The Absolute in itself—Yahveh's 'I am that I am'—is a
logical idea which is non-temporal; if we try to conceive of the
wholly indeterminate, Being passes into Not-being. Being and
Not-being each disappears into its opposite; their truth is thus the
'immediate disappearing of the one into the other'. Movement from
Being to Not-being and back is Becoming: which is thus the synthesis of Being and Not-being, their ultimate unity. So the concept of
the Absolute as Being is really the concept of the Absolute as Becoming: which is self-development.

This bears directly on Hegel's philosophy of art, wherein spirit and
matter, subjectivity and objectivity, merge in the dialectical process of
becoming, which is self-realization. Historically, he regarded the
evolution of art as itself a dialectical process. The first stage, conceptually but not necessarily chronologically, he calls *symbolic*, in which
meaning is suggested rather than expressed; most primitive art comes
into this category, though Hegel educes as his supreme example
ancient Egyptian art, wherein the Sphinx is the 'objective riddle', the
'symbol of the symbolic itself'. The second stage he calls *classical*,
wherein Spirit is rendered 'concrete' in the self-conscious individual
spirit, whose sensuous incarnation is the human body. Anthropo-
morphoid Greek art, especially sculpture, is the prototype. The third
stage Hegel terms *romantic*, wherein the infinite Spirit tends to overflow its sensuous embodiment. This is not because, as with symbolic
art, Spirit remains an enigma, uncomprehended and incomprehensible; it is rather that Spirit, having been apprehended for what it is, the

infinitude of God, cannot be materially contained. This is why Hegel believed that romantic art must involve movement, conflict, growth. Spirit must die in order to live; and in this sense romantic art must be inseparable from religion, and from Christianity in particular. Hegel's view of spirit has thus grown far beyond the traditional equation, common to the Greeks, to Pauline New Testament theology, and to Kant, between spirit, reason and the power of moral judgement. Spirit is now also a supernatural power beyond reason; it is knowledge which is also vision, capable even of physical manifestations such as glossolalia and prophecy. Romantic art, in Hegel's sense, is effectively incarnate in poetry (he mentions Shakespeare as the supreme exemplar, and might have added bardic Blake); and still more in music, an art which, since it can exist only in time, has no choice but to be a process of Becoming.

Of all musicians none answers more comprehensively to Hegel's prescription than Beethoven. That he was an *unglückliches Bewusstsein* is evident throughout his life. Goethe's Faust exclaims 'From desire I rush to satisfaction; and in satisfaction I yearn after desire'; this Faustian duality embraces the aspirational and inspirational 'two selves' within Beethoven, wherein the most violent contradictions could co-exist. We have noted his social ineptitude, even in childhood, before deafness extenuated his boorish behaviour. As an adult his personality seems no less contrarious; and it is significant that, although we know a lot about Beethoven as a human being, since he was the kind of man who, once met, could not readily be forgotten, accounts of him by his contemporaries, though vivid, tend to be contradictory. This applies to superficial matters such as his personal appearance. Some commentators say that he dressed elegantly, even foppishly, in youth; others see him always in the daimonic disarray typical of his later years. Some find him scrupulously clean, even neat, through the period when his eccentricity of dress was most pronounced; others excuse his physical filthiness only in relation to the presumed cleanliness of his soul.

It is the same, at a deeper level, with his piano playing. Cherubini dismissed it in one word, 'rough'; Cramer complained that it was inconsistent: now expressive, now moodily muddled. Clementi found it unpolished, but 'always full of spirit'. Rellstab says that Beethoven played 'with irresistible fire and mighty force'; whereas Schindler found his playing restrained, with minimal movements of hands or body. Czerny thought it 'not elegant or brilliant, compared with some'; Karl Varnhagen found his performance 'beautiful, devout, serious, as if he had been kissed by a god'. Most of these comments were uttered as general statements rather than in response to a particular performance; clearly they and many more conflicting accounts might have been true in differing circumstances, at various times in Beethoven's life, and at various phases of his deafness. Yet it would seem to be undeniable that Beethoven, as pianist, was a Proteus. There was little agreement as to the nature of his piano playing, but everyone agreed that, even when he was too deaf to hear the sounds he produced from a piano, he could 'exercise a magic spell on every one who heard him'. What Czerny said of his improvisation was probably true of his playing in general: 'his improvisation was brilliant and striking, frequently not an eye would remain dry, while many would break into loud sobs: for there was something wonderful in his expression in addition to the beauty and originality of his ideas'. Clearly Beethoven gave to the performance of his own music the 'total commitment' he asked for, but seldom obtained, from singers. It is interesting that the one point on which all commentators agree is that in adagios and lyrical legato playing, even in chordal passages, Beethoven had 'never been surpassed by anyone'.

In biographical terms Beethoven's divisiveness is most movingly evident in the so-called Heiligenstadt Testament, that extraordinary document, half valedictory will, half spiritual confession, that Beethoven penned in 1802, at his country retreat, when on the verge of breakdown. Self-pity (he could no longer evade the fact of his encroaching deafness) and self-confidence (his ability, even success, as an artist was proven) could co-exist inextricably; hostility to the outside world was almost a condition of his faith in the inner world of his art. He had recently completed his triumphant Second Symphony; though he now seemed to be at a nadir of spiritual health, it was from this *de profundis* that he was already gestating the Third Symphony, the work that was to prove a watershed in European history as well as in Beethoven's own development. The composer's two brothers, to whom the Testament was addressed, must have been bemused; ordinary fellows, without the malice Beethoven later imputed to them, they were impotent to help, because incapable of comprehension.

There is a comparably puzzling divisiveness in Beethoven's sexual life. Indeed the mystery that surrounds his relationships with women is extremely odd, given his celebrity. He was a legendary figure in his lifetime; most people thought him susceptible to feminine charm and suspected that he was of exceptional virility. Von Breuning said that he always had 'a great deal of success' with women; Wegeler tells us that there was never a time when Beethoven was not 'in love, and that in the highest degree', and credits him with amorous conquests that would have been difficult if not impossible for many an Adonis. Yet there is no proof of casual sexual encounters in youth; no evidence whether any of Beethoven's physical distresses were syphilitic in origin; no documentation of the precise nature of his numerous 'serious' emotional involvements, including the several rejected proposals of marriage; and still, after a hundred and fifty years' probing, no definitive evidence as to the identity of the Eternal Beloved, to whom Beethoven wrote, but probably did not send, those deeply moving though only partially articulate letters. Candidates for the role of this Beatrice-like beloved litter the ground, new ones being periodically unearthed after others have been eliminated by scrupulous detective work on dates and locations. Yet the mystery remains. None is demonstrably the real solution, and the beloved's identity is less important than the fact that Beethoven projected her into Leonora who, in *Fidelio*, is simultaneously the woman Beethoven could have loved (and surely did love, or she would hardly be so vividly incarnate) and the symbol of an ideal. Perhaps the most moving and revealing of all the stories about Beethoven and women is the strangest. Ries tells us that one evening he visited Beethoven and found 'a handsome young woman sitting on the sofa beside him. Thinking that I might be intruding I wanted to go at once. But Beethoven detained me and said: "Play, for the time being". He and the lady remained seated behind me. I had already played for a long time when Beethoven called out: "Ries, play some love music"; a little later, "something melancholy", then "something passionate", etc. From what I heard I came to the conclusion that in some manner he must have offended the lady and was trying to make amends.... At last he jumped up and shouted: "Why, all those things are by me!" The lady soon went away; to my great amazement Beethoven did not know who she was.'

Scarcely less puzzling than Beethoven's relationships with women is the disparity between the man who indulged in pawky practical jokes; who behaved with churlish suspicion to his well-meaning brothers, with near-pathological venom to the sister-in-law he dubbed 'the Queen of Night', and with near-paranoid protectiveness to his nephew; who engaged in ferocious litigation with men (such as

Lobkowitz, Kinsky and Mälzel) who had befriended him; who haggled shiftily, if not downright dishonestly, over terms for what he regarded as his most sublime composition; and the man who genuinely aimed to live in the light of Kantian duty and freedom, and was capable of exceptional benignity and munificence. 'This reputedly savage and social man', as Varnhagen put it, 'proves a magnificent artist with a heart of gold, a glorious spirit and a friendly disposition'; if his judgement in the affairs of life was shaky, that was because his art's search for self-realization ('Man, know thyself') was totally engrossing. The world could offer no 'eternal' beloved precisely because it was temporal; his search for a beloved son in his nephew foundered because, being in Thayer's word 'idolatrous', it drove the object of love to attempted suicide. Such painful contrarieties were manifest too in Beethoven's physical appearance. In youth he was often referred to as ugly; yet his swarthy complexion, derived from his Flemish descent, gave him a magnetic, gypsy-like fire that earned him the soubriquet of 'the Spaniard'. Later in life Sir Jules Benedict saw him at Baden, 'his white hair flowing over his mighty shoulders, with that wonderful look, sometimes contracting his brows when anything afflicted him, sometimes bursting into forced laughter, indescribably painful to his listeners', and was 'touched as if King Lear or one of the old Gaelic bards stood before me'. Klöber too, seeing him striding in the open air, his grey hair wafting in the wind, found him 'Ossian-like and aweful', yet 'in friendly conversation he took on a genial and mild aspect.... Every mood of his spirit was immediately and violently expressed in his countenance.' Seyfried, on the other hand, writing between 1800 and 1805, found it 'difficult, yes utterly impossible, to tell from his features whether he was pleased or displeased.... His mind was at work ceaselessly, but the physical shell was like soulless marble.' Schindler's description is a compromise between these extremes, for he says that 'his brown eyes were small, almost retreating into his head when he laughed. They could however suddenly become unusually prominent and large, either rolling and flashing, his pupils almost always turned upwards or, not moving at all, staring fixedly ahead when one or another idea took hold of him.' The ambiguity of the outward physiognomy reflected the inner man. Beethoven's 'two selves', real and ideal, dark and light, inspirational and aspirational, were necessary the one to the other. To have destroyed one would have destroyed the whole. To discover the Whole, through his music, was Beethoven's life-task; and it may be

that even his deafness, which we normally think of as an affliction
peculiarly terrible for a musician, was a condition of his supreme
achievement. At once a physical fact and a spiritual allegory, it shut
him off from external reality, and helped him to concentrate on his
internal reality of sound.

So Beethoven's life, like Hegel's conception of reality, is a Becoming that advances only through negation and contradiction. His
life was a flux, a manifestation of Hegel's *Unruhe*; but its goal was rest,
at a point where man, having become aware of the dialectical process
within him, has become truly free. The analogy extends to Beethoven's art; there is an obvious parallel between the dialectical triad of
thesis, antithesis and synthesis which Hegel derived from Fichte, and
the exposition, development and recapitulation of the sonata principle,
and there is a still closer parallel between Hegel's later triad of opposition, synthesis and transcendence, and the precise form which the
evolution of sonata assumed through Beethoven's life. It is hardly
extravagant to call Beethoven the first modern composer, in that he
seeks, through the dialectical process of his music, the forms of truth.
The structures of the classical baroque age—tonal fugue, binary dance
movement, ternary aria de capo—were closed forms that 'stood for'
absolute concepts and public assumptions, however much an
individual composer might modify or even undermine them. Beethoven's forms, on the other hand, are discovery: themes and motives
become what they are not, on the basis of what they are. It is relevant
to note that Beethoven must be the first composer in history
consciously animated by a desire to be original. According to
Tomaschek, Beethoven told a young lady admirer that he didn't
know Mozart's operas, because he preferred not to listen to other
composers' music lest it impair his pristine individuality. This must
have been partially a jape, since he had played the viola in some
Mozart operas, and certainly knew *Don Giovanni*, and *Figaro* and *The
Magic Flute*. None the less it was a significant joke for Beethoven to
make, and it ties in with his famous and more general pronouncement to Prince Lichnowsky: 'Prince, what you are, you are through
accident of birth; what I am, I am through my own efforts. There
have been thousands of princes and there will be thousands more;
there is only one Beethoven.'

There is a philosophical dimension to this: an artist ought to be
original because, as Rousseau put it, though man is 'everywhere
enchained, he is born free'. There is also a political dimension because,

as Hegel saw, dialectical process involved an archetypal struggle between master and servant in the forging of the new, post-Revolutionary world. Beneath both, however, there is a psychological and ultimately religious dimension, since the basic question posited by emergent democracy was that of self-responsibility. If man is answerable neither to God nor to the State, he must also recognize that he cannot be free simply in relation to himself. As Merleau Ponty, paraphrasing Hegel, has put it: 'my consciousness of another as an enemy comprises an affirmation of him as an equal. . . . The other whom I first saw as a rival is a rival only because he is myself. . . .' 'I discover myself in the other' applies both to other people and to opposing categories of experience. Beethoven's acceptance of his two selves makes him the supreme composer who, without evasion, confronts chaos. Hegel speaks of 'an underground source in the inner spirit whose content is hidden and which has not yet broken through the surface of actual existence, but which strikes against the outer world as against a shell and cracks it because such a shell is unsuited to such a kernel'. Such was Beethoven's impact on the shell of civilization and its music. He is Hegel's 'world-historical individual'. Moreover, within the context of each work, at least from the *Eroica* Symphony onwards, Beethoven's themes and motives likewise behave as world-historical individuals. They are consciousness coming to birth, obliterating the opposites in recognizing that the Other is in me. As Hegel put it, 'At that point where its appearance becomes equal to its essence, consciousness's presentation of itself will converge with this very point in the authentic science of spirit. And finally when consciousness itself grasps this essence, it will indicate the nature of absolute knowledge itself. Real knowledge of beings means the absolute knowledge of the Absolute in its absoluteness.'

Beethoven owned a volume or two of Hegel and must have regarded him with empathy, though he had not the abstract intellectual capacity to comprehend a writer whom trained philosophers find difficult. But he did read and quote Schlegel, who said 'every concept of God is empty prattle, but the Idea of God is the Idea of all Ideas'; and he would have agreed with Schlegel when he defined freedom and immortality as man's ability to 'bring forth God and make him visible', or audible. 'One lives only in so far as one follows one's own Idea. Individuality is the original and eternal in man'; in finding himself, the artist finds God. For Schelling too, whom Beethoven also read, the artist is an instrument of revelation; the created product is

greater than the creating mind, for 'the Self is conscious in its production, unconscious in its product'. The philosophy of art is thus
the 'single and eternal organon' of all philosophy; through it
the Enlightenment attempted a synthesis of metaphysical religion
and physical science. This dynamic concept of thinking, and this
morphological approach to culture, hark back to Vico's *Scienza Nuova*
and to Herder. Kant defined an organic structure as one in which every
part 'is reciprocally means and end'. Schlegel distinguished mechanic
form which is predetermined from organic form which 'shapes and
develops itself from within'.

Still more significantly, Goethe, the supreme poet of the time as
Beethoven was the supreme composer, was passionately concerned
about science, especially botany and biology, as well as art, and saw the
'laws' of Nature and of the human psyche as related, if not identical.
Inorganic nature was for him symbolized by stone and crystal; organic
nature by shell and flower, equated with the world of higher forms
characterized by a higher geometry. The wise man will 'bring to full
realization the inherent forms of his being' only if he 'harkens to the
involuntary promptings of his nature' and allows them to grow like a
spiral, which is an organic curve, or to flower like a plant. What we
know of Beethoven's methods of work, both from the Sketchbooks
and from recorded comments, suggests that such was, or became, his
approach to creation. 'My dominion is in the air,' he wrote to Count
Brunswick in 1814; 'the tones whirl like the wind, and often there is a
whirl [a spiral] in my soul.' Similarly to Louis Schlösser he said in
1822: 'I carry my thoughts about for a long time, often a very long
time, before I write them down. . . . Inasmuch as I know exactly what I
want, the fundamental Idea never deserts me. It arises before me . . .
like a cast, and there remains nothing but the labour of writing it
down.' Musical 'ideas', that is, may be 'snatched from the air, in the
woods, in the silence of the night'; they are 'tones that roar and storm
about me until I have set them down in notes'. The process of transference is organic, like a 'law of life become audible'. Considering a
passage such as the coda to the first movement of the piano sonata opus
111 we may say that, although Beethoven could hardly have achieved
that miraculous metamorphosis of tempest into music except through
the struggle within his psyche, yet what is born in the music is
something other and greater than the creating mind. It is 'absolute
knowledge of the Absolute in its absoluteness', independent of anything that happened to Beethoven, though realizable only through

him. Not Beethoven's personal crisis but what Hopkins (in his noble sonnet on Henry Purcell) calls 'meaning motion' here fans Beethoven's wits 'with wonder and awe'. In the few bars of this coda musical motion is 'freedom in prospect, necessity in retrospect', to use the terminology of Zuckerkandl in his great book *Sound and Symbol*.

Indeed Zuckerkandl takes us to the heart of this organic metaphor as applied to Beethoven's principles of composition. The tones, he says do not *stand for* emotion but are themselves *in* emotion, which is that of the tones. 'The art of hearing is itself an art of feeling (of being in emotion) and of understanding (perceiving the dynamic qualities of the tones and the relationship of this to that). A piece of (good) music is a meaningful entity of tones because its structure is organic in the exact biological sense of the term. To hear a composition is therefore directly to perceive organic structure; the act of hearing is itself organic.' Certainly in this coda something is, in the sounds, 'brought forth'. 'Something is done, something is made; and this doing consists in thinking. This thinking is not that of a man who acts, this doing is not that of a man who thinks. Doing and thinking are wholly fused in one; not existence on the one hand and thinking about it on the other, but a thinking that by itself creates existence.'

This seems close to Hegel's identification of self-consciousness with Spirit, and of that with the Absolute. Certainly anyone who creates music, Zuckerkandl continues, 'thinks not only in tones but out of tones. They stand before us wholly the product of human thought. Conceptual thinking [like Hegel's] is cognitive, its purpose to add to our store of knowledge; musical thinking is productive, its purpose to add to our store of reality.' It follows that the closest analogy to the functioning of a musical composition is the functioning of a human life. 'We act as we do because we are what we are. We become what we are because we act as we do. The process is one of gradual progression from amorphous beginnings to ever more sharply defined forms, and is complete only when the last step is taken. A man's death might be compared to the moment when a melody has ceased to 'grow' and enters actual existence. Musicality is thus not an individual gift but one of man's basic attributes. In music man does not give expression to something (his feelings), nor does he build autonomous structures: he *invents himself*. In music, the law by which man knows himself to be alive is realized in its purest form.' Of course some lives are 'better than' others in that more self is invented. No man ever had more self

than Beethoven or manifested more 'thought' in the process of inventing it.

However generally valid Zuckerkandl's account of the nature of
music may be, it is clear that it is precisely apposite to the Hegelian
dialectic of Beethoven's life and art, both intrinsically and in their
interrelationship. While Beethoven could not have theorized about his
musical thought and did not need to, he did make several pronouncements that lend direct support to this approach. The most remarkable
is a long conversation transcribed in 1810 by Bettina Brentano, a
romantic young lady who, being a lion-hunter with a highly coloured
imagination, is usually considered an unreliable authority. This quotation none the less *sounds* authentic; Thayer explains that she had pieced
together notes she had written at the time. According to Bettina,
Beethoven said:

This is harmony, this is expressed in my symphonies in which the
confluence of many-sided forms surges along in one bed to its
destination. In them, one can feel that something eternal, infinite,
never to be wholly comprehensible, is contained in every product of
the human spirit, and although my works always give me a feeling
of having succeeded, I feel an insatiable hunger to recommence like
a child, even though the last work seemed to have been exhausted
with the last beat of the kettle-drum which inculcated my joy and
my musical convictions upon the audience. (Speak to Goethe about
this, tell him to listen to my symphonies, for then he will admit that
music is the only entrance to the higher world of knowledge which,
though it embraces a man, a man cannot grasp.) A rhythm of the
spirit is needed in order to grasp the essence of music: for music
grants us presentiments, inspiration of celestial sciences, and that
part of it which the mind grasps through the senses is the embodiment of mental cognition. Although minds live on it, as we live on
air, it is still a different thing to be able to grasp it intellectually. Yet
the more the soul takes sensuous nourishment from music, the
more prepared does the mind grow for a happy understanding with
it. Yet few ever attain this stage; for just as thousands marry for love
and love is never manifest in these thousands, although they all
practise the act of love, so thousands have intercourse with music
and never see it manifested. Like all the arts, music is founded on the
exalted symbols of the moral sense: all true invention is a moral
progress. To submit to these inscrutable laws, and by means of

these laws to tame and guide one's own mind, so that the manifestation of art may pour out: this is the isolating principle of art. To be
dissolved in its manifestations, this is our dedication to the divine
which calmly exercises its power over the raging of the untamed
elements and so lends to the imagination its highest effectiveness.
So art always represents the divine, and the relationship of men
towards art is religion: what we obtain from art comes from God, is
divine inspiration which appoints an aim for human faculties,
which aim we can attain.

We do not know what it is that grants us knowledge. The grain of
seed, tightly sealed as it is, needs the damp, electric warm soil in
order to sprout, to think, to express itself. Music is the electric soil in
which the spirit thinks, lives and invents. Philosophy is a striking of
music's electric spirit; its indigence, which desires to found everything upon a single principle, is relieved by music. Although the
spirit has no power over that which it creates through music, it is yet
joyful in the act of creation. Thus every genuine product of art is
independent, more powerful than the artist himself, and returns to
the divine when achieved, connected with men only in as much as it
bears witness to the divine of which they are the medium. Music
relates the spirit to harmony. An isolated thought yet feels related to
all things that are of the mind: likewise every thought in music
is intimately, indivisibly related to the whole of harmony, which
is oneness. All that is electrical stimulates the mind to flowing,
surging, musical creation. I am electrical by nature.

In this extraordinary passage Beethoven touches on all the philosophical and psychological issues we have explored in this chapter:
the Hegelian process of dialectic, the confrontation of chaos, the
'morphological' concept of form, the independence of the creation
from the creator, and at the same time their identity in the unity that is
God. In one particular, indeed, in extending the morphological
metaphor into the field of electricity, Beethoven ventures further than
we did, seeming to anticipate very recent theories about the nature of
the human mind. There is something awe-inspiring in the fact that
Beethoven, employing a key-word of his time which was then imper-
fectly understood, should prophetically have hinted at truths of which
we are just becoming aware. His 'sublimation' was born, through the
techniques of his late music, of the pain of consciousness; and affinities
between Hegel's definition of Spirit, Zuckerkandl's account of the

process of musical creation, and the dialectic of musical 'thought' in Beethoven's last works, cannot conceivably be fortuitous.

One of the wellsprings of Marx's thought was in Hegel's doctrine of alienation, though he complained that, in ultimately handing back dialectical process to metaphysics, Hegel denuded theory of human manifestation. Beethoven's 'third period' music is certainly a religious rather than a political act; yet it does, in Marx's words, abolish 'human self-alienation, and is thus the real appropriation of human nature through and for man. . . . It is the definite resolution of the antagonism between man and nature, and between man and man. It is the true solution of the conflict between existence and essence, between objectification and self-affirmation, between freedom and necessity, between individual and species. It is the solution of the riddle of history, and knows itself to be such.' To substantiate this large claim, in the terms of Beethoven's music, will be the aim of this book.

Beethoven's life embraces three stages which are relatable to the Hegelian triads. In his first period Beethoven accepted social and musical precedents from the past, yet energized them with Hegelian negations and contradictions more violent than those of any previous composer using the sonata principle. As early as 1795 he wrote in a diary that 'even with the frailties of my body, I will seize fate by the throat, it will never wholly subdue me'. In his second period he transformed this iconoclasm into a moral force, creating through the symphony orchestra a music of democratic principle, and exerting on mass audiences the exceptionally potent impact which it has preserved unweakened until the present day: 'Power', he said in a letter of 1798 addressed to Zmeskall, 'is the morality of those who stand out from the rest, and it is mine.' In this phase of his life Beethoven's threat to autocratic Establishment became public affirmation: which is the closest he came to political manifestation. But in his third period Beethoven yet more wondrously proceeded not merely to a triumphant assertion of human rights and responsibilities, but to an exploration of their spiritual roots within the psyche, thereby demonstrating that, as he again put it, 'A true artist has no pride ... art has no bounds. . . . Nothing must bind me to this life' (letter to Emilie M., 17 July 1812). So Beethoven, like Hegel, would seem to hand dialectic back to religion and metaphysics, for his late music is the creation of a man who, though 'often darkly led to evil by passion', has returned 'through penance and purification, to the pure fountain' (from a diary dated 1815). There is, however, a crucial difference between

Beethoven and Hegel, which the composer himself pinpointed when he explained why philosophy, in comparison with music, is 'indigent'. The difference is that Beethoven's metaphysical reality also has physical flesh, in that it is incarnate in sound. In the sublime simplicity of the Arietta of opus 111, in the unity his late fugues achieve from the fact of alienation itself, Beethoven offers hope, and even 'happiness', for man who is born alone, to die alone. Beethoven, the sufferer and scapegoat, was also the man of affirmation, every note of whose music justifies his Fare-well, in a letter to Breitkopf and Härtel dated 26 July 1809: 'I wish you all that is good and beautiful, as far as our wild century permits.'

During the fallow years preparatory to his third period Beethoven made an entry into a diary of 1815 as significant as it is apparently surprising. He who, in his middle years had been a new kind of public composer, whose symphonies made, as well as reflected, history, wrote that he yearned for a 'small court and small chapel' to work in, with a 'small orchestra, with music by me for it, *performed to honour the Almighty, the Eternal, the Infinite*' (italics added). Clearly that small court didn't imply a return to the conditions of patronage under which Haydn had worked at Esterházy; Beethoven expressed it in those terms because he had no other standards of reference. The court he wanted was, like the Kingdom of God, 'not of this world' except in the sense that it was a temple within Beethoven's spirit, its 'orchestra' being a concourse of sounding instruments within Beethoven's deaf ears and liberated mind. Russell Hunter, who heard Beethoven play the piano in 1825, spoke touchingly of the gulf between the real and the ideal in the sounds, or occasionally silences, which Beethoven produced:

> The moment he is seated at the piano he is entirely unconscious there is anything in existence but his instrument, and considering how deaf he is, it seems impossible he should hear all he plays. Accordingly, when playing very *piano*, he often does not bring out a single note. He hears it himself in his mind's ear. Whilst his eye, and the almost imperceptible motion of his fingers, show that he is following out the strain through all its dying gradations, the instrument is actually as dumb as the musician is deaf.

At one level this anecdote simply means what it says: Beethoven's defective ears couldn't hear the sounds he was not playing. But at a deeper level the story reflects the dichotomy between the Beethoven who so clumsily lived and moved on the terrestrial earth, and the Beethoven who 'had his being' in his music. Often, alive in his inner world, he became dead to the world in which he was supposed to exist: as when, sitting for his portrait, he suddenly leapt at his piano to discover, through improvisation, the reality of his art, which obliterated the materiality of room with attendant and momentarily frustrated painter; he 'did not even realize any more that anyone was in the room'. There is a further strand to this allegory in that most of Beethoven's late music was created for instruments that had not yet been invented, or were even incapable of materialization. Those sounds he didn't make audible were heard, as the phrase has it, in 'the mind's ear'; if they were inapprehensible it was because 'inner' and 'outer' planes of consciousness couldn't cross. When Beethoven expressed dissatisfaction with the piano as a medium, he must have done so in this ultimate sense, for no man ever wrote for the instrument with more profound and developing creativity, discovering new technical potentialities that were inseparable from his spiritual adventure. The point he arrived at was immaterial in that it could not become totally articulate: 'words fail me', we say, confronted by transcendent experience. Yet this immateriality is a distillation, not a denial, of Beethoven's physicality, which is that of the supreme 'activist' in European music. It is now time for us to look back at the achievement of his early years, so that we may accompany him on his first sturdily challenging steps towards that magical court or temple wherein he sees his ultimate vision of an Eternal Return: or rather, to abandon the inappropriately visual metaphor, wherein he hears the Hidden Song referred to by Schlegel:

> Through all the tones there sounds
> Throughout the colourful earth
> A gentle tone, sustained
> For him who secretly hears.

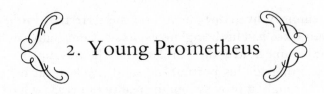

2. Young Prometheus

Piano sonatas
opus 2 no. 1 in F minor
opus 2 no. 2 in A major
opus 10 no. 3 in D major
opus 13 in C minor (Pathétique)

History books are often unsure whether to allot Beethoven to the classical or the romantic age; the reason is that conceptually as well as chronologically he overrides both. He was trained in classical traditions; revolutionized them in a search for freedom; discovered that freedom is apprehensible only in the light of order re-created. In many ways his first piano sonata, or at least the first he admitted to the canon of the thirty-two, is a startling piece, romantic in its vehemence; yet in choosing F minor as its key Beethoven is following Baroque precedent which related F minor, the flattest, darkest minor key then in common use, to the infernal regions, just as E major, the sharpest major key in common use, was associated with heaven. At this stage the devilish character of the young Beethoven is no more than skin-deep. He treats the dualism of the classical sonata with economy, even with formality, for the first movement of this sonata is structurally more conventional, and simpler, than the mature sonata movements of Haydn or Mozart. None the less, this F minor sonata is a subversive piece, and its subversion may be defined in terms of Hegelian negation: its first movement, and still more disturbingly its last, is remarkable for *avoidance* of lyrical song. Frustration dialectically promotes growth; and we will discover that Beethoven's life-work may be described as a search for the song that lyrically fulfils, making us whole, hale and holy. That long journey is enclosed within the first movement of this first sonata, and the Arietta that is the second and final movement of the last sonata.

The F minor sonata, opus 2 no. 1, opens with a physical gesture that was also a cliché of the new demotic music of what purported to be a socially enlightened community. The bouncing upward arpeggio,

striding across the strings, is a violinistic technique that was developed
by the Mannheim orchestra, financed by the rising merchant class
rather than by the aristocracy. This particular device was, for obvious
reasons, known as the Mannheim skyrocket; despite its physical ebul-
lience, it is enclosed within the arpeggio, and so resists the impulse
lyrically to sing. Negation is the more evident in this case because the
bounding arpeggio, unexpectedly quiet in dynamic, is rounded off, at
the top of its crest, by another cliché, which the Mannheimers called a
'birdie'. The effect of this tweeting turn, after so confident an upthrust,
is chirpily derisive; the more so because the birdie is tethered to the
ground by the chugging minor triads that form the accompaniment,
scored as though for hound-barking horns. The next two bars repeat
the figure on the arpeggiated dominant seventh; and the following
two bars more agitatedly telescope the previous four, since birdies, first
on a tonic minor triad, then on the dominant seventh, also suggest
the upward arpeggio by grace notes leaping up a sixth and a seventh. In
apparent finality the upward prancing motive reaches its goal, the high
C, in the next bar, only to droop down the scale to a half-close,
decorated with a turn that is the birdie inverted, on the dominant:

Ex. 1

At this point Beethoven inserts a pause mark over the rest; this is the
first subversive moment in the sonata, since the thrust of the opening
motive seems to have collapsed in a manner that would be inconceivable in a Mozart allegro, and improbable, at least so early in the
movement, in a similar work of Haydn. It is instructive to contrast
Beethoven's first sonata allegro with the finale of Mozart's great G
minor symphony, which also has a Mannheim skyrocket as theme: for
whereas Beethoven's rocket fizzles out, Mozart's bounds on as well as

up, acquiring chromatic elements, building sequentially into long paragraphs that lyrically sing. After the collapse of his half-close Beethoven, however, tries again. The skyrocket mounts in the hopefully sharper dominant, yet darkly, in bassoon register. Moreover, the sky-rocket occurs once only; the birdies take over, gently, in a chain of declining sevenths, 'orchestrated' as though for woodwind. The suspended sevenths mollify the music not only through their enveloping sostenuto, but also because they effect a modulation from C minor to its passively flat submediant, A flat major, which is also the relative of the home tonic, F minor. Five transitional bars of falling scales, syncopated or tied over a rising chromatic bass, establish the new key over a rocking dominant pedal, above which droops the second subject:

Ex. 2

This is hardly a new idea, since it is a falling instead of a rising arpeggio on the dominant seventh. But the inversion of the original motive is emotional as well as technical; far from springing upwards, it swoops down from a dissonant appoggiatura of F flat to a scrunching double appoggiatura on the strong beat, each two-bar phrase naggingly repeating itself. So the second subject is not so much a contrast as a rudimentary Hegelian negation. Over the next eight bars the music attempts to rise again, since the falling bass is counteracted by rising figuration and by what Tovey calls an 'enhanced dominant': an intensifying of the dominant's 'upward' implication by passing references to the dominant's dominant. The animation, being broken by rests, is, however, agitated rather than affirmative; resolution is achieved, or seems to be, only when the bass returns to its rising arpeggios, while the treble part flows in quavers. But even in this there is an element of anxiety, since the arpeggio is syncopated, with fierce cross-accents, while the quaver scales intermittently bump in semitonic dissonance against the left hand's melody. Eight bars of codetta then fuse the first and second subjects, which we have seen freely to mirror one another. Leaping sixths and diminished sevenths, either within the contours of the melody or inserted as grace notes, recall the energy of the initial motive again; each leap is answered by a declining scale or fifth. The chords—diminished seventh, 6–4 and dominant seventh of A flat—are off-beat barks, reminiscent of the snarling 'horns' of bars 2 and 3. The phrase is played three times, in two octaves. Such assertiveness carries a hint of desperation; the final cadence, telescoping dominant with tonic, denies progression.

After the double bar and the repeat, Beethoven begins his development with the original skyrocket, in A flat major. Initially jaunty, even fierce, it sounds bland in the relative major, and so reminds us that one of the essential characteristics of the new sonata music, as compared with the closed forms of the Baroque, is its irony. A society that is founded on the stability of an accepted faith, religious or civic, is unlikely to undermine its beliefs with a 'recognition of other modes of experience that may be possible', though this does not preclude humour or wit. A society that, on the other hand, is precarious, unsure of its direction, will tend to ambivalence. 'Meaning' cannot be absolute, since it is a process of discovery; and in the mildly pretty form the skyrocket assumes at the opening of the development, Beethoven is asking whether his originally defiant gesture might not be a sham. From one point of view the skyrocket is no more than Rococo small-talk, which may be why, after this initial somewhat deflatory statement, Beethoven banishes it from his development. This recharges its energy by returning to the tonic minor and then, by way of a chromaticized German sixth, to F minor's subdominant and the drooping arpeggio of the second subject. The minor ninths of this motive grind over the rocking quaver octaves, teetering between subdominant and dominant minor, and descending sequentially, in baritone register, to A flat *major*. An attempt at reaffirmation is painful, since cross-accents dislocate the metrical pulse.

But a long dominant pedal is established, over which sound broken fragments of the motives: falling thirds or fifths and minor seconds, first plain, then trill-decorated. The dynamic level subsides until there's nothing left except reiterated dominant Cs, at first alone, then intensified with semitonic suspensions, over which birdies begin tentatively to cheep. Both pulse and birdies gather energy until we arrive at the recapitulation, which opens loudly and angrily, instead of in suppressed agitation as in the exposition. This time the 'bassoon' register entry after the half-close starts in the tonic instead of the dominant, so the second subject material also stays in F minor, with grimmer effect. The coda, as compared with the codetta, is slightly changed, a German sixth being assuagingly substituted for the conventionally 'horrendous' diminished seventh. It is also extended, since the threefold repetition is rounded off by a fiery cadence in B flat minor, followed by a silence, and a cadence in the relative, A flat. Three final bars of savage chords return us, with dislocated accents, to the tonic. So the coda is a microcosm of the tonal structure of the movement; the last bars are gruff, dismissive rather than consummatory.

Beethoven has created a structurally conventional, not very extended sonata allegro, the subversive tendencies of which consist in its dynamic rather than lyrical nature, and in its impulse to frustrate, even to destroy. For his second movement he offers what appears to be a throwback to the old, aristocratic–autocratic world, in the sense that it is an arrangement of an 'old-fashioned' movement from a piano quartet written ten years previously, when Beethoven was only fifteen. Even so, there is an ambivalent element in the movement, which isn't heroic like an aria of Handel, nor sublime like an aria of Bach. Its graciousness is in the manner of Bach's sons, for it cultivates an aristocracy born of feeling rather than of titular right. The new aristocracy consists of men of Sensibility, of Connoisseurs and Amateurs, those who know and those who love. In such an attitude there's a hint of self-congratulation: which may not be far from self-indulgence. There may be a suspicion of this in Beethoven's initial phrase, with its upward-yearning sixth followed by the quasi-vocal turn and the decline down the scale to the 6–4 resolution, especially when reinforced by the sighs of the answering clause, and by a repeat decorated with flowing semiquavers. The second eight bars, with a gentle Alberti bass, are conventionally Rococo; sighing appoggiaturas lead to a more lacerating double appoggiatura on the subdominant triad, and a triple suspension over the tonic to conclude.

The middle section begins in the relative minor, with a suggestion of operatic nobility. A rising fourth and repeated notes in dotted rhythm counteract the sighing suspensions, over an accompaniment of warm parallel thirds; the immense leaps in the theme from the high

D to the D in the bass clef are an extravagant extension of the gradilo-quent leaps Mozart gives to his operatic basses. The second half of the section moves to the dominant major and to coruscating figuration in demisemiquavers, still with sighing suspensions in the inner parts. The movement's opening bars are recalled, in the dominant, as a 'cadence theme'; entwining triplets lead to a repetition of the dominant cadence, which is cancelled by an intrusive flat seventh leading back to the tonic. The da capo is ornamented both with semiquaver sighs and with chromaticized triplets. It is at this point that a sense of emotional dubiety becomes evident. It would be going too far to say that the ornamentation sounds faintly comic, and it certainly wasn't intended parodistically by the fifteen-year-old Beethoven. None the less, we cannot take it merely at its face value, as we would be invited to in a comparable movement of C. P. E. or W. F. Bach; the coda intensifies this unease, for after an extended passage of chromatically quivering demisemiquavers, we approach a cadence by way of sonorous semi-quavers in parallel sixths, only to return to the broken triplet figura-tion, which is then repeated at twice the speed! The effect is incorrig-ibly skittish, so it's difficult to take the cadential triple suspension with the solemnity it had asked for on its initial statement. Baroque *affect* has become Rococo affectation; when, after a silence, the triple suspension is followed by a simple dominant–tonic cadence, the chords separated by quaver rests, it's hard to suppress a smile, perhaps more wry than affectionate. Beethoven's threat to the old autocratic world was not always, even in adolescence, by way of direct assault.

There's a whiff of threat in the third movement also. Beethoven calls it a Menuetto, which was originally an aristocratic dance, though Haydn and Mozart had tended to equate it with the Ländler—with the peasant or middle-class world of beer-garden and café. Beethoven's minuet, back in the tonic minor, is quicker than the aristocratic dance; moreover, its essence lies in its cross-accents, which make corporeal elegance awkward, if not impossible. The first period consists of fourteen instead of the conventional sixteen bars. The tune's lift up a tone and down a minor third is doubled in parallel sixths, with a cheeky staccato offbeat in the bass. The four-bar phrase is sequentially repeated in the relative; and rounded off by small bows from 6–4 to dominant seventh to tonic of A flat major. The reiterations of the phrase, with offbeat sforzandi and clinking acciaccaturas, hint at com-edy rather than ceremonial hauteur. After the double bar the stepwise rise changes from tone to semitone, and the parallel sixths become thirds, answered by inversion and across the beat:

Ex. 3

Sequential modulation into B flat minor cadences into a repeat of the 'bowing' motive; but gentility, even mock gentility, is swept away by a flurry of octave scales in sudden fortissimo. This takes us back to the initial phrase which, now answered by inversion, stays in the tonic minor; the bows are followed by two bars of straight dominant–tonic cadence, still, almost grave. Though unassuming, the piece certainly embraces 'other modes of experience that may be possible'.

This becomes more subtly evident when the 'gravity', if that's what it is, leads into the trio, conventionally in the major. It opens with a Ländler-style arpeggiated motive in the left hand, with equally flow-ing quavers on top; rising sixths dreamily recall aspects of both the previous movements. After the fourth bar there's some vestigial double counterpoint, for the right hand takes over the rising arpeg-gios, while the left hand chromaticizes the stepwise-moving quavers. The first section ends with a conventional modulation to the domin-ant. After the double bar the double counterpoint continues over a pedal C: but leads, with the intrusion of the flat seventh and the return to the tonic, to fortissimo parallel thirds and 6–3 chords: an abruptly wild organum (fingered by Beethoven in such a way as to achieve maximum ferocity) which ironically cocks a snook at the purling cosiness of the opening:

Ex. 4

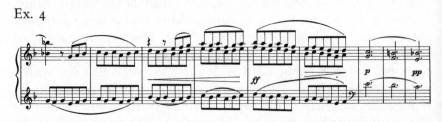

The outburst subsides as suddenly as it began; three 'corny' bars of dotted minims take us back, by way of sequential dominant sevenths, to a da capo, the first four bars of which are literal except for the sharpened B in bar 2, effecting a momentary dominant modulation. The second half modifies the arpeggiated tune, now on top, so that it flows in waves. It stays in the tonic, and leads to a restatement of the minuet.

So Beethoven has given us a first movement allegro, an aria da capo, and a minuet and trio, all within established precedents, yet all containing elements of subversiveness, which in the finale becomes overt. This is evident in the fact that the movement is difficult to categorize. It looks more like a sonata movement than anything else: certainly it has an exposition with first and second subjects conventionally related, and a recapitulation in which the same material recurs in the same order, with the conventional modifications of tonality. Yet we have to admit that what ought to be the development behaves very oddly and, indeed, might be more accurately described as an anti-development. Only when we consider the movement in retrospect, in relation to the whole sonata, do we realize that this irony is the point.

The exposition is characterized, even more than that of the first allegro, by an absence of song-like melody or even of anything worth dignifying as a theme. The prestissimo alla breve tempo indication is unusual; the consequent speed of the triplet figuration (with accents dislocated from the strong beats), and the violence of the barking tonic and dominant ninth triads, outweigh any attempt to establish a tune. Even the repeated-note figure, followed by a rising fourth, though it carries us positively to the relative major, is too puerile to count as song. Moreover its alleviation is momentary, since it transports us, by way of a syncopated accent, to the dominant minor and a return of the whirring triplets and barking chords. A transitional theme consists merely of a chromatically revolving cam around the dominant of the dominant, wriggling through the triplets. When a more song-like tune, an ostensible second subject, does emerge, still in the dominant, with touches of its relative major, it is so rudimentary, being a plain descent down the scale, as to be almost risible. In any case it is brusquely banished by a return of the barks and snorts, and a primitive modulation back to the tonic, for the repeat.

The transition from the C minor close is then even more comically gauche: we subside gracelessly to the flat submediant by way of three thumping dominant sevenths, separated by rests. Though A flat major may be a positive key in relation to its relative minor, the home tonic, it is a key of passive relaxation in relation to C minor. The beginning of what should be the development sounds almost like a parody of the opening of the first movement's development, in the same key. There is now a 'tune', which bears no relation to what we've heard in the exposition, though its guileless rising arpeggios recall the fierce arpeggios with which the sonata had started. But the feeling could hardly be more different. Though the tune may be song-like, it is not a song achieved through contrariety, but is rather prettily Rococo, like pre-teenage Mozart, with gentle appoggiaturas, cooingly vocal turns, and a repeated chord accompaniment that blandly and ironically echoes the barking triads of the first movement:

Ex. 5

The tune is self-contained, with no modulation through the first twenty-nine bars, apart from a touch of B flat minor at the approach to the cadence; it is self-indulgently repeated an octave higher, with more caressing appoggiaturas. Though there are now brief modulations to the subdominant and its relative, the tune's infantile innocence is unsullied. As the repeat of the tune cadences, however, the whirling triplets return very softly in the bass, above which right-hand octaves steal in, pianissimo, with the rhythm of the original barks. Two bars of this figuration alternate with two bars of Edenic song, with repeated triad accompaniment, and liberating octave leaps, introduced by a melodic turn. The leaps become anchored to triads and dominant sevenths of D flat, the flat submediant; sforzando accents on each strong beat suggest desperation or frustration, or both. Finally the bass moves from D flat to settle on a dominant pedal; and the sizzling triplets and snapping ninth chords banish the childish song and re-establish the furious prestissimo. The recapitulation is orthodox, as we might expect since nothing has happened to disturb it. The descending scale second subject, conventionally in the tonic minor, now sounds slightly threatening rather than inane. The final barks are abrupt, brutish and short; and the ultimate cascading arpeggio must be the first piece of piano music to require, for its adequate realization, ten fingers and a lock of hair!

Ex. 6

The subversiveness of this youthful sonata should not, of course, be taken too seriously. Beethoven is offering his fashionable and still aristocratic public a music of which the structural bases are readily apprehensible, according to precedents: to which he gives a disturbing twist. In the last movement, indeed he comes near to inverting trad-itional values, equating himself with the fuming tiger who savages through the toccata-like figuration, while almost insultingly offering his public the palliative of the babyish tune which, he implies, is all they're fit for.

So Beethoven's first sonata has begun in a mood that is fashionably stormy and stressful, has acquired elements that are ironic and even parodistic, and ends in tempestuous ambiguity. Its companion piece, opus 2 no. 2, opens in overt comedy, while demonstrating that Beethoven's comedy may be no less subversive than his rhetoric. The key is A major, the initial motive a perkily descending fourth across the 2/4 beat, followed by a demisemiquaver scale filling in a falling fifth; a dominant seventh arpeggio then descends in staccato crotchets. These descents are balanced by a rising triplet arpeggio, flowing into ascending scales contrapuntally imitated in parallel tenths and sixths. Counterpoint is here happy, and prompts too a conventional modulation to the dominant, serenely pianissimo. The sharpwards modulation is, however, cancelled by a return to the tonic, for a repeat from which the falling dominant arpeggio is omitted, though the contrapuntal rising scales are extended, incorporating skittish triplets that become hilarious when they are chromaticized.

The dominant modulation recurs, later; and after it has subsided on a sustained pedal, it peters out on a spread chord of the dominant ninth, to introduce the second subject in the dominant minor instead of major. Melodically it consists of an undulating turn derived from the arpeggiated minor ninth; but its prophecy of song is false, both because its accents are dislocated, and because the theme modulates every two bars through rising mediant sequences: E minor, G major-minor, B flat major, D major, F sharp minor, and so back to E. All this happens not at an advanced stage in the development but in the exposition! If the piece is funny, and it is, it is also shocking, and must have seemed wildly so to contemporary audiences, who would hardly have been mollified by the assertion of the real dominant in the frisky triplet arpeggios of the codetta theme. Here is that second subject and its (fairly) safe landing:

Ex. 7

The end of the codetta, however, is ambiguous again, for although it is stably over a pedal E, its mood is a sudden recognition of 'other modes of experience'. The rising quaver scales are twice augmented to minims, which quietly descend in the top part. When, after the repeat, the minims, hymnic in manner, are succeeded by silence and a pianissimo E minor third, we're at once expectant and puzzled.

What in fact happens, to launch the development, is an abrupt dismissal of that hint of solemnity. The original motive returns, loud, in the upper mediant, C major; and is extended in C major's flat submediant A flat (remote from the initial A major), and so into its relative F minor. After a pause on the dominant (bar 160), the rising scale section of the first subject reasserts its counterpoint in F major (again a flat submediant in relation to A), and prances into wittily overlapping canon, pianistically both original and risible:

Ex. 8

The canons eventually leap their way to a dominant pedal on E, with explosive cross-accents and grinding dissonance; and so, after a longish silence, to the recapitulation, which is orthodox, the second subject's multiple modulations being repeated in the same relationships, but in the new keys. The codetta ends with its hymnic minims drooping over the rising quavers, and fades out on a bar's silence, wherein we hear a question mark. Silence may indeed be audible!

What the question might be asking is inherent in the rondo-like slow movement, which the young Beethoven boldly but justifiably marked *largo appassionato*. For it is not, like the slow movement of opus 2 no. 1, a relapse into Rococo affectation, but the first of those noble arias which, during Beethoven's middle and later years, are to embrace the heart of his humanistically religious experience. The theme, beginning on the third of the tonic D major, undulates after three repeated notes down and up a step, faintly suggesting the ceremonial sarabande rhythm in the second 3/4 bar. Three-part harmony is resonant, in the middle of the keyboard; the bass is melodic, in the style of a pizzicato cello. The melody lifts a fourth to the subdominant triad, the accompanying parts flowing in tenths; cadences in a double appoggiatura; modulates with trills and a turn to the dominant; and returns to the original phrase with the sarabande syncopations more strongly marked, the texture now wide-spaced:

Ex. 9

The next episode modulates more luxuriously to B minor and F sharp minor and, by way of F sharp's Neapolitan G major, to E minor; and thence back to D major for the next statement of the hymn. A passage in flowing quavers and semiquavers, often chromaticized, seems like another episode, but the hymn tune does not reappear as expected. Instead it returns in sudden fortissimo in the minor, the 'pizzicato' bass now grimly stamping; modulates again to the flat submediant (B flat); and arrives back at D major by way of a dominant pedal, tinged with crying appoggiaturas, *sfp*. The final statement of the hymn is melodically the same as its first statement, but an octave higher, with the semiquaver appoggiaturas whimpering in an inner part; the pizzicato bass is also gentler, because higher. The final dominant–tonic cadences are almost courteous, which may be necessary, after the hymn's solemnity and the violence of its D minor eruption, if the sonata is to re-establish socially biased comedy for the next movement.

Beethoven calls it Scherzo, though its relation to the aristocratic minuet and trio is still discernible. Like the first movement, it begins with an arpeggiated figure, a rise to the dominant and immediate return to the tonic. Rhythmic structure is elliptical; and after the double bar the little arpeggio modulates rapidly to F sharp minor, C sharp minor and G sharp minor. Here there's an attempt at songfulness, with a theme incorporating repeated notes and a rising and falling undulation, as in the slow movement's hymn. After six bars, however, this peters out in romantically drooping sequential sevenths; and leads, after another silence embracing a question mark, to a repeat of the first period:

Ex. 10

The relatively strenuous trio, in the tonic minor, tries to create a more continuous tune from the stepwise undulation, but holds itself together only by way of a dominant pedal, over which the undulation often dissonantly grinds. The da capo of the scherzo releases laughter in its bubbling arpeggios, though the question marks remain.

They're not fully answered even in the lovely finale, which seeks a synthesis of the first movement's disruptive wit and the slow movement's lyrical gravity. It's a rondo, marked *grazioso*, and begins once more with a rising A major arpeggio which would flower into song. It lands on the high E, which is repeated twice, descends through a sixth extended into the lower octave, and after a slight hiccup, rises up the scale. The tempo is easy, no faster than *moderato*. The four-bar phrase is then repeated with the descending sixth changed to a seventh, and cadences in the dominant:

Ex. 11

The succeeding interwoven quaver scales recall the contrapuntal scales of the first movement, but are more hazily romantic since they clash with a dominant pedal. Each repetition of the rondo tune is delicately decorated, a variation technique which overflows into the following episode. The first real episode, in the dominant, floats in paired quavers, which become agitated in syncopation, only to be healed by a smiling return of the rondo song, lilting in a dotted rhythm.

The next episode is, however, of a sterner metal. In the tonic minor, it hurls a leaping triad and rigid dotted rhythm in the left hand against chromaticized triplets in the right. The hands and material are inverted as the music modulates to the relative, C major. After a double bar the chromatic triplets are combined with sighful appoggiaturas, at first fortissimo, then echoed in wistful pianissimo. This tight music climaxes in sforzando cross-accents until, with a rapid pianissimo scale from nearly the bottom to the top of Beethoven's keyboard, the rondo song languidly resumes, exquisitely garlanded. The first episode returns, in the tonic, as in a sonata recapitulation; and after the rondo tune has floated into a Neapolitan F major, it manages to fuse even the ferocious second episode into its lyrical grace. B flat major functions as a Neapolitan to A, as had F to the dominant, and the screwed-up dotted rhythm dissolves in flowing scales, and so into the last, most flowerily elegant (almost Chopinesque, rather than Hummel-like) version of the rondo tune, beneath which chromatic passing notes sensuously colour the momentary modulation to the relative. Beethoven has civilized wit into *cortesia*, which is both a social and a spiritual quality; in so doing he has heard, however distantly, the hidden song that makes the heart whole.

Since the experiential pattern of this beautiful sonata—so maturely subtle an achievement for a young man—is the core of Beethoven's later work, it is not surprising that it is echoed in several early sonatas. There is a suggestion of it even in the third of the opus 2 sonatas, which boldly juxtaposes a first movement allegro that plays rhythmic, harmonic and tonal jests with material revived from Beethoven's teens, with a nobly expressive adagio in E major (the upper mediant), only to demolish pathos in a wittily imitative scherzo and rampageous trio. The rondo-sonata finale is again equivocal, however; for although it is very fast, in a gossamer-textured 6/8, and jokes outrageously in tonal puns and metrical contradictions, it ultimately dissolves in flickering chromatics and bell-like trills that are the first intimation of the 'celestial' trills typical of late Beethoven. Moreover, the trills fade into silence, followed by an echo of the theme in the lower mediant (A major): a glimpse over the horizon, or a murmur of the hidden song, which is bluffly dismissed by contrary motion scales in octaves and the bump of a dominant–tonic cadence, on the beats.

The E flat sonata, opus 7, though on a grander scale, is even closer to the 'pattern' of opus 2 no. 2. The first allegro is itself relatively song-like, though its lyricism is disrupted by cross-accents such as the syncopated pedal-note in the codetta. The magnificent slow movement is marked *largo, con gran espressione* and preserves in its arching though broken lines and its double-dotted rhythm, the heroic note of the old Baroque world, while imbuing it with Beethovenian expressivity so that it becomes, again, a humanistic hymn. The scherzo has an arpeggiated theme which remains seductively lyrical, even when it's irregularly fragmented, and which sounds still more songful when it returns after the tempestuous E flat minor trio. The final sonata-rondo, though again on a larger scale, repeats the pattern of the finale to opus 2 no. 2: for the easy-going melody, wistful with sighing appoggiaturas and flushed with chromatic passing notes, is disturbed by episodes of harmonic and rhythmic violence, returning after each assault more delicately ornamented, more vulnerable in its songfulness. The coda's pianissimo modulation to E (really F flat) major and its dissolving arpeggios are harbingers of pianistic romanticism: nostalgia for the song of the Forgotten Garden which Beethoven cannot yet recover.

Most crucial of all these early song-seeking sonatas, however, is the third member of opus 10, in D. Again the first movement starts by playing witty games with rudimentary material, a rising and falling scale in presto crotchets. It turns out, however, to be a quite long and complex movement, for the introduction of a 'darker' tune in B minor and of a hymn-flavoured codetta theme in minims means that Beethoven has to enlarge his exposition in order adequately to establish the dominant. It also means that, after the tonal pranks and the bizarre metrical dislocation just before the recapitulation, he needs to expand that section into an extraordinary coda wherein an extended version of the hymn-like motive is brushed off by fragments of the crotchet scale in contrary motion, and by a flurry of quavers over a pedal which stops, rather than ends, on an offbeat, followed by a (notated) bar of silence. The expectant, questioning character of this movement depends on the pervasiveness of upbeats and offbeats, which seem to be countered by the heavily downbeat nature of the following *largo e mesto*, in the tonic minor and a slow swinging 6/8. This is justly the most celebrated of Beethoven's first period slow movements; it combines hymnic gravity with quasi-operatic passion.

The thick, dark texture of the D minor opening—a chromatic undulation that rises through a minor third and falls through a diminished fourth, expanding into throbbing diminished sevenths and minor ninths—is alleviated by the second eight-bar clause, which is operatically lyrical over an Alberti bass. But having arrived at the dominant (A minor) by way of C major, the music finds that its severity has been intensified as well as enriched by its infusion of operatic passion. The diminished sevenths (marked *ffp*) and syncopated cross-accents are savage; and a middle section, resonantly spaced in F major, soon splinters in sequential modulation through G and A minor, with ghostly demisemiquavers beckoning back to the tonic. There are two more complete statements of the aria-hymn, the first of which resembles a sonata recapitulation in that its second eight-bar clause stays, by way of a Neapolitan modification, in the tonic instead of modulating to the dominant. The final statement, beginning at bar 65, is darkly in the bass, supporting undulating arpeggios in demisemiquaver triplets, dissonantly intensifying. At bar 72 these arpeggios dissipate into flickering, broken demisemiquavers, and so into a thinly scored coda wherein the original thematic motive is splintered into a falling diminished fourth, followed by a rising chromatic semitone. Broken from the rest of the phrase, this semitone becomes an appoggiatura which is paradoxically unaccompanied. That's what is left after a brief return to the muddy texture of the opening, with passing notes grating against a tonic pedal. After it the appoggiatura sounds the more forlorn, suspended over space and silence.

This is Beethoven's first indubitably tragic movement, and in a sense it proves too much for him to undertake at this stage, in the context of this work. For the minuet and trio (so titled; its character is less scherzoid than that of the comparable movements in the other early sonatas) is light-weight, though subtle in the metrical ambiguities occasioned by the initial upbeat tied across the bar. Although the rondo starts from a chromatic semitone and rising third, clearly recalling the theme of the aria, it is the most fragmented of these song-seeking finales. Any reminiscence of the aria is punctured as the would-be cheeky little phrase ends, again and again, in mid-air, in a rest or on a pause, or is bamboozled by extravagant modulations, or by a weird chromatic unison, as in the passage at bar 50. When the motive, which itself sounds like a question, is answered by inversion in semiquavers (bars 85 ff.) the effect is at once comic and pathetic. At bar 100 it dissipates in contrary motion stretti, and in oddly syncopated sequential sevenths, before flickering out over a tonic pedal, with a haze of chromatic scales and a wash of dominant and tonic arpeggios.

This astonishing sonata 'fails' in its quest for the Hidden Song only because in its slow movement Beethoven has, perhaps for the first time, fully faced the tragic implications of being human, yet cannot, at this stage, go 'through' tragedy not simply to 'happiness', but to a paradisal joy. Opus 10 no. 3 is so significant a work in his life because through it he learned, or became intuitively aware, that the playfully ferocious tigger cub of his first (F minor) sonata had to grow into the Blakean Tyger of the first movement of opus 111, for ultimately democratic revolution involved more than a conflict between the self and external authority, however adumbrated. The real conflict—as was suggested in the previous chapter—was between divided elements within the psyche; before democratic man could assume responsibility for other people's destiny he had to put his own spiritual house in order. Sonata had always been a principle of composition rather than a formal mould into which 'content' could be poured; in the hands of the masters, notably Haydn and Mozart, it had sprung from a tense equilibrium between the private and the public life. This equilibrium is not shattered by the young Beethoven, though we have seen how it begins, both comically and tragically, to founder. After the admission of tragedy into opus 10 no. 3, Beethoven was forced to admit that he had far to go before he could encompass the hidden song that is the self undivided. It is not fortuitous that his next sonata, opus 13, returns to his strifeful key of C minor, and is the first of his sonatas to introduce a structural modification, over and above intermittent harmonic and rhythmic perturbations, into the classical form.

The first movement allegro of the *Sonate Pathétique* (the tag, which is Beethoven's and therefore appropriate and significant) is built on an imposing scale, and is prefaced by a slow introduction that recurs, with modifications, throughout the movement. The procedure is irregular, though to precede a sonata allegro with a solemn introduction was a convention long established. When Haydn and Mozart employ such an introduction the point is clear enough: the prelude reinvokes the world of aristocratic autocracy, often incorporating the ceremonial dotted rhythm and the stilted gait of the Lullian operatic overture, to which the King and nobility had made a regal ingress. The sonata allegro then sweeps aside this spiritual and technical archaism; or at least recreates it in a new, democratic reality, springing from dualistic conflict rather than from an order externally imposed. It isn't a simple case of black against white, for the glory that was Greece (or Versailles) is admitted to be glorious. None the less, we cannot listen to a mature symphonic allegro of Haydn, after its slow introduction, without feeling that the 'becoming' of the allegro is a new order that to some degree discredits the old.

Beethoven, in his introduction to the *Pathétique* sonata, preserves the traditional grandeur of the genre, even to the conventional tightly dotted rhythm. Yet one could not mistake this music for a Haydn or Mozart operatic or symphonic *grave*; and one can define the difference in terms of the interior tension typical of Beethoven. The dotted rhythm has become not so much an exhibition of rhetorical panache, directed outwards to the world, as a tightening of the nerves and sinews, which is the more potent because the opening phrase is at once restrictive and generative. The sustained minor triad, thickly registered in the lower reaches of the keyboard, thrusts up through a minor third in the top voice, with the same third inverted as bass. Having attained the E flat, it is harmonized with the diminished seventh of G minor, which the bass approaches by a leap through a tritone. The diminished seventh itself—traditionally a chord of horror in Baroque opera, since its interlocked tritones are harmonically neutral and thus undermine tonality—resolves on to G major, which becomes domin-

ant to C minor. Never before had Beethoven started a work with so
germinal a seed, for from the rising and falling minor third, and from
the diminished fifth *rectus et inversus*, is derived all the material of the
introduction; and the allegro is an explosion, and a reinterpretation, of
the same motivic tension. There is no longer the classical dichotomy
between the introduction and the allegro. If the introduction is heroic,
and it is, the Hero is no longer the King as God's surrogate; he is the
Beethoven who said, pointing to his head and heart, '*My* nobility is
here, and here'.

Ex. 12

The rise in the dotted rhythm through a minor third, which reaches a
diminished seventh and resolves on the dominant, is followed by a
silence. The figure is then repeated a fourth higher and therefore in C
minor, but with the harmonic process inverted; we now *start* with a
diminished seventh and resolve, in a painfully dissonant triple suspension, on the first inversion of the tonic. The next bar intensifies the
process by doubling the harmonic pulse-rate: the dotted-rhythmed
thirds occur twice in the one bar, moving from the G minor
diminished seventh back to the dominant of C. The next bar augments
the pulse to quavers and crotchets, expanding the melody while tonality falls to a first inversion of the subdominant, F minor. Up to this
point the screwing up of harmonic and rhythmic tension has been

incremental; now tension is released as the expanded melody transforms its subdominant resolution into a 'real' modulation to the
relative major, E flat. The cadence is also a quasi-operatic cadenza: a
roulade of hemidemisemiquavers that ends with the motivic tritone.
In the new key, powerfully 'positive' for Haydn and Mozart as well as
Beethoven, the motive of a rising third sings again, pushing through a
major instead of a minor third over a pulsing accompaniment of tonic
triads. In this major form the dotted motive, though still urgent, seems
less tight; the appoggiatura over the subdominant triad is a sigh but
also a release. Songfulness is then abruptly obliterated as the right hand
pounds out the dotted rhythm fortissimo, back in C minor, while the
left hand descends heavily through the minor third. The same pattern
is repeated sequentially through the next few bars, each reiteration,
through C minor, D minor, G minor and back to C, stressing the
aspiration of the dotted-rhythm scales and the anguish of the appoggiaturas, which at first resolve downwards, then upwards. The shift
from downwards to upwards resolution in bars 6–9 gives the music a
fervent intensity that anticipates Wagner's *Tristan*, which is hardly
surprising, given Beethoven's conviction that he alone could be
responsible for his destiny; long before *Tristan* Beethoven had admitted that it was 'I myself who brewed the potion'. But Beethoven does
not continue to project an inner distress into operatic rhetoric. The last
chromatic upthrust on to the dissonant appoggiatura resolves on to a
dominant seventh of C minor, which moves to a half-close on an A flat
major triad. Three beats of silence are passion-fraught: until an elaborately decorated cadence—an expansion of the earlier cadenza into the
relative—carries us chromatically to a descending diminished seventh
in the dotted rhythm. The pause which Beethoven indicates on the top
note should not be so long that we fail to recognize the genesis of this
rhythm and harmony, which serve as springboard to the sonata
allegro.

The 'scoring' of this prelude is as interesting as its thematic and
harmonic content, from which, of course, scoring is indivisible.
Beethoven's early piano music is well written for the instrument, in
that everything lies under the fingers and creates resonance; but it is
not essentially pianistic, as is the idiom of a middle-period work such
as the Waldstein Sonata or the triptych of the last three sonatas. In
playing the F minor sonata from opus 2 it is, we observed, often
helpful to think of the timbres, dynamics and textures of the Mannheim orchestra: the bounding string arpeggios, the repeated note

figurations on woodwind, the barking horns. More remarkably, the slow introduction to opus 13 harks back to the sepulchral trombones and horns of Mozart and Gluck, and at the same time orchestrally anticipates the full flush of Romanticism. The upward yearning motive seems to sing on violins doubled by flutes and oboes, the lower strings and woodwind to play the repeated notes of the accompaniment, and horns and trombones to underline the diminished seventh cadences. When the allegro bursts upon us we return 'orchestrally' to the world of Gluck, but with a precise vehemence approached by no earlier composer.

Superficially the allegro alla breve seems to be poles apart from the introduction, and is so in the sense that it's a new world of feeling. Yet that it is also an implosion and explosion from the introduction's tension is manifest: for its first bar changes the prelude's minor third ascent to a major third, and the second bar ascends from F to A flat at the same pitch as in the introduction. In bars 3 and 4 this pattern is repeated, an octave higher:

Ex. 13

Moreover, tritonal tensions are present in the inner parts, enhanced rather than relaxed by the fact that the bass consists of a tremolando tonic pedal, holding on for grim life, as it were. The bass rises scalewise as the upper parts descend to cadence by way of a diminished seventh. These eight bars are repeated, given greater impetus by the fact that the upward spring is launched by a syncopated accent on middle C. This time the cadence on the dominant is followed by reiterated Gs, tightly offbeat: an attempt to rein in the explosiveness, though the rising minor third is still present, syncopated in the tenor register.

Descending dominant seventh arpeggios flicker through an Italian sixth approach to the cadence. Again the phrase is repeated, with an effect not of architectural balance, but rather of nagging desperation: there may be a Hegelian paradox in the fact that the repeats simultaneously madden and affirm. The semitonic and tritonal motive then bounces up over a dominant pedal: which shifts to the flat submediant and, by way of a diminished seventh of B flat minor, to a dominant pedal of E flat, the tritones emphasized on the offbeats.

   This pedal initiates the second subject, which although more song-like is not simply a release, since its tonality is unexpectedly the *minor* of the relative. Moreover, it is not a new concept since, if it aspires to song, it does so merely through the addition of a B flat a fourth below the original motive of rising minor third (bars 51–63). The song remains frustrated: partly because it is still anchored to a B flat pedal, more because the brief, though potentially lyrical, motive still nags impotently. Each stepwise rising minor third is immediately counter-acted by a descent through the *interval* of a third, prefaced by a grace note painfully lifting through a minor sixth. The darkness of the E flat minor tonality and the division of the phrases between baritone and soprano registers also inhibit release. Only when the tune is repeated and the bass falls to A flat is there a partial relaxation, for the key luxuriously sinks to D flat major and the upward yearning sixths in the melody expand from minor to major, and then open to sevenths:

Ex. 14

Relaxation is only momentary, for the D flat major modulation proves to be an approach to B flat minor, its relative and E flat minor's dominant. Sharpward cyclical modulations from B flat to F to C minors increase energy: but not in an unambiguously positive manner, since the minor thirds of the tune are now contracted to seconds which, phrased in pairs decorated with a querulous mordent, droop down the scale after the upward leap of the seventh.

Some kind of resolution occurs, however, when the key changes from C minor to its relative E flat major, and Beethoven introduces the codetta theme (bar 89). The bass descends down the scale, arpeggiated quavers rock in the middle parts, the top voice sustains minims across the beat—a 'holding on' effect extended, perhaps, from bars 17 and 18. The top voice moves chromatically upwards while the bass descends diatonically to effect a conventional IV–V–I cadence; when the passage is repeated the cadence is slightly modified into II first inversion–V–I. The next eight bars seek to evade Beethoven's inner fury, for they chatter through a VI–IV–V–I peroration with cheery Rococo scales on top (bars 113–21). This may be 'another mode of experience that is possible', perhaps even desirable, for lesser mortals; but one wouldn't expect it to be a conclusion to Beethoven's exposition. Nor is it; for the upward-springing motive with its thirds and tritones recurs, at first in the relative major, but soon descending through the bass to a strenuous C minor, with sforzando accents and with hammerblow semibreves in sixths and thirds, plunging through an octave to the exposition's repeat.

This repeat is usually taken from the beginning of the allegro, which accords with eighteenth-century practice. There is, however, nothing in any published score to indicate that the repeat should not include the introductory *grave*; and Rudolf Réti believes that to do so makes better sense, since the introduction's tension inevitably generates the allegro. Against this view is the fact that to incorporate what amounts to a longish slow movement into the middle of a sonata allegro severely taxes a player's ability to sustain momentum; and one might say that fully to repeat an embryonic psychological process makes no sense at all. An explosion, once generated, has occurred; one can hardly repeat its genesis, though one might fragmentarily recall the psychological events that had led to it. This, anyway, is what Beethoven does after the repeat of the exposition, and before the development proper: he returns to the *grave*, in the dominant, G minor, and modulates in the third bar, by way of an enharmonic pun that changes the E flat of the G minor diminished seventh to D sharp, to a mysteriously remote E minor. If this is a glimpse over the horizon, *another* mode of experience that might be possible, its solemnity evaporates in sonorously falling seventh and ninth chords over a syncopated dominant pedal. The allegro development reasserts man's desperate humanity, as though affirming Wallace Stevens's words:

> To say more than human things with human voice,
> That cannot be; to say human things with more
> Than human voice, that, also, cannot be;
> To speak humanly from the height or from the depth
> Of human things, that is acutest speech.

Beginning in E minor, a lower mediant to G and upper mediant to C, and so prophetic of many violent mediant relationships in Beethoven's later music, the motivic fourths and tritones at first leap above a tonic pedal. The balancing clause in bars 3–5 is, however, a literal quotation of the introduction's rising third and drooping appoggiatura, with the crotchet pulse more or less equivalent to the prelude's semiquaver. This also reveals an affinity between the cantabile phrase from the introduction and the allegro's second subject. But whatever the opening of the development may suggest, there is no synthesis of dynamic drama and lyrical song. The bass descends chromatically to D, and the passage is sequentially repeated in G minor (bar 143). The semitonic motive, phrased across the beat, takes over as texture thins and the music flickers through sequential modulations vacillating between F and G minor, B flat and C. Dynamics decline to pianissimo as we seek the stability of a dominant pedal, around which shimmering chromatics are entwined. From this the original springing motive spurts, to climax on sforzando accents, treble and bass widely separated. The sonority is rugged, and sounds more desperate when repeated, extended from two bars to six, still over the dominant pedal, with searing trills. The pedal remains implicit after it has ceased to be audible, and the right hand descends in a cadenza that chromatically embellishes a dominant seventh. When the cadenza reaches its low C we are already swept into the recapitulation (bar 195).

Though much has happened in this development, it does not chronometrically last long, and does not need to, since both exposition and recapitulation involve developmental elements. Thus the passage in the exposition wherein, after the second upward spurt, minims fall over a rising bass, is extended, in the recapitulation, from two to twelve bars. These effect fairly abstruse modulations, first to a Neapolitan D flat major, then to E flat minor (the original key of the second subject), and then to F minor. This subdominant to the home tonic now carries the second subject, a tone higher than in the exposition, and subtly changed in that the leaping sixths in grace notes become liberating octaves. When the bass descends to G, the second subject sings in the tonic minor. Similarly the codetta theme is now in C minor, with momentary modulation to the subdominant. The passage of Rococo frivol sounds, in the tonic minor, less evasory: darker, even a shade frantic, preparing us for the climactic statement of the upward spurting figure and the hammerblow of the plunging octaves, which land on a ferocious diminished seventh of G minor. A retrospect of the introduction sounds from a distance, falling cyclically from G to C to F minor, and so to a measured cadence, in steady quavers, to the tonic. Finally the allegro theme bounds up in an immense crescendo, concluding in short, sharp chords of G minor diminished seventh, 6–4, dominant seventh, and tonic of C minor, separated by silences, and followed by a pause bar in which silence should be audible!

This is a powerful end to the movement, but it is not and could not be a conclusion to the sonata. Though it reminds us what fury the *grave* has released, that fury remains unresolved. Only in relation to the adagio and the rondo finale can we fully understand the first movement; such an organic interconnection between the parts and whole has been discovered by Beethoven in the brief years since his opus 2. We have seen that in the F minor sonata there is point in the fact that the last movement renders overt some parodistic elements that were latent in the previous movements; but there is no inevitable reason why that first allegro had to be followed by precisely that aria and minuet. In the A major sonata of opus 2, the D major of opus 10, and the E flat sonata opus 7 there is an approach towards an 'experiential' relationship between the movements, in that all these sonatas are a quest for song. But, even more than the *largo e mesto* of opus 10, the slow movement of opus 13 is inevitable to the total design, both because it has motivic relationships with the allegro, and because its function is positive, as compared with the tragic and ultimately frustrating pathos of that *largo*. Here the 'hymnic aria' hinted at in those earlier slow movements is fully consummated. It is a type of melody which Beethoven created or perfected, for there are no precedents for these noble tunes except possibly in Mozart's Masonic musics and in Gluck's monumental choruses. That gives us a clue as to the kind of experience they are. They are not concerned with the heroic grace of an aristocratic world—which Beethoven still refers to, in more introverted terms, in the introduction to the allegro; they are concerned with a heroism of the spirit, with a love that binds men in fraternity. Melodically, an eighteenth-century elegance is preserved in the symmetrical contours, but Baroque ornament is avoided, either in the form of melismatic decoration or of dissonant appoggiatura. Part-writing is 'real', but eschews complexity; harmonically, triads favour root position. Later, Beethoven was to discover metaphysical and mystical overtones to this ethical humanism, as is manifest if we compare this noble tune with the still sublimer hymn-aria that is the theme of the variations in opus 109.

The key of this adagio is A flat major, the passively flat submediant to C minor. Its form is a cross between rondo and variation, in that the episodes between the statements of the song affect not only how we hear it, but also its intrinsic figuration. Though the song doesn't grow like a sonata movement, it is not entirely static; it attains the repose of a man who could create the sonata allegro. The balm-dispensing qualities of the music, as compared with the first movement's violence, are manifest in the first eight-bar clause, which is harmonized in three real parts, spaced in the middle of the keyboard. The inner part enriches the euphony with Alberti figuration, but is not for that reason less melodic; indeed when in the third bar it introduces a modulatory D natural, it crosses over to become, in effect, the upper part. Moreover, the hymn theme itself implies a crossing and dovetailing of parts; the basic motive of descending third (inverting the motive of the *grave*) rings through C, B flat and A flat, resonantly doubled in sixths or tenths. The second half of the hymn also recalls the second half of the *grave*, in that falling perfect fifth is followed by falling tritone, effecting modulations that balance the rising and falling contours of the tune. Thus after the first two self-enclosed bars the melody mounts through a tonic arpeggio and modulates to the dominant. Tonality flattens again as the melody falls through its perfect fifth, but sharpens when the tritonal descent prompts a dominant seventh approach to B flat minor. This is not a 'real' modulation, but a II–V–I approach to a tonic cadence; the hymn is then repeated an octave higher, with an additional Alberti-style middle part to fill in the texture. The sonority glows:

Ex. 15

After the cadence, which telescopes dominant with tonic, the flowing accompaniment turns into repeated notes or chords, in the relative minor. The theme of this first episode reiterates an inversion of the *grave*'s scalewise thirds. The texture of the hymn suggests singing strings with some woodwind doubling and sustained horns in the middle, and the solo melody is here oboe-like, melancholic, even bleak. But after a sighing appoggiatura we modulate, by way of a vocal turn, to C minor and then, through an ornamented miniature cadenza similar to that in bar 4 of the first movement's introduction, to C minor's relative, E flat major. Five and a half bars of alternating tonics and dominants, supporting gentle semiquaver appoggiaturas, re-establish the warm texture, and lead to a restatement of the hymn, unaltered. The next episode, prompted perhaps by the weeping semiquavers, moves darkly in the tonic minor of A flat. Melodically it links the falling thirds to the tritone, inverted. The bass line extends the weeping into slightly more agitated triplets, the two-part accompanying chords in the middle also being in triplets. The hymn tune resembles a cello melody singing in tenor register, and we may think of this episode as a duet for clarinet and bassoon, with string accompaniment. The darker tone-colour gives this episode something of the effect of a sonata development: the more so when the music modulates dramatically through the mediant, from A flat to F flat (notated as E) major, and then from F flat to a hint of C flat (= B) major. The melody acquires wings, leaping from arpeggiated triplets to sustained notes, with the triplet accompaniment thickly scored:

Ex. 16

After this climax, the rising and falling third theme sounds again, quietly, as though in duet for oboe and bassoon. Blissful E major behaves again as F flat, becoming a Neapolitan approach to a cadence in E flat minor. Diminished sevenths rise in arpeggiated triplets, slightly minatory, as though for pizzicato double basses. An F flat in the bass leads into a cadence back to A flat major; and the hymn chants again, at the original pitch, but garlanded with the triplet figuration of the last episode. This makes it more animated, though not more agitated.

As before, the melody is repeated with an additional inner part, also in triplets. After the dominant modulation the bass's rising arpeggios recall the quasi-double bass pizzicati of the episode, but are now devoid of threat. A coda, built over repeated note triplets, extends the introduction's cadential motive: a three-note rise up the chromatic scale floats down from a dominant ninth and cadences in a turn (bar 67). This dams the hymn's flow, and is repeated with the addition of the higher octave. The end is curious: a dominant–tonic cadence, garlanded with triplets, is repeated three times, a ceremonious bowing. It is not exactly a return to the 'old' world, though it is significant that an early, as opposed to a late, Beethoven hymn should end up sounding social and civic, rather than religious.

The finale is called a rondo, but has some of the attributes of a sonata allegro. It synthesizes the dynamism of the first movement with the adagio's rich repose, and its tempo, though marked *alla breve*, should certainly be less hectic than the *alla breve* of the first movement. Beethoven does not want its graciousness sentimentalized; on the other hand he expects us to recognize the music's relationship to classical tradition, for instance to Mozart's great C minor sonata with the Fantasia. The theme begins with the three notes that initiate the first movement's second subject; after this upbeat, it sings the scale-wise third in inversion, with two embellishing notes. In its third and fourth bars it settles on dominant Gs, as did the first allegro after its two upward explosions. Bars 5 and 6 call on the basic motive of descending tritone and perfect fifth; bars 7 and 8 return to the declining third:

Ex. 17

The falling perfect and imperfect (diminished) fifths are directly related, in inverse order, to the second half of the hymnic adagio. Repeated, the passage hints at a subdominant modulation, but cadences in the tonic.

The first episode opens (bar 18) with a third inversion dominant seventh of F minor sustained through a bar, then bounces up in arpeggiated quavers, and cadences through a repeated chord figure in the left hand. The passage is sequentially repeated a tone lower, but in the major. This relatively cheery music recalls the codetta theme of the first movement; and is readily reconcilable with the relaxed manner of this rondo finale. It leads into a motive of wriggling triplets, which may be a frivolous version of the ceremonial bows at the end of the adagio. The rising fourths of the triplets merge into an E flat version of the repeated note figure, harmonized in four parts, as though for woodwind. The motive of rising fourth and fifth has been elevated into a theme, even a faintly hymnic tune; but a recurrence of the wriggling triplets explodes in a scale, descending from the high F over a dominant seventh, to swirl back into C minor. The rondo tune is restated, unchanged.

The next episode descends to the flat submediant, A flat, spaced in the middle of the keyboard (bar 79). There is now no ambiguity about its recollection of the adagio's fifths and fourths, and the music's hymnic character is still clearer when the passage is repeated in freely syncopated canon. The two or four parts are 'real', suggesting embryonic fugato:

Ex. 18

Texture is lucent, yet resonant, until an undulating dominant pedal (bar 107) leads to a resurgence of the triplets, another cascading scale over the dominant seventh, and a return to the rondo tune. The first part of this restatement is literal, though the falling fifths are then transferred to tenor register, with broken arpeggios on top. The merry Rococo passage, the canonic triplets and the four-part harmonized tune reappear in the tonic major, as they might in a sonata recapitulation. Though all this, in tonic major recapitulation, sounds radiant compared with its first presentation, the gaiety remains classically restrained. The episodes haven't really functioned like a sonata development, though enough has happened to provoke a typically Beethovenian coda.

This begins when, on the path back to the rondo, a semitonic motive A sharp to B, grows obtrusive (bar 167), for although it seems that the rondo tune will be repeated unchanged, it gradually garners chromatic passing notes. The wriggling triplets become aggressive rather than cheerful, with thick chords interjected in offbeat syncopation. Climax comes with the syncopated chords followed by scales falling through a fifth in semiquavers, and therefore in diminution (bar 193). The passage is repeated and screwed up to a Neapolitan D flat which, instead of returning to the dominant, becomes a real modulation to A flat major, succeeded by a pause. When, after a cascading scale, the rondo theme sounds again, with the first note of its upbeat omitted, its relationship to the adagio hymn is patent. It peters into silence; lifts brokenly to a German sixth, through an augmented fourth; and then through a perfect fifth to a scarcely audible C minor 6–4. The triplets swoop down fortissimo; the end is abrupt, not triumphant.

In total effect Beethoven's opus 13 equivocates, renouncing the grand gestures it had started from. Compared with the first movement theme, the rondo tune gracefully sings, and builds up its clauses cumulatively. It also dances, implying corporeal energy. Yet the tune is not, despite its classical symmetry, entirely self-contained; the mere fact that the episodes *are* episodic is a recurrent frustration. The rondo does not, like middle-period Beethoven, achieve or even seek resolution through the force of the human will nor, like late Beethoven, does it flower in consummated song. The sonata begins by rejecting precedents, and ends by partially reinstating them. Yet though Beethoven is biding his time, the rondo's coda tells us that he knows that he cannot look back. The ultimate challenge, from which he has to remake the very nature of sonata, is not far off. Meanwhile he says farewell to classical tradition, in creating three sonatas which can be characterized as happy works though their joy is also a disturbance. The last of the trio, the sonata in B flat, opus 22, is both the biggest and the most life-enhancing. Beethoven was justifiably proud of it, for it was a dynamo of stored power and lyrical grace, out of which he could launch himself into a holocaust. Appropriately, it was composed at the turn of the century, in 1800.

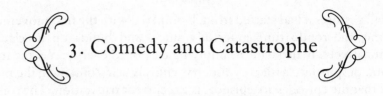

3. Comedy and Catastrophe

Piano sonatas
opus 22 in B flat major
opus 27 no. 2 in C sharp minor (Moonlight)

Cast on a generous scale in the familiar four movements, opus 22 consists of a sonata allegro, an operatic aria in sonata form, a minuet and trio, and a rondo-finale that is halfway to sonata. The first movement, *allegro con brio*, begins in 4/4 with a motive of rocking thirds identical with the motive that, years later, is to initiate the titanic drama of the Hammerklavier Sonata opus 106, in the same key, B flat. The rocking thirds, in crotchets, are at first soft, accompanied by a semiquaver figure that begins with a semitonic wriggle, descends a fourth and leaps a sixth. The bass reiterates two tonic octaves, quasi pizzicato. The upbeat at the end of bar 2 launches the crotchets into a rising bugle-style arpeggio, still accompanied by the wriggle, so the effect of this opening clause is a positive, jaunty version of the Mannheim skyrocket and birdie we commented on in the first, F minor sonata:

Ex. 19

The answering clause, however, is very different in mood, for it flows by step, *sostenuto e cantabile*, like a Rococo operatic aria, and is accompanied by the polite cliché of the Alberti bass:

Ex. 20

Singing lyrically, the tune declines in a suspension, E flat to D; and the elegant pathos is enhanced when, in the answering period, A natural sinks to A flat, suggesting a subdominant modulation which doesn't materialize. The wriggle returns in parallel octaves, and an upshooting scale carries us briskly to the dominant, emphasized by a downward leap through two octaves. This too proves a feint; for after a beat's silence the rising arpeggio and wriggle bounce up again in the bass, land on the F above middle C, and decline through a passage of four-part chromatics, languorous, even lachrymose (bars 13–15), as compared with the earlier vivacity. Surprisingly this leads into a long, conventionally Rococo dominant pedal, with semiquavers clinking on top. Passing notes bump dissonantly into the pedal note.

This terse statement of the first subject material has thus already embraced a variety of moods, from demotic exuberance to aristocratic elegance to 'subjective' pathos; an ironic admission of contrary modes of experience is held in a subtler, more precarious equilibrium than in earlier works. The material presented in the newly established dominant enhances this effect. A rising semiquaver scale ends in a semitonic undulation, and an arpeggiated melody, mostly in parallel thirds, floats over gently rising scales and written out trills, which are the 'wriggle' rendered static (bars 22–5). For four bars there is no harmonic movement, and virtually no melodic movement either, since the tune is simply a spread triad of F major. The melody is open to the sun, as it were; it smiles, while the accompaniment purrs. In bar 26, however, the triad unexpectedly shifts from F to the dominant seventh of G minor, the supertonic, and the semitonic wriggle, descending in the bass, acquires a hint of threat. Such a relatively abstruse modulation might be expected in a development section rather than an exposition; it proves to be another Beethovenian feint, for the bass, having sunk to a low oscillation of C sharp and D that now sounds more like a growl than a purr, rises chromatically to effect a real modulation to the dominant. What follows (bars 30–8) is the main section of the second subject, which returns to the thirds of the opening, now all in descent, and in a rhythm suggested by that of the F major triad motive. The trumpet or horn-like sonority hints at heroism and is vigorously assertive, the more so since the parallel thirds and sixths incorporate a dotted rhythm that marches down the scale. When the parallels cease, the four-part texture, modulating to D minor, is hymnic; but the simple F major cadence, though not bathetic, clears the music of portentousness. In repetition the second subject acquires syncopated accents that impart an air of hilarity to its grandeur:

Ex. 21

This time the D minor cadence is resolved in wave-like arpeggios that, at their crests, more tensely recall the original semitonic wriggle. Sequentially we move from D minor to C to F minor; and so back to the dominant major, a I–VI–IV–V cadence being defined by thematic minims in the bass. In the codetta theme, over a rolling dominant pedal, Rococo vivacity is darkened by the flattened subdominant. The dotted rhythm is followed by the wriggle augmented to quavers, oscillating between G flat and G natural, uncertain whether to press dissonantly down to F or to rise:

Ex. 22

Beethoven doesn't resolve the ambiguity, but brushes it aside with a fortissimo, and pounds out the march's dotted rhythm in parallel octaves, stumping up the scale, only to thump down again. Since this march marches nowhere, the final statements of the wriggle in repeated dominant–tonic cadences sound like Rococo cliché, and are meant to. The potentially heroic second subject and the potentially mysterious codetta theme have been dismissed by a trumpery trumpet.

The development begins mildly with the wriggle and leaping sixth bandied between the hands, but sweeps the figure away with the dotted-rhythmed march in octaves. This time the march doesn't inanely revolve on itself, for it modulates to G minor: precisely that tonal adventure which had been anticipated in the exposition. Having reached a dominant pedal of G minor, the right hand extends the undulations of the codetta theme (which is the wriggle at half speed); and this time the figure's latent mystery and drama are not evaded. The march's dotted rhythm returns fortissimo in freely canonic sixths and thirds, answered by inversion, with grinding dissonance: a passage distantly prophetic of the fugato sections in opus 101 and 106.

A cadential diminished seventh sends the semiquavers seething to the heights, and the clause is repeated in cyclically descending fifths from G to C to F minor. By now the drama is real: the left hand sustains slow arpeggios undulating through fifths, while the right hand mingles the semiquavers, now fierce, with clattering arpeggiated triads (bars 92–104). But if we think that the descent to B flat heralds the recapitulation we are in for a further surprise, for the bass falls from the dominant F to F flat, and so to E flat, supporting a dominant seventh of A flat major. The semiquaver arpeggios become a quiet moto perpetuo; in the left hand the dotted rhythm is transformed from a march into a wave-like undulation, potentially song-like, moving to the flat seventh and back. In hushed darkness the arpeggios change to dominant ninths of F minor, while the scale undulates from the low C:

Ex. 23

The sonority suggests a distant storm like that which, in the same 'lugubrious' key, accompanies Schubert's 'Junge Nonne'. In still more mysterious, perhaps minatory, quiet the bass descends to the low F, and the right hand arpeggios become dominant ninths in B flat minor.

What happens then is extremely odd, for after one scalewise undulation up and down, the bass gets stuck on its low F. Four more times it sinks down the scale from C to F, while the right hand's dominant arpeggios murmur on (bars 116–22). It is like a spinning top running down; and although the scale eventually rises again, it does so only in dissipation. There is no change in harmony, or much in dynamics; the scale simply fades on the dominant seventh. Drama and mystery are liquidated, the metaphor being peculiarly appropriate to Beethoven's piano sonority.

After this frustrated development there is a pause on a pianissimo dominant seventh, followed by a recapitulation wherein the ironies become more telling because so many expectations have been defeated. In itself the recapitulation is orthodox, except that in bars 138–40 texture is thickened by combining the rocking thirds simultaneously with the wriggle. The passage ends a minor third higher than in the exposition; the four-part chromatic languishment is extended from two to four bars. In the rococo transition passage the triads are intermittently flattened, reminding us of the darker codetta theme, which now appears, along with the other second subject material, conventionally in the tonic. The final assertion of the dotted-rhythm march is no less perfunctory than it was when first we heard it; yet it's oddly more disturbing, perhaps because, after the development, we know what is at stake. It is worth noting that the close of the movement, though of course in the tonic instead of dominant, exactly mirrors the close of the exposition. There is no coda, for any consummation would be irrelevant. The movement owes its electrical vitality to its equilibrium between strength, wit, pathos, mystery and something (in the top-spinning approach to the recapitulation) that is not far from farce. This emotional complexity is not belied, but is rather rendered more dangerous, by the fact that the movement ends in deliberate banality. Even physically, it's difficult to play those final cadences (bars 197–9) without a shrug of the shoulders.

Beethoven's serious answer to this mysteriously comic piece sounds at first like a reversion to the past, for the slow movement is an Italian operatic aria, less equivocally related to its source than is the rococo aria in opus 2 no. 1, or the hymnic aria of opus 13. Yet this Italianate operatic music looks forwards to Rossini and even Verdi, rather than backwards to Handel and Scarlatti, and it turns out to be an aria not in the traditional 'closed' da capo form, but in the developmental form of sonata. Moreover, its operatic flavour prophetically suggests the transference of vocal styles into pianism such as we find in the nocturnes of Field and Chopin. However outward-going its rhetoric may seem, the piece is concerned with growth, and incipiently with conflict, within the mind. Though sensuous passion is expressed in physical gestures, this outer drama romantically projects an inner strife.

The key is E flat major, B flat's subdomiant. The 9/8 pulse breathes slowly but regularly, like a heart-beat. Over the resonantly scored tonic triads the melody opens with a hiccuping acciaccatura that urges the line up by step: first to a dissonant appoggiatura, A natural to B flat, then, with a shift to dominant seventh harmony, to a B natural appoggiatura. This, clashing with the harmony and ornamentally resolved in a sobbing sixth, creates an almost Verdian plangency. The answering clause, still over a dominant seventh, extends the semiquaver melismata and cadences on a double appoggiatura, F sharp feeling painfully up to G, with the tenor A flat drooping to the G an octave below. This resolution on the tonic triad releases the pain, and the tune rises through a tonic arpeggio whilc the bass fall to a first inversion of the tonic chord. The tune floats down an arpeggio and, having reached middle C, leaps through two octaves. Tension is maintained because the tenor, at the top of the left hand's chugging chords, rises chromatically. The 6–4 cadence begins with a falling appoggiatura, and a trill and turn over the dominant seventh:

Ex. 24

Between bars 8 and 11 this cadential figure is stated three times, falling through two octaves: which politely, almost ceremoniously, deflates operatic passion. After the gradual build up of melodic and harmonic urgency, the music subsides of its own weight, the pendulum swinging to rest. Resolution is not, however, complete, for the final (also threefold) reiteration of the dominant–tonic cadence is disturbed by cross-accents, and another triple appoggiatura (bars 11–12).

After a double bar, an extension to the first subject theme starts with the rising tonic arpeggio of bar 12, leading into the 6–4 cadential formula, scored as though for conversing cellos. When the phrase is repeated, however, it introduces a chromatic passing note, which provokes a chromatically rising bass, supporting sighing appoggiaturas in the right hand. This carries us to the dominant, B flat, and re-establishes an ostinato of pulsing quavers. Above these flows the second subject, which balances the first subject's chromatic rise with a relaxed diatonic descent. The melody notes clash dissonantly, however, with the unmoving pedal, and pain is assuaged only when the middle parts drop out, and the isolated pedal note supports a delicate upward efflorescence of the theme, with a vocal turn, a lifting grace note, and a fluttering chromaticized E natural. The rich texture returns as the music cadences in sonorous parallel sixths and a down-flowing scale. Broken, upward-resolving appoggiaturas balance the falling chromatic appoggiaturas that had appeared in the transition to the second subject; and a 6–4 cadence, moving more slowly than the similar cadences in the first section, is repeated, with arabesques in demisemiquavers. A codetta phrase takes over the rising arpeggio of the second part of the first subject, but resolves it more acutely in a diminished seventh (bar 27). The cadential 'bowing' phrase also recurs, more intensely, since its cross-beat incorporates a dotted rhythm: first dotted semiquaver–demisemiquaver, then dotted quaver–semiquaver, twice. The final cadence into the dominant is a triple appoggiatura on the beat, ornamented with a turn. So, despite its similarity to the end of the first section (bars 10–12), the conclusion of the codetta (bars 28–30) hardly swings to rest 'of its own weight'; we are aware rather of an inner stress which is held in check.

Because of this, the silence that fills the rest of the cadential bar is significant. Out of the silence, the softly pulsing pedal-note quavers resume on G, sounding mysterious because their tonal implications are obscure. When on the third beat the melody enters on B natural it

forms a G major triad in false relation to the B flat major cadence (bar
31). In fact, however, the low Gs prove to be dominants of C minor,
into which key the music moves by way of Tristanesque chromatic
appoggiaturas, with minor ninths painfully falling, and sharpened
elevenths and thirteenths pressing upwards:

Ex. 25

The passage is similar to that in the slow introduction to opus 13,
though slightly less startling because here the operatic context is
explicit. The upward yearning of the melody is counterpoised by
descending sequences in the tonality: for after the semiquaver motive,
with the original acciaccatura, has been repeated in octaves, ripely
scored with seventh chords, the tonality declines from C to F to B flat
to E flat to A flat minor, each descent marked by a sforzando on the
bass's first beat. By the time we have reached A flat minor the semiquaver figuration is continuous, undulating in sensuous parallel sixths
and tenths (bar 39). At this point we may become subconsciously
aware that this semiquaver figure is a metamorphosis of the wriggle
that initiated the first movement. Certainly the passage is affirmative,
even though the broken appoggiaturas sigh, oboe-like, on top, above
the semiquavers' resonance. Moreover, we have risen from the darkness of A flat minor to E flat minor, with a touch of 'enhanced
dominant' over a long dominant pedal; and when this ceases, a solo
arabesque in the running semiquavers re-establishes E flat major and
the aria. The da capo is also a sonata recapitulation.

As in the first movement, the recapitulation is orthodox, though the
first theme is elaborately decorated, much as it would have been by a
solo singer in a High Baroque opera. Ornamentation enhances rather
than dissipates passion, especially when the wide-flung arpeggiated
phrase embraces chromatic appoggiaturas within its descent. The
repeated cadences are unchanged. The second part of the tune, the
transition to the second subject, surprisingly darkens to tonic minor
and extends the chromatic sighs from two to four bars, making a

Neapolitan return to the tonic major (bars 64–5). In this key the second subject sounds more relaxed in its declensions, more airy in its fioriture. Its recapitulation is strict, as is that of the codetta, apart from a few changes of registration. Like the first movement, the adagio merely repeats its codetta material; there is no expansion or consummation in a coda.

The textures of Beethoven's sonata allegro in opus 22 are sharp and clear; even the potentially heroic second subject is open in sonority, chiming in parallel thirds. Complementarily, the sonata adagio is thick in texture. Beethoven does not dissolve the accompaniment, as Field or Chopin would have done, into watery arpeggios, and the pulsing triads, warmly spaced in tenor register, sound almost viscid as the melody expands through its double and triple appoggiaturas. Both movements are of the earth, earthy: bouncing with sheer physical exuberance in the allegro, in the adagio suggestive of the opera singer's head tossed, arms outstretched in the throes of passion. Both movements fascinatingly complement the comparable movements in the later B flat major sonata, opus 106. The two allegros start from the same motive of rocking thirds: but whereas opus 22 exploits the brief motive to 'debunk' classical precedents, the oscillating thirds of the opus 106 allegro generate an apocalyptic drama of mediant relationships. Opus 22 exhibits an active mind and energetic body profiting from tradition while at the same time gleefully undermining it; opus 106 fights an inner battle for the salvation of 'unaccommodated man'. Similarly the adagio of opus 22 never loses contact with the gestures of operatic performance, even though its concept as sonata renders its rhetoric subjective, even romantic. The adagio aria of opus 106 is also a sonata movement, and is also related to Italian bel canto and to Chopinesque fioriture. Yet it is no longer 'operatic' in inverted commas. The immense length of the melody and ecstatic nature of its arabesques make the music air-borne. Opus 22's adagio lyrically accepts its earthly passion, finally trammelled in the codetta's reiterated bows, pedal notes and multiple appoggiaturas; opus 106's adagio lyrically seeks, though it does not consummatorily find, release through a dissolution of the physical.

This, however, is to apply criteria that are not relevant to Beethoven's opus 22, a work of which the young composer was justifiably proud. What makes the sonata so impressive on its own terms is that the two final movements resolve the contradictions of the first two, with a maturity of which Beethoven had not previously been capable.

The third movement is called a Minuetto, to which it is closer than to a Beethovenian scherzo-joke. Yet it lacks the sociable formality of the aristocratic dance; its grace is personalized in the sense that it at once sings and dances, fusing the first movement's body energy with the second movement's lyrical passion. It is hardly a question of overt thematic relationship, though the first phrase reiterates the allegro's rising third at the identical pitch, following it not with a descent, but with an upward semiquaver wriggle. This not only resembles the semiquaver groups of the allegro; it also, being launched by an acciaccatura, recalls the beginning of the adagio aria. Such thematic affinities may be elusive, but are not illusory; although seldom consciously contrived by their composers, they are unconscious evidence of the functioning of compositional unity, and are audibly intelligible to the listener.

The art of music depends of its nature on memory. In this context memory must operate in order that we may appreciate how different the menuetto theme is from the melodies or motives it reminds us of! For whereas the appoggiaturas imbue the adagio's upward thrusts with pain, the ascent in the minuet is a delighted release. Chromatic passing notes in the accompanying quavers enhance animation, which flows into the insouciant dotted rhythms of the third bar. Though the double appoggiatura into the dominant in bar 4 may be an acute dissonance, it feels, as climax to the lilting line, like pleasurable excitation rather than pain:

Ex. 26

The answering four-bar clause declines from this high point. The semiquavers run up to a falling perfect and then an imperfect fifth, the former over a spread dominant seventh, the latter over a spread minor ninth. That chord prevents tension from evaporating into blandness; but the clause ends with three semiquaver groups rising to dominant *major* ninth. This smiles wide-eyed or open-eared: yet is not complacent, since it is followed by another double appoggiatura cadence, this time *falling* to the tonic. The equilibrium of melodic clauses and harmonic tensions makes the opening eight bars sanely satisfying, rather than euphorically merry.

After the double bar there is an eight-bar middle section which amounts to a miniature development. Abruptly modulating to the relative minor, it induces surprise, even a mild shock, without compromising the music's happiness. At first the semiquavers seem to have been trapped in chromatic oscillation; but they are freed by a martially rhythmed cadence, again with double appoggiatura. Freedom, however, proves illusory: for the passage is sequentially repeated in what looks like E flat, but turns out to be C minor, only to cadence on a 6–4 in B flat major, and so to a da capo of the original eight bars. The left hand's spread chords are now filled in with semiquavers, enhancing the lilt. In repeat, the semiquavers are wittily imitated in an alto part, and in a codetta dominants and tonics oscillate in a 2/4 cross-rhythm against the 3/4 pulse (bars 27–30). This repeats an effect from the codettas of both the allegro and adagio, and gives the lyricism of the minuet a gentle undercurrent of irony: its gentility isn't quite what it seems.

This anti-lyrical cross-rhythm makes, however, an unexpectedly violent impact on the trio, which is in the relative (G minor), and is related both in key and in ferocity to the 'martial' passage in the middle section of the minuet. The left hand's impetuous semiquavers are an inversion of the wriggle, now in continuous momentum. The right hand punctures them with dominant and tonic triads, always offbeat, out of alignment with the semiquavers' rhythm. At the end of the eight-bar period Beethoven modulates to D minor, G minor's dominant, only to be wrenched back, after the double bar, not to the tonic but to the subdominant (bars 38–9). Indeed the effect is even subtler, since the canonic entries of the semiquavers could be in E flat major, serving as Neapolitan to D minor. Only at the end of bar 39 do they reveal their C minor identity, and lead back to the tonic minor for a da capo of the first section. This time, with the help of a Neapolitan flattened A in the bass, it stays in the tonic for the final cadence, which at last ties up the metrical ambiguity and reveals that we have been hearing the trio in 3/4, but with accents dislocated across the

metrical pulse, with two tipsy bars of 2/4 to conclude. This gives a
touch of hilarity to the semiquavers' fierceness: an effect that would be
impossible but for the eight-bar symmetry of both minuet and trio.
The da capo of the minuet is unchanged, except in so far as we hear it
with different ears since we now know that the trio's violence was
implicit within it.

   The finale is a rondo of substantial dimensions: more relaxed than a
sonata movement, yet embracing enough sonata-drama convincingly
to round off the work. Flowing in a 2/4 allegretto, it resembles the
finales of opus 7 and opus 10 no. 3, in that it lyrically resolves the
allegro's exuberant comedy, incorporating the adagio's pathos and the
minuet's grace. The smiling tune opens in semiquavers, moving up a
tone, and flowing down the diatonic scale. It is therefore an extension
of the wriggle, rendered song-like, and recalls the adagio in cadencing
on a dominant seventh, by way of an upward-pushing chromatic
appoggiatura:

Ex. 27

Repeated a tone higher, the tune cadences on the tonic, then oscillates
between tonics and dominants, a reflection, in harmonic terms, of the
wriggle itself. This takes us, in the eighth bar, to a dominant modulation which is cancelled by a repetition of the whole clause, the melody
now in octaves, the accompaniment an octave lower. The oscillating
passage is rendered more sensuous by the addition of a chromatic alto
part. Delicate sensuality is implicit too in the chromatic demisemiquavers that approach the tonic cadence (bars 16–17).

The first episode breaks lyrical flow with two-bar phrases stretched across the beats. At first, modulating from tonic to dominant, they are metrically rigid, even though ornamented with cadential trills in dotted rhythm. During the next ten bars, however, spread arpeggios, ties, syncopations and chromatics imbue this music too with sensuality, the bass moving diatonically down from D to F while the treble, tied over the beats, pushes up chromatically.

A graver note emerges when, the dominant clearly established, the left hand spreads sustained chords in quavers, while the right hand adds demisemiquaver roulades. Both figuration and harmony recall the development of the first movement, especially when the bass descends from F to E flat to D flat, and cadences back to an F major triad by way of a German sixth on G flat. But this serious, developmental feeling is whimsically belied when the opening phrase—the extended form of the wriggle—is bandied in dialogue between the hands, at first on C, then trill-decorated on E flat, then in tail-chasing stretti, winding itself up from semiquavers to triplets to demisemiquavers (bars 40–9), and so to a restatement of the rondo, again with the embellished repetition.

The second episode begins with the same offbeat dotted-rhythmed phrase as the first, but in the tonic minor, and without the mollifying turns and trills. The second chord is, moreover, intensified into a first inversion of a Neapolitan C flat: a dramatic stroke the more powerful because it is, in so apparently benign a piece, unexpected. What follows has the potency of a sonata development. Modulating with cross-accents to the dominant minor, a texture of thick parallel thirds, moving scalewise through a fourth, chugs in the left hand (bar 72). These scales echo the opening motive of the rondo tune, and possibly the faster semiquavers of the minuet's trio also. Above this, the right hand executes flickering demisemiquavers: a wilder version of the first movement's transitional passage over a dominant pedal. The cadence is by way of fierce syncopations leaping through an octave and then a sixth, followed by diminished seventh arabesques over murkily telescoped tonic–dominant–subdominant chords. Again there is a sudden change in texture: the 'rigid' phrase, with its thrusting dotted rhythm, is metamorphosed into a screwed-up three-part invention, modulating down the cycle of fifths from F to E flat minor. This severity is then extended in canonic parallel thirds, moving from E flat minor to D flat major to B flat minor:

Ex. 28

False relations are aggressive, though in total effect the sturdy texture of parallel thirds recalls the first movement's near-heroic second subject. In a manner typical of this sonata, however, development is frustrated. Beethoven proceeds neither to evolution from the parallel thirds nor to an orthodox recapitulation, but rather to a repetition of the previous episodic passage. The parallel-thirds scales, the clattering demisemiquavers and the syncopated peroration now appear in the tonic minor; and again drama dissipates in pathos (which later becomes once more comic). The opening phrase reappears, unaccompanied (bar 103), modulating in the left hand from B flat minor to G flat major; cadences in A flat minor; then repeats itself a note higher, as in its original statement. The A flat inches up to A natural, harmonized with a pianissimo diminished seventh in B flat. The top notes wriggle between G flat and F, and then change into a written out demisemiquaver trill, which in turn reaches up to become a trill between F and G natural.

This teetering recalls the oscillations at the same pitch in the codetta to the first movement. Now it leads into a restatement of the rondo, beginning in tenor register, in parallel sixths and thirds, with an accompaniment of delicately floating octaves. Arrived back in the treble, the tune is embellished with demisemiquaver arabesques. The next episode opens identically with the first, but stays in the tonic. The copious material of the first episode—spread chords, chromaticized syncopations, sustained arpeggios with demisemiquaver roulades— is all repeated, centred on the tonic, as in a sonata recapitulation. Yet the episode does not really function as a recapitulation, partly because we have already had a recapitulation of the second episode material, but more because the dramatic implications of that material have been so comically contradicted. The same happens with this episode: frustration has become so much a 'recognition of other modes of experience that may be possible' as to become a source of mirth. The comedy takes the form of a 'false' recapitulation: since the dominant episode has brought back the rondo tune in the tonic, the repeat of the episode, followed through literally, must carry the rondo's recurrence into the subdominant. This starts off merrily enough; realizes it is moving in the wrong direction; breaks off, finding itself in C minor, in tentative dialogue between the hands; and hesitantly winds its way back to the tonic through chromaticized triplets and demisemiquavers over a dominant pedal:

Ex. 29

The tune seems delighted at having recovered from its false start, for its final statement in the tonic is ornamented with cross-rhythmed triplets and chromatics that make the music skittishly laugh; when broken triplets are introduced into the octaved repeat the effect is almost a chortle (bar 178). The rigid offbeat phrase from the first episode is then transformed into a coda, which all three previous movements lacked. Stabilized by complementary touches of dominant and subdominant, and more thickly harmonized, this coda hints at the vigorous, even youthfully heroic tone of the first movement, though the heating up of the 'wriggle' from semiquavers to demisemiquavers ensures that gaiety prevails. After an almost grand 6–4 cadence, approached by a German sixth, the throwaway return to the opening scale-motive pricks any bubble of pretension. In the first movement heroism is tempered, and strengthened, by irony; in these final bars the effect is inverse and complementary, for a comic-pathetic hesitancy is replaced by canonically continuous scales, warmly spaced on the keyboard. Though the two final dominant–tonic cadences, the first soft, the second loud, are funny, they are not deflatory. As a whole, the movement carries a stage further the search for the Hidden Song that was initiated in the rondo finales of opus 2 no. 2, opus 7, and opus 10, no. 3. The sonata does not embrace tragedy, as does the largo of the D major from opus 10, but it explores dimensions within comedy that had been hitherto unsuspected. Opus 22's reconciliatory qualities were essential to Beethoven's maturation.

Opus 22 has been called Beethoven's farewell to the classical sonata: a point emphasized by the fact that the next sonata, opus 26 in A flat, begins with a set of variations and contains no movement in sonata form. It is famous for its A flat minor funeral march on the Death of a Hero: a prototype for the funeral march in the Eroica Symphony, which was to be one of Beethoven's most epochal creations. In this small sonata, however, the funeral march, remarkable though it is, cannot have the dramatic and evolutionary significance it acquires in the context of the vast symphony; and the turning point in Beethoven's piano sonatas is rather the opus 27 pair, which followed in 1801, appropriately in the first year of the new century. Beethoven described these sonatas as being '*quasi una fantasia*', thereby admitting that they did not even look like sonatas according to eighteenth-century recipe. The previous sonata, opus 26, we have remarked, has no movement in sonata form. Nor has opus 27 no. 1; and although the second and more famous of the opus 27 sonatas does include a full-scale sonata allegro, it places it at the end, preceded by two relatively short movements that serve as prelude and interlude. The experiential relationship between these three movements is more 'organic' than anything in Beethoven's previous work; neither the prelude nor the interlude has a completely autonomous existence, apart from the sonata into which it explodes.

The sonority of the opening movement of opus 27 no. 2 is a shock. Beethoven directs that it be played *senza sordini* (which means without dampers, that is, with pedal) throughout; he also played it *una corda*, Czerny tells us, except for the crescendo in the middle section. Beethoven's piano had three strings to every note, and his *una corda* effect was more ghostly, and could be more subtly graduated, than on a modern instrument (see Appendix A). The pianist Roger Woodward has tried the experiment of playing the movement on a large modern piano, with both pedals sustained throughout. Though certainly mysterious and astonishing, the effect hardly approximates to the sound Beethoven had in mind. Whatever the sonority, the *adagio sostenuto*, which earned the sonata its misnomer of 'Moonlight', is mysterious intrinsically. It seems serene, because the bass moves slowly and in stable diatonicism, descending from the tonic stepwise to the submediant, then to the subdominant, and so to the dominant–tonic cadence in C sharp minor, while the arpeggiated triplets of the accompaniment flow in unperturbed regularity:

Ex. 30

Yet even in these introductory bars tranquillity is deceptive, since in bar 3 the bass's F sharp is harmonized not as a subdominant but, with the quaver triplet's D flattened, as a first inversion of the Neapolitan chord of D major. The implied progression from D natural to the cadential B sharp delivers a small stab to the nervous system, anticipating the disturbance of diminished thirds later in the movement. The story that, shortly before composing this adagio, Beethoven had been playing over the passage in Mozart's *Don Giovanni* depicting the death of the Commendatore, may or may not be true. But it is certainly pertinent that affinities between the two passages—the rocking triplets over a pedal, the wailing appoggiaturas, the lacerating Neapolitan—should exist: for in the Commendatore's death an aristocratic Hero and an old world expire, and in Mozart's opera new worlds are in travail. In potent microcosm Beethoven's adagio is also an elegy in which death-throes are inseparable from the pangs of birth. What is in travail is not, however, in this sonata fully manifest.

The relationship between this adagio and the Mozart passage bears on the tricky matter of tempo. The autograph and most, though not all, the early editions have an *alla breve* time signature. This would suggest that a tempo approaching the slow 12/8 often adopted must be alien to Beethoven's intentions; on the other hand a tempo fast enough to suggest the dramatic action of the Commendatore's murder would be absurd. In Beethoven's adagio the violence must remain always latent beneath a surface of glassy calm; the triplets must be triplets, not 12/8 quavers, but the crotchet pulse must surely be as slow as can be convincingly sustained. The slower the pulse, the more dangerous the inner tension, as becomes evident when, after the momentary and apparently slight disturbance of that Neapolitan D natural, a tune emerges, pivoting slowly up a semitone and down a tone around the dominant G sharp.

Its initial dotted rhythm, conflicting with the accompanying triplets, emphasizes the separateness of the melody, which sounds like a distant horn or trumpet, calling across the undulating water, hanging on to its ♪♪♩. rhythm (traditionally a representation of fortitude) and its sustained dotted minim, as though to offset whatever threat the waters may offer. So far, the only hint of threat has been the intrusive D natural in bar 3, and even that seems to be banished once the tune is under way. The melody, in its narrow compass, is both restricted and restrictive, yet seems for that reason 'safe'; it appears to reach a haven as the bass moves from tonic to first inversion dominant seventh, back to the tonic, and then to a real subdominant, and so to a 6–4 cadence into the bliss of the relative, E major. Blissful is what it would have seemed to contemporary musicians, since E major, the sharpest key in common use, was in the High Baroque period traditionally the key of heaven. In this context the passage, resonantly spaced in the middle of the keyboard, hardly sounds celestial; it does, however, promise peace, as the triplets warmly envelop us.

Unsullied calm lasts through the bar of E major triplets, after the melody has broken from its G sharp obsession to rise to B, and to fall to the new tonic. In the next bar, however, the triplets change from major to minor, and the trumpet-call enters, muted in its dotted rhythm, on G natural instead of G sharp. The bass descends down the scale from E to C *natural*: so we find we have modulated, by way of a second inversion dominant seventh, to C major, remotest possible point from the initial C sharp minor! It would seem that, despite the music's quietude and the Bach-like consistency of its figuration, these unruffled waters hide a turbulence, already latent not merely in the substitution of minor for major triad, but still more in the distant, apparently rudderless, modulation.

This irony, if that is what it is, is more fearful than funny. None the less fear is at this stage conquered, for the modulations, however mysterious, prove to be not rudderless after all. The C natural the bass has arrived at is a real modulation while it lasts; but its duration is brief, since it turns into a Neapolitan approach to B minor, E's dominant, and subdominant of the subdominant of C sharp minor. This cadence occurs by way of a modification to the pivot figure: the melody rotates around the current dominant, F sharp, moving up a semitone, down a minor third, the bass answering by inversion. The rocking minor thirds try plagally to stabilize the bass, while the melody transforms the minor into a *diminished* third, C natural to A sharp, both tones clashing fiercely with the pedal notes of the arpeggiated triplets (bars 16–18).

It is now evident that the seeming immobility of this adagio—its very slow harmonic movement, its prevalence of internal pedal notes—is inseparable from its latent pain: the more so when the dissonant double appoggiaturas are repeated. The derivation of the diminished third in the theme from the descending Neapolitan bass in bar 12 suggests that we should construe this passage as a plagal cadence to B minor, rather than as being in E minor. In any case the melody settles on B and declines down the scale as the bass, falling in thirds, forms an explicit Neapolitan cadence into F sharp minor. At last the implications of that single chromatic alteration in bar 3 are manifest; and the manifestation suggests progression and disturbance within a music that appears deceptively calm. Indeed the diminished thirds in the theme, poised against the stabilizing minor thirds in the bass, have some of the characteristics of a sonata second subject; and when the arpeggios flow over the F sharp minor triad, and the dotted note melody reappears on top, there are intimations of sonata-style development. This time the horn or trumpet call promotes sharp-wards modulations back to C sharp minor and then to G sharp. The pivot notes and the minor thirds both appear melodically; the bass is thickened at the approach to the G sharp major triad, which immediately becomes a dominant to the original tonic.

Over a long sustained dominant pedal, the triplet waves undulate in rocking thirds, as though seeking triadic stability. Gradually, however, the wave figuration dissolves into tritones, which suggest dissolution, especially since, however levelly we play them, our ears begin to hear them as grouped in twos against the triple flow. We might lose mooring totally, were it not for the deep anchorage of that G sharp pedal; and threat becomes acuter when an inner part within the triplets irregularly reiterates the scalewise falling third, at first minor, then diminished. The pitches are again the crucial D natural to B sharp: an event which at last prompts the bass to move, at the end of this cadenza-like section, from G sharp to A to F sharp and back to the dominant. This bass is a permutation of the original pivot motive in the horn or trumpet call; when it finally falls from dominant to tonic it embarks (the maritime metaphor seems appropriate) on what we need not hesitate to call a sonata-style recapitulation.

This time the modulation into the ostensibly heavenly E major is not cancelled by the E minor triad. Instead, it returns to the C sharp minor tonic, emphasizing the diminished third in the Neapolitan cadence, and leading to the quasi-second subject of rocking thirds in the bass, diminished thirds in the melody. The stabbing dissonances of minor ninth and major seventh again effect plagal cadences, this time to C sharp minor. There's a touch of E major, in bars 55–6, as the bass inverts the thirds to leap a major sixth; but the pivot notes, rising in the melody, descending in the bass, rest on dominant G sharps and a 6–4 cadence to the home tonic. During a ten-bar coda the dotted rhythm motive is submerged in the bass, still on G sharp, but unable to rotate even to its pivot notes. It sounds slightly minatory as it echoes cavernously on its unchanging pitch, while the waters of the triplet arpeggios flow over it. There is a hint of the cross-rhythms of the 'deliquescent' cadenza, but the final descent to the low C sharp is through unambiguous minor arpeggios. The repeated triads at the end sound as though one has never heard a minor triad before: which perhaps is the essence of genius. As Ezra Pound put it, 'literature is news that STAYS news'. The figuration looks as regular, as consistent, as faithful as that of a Bach prelude, but it masks, as we've seen, sonata-like contrariety and incipient violence. Certainly threat broods over those final minor triads, which sound desolate rather than serene, and therefore not final at all. Indeed Beethoven's notation indicates that this end is no conclusion. He sustains the pedalling; and instructs the player: *'attacca subito il seguente'*.

Yet what follows appears to be not a consequence of threat, but its alleviation. The tenebrous dark of those C sharp minor triads is suddenly illuminated into the tonic major, enharmonically notated as D flat instead of C sharp. The change of notation is perhaps not fortuitous: for whereas very sharp keys tend to be associated by Beethoven with states of joyousness (for instance the F sharp major sonata opus 78), very flat keys tend to dreaminess and sometimes, by implication, to illusion. Certainly there is in this scherzo-minuet and trio a quality one might call illusory. It is as though the distant horn-call theme of the first movement were transformed into an Edenic dream-song, for there is a distinct affinity between that first movement theme and the minuet, as is evident if the pitches are transposed:

Ex. 31

In its new guise the theme is at once playful and wistful. Although phrased in four-bar periods, the song is wispy, fragmented by rests. Similarly, though it modulates sharpwards in the fourth bar, it turns back immediately to the tonic and, apart from one momentary sequential darkening, doesn't venture beyond tonic and dominant oscillations throughout the piece. The contrast with the abstruse modulations that undermine the apparently tranquil prelude is extreme.

When the two four-bar phrases are repeated the melody notes are no longer broken, but are syncopated by ties across the bar-lines. The playfulness is compromised by miniscule sighs, the final appoggiatura petering out with a hint of tipsiness: note how the alto part disappears,

leaving the treble suspended. After the double bar, eight bars of
'middle section' produce a slight intensification through chromatic
passing notes and sequential references to A flat minor. Immediately,
however, the tonic major is re-established; in so far as modulation
occurs, it suggests a momentary relinquishment rather than a dramatic
event. After sighing parallel thirds and a 6–4 cadence in the tonic
major, the initial minuet phrase is strictly repeated, though more
widely spaced on the keyboard. The concluding phrase is subtly
modified, since the 6–4 cadence is approached by a sforzando
diminished seventh. This touch of heat, in so cool a piece, is unexpected; it serves to make the rudimentary dominant seventh–tonic
cadence of the two final bars the more touching. After the veiled
suspensions, it sounds so homely as to be hardly credible.

Nor is it altogether credible as the minuet is followed by the trio,
which is riddled by syncopated cross-accents that disguise the beat,
over a bagpipe drone. This is Beethoven's more mysterious version of
the beer-garden musette trios of Haydn and Mozart, which were
themselves a demotic transformation of the bagpipe-emulating dances
of aristocratic composers such as Couperin and Rameau. Beethoven
disrupts his trio with offbeat sforzandi; but its manner manages to be
sensuously dreamy as well as fierce, and after the double bar the
harmonies dissolve not in real modulations but in sequential dominant
sevenths, while the tune remains syncopated, falling through fifths:

Ex. 32

This hazy, almost hallucinatory, passage presages romanticism: the offbeat syncopations, the sequences falling cyclically from E flat to G flat, the cavernous pedal notes, obscure the light of common day; disturbing too are the intermittent sforzandi within a pervasively soft and sensuous texture. When the little minuet sounds again after the trio, its frailty affects us more deeply than its happiness. Though it seems to reveal a smiling innocuousness within the melody that, in the 'prelude', precariously rode on the waters, we now know that that gaiety exists only in dream. The reality that lurks beneath the waters bursts upon us, inexorably, in the sonata finale.

Beethoven's tempo indication for the finale is *presto agitato*. A glance merely at the printed page, or better at Beethoven's original autograph, reveals that the water-wave metaphor employed in reference to the first movement is no less valid here: only whereas the first movement's waves rocked gently in the centre of the keyboard, the finale's waves pound upwards in turbulence, through a tonic and then dominant arpeggio, in both cases landing on sforzando triads disruptively on the last beat. The next two bars shift through a rocking dominant seventh in the bass to the subdominant and then dominant, with a sforzando offbeat in each bar, instead of every other bar. In or rather on the dominant, a tenor part wriggles between a pedal bass and a chittering of semiquavers in the right hand:

Ex. 33

There is still nothing one could call a melody, or even a theme, though the tenor part's stepwise movement and the sustained pedal-note counteract the initial explosiveness. The storm is momentarily halted as the dominant triad plunges to sustained G sharps (bar 14). What

follows looks like a repeat da capo: but the explosions are less violent,
culminating, at the crests of the waves, in bare octaves instead of triads.
This time we land in, not merely on, the dominant, approached by a
turbulence of diminished sevenths. At bar 21 we have arrived at a
second subject which is not only recognizably a theme but also, at least
potentially, a song. Significantly it oscillates through the interval of a
third, transforming the would-be stabilizing thirds of the first movement (its bars 16–17 and 30–1) into cantabile melody:

The thirds are rounded off, indeed, by a cadential appoggiatura with
quasi-vocal turn; are inverted into sixths, tightened to fifths, then
fourths, each reiteration resolving on a sighing appoggiatura, while
the semiquaver storm flickers in the left hand. From bar 25 this passage
is repeated, agitated by syncopations. Upward-screeching cadential
trills explode on the Neapolitan chord of A major: a scarifying consequence of the discreet Neapolitan D natural that had crept into the
third bar of the prelude's calm:

Ex. 35

Shooting scales are accompanied by hammered horn-barks on the A
major triad in first inversion: the Neapolitan explosion is repeated an
octave lower with lacerating syncopations, and it cadences as the bass
rises chromatically into a firm dominant.

   At this point the semiquaver whirring is superseded by a figuration
of repeated quavers. Though they are related to the hammering
motive, they are soft in dynamic, and suggest a somewhat desperate

affirmation merely through their regularity. Moreover, although the
potential song of the second subject seems to have vanished, the
codetta theme at least offers the possibility of triumph for, hidden
within its harmonic progression, the first movement's pivotal 'horn'
or 'trumpet' melody rings clear:

Ex. 36

As yet, we are not engulfed beneath the whirlpool. That this movement, for all its dualistic vehemence, is until its coda an orthodox
classical sonata, is to the point, for it is the artifice that prevents chaos.
The repetition of phrases and motives, often in two-bar periods,
contributes to the effect; far from being rococo small-talk, a filling-in
of empty time, the repetitions are necessary because the fury is intense.
This is manifest at the end of the codetta, when the semiquaver storm
returns softly in the bass, over a dominant pedal. The right hand
melody attempts to reinstate the song-like second subject, combining
the falling third with the drooping appoggiatura, followed by reiterated dominants of the dominant in crotchets, one on each beat. An
octave higher, the D sharps become minims, twice as slow,
approached by upward arpeggios for emphasis. Beethoven hangs on
to these dominants, grimly hopeful, as 'theme' disintegrates and the
swirling waters take over for the exposition's repeat.

  After the double bar the upward-seething arpeggios, with a yell on
each final beat, move flatwards to the subdominant. For the most part
the development is quiet, aspiring towards the song-like second subject. The texture is thinly in two parts, first with the tune on top and
the semiquaver storm beneath, then the other way up. But although
dynamics are subdued, tension persists, for dissonant appoggiaturas

between the melody and the storm figuration may be more acute
when presented in linear terms. When the song appears in the tenor
register the rocking thirds are again inverted to sixths, naggingly
repeated, and lead at bar 79 to a modulation to G major, the flat
supertonic of F sharp minor.

This again is a long-range consequence of the Neapolitan chromatic in the third bar of the prelude. It would be extravagant to point out
that G major is often, for Beethoven as for Bach, a key of blessedness,
and is the benedictory goal of his *Missa Solemnis*; but it is a physiological and psychological event that, in the context of this sonata, the G
major modulation remotely hints at a peace that 'passes understanding'. The effect is transitory, for the music soon sinks back to F sharp
minor, and the lyrical melody is transformed into those rocking
thirds which, in the first movement, had tried to stabilize chaos. Here
they boom in the depths of the keyboard, with sforzando stresses
(bar 83), frightening, but exerting control and leading to a long
dominant pedal, over which move stepwise undulations in rigid
rhythm derived from the transitional passage (bars 9–14). Stabiliza-
tion seems to be not so much victory as exhaustion: for dynamics
quieten and a V–VI–IV–V cadence stills the movement in two bars of
sustained semibreves (bars 95–101). From this deceptive moment of
repose the recapitulation sizzles, beginning *fp*, but with cumulatively
increasing vehemence.

The recapitulation is regular, with the song-like second subject
conventionally in the tonic minor. The Neapolitan explosion is now
(bar 128) explicitly on the triad of D, the original pitch of the
chromaticized D natural in the prelude. Similarly the codetta theme is
now in the tonic minor, so we hear the prelude's pivotal melody at its
original pitch (bars 137–50). Not surprisingly it is now, though still
disguised, more readily recognizable. The second half of the codetta
theme strains up to high G sharps, again the identical pitch around
which the first movement's 'horn' theme had obsessively gyrated.
This time, the waters of the unconscious prove stronger even than
Beethoven's Morality of Power, for at the orthodox end of the
recapitulation Beethoven throws orthodoxy to the winds and
launches into a large-scale coda. He begins with a bursting of the dykes
in a swirl of diminished sevenths, marked *con sordino* in the autograph
(bar 163) and with pedal (bars 165–6); there is no passage in music that
more tellingly reveals why this tonally neutral chord was considered
horrendous by the classical age.

After this outburst Beethoven tries again to establish his song theme, quietly, still in the bass as in the development, but in the tonic minor. Song fails to win through; the octave repetition of the tune explodes in triplet arpeggios, on the subdominant triad, on the Neapolitan D major, and on a diminished seventh approach to a 6–4 and cadenza. Chromatic scales whirr up to trill on a dominant ninth, descending in grace notes that distantly recall the cadenza-like tritonal arpeggios in the first movement. Deep in the bass, the resolution is on a dominant G sharp, approached by a semitone appoggiatura (bars 185–90). Again this is a moment of deceptive repose, or rather of stillness, for the two adagio bars are electric with expectancy. As well they might be: for in the tonic minor the storm softly resumes in the left hand's semiquavers, while the right hand asserts, with growing desperation, the stabilizing dominant G sharps. The motive has become the defiance of the Beethoven who cried 'I shall seize fate by the throat, it will never wholly subdue me.' Beethoven has justified his assertion, although in this sonata the Hidden Song is defeated, and even the reiterated G sharps cannot attain a fortissimo, but disappear in a cloud of tonic minor arpeggios that descend to the keyboard's depths. The tenebrous sonority of the prelude's end blows up, or rather down, in acrid smoke. Pain is not absolved, though since Beethoven appends two suddenly savage C sharp minor triads, it would seem that he lives to fight another day.

In later life Beethoven deprecated the popularity of the Moonlight, maintaining that he had composed many finer sonatas, such as the relatively cheerful F sharp major opus 78. Yet there is seldom smoke without fire, and the Moonlight, like those other soubriqueted warhorses, the Pathétique, Waldstein and Appassionata, is a work of exceptional potency, even for Beethoven. This power must be intrinsically musical, independent of adventitious associations with moonlight or anything else; if it were not, it could hardly have maintained its impact through so many years, and so many inexpert, as well as expert, performances. It 'struck a chord', as the saying is. It was deeply significant to his age, because it was so to Beethoven, he being not just *a* but *the* 'point at which the growth of the mind' showed itself. That Beethoven 'lived to fight another day' is patently true: for although at the time of the Moonlight he went through what we would call a nervous breakdown, the work itself is not a breakdown. It would not be far out to say that the rest of Beethoven's life was an (ultimately triumphant) attempt to heal the dualistic violence of this sonata; and

the process had started even during his months of psychological stress.
Beethoven's ends are usually also beginnings. From within his 'breakdown' he gestated the Eroica Symphony: a work which he rightly
believed to be a turning-point not merely in his own life, but also in the
chequered history of Europe.

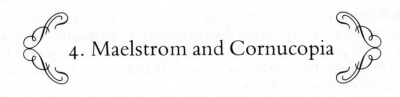

4. Maelstrom and Cornucopia

Piano sonatas
opus 57 in F minor (Appassionata)
opus 53 in C major (Waldstein)

Even in Beethoven's own day the Eroica was recognized, as was the Moonlight Sonata, as a remarkable work; the power of the music could not be gainsaid, though it was not necessarily approved of. In both works the main structural departure from tradition is a vast expansion in the sonata movements' codas; contemporary audiences found the Eroica's 'morphological' form not only too dissonant, as is usual with new music, but also too discursive. In fact one might claim that the Eroica is not only the most rigorously organized large-scale composition in Beethoven's work up to that point, but also in the history of music. The greater the violence that Beethoven's 'bursting of the dykes' released in the psyche, the greater proportionally became the necessity for control. The Eroica Symphony was, by contemporary standards, very long: but it needed its length to achieve its goal, the discovery of the Promethean chaconne theme of the finale. That Beethoven had used the theme before, in his Prometheus Variations, emphasizes rather than refutes this: for Beethoven's spiritual crisis is an act of rediscovery, tracing the process whereby his talismanic theme had been forged. Humpty Dumpty, regardless of kings and horses, puts *himself* 'together again', which is psychologically a near-miracle. Here Beethoven's technique of motivic transformation, whereby the form of a work is the discovery of its themes and the resolution of its contrarieties, is first maturely manifest.

By the time of the Fifth Symphony the process can be effected not more economically (for there are no supererogatory notes in the Eroica), but more trenchantly. The Fifth is 'about' the birth of the theme latent within its motto and throughout the first three movements, but overtly heard only in the major apotheosis of the finale. Beethoven reserved the heroic solemnity of trombones for the occasion; at the end he has transcended even the painfully won theme, since the final twenty-nine bars reiterate the mere C major triad some fifty times, and the reiterations are neither one too few nor too many. An acoustical fact, the major triad's dismissal of the ambiguities inherent in the minor triad itself, in this context epitomizes the symphony's pilgrimage.

It is not fortuitous that the instrument for which Beethoven in youth composed his most revolutionary music was the piano, for the piano is a one-man band, responsive to individual experiment, especially for a composer who thinks harmonically, in long-range tonal argument. Yet if Beethoven's early fame was as a keyboard improviser, by the time of the Eroica, already growing deaf, he tended to favour a medium less dependent on the vagaries of personal sensation. The will's imposition of order on the fragmented psyche calls for a medium of greater objectivity, combining power with precision. 'Power', Beethoven remarked at this period of his life, 'is the morality of those who are different [or stand out from the rest], and it is mine.' No medium could have been more pertinent to this Morality of Power than the symphony orchestra at its then stage of evolution. It was the loudest noise available to Beethoven, the most powerful in decibel content. More importantly, it comprised not merely the varied sonorities of which a piano is capable, but many different instruments, each operated by a separate player, coordinated by the wilful dominance of a single man, appropriately called a con-ductor. By the time of the Eroica Beethoven seldom, and then disastrously, conducted his symphonies, because of the incidence of his deafness. Yet this change-over from composer to professional conductor or maestro reinforces an apparent paradox: that whereas Beethoven played his early piano music before small, private and often aristocratic audiences, his symphonies were performed in concert-halls before audiences increasingly large and democratic. This view of the symphony as a 'public' medium was embryonic in Haydn and Mozart, who favoured a direct unfussy style in symphonic performance (as compared with the subtleties of their chamber music), and who preferred, though they seldom obtained, large orchestras, heavily weighted in the bass, to small chamber bands. Even more, Beethoven believed that his private 'message', the battle within his psyche, was of public relevance, not merely at a political level (though the Fifth Symphony refers to French Revolutionary music), but simply and profoundly because the more people could vicariously experience Beethoven's inner victory the better—for themselves, for Europe, and of course for Beethoven.

Obviously the advantage to Beethoven was economic as well as spiritual; and the economic factor is not trivial, since if music is an act of communication, as Beethoven believed, it cannot function unless the communicatees, the public, want what is offered. The scope of Beethoven's symphonies presupposed a fairly large democratic audience, animated by aspirations comparable to Beethoven's, though less potent and complex. Indeed his orchestra was made possible only by technicological skills developed in a semi-industrialized semi-democracy, so it is not surprising that during his middle years, when he believed that an equation between the private and the public life was both possible and desirable, he rejoiced in the symphony orchestra as his essential medium. This belief waned during the later years with which we, in this book, are principally concerned. For his ultimately 'religious' experience Beethoven returned to the solo piano, but to a piano idiom radically trans-formed; and to the string quartet, which Haydn had rendered a medium for intimate conversation. Beethoven's conversation becomes self-communion; the intimacy and, in Beethoven's religious sense, the communication, remain.

Even during his middle years, when the orchestra was the core of his self-discovery, Beethoven did not cease to compose for his own instrument; the three greatest concertos, which combine piano with orchestra, belong to this period. The most celebrated of the solo piano sonatas he wrote in these years are, not surprisingly, the most orches-tral in concept among the thirty-two. Both works were written in the same year as the Eroica Symphony, 1804, though one of them was much revised and not published until 1807. I will discuss them in the reverse order of publication, though not perhaps of composition, since the Waldstein Sonata is more prophetic of Beethoven's future than the climactic Appassionata. Both pieces are crucial and complementary; again we cannot escape a link between popularity (at least on a long-range basis) and significance.

If there is some validity in the crude statement that Beethoven's life-work is consummated in the mandala of the Arietta which forms the last movement of his last sonata, then it might also be legitimate to equate the Appassionata Sonata, standing midway in his composing life, with a maximum psychic disruption, for its essence and structure are a denial of song. The key is 'flat' F minor, traditionally dark key of *chants lugubres* and of the infernal regions; the initial motive consists simply of a spread minor triad which, exploiting the acoustical

properties of the chord, roots us to the earth, descending in the left
hand to cavernous regions:

Ex. 37

It is cunningly scored, the theme being doubled at the distance of two
octaves, so that the harmonics of the lower hand sound ghostily in the
gap. Counteracting the effect of the arpeggiated triad, however, is the
expansive 12/8 rhythm, which begins unobtrusively on the upbeat,
and floats, rather than thumps, through double-dotted metres that
quicken as the arpeggio rises. It is as though the earth-bound triad
would like to wing and sing, if it could; and having reached the
dominant C, the arpeggiated movement succeeds in becoming a
whole-tone undulation from C to D, rounded off with a quasi-vocal
trill. Beneath this the tenor and bass also undulate, but through semitones instead of tones; the triads are thickly scored, never in root
position.

If the theme seems to be growing towards song, it is frustrated. The
trill and turn on the dominant are followed by silence. The opening
phrase is repeated on G flat, a Neapolitan screwing-up which Beethoven is prone to when composing in his daemonic F minor; the most
remarkable example is in the first movement of the opus 95 quartet.
Again the resolution of the cadential trill and turn is succeeded by
silence, this time filling all the rest of the bar. The D flat triad serves as
submediant of the tonic, with a touch of its subdominant, B flat minor.

Back in F minor, the trill and turn are repeated and answered by a contraction of the whole-tone oscillation to a semitone. This becomes a foreboding drum-tap, D flat to C, in the bass, which is expanded and inverted into a minor third which, suddenly forte, explodes in semiquavers splattering through an ambiguous dominant seventh. The cadence, moving abruptly back to piano, is again in first inversion, without finality.

After a pause Beethoven embarks on what appears to be a repeat of this exposition material, with the sustained notes of the arpeggio theme filled in with ferocious, thickly scored triads in syncopation (bar 17). Instead of breaking off after the cadential trill, however, he repeats the undulation, moving the bass down semitonically to effect a modulation to A flat. At first this is not an unambiguous relative major. An ostinato of quavers on E flat (bar 25) softly supports triads of A flat *minor* and F flat major, thereby extending the 'Neapolitan' intensities of the opening bars. The drooping appoggiaturas hurt, and their resolution is rhythmically fragmented, syncopated on the third quaver of the groups. Only after energy has dispersed, and tonality has disintegrated through a chain of diminished sevenths falling through the persistent E flat pedal, is the true relative major established (bar 35).

Since the exposition of the first subject material has contained developmental elements, it is not surprising that the second subject is neither altogether new nor contrarious. It is the arpeggiated motive of the first subject, floating over warmly spaced A flat triads in the left hand, and acquiring song-like qualities because its arpeggios now embrace stepwise motives, as the rising third falls through a fourth. It is by far the longest melody we have so far heard, and the lyricism of its wave-like arches is heart-easing. Yet after it has risen through two octaves (note how subtly Beethoven preserves the enveloping texture of the accompaniment as the pitch rises) the song ends in frustration: not because it is threatened by assault from outside, but rather through inanition. The rotating accompaniment stills once more on a first inversion of a tonic triad of A flat; the melody droops through a fourth, then a third, on the Neapolitan chord of B double flat; and thus to a cadence in A flat minor. So the dark key of the transitional section, before the songful second subject could raise its head, proves stronger than the lyricism, which fades in unaccompanied trills and turns into a codetta theme in A flat *minor*. The downward arpeggios of the first subject now spring *up* in the left hand, only to droop through an appoggiatura, while semiquavers shimmer in the right, recalling the figurations that in Schubert's songs often depict a tempest or night-mare ride. Triads alternate between tonic minor, flat submediant (F flat), and the Neapolitan B double flat; diminished seventh arpeggios bound up, to hammer the semitonic motive D flat to C, or F flat to E flat. Texture thins out and dynamics quieten through a threefold repetition of a scale from D flat to A flat, ending with a gap of five octaves between the hands. These A flats change enharmonically to G sharps; and the development begins with the first subject pianissimo, remotely in E major, which is really F flat, A flat's flat submediant.

For a while the song, though still intermittently broken, acquires a hymnic gravity, moving sequentially from E major to F sharp minor, then back to E, with a harmonious 6–4 cadence. But the sequential repetitions are of little avail: for in sudden forte E major changes to E minor, which seems inconceivably remote from the original F minor, however logical its mediant relation to A flat; and an expanded version of the first subject swells from the E below the stave to the F above middle C. The right hand whirrs in its storm-thirds, which cross over with the rising melody to form an arpeggiated descent:

Ex. 38

This cross-over of waves, a brilliantly pianistic device, despite Beethoven's 'orchestral' sonorities, is at once liberating and frightening: the more so since the storm figuration changes to quintuplets which tend to loosen, though not disguise, the beat. Moreover modulation is now rapid and unstable, at first through descending mediants (E to C to A flat), then in an oscillation between D flat major and its relative B flat minor. At this point (bars 90–3) the hands are widely separated, the top line twanging on its high G flats, the left hand's alternating A flats and A naturals reverberating like gigantic bells.

Cadenced on a dominant seventh of D flat, the dynamics suddenly quiet, Beethoven takes up the transitional passage from the exposition (bars 24–34), the dominant pedal of reiterated quavers now being A flat. The syncopated appoggiaturas and the chain of diminished sevenths are both repeated without further modulation, and the A flat pedal note still rings through an additional passage of scalic undulations, the hands widely separated. Out of this the song-like metamorphosis of the theme that forms the second subject nobly arches, still in D flat major, F minor's 'passive' flat submediant (bars 109 ff.). Melodically the spacious melody is unchanged; but it is developed in that, instead of expiring on its falling fourth, it flows on, over the rocking accompaniment, through a series of modulations. Suddenly, D flat major changes to its relative and lower mediant, B flat minor; then to G flat major (another flat submediant), which changes enharmonically to F sharp major, and becomes in turn a dominant to B minor. The submediant triad to B, G major, is then transmuted into a dominant of C; and this spells death to the development's sustained approach to songfulness, first in the long lyricism in D flat major, then through the modulations which, in association with the openly singing phrases, are a release rather than exacerbation. The destructive agent is, once more, a tempest of diminished sevenths in fortissimo; Beethoven directs that they should be pedalled throughout, so that linear definition, let alone song, dissipates in a swash of waves (bars 123 ff.). Through the storm the hammer motive, in its most ferocious form, returns as the music sinks to a dominant pedal on reiterated low Cs. It is interesting that in this movement, as in the finale of the Moonlight Sonata, an extremity of violence should be girded and guarded by rigorous assertion of ostinati and pedal notes.

As the recapitulation steals upon us, pedal notes on low Cs give the music a more purposeful momentum than it had in the hollowly scored exposition. But they also increase its threat, especially when the pedal is doubled into a devilish tritone (bar 143), and D flats ominously pulse against the Cs. The repeat of the first clause, with the fiery syncopations, begins unexpectedly and devastatingly in the major; returns to the tonic minor for the fragmented transitional passage over a dominant pedal; and follows classical precedent in introducing the more song-like second subject in the tonic major, *dolce*. As in the exposition, song is frustrated by the intrusion of a Neapolitan triad in first inversion; since the Neapolitan to F minor is G flat, this harks back to the original semitonic repetition that begins in the fourth bar. After the effacing trills, the monodic scales flowing through four bars are repeated freely, in the tonic minor: so is the whole of the codetta. As in the Moonlight Sonata and the Eroica Symphony, the most structurally subversive aspect of the piece is its large-scale coda: for the arpeggiated theme descends into the lowest reaches of Beethoven's keyboard, with the storm figure softly whirring high aloft, and then slides yet again into the flat submediant, D flat major, moving more freely in metrical diminution. It is as though Beethoven were remembering how nearly his second subject song had come to fulfilment in the development's D flat major episode. But the memory is soon clouded; song darkens as it moves through a chain of diminished sevenths, through G and C minor back to F minor, when thematic identity is sundered in broken arpeggios, launched by the original Neapolitan G flat. A maelstrom of kaleidoscopic arpeggios, abetted by Beethoven's *sempre pedale* indication, induces chaos. But the arpeggios simmer down, and the hammer motive, both in semitonic descent and in rising minor thirds, slows to adagio. If Beethoven's pedal direction is adhered to, the pedal Cs and their D flat appoggiaturas will be blurred; even their dissonant pain will sound directionless (bars 235–8).

Only momentarily, however; for suddenly *più allegro*, Beethoven starts off on the final phase of the coda with the second, more song-like version of his theme, now in the tonic minor. Because of the key, and because it is faster, it sounds less song-like and more agitated; tonally too it alternates naggingly between F minor and its subdominant B flat minor. Finally any attempt at song is swept away by a furious pounding of triads, alternating between the hands, sometimes creating an effect of cross-rhythm; the C–D flat–C motive is obtrusive at the top of the syncopated chords:

Ex. 39

These fortissimo barks are abruptly followed by a return of the storm's thirds and of the original arpeggio motive, rising to F *in alt*, and falling to the low F at the bottom of Beethoven's piano. The low Fs are sounded five times in progressively augmented time values, while the storm-thirds softly shiver. Though the end is quiet, it is not resolved. Even more than at the beginning, the overtones of the sepulchral Fs echo through the gap between right hand and left. So the coda, having transformed the potentially song-like version of the theme into tempest, leaves us on the brink of an abyss: a scary state which the slow movement, an apparently simple air with variations, does little to assuage.

In the first movement of the Appassionata Sonata Beethoven carries us through the Tempest that would destroy Music, using the metaphors with the significance they have in Shakespeare. The carrying *through* is Beethoven's genius, and is the reason why the discipline of his art is necessary. Indeed such a raw openness to experience as Beethoven attains in the Appassionata might seem to suggest that 'reality' and 'meaning' were for him at this time 'absent gods', were it not that his yearning for them alone made life ethically possible. As George Lukács has put it, 'the achievement of form is the articulation and stilling of that longing. Form-giving is a judging force, an ethic; there is a value judgement in everything that has been given form. Every kind of form-giving is a step in the hierarchy of life's possibilities; the all decisive word has been spoken about a man and his fate when the decision has been taken as to the form his life-manifestation must assume.' In Beethoven's music the ultimate crown of the achievement of form is the rediscovery of song; but the second movement of the Appassionata, though superficially song-like, is not this pearl without price. For though a song, it is not a particularly rich one. This is not a pejorative comment on the movement in its context. A better song would have been worse, because inapposite to or inconceivable after the searing experience of the first movement: an experience which Beethoven had uncompromisingly to face if the Psalmist's New Song were ultimately to be born. Here, the self-contained song movement, the simplest type of air with divisions, serves as a momentary and illusory respite between two tempests, both in sonata form, the second even more violent than the first. In this sense the air in opus 57 and the Arietta in opus 111 exemplify T. S. Eliot's distinction between a dream and a vision. Analysis will give technical corroboration to what sounds like a metaphysical statement; for the moment it must suffice to say that the difference lies in the nature of the two melodies and of the variations stemming from them. The tune of the opus 57 andante is of limited melodic and emotional range, its variations being in the strict sense divisions: the tune, substantially unchanged, proliferates into smaller note-values. The opus 111 theme, though hardly less simple, is of seemingly limitless emotional range, and its variations, though in the technical sense divisive, stimulate flight.

The whole-tone undulation from the fifth to the sixth degree of the scale had, in the Appassionata's first movement, aspired to release us from the earth-bound minor arpeggio that forms the first segment of the theme. In the *andante con moto* the tune opens with precisely this undulation, but it is now metrically regular, in a moderate 2/4 pulse, harmonized with tonic, subdominant and dominant triads in root position, instead of first inversion:

Ex. 40

The key, D flat major, is again the flat submediant to the main tonic, F minor; given the rhythmic regularity and harmonic solidity of the theme, the effect of the submediant tonality is slightly depressive in its passivity, especially since the second two bars melodically 'stay put' on the fifth, moving from the dominant chord back to the tonic with a dotted rhythm in the bass. The second four bars invert the procedure of the first four, since the tune opens with four tonic D flats and cadences by the stepwise undulation, now semitonic and in inversion. Symmetry is inherent in the harmony too, since the I–IV–I–V–I progression of the first four bars is repeated in the second four, except for the slight intensification of the chromatic passing notes in bar 6. In the last bar the bass's dotted rhythm tails off from the first beat instead of moving towards it. The tune is anchored to its recurrent A flats, to its repeated tonics and dominants, to its sonorously spaced four-part harmony, and to its metrical regularity. It is therefore stable, secure, and in a post-eighteenth century sense hymnic; but unlike the Arietta of opus 111, it does not hint at the visionary. The bass's dotted rhythm remains physical, as indeed it had been in the seventeenth century when, in French music of the Heroic Age and its English imitations, it was allied to the corporeal movements of the dance, which incarnated man's pride in being human, able to stand, walk, jump, prance, whirl, and glide on his own feet.

Beethoven's lilting rhythm is no more than a remote echo of the past. None the less, that the rhythm is there, and always in the descent, testifies to the earth-bound character of this movement, which offers a dream of physical contentment, within the reach of ordinary mortals, rather than a vision of transcendent bliss. After the double bar the dotted rhythm appears in the tune itself, so the melodic shape has slightly more animation. Having begun with the repeated dominants, Beethoven leaps through a fourth to the semitonic undulation and, in the second two bars, through a sixth which falls to the tonic. In the last four bars the repeated A flats extend their leap to an octave. This is a climax, though hardly an obtrusive one, since the pull of the dominant–tonic axis is never broken. Nor is it threatened harmonically and tonally, for although the harmony of the second half is more positive than that of the first half there is, apart from one first inversion of the supertonic in the cadence, no alleviation of the oscillation between tonic and dominant. Throughout the sixteen bars of the air there is no modulation at all: a phenomenon very rare in Beethoven's 'activist' music.

The faint hint of enhanced animation in the second half derives from the fact that the harmony is in five homophonic parts instead of four; from the fact that the triads tend to be in first or second inversion instead of root position; and from one scrunching dissonance (a dominant thirteenth) caused by the high F. This is not sufficient, however, to suggest development: the essence of the *andante* lies in its static nature, as contrasted with the dynamism of the first movement. Moreover, the first variation counteracts any sense of progression, since the harmonic texture is broken into syncopation between the hands. Both tune and harmonies are unchanged; but the fragmented effect, each right hand chord separated by quaver rests, the left hand's melody dislocated offbeat, inevitably, even risibly, disrupts song. The

second variation does aspire to lyricism: the original bass line, without
the dislocated accents, becomes a cello-like melody, while the right
hand chords are spread into flowing semiquaver arpeggios. There is
no change in the harmonies, not even in the details of passing notes;
nor is there in the next variation, which speeds up the divisions from
semiquavers to demisemiquavers. Though the rapid figuration makes
the music brighter, the song doesn't 'take off', perhaps because the
theme is enunciated offbeat. The cadence to the first half is fleetingly
disturbed by passing diminished sevenths; in the written out repeat the
demisemiquaver figuration is transferred to the right hand, while the
left hand plays the offbeat theme in richer, usually three or four-part,
chords. But there is no change in the harmonic fundaments; nor is
there in the second half, when the demisemiquaver figuration climbs
to the higher reaches of the keyboard. Though textures shimmer, the
tune itself remains untransformed; indeed its regularity and symmetry
and its reiterated A flats sound, sparsely presented, almost simple-
minded! The demisemiquavers descend in a scale to the lower range of
the keyboard and to a repetition of the theme, without repeats,
unchanged except that the dotted rhythm in the bass line has been
ironed out to straight semiquavers, and the registration of the two-bar
phrases alternates between octaves, with antiphonal effect. These
changes, though slight, are significant: the level semiquavers sound
less 'corporeal' than the dotted rhythm, reflecting the variations'
abortive aspiration to song; the antiphony suggests illusion, or at least
a division within what purports to be whole. That the andante's
simplicity and security may be a cheat is implicit in the famous end to
the movement, which substitutes for the tonic chord resolving the
II–V–I progression a pianissimo diminished seventh in F minor,
slowly spread so that the ambiguity of the D flat at the top, which
ought to be the tonic but isn't, sounds the more mysterious:

Ex. 41

The chord is repeated fortissimo, only the left hand being arpeggiated, to produce a pounce on to the right hand chord marked *secco* by Beethoven. The diminished seventh—consisting of two interlocked and devilish tritones, and also built from stacked minor thirds, as was potently demonstrated in the first movement—then releases the fury of the finale. Like the first movement, this is in sonata form, kinetic and dynamic rather than resolutory.

The diminished seventh, traditional operatic chord of terror, swings us back from our dream of contentment, which comes as close to being static melodically, harmonically and tonally as is feasible for Beethoven, to a maelstrom which is all motion; moreover it is enunciated in a 'corporeal' dotted rhythm: first dotted crotchet and quaver repeated, then dotted quaver and semiquaver repeated thrice. These hammer blows let loose a flood of semiquaver scales, wherein the stressed notes on each beat of the fast duple time form descending diminished sevenths. We reach a low growling in octaves, which is the first movement's semitone undulation, *rectus et inversus*. Beginning on the dominant, the semiquavers descend to the low tonic, and the first subject proper seethes up, softly but minatorily. The theme consists of a rising F minor arpeggio, with the familiar C–D flat–C undulation on top. The first note of each beat defines a descending minor triad; after four bars the pattern is repeated, on a Neapolitan G flat:

Ex. 42

So all the elements of the first movement's opening subject are present, thematically, harmonically and tonally, pared to their bare bones. There is no song, hardly even a theme: only a moto perpetuo of storm figuration, within which fragments of the first movement material are tossed and torn. Even the V–VI–IV–V–I cadence has its bass notes separated by rests, in sinister quasi pizzicato. An extended repeat brings back the brokenly falling thirds of the first movement, presented in double counterpoint divided between the hands. Within the violence and fragmentation, however, the surge of semiquavers remains anchored to its tonic F minor, with only fleeting touches of subdominant minor, and the moto perpetuo is continuous. So although the effect is scary, it is also undefeated, and carries us, when the original motive appears two octaves higher accompanied by rocking F minor triads, to the first real modulation (bar 72).

What follows, in the dominant, C minor, is presumably a kind of second subject, though it offers no contrast. Both hands present versions of the motivic 'undulation', either whole tone or semitonic; the left hand moves in parallel thirds in dotted crotchet–quaver rhythm, while the right hand continues the running semiquavers. The passage opens on the Neapolitan chord of D flat, recalling the obsessive Neapolitan relationships of the first movement: the more so since the two-bar phrase is naggingly repeated. These reiterations thrust us into a codetta theme, or rather motive, which again is not a new idea but the original rising arpeggio plus semitone undulation, now in C minor and in close canon, answered by barking dominant–tonic chords, rigid in quaver rhythm. Beneath the barks surge semiquaver scales which, on the first note of each bar, themselves define a whole tone undulation. The barks move flatwards back to F minor, then down another fifth to B flat minor. The arpeggiated diminished sevenths return, leading without repeat of the exposition into the development.

The original storm figuration now forms a soft dominant minor ninth of B flat minor instead of a straight tonic; and a quasi-canonic two-part passage introduces the semitonic undulation, both ways up. The original form of the first theme, now in the subdominant, is restated over a first inversion pedal, and is repeated with the Neapolitan shift (now to C flat). Augmented to crotchets, the semitone wriggle appears in interlocked canon, *rectus et inversus*: a screwing up that leads, painfully, into a transformation of the undulation, syncopated, with dissonant clashes between G flat, E natural, and the dominant pedal:

Ex. 43

The effect here is more subtly disturbing than that of mere syncopation, for we hear the motive as though in 2/4 (crotchet followed by two quavers), but overlapping each bar since each time it begins on the second quaver. This screw-necked dislocation sounds fiercer when repeated with octave doubling, and leads at bar 158 to what seems like the beginning of the recapitulation, since the original theme reappears canonically in the tonic, followed by its repetition in the Neapolitan G flat. But recapitulation is denied by the first interruption of the semiquavers' continuity. Octaves over a dominant pedal, widely and weirdly scored, explode in Neapolitan arpeggios, succeeded by a bar's silence (compromised by Beethoven's sustaining pedal). Dominant seventh arpeggios are similarly followed by an empty, but pedal-haloed, bar. Then, suddenly piano, diminished seventh arpeggios return, broken, slowing down from quaver triplets and semiquavers to quavers; ascending fraily to the heights and descending sepulchrally to the lowest reaches of Beethoven's keyboard (bars 184–204). All this passage is enveloped in a haze of pedal, which is changed only when the low C emerges pianissimo as fundament, above which dominant seventh chords are poised, covering four octaves, separated by brief rests:

Ex. 44

Eventually the low C slides into the real recapitulation, which presents the original material in a darker texture, with the traditional modifications of tonality, so that the second subject motive is now in the tonic minor, with its Neapolitan screwing up once more on G flat. The codetta is in the tonic minor also, barking from dominant to tonic; and there is point in the fact that, in such violent music, recapitulation should be thus orthodox. Tonal stability, consistency of figuration, regularity of rhythm, prevalence of pedal notes and ostinati are the means whereby Beethoven (just) keeps nightmare at bay. Even more than in the first movement, 'form-giving' is here, as Lukács has put it, 'a judging force, an ethic'. Perhaps it is pertinent to note that Beethoven's tempo directive for this movement, probably the most vehement in his piano music, is *allegro ma non troppo*.

Beethoven's 'judging force' bears on another notorious crux: the fact that he directs that the development and recapitulation be repeated. In minor Rococo music repeats had a crudely functional purpose: sections were played twice because composers did not expect them to be listened to the first time round. With the great Viennese classical composers one can see the point of repeating expositions since, apart from matters of architectural balance and proportion, repetition is an aid to memory when the musical materials involved may be complex. Even with Haydn and Mozart, however, repeats of development sections tend to be problematical, for since the essence of sonata development is growth through conflict, it seems at best tautological, at worst inane, to evolve from A to Z, only to return to one's starting point, to be identically reborn! Beethoven did expect to be listened to, and by his middle years seldom repeated his developments; when he does so—and the evidence of this autograph is unmistakable—he must have a reason, the more so because in this case the exposition has not been repeated. Tovey suggests that Beethoven 'values the interrupted close and the effect of the subdominant that will follow', and wishes to 'delay the appearance of the entirely new theme in the coda'. (I don't think it is 'entirely new' [see the following pages], but it is certainly renewed in impact, so Tovey's point is valid.) One

might claim that the repeat is here necessary because of the movement's lack of thematic definition. It needs scope to build up for the
coda, and since it is a moto perpetuo, energetically propelled in consistent figuration, the development will serve as well for repetition as the
exposition: perhaps better, since the figurations are more potently
exploited. Only the strange passage of diminished seventh breakdown, blurred by Beethoven's pedal effects (bars 179–211) fails
adequately to function on this account. Tovey calls it the Death of a
Hero, and it sounds like an expiration of breath. To re-enact a death is
difficult, though not impossible. Perhaps one can say that though the
moto perpetuo is a tempest that cannot grow into song, it can, given
the courage of the human will, be withstood: which is what Beethoven
is doing in experiencing the development's crisis a second time. The
toccata-like quality of the figuration is thus itself ambiguous. It tells us
that the slings and arrows of outrageous fortune are impervious to our
aspirations and desires; and the repeat suggests that it's foolhardy to
think that, because a storm seems to have passed, it won't return. At
the same time the consistency of figuration works the other way
round, since it affirms that, even in the face of those slings and arrows,
man may have the strength to *go on*. He may even die twice, or three
times or four; he must sustain many little deaths before he can achieve
the 'transcendent' dying–into–life which Beethoven is to explore in
later years.

However this may be, there can be no doubt that the repeat of the
development enhances the power of the extraordinary coda. The
second time round there is a bridge passage built on the barking chords
and whirling scales of the codetta, and incorporating the semitonic
undulation. Tempo increases to *presto*, a direction never lightly used
by Beethoven, and the semiquaver storm figuration disappears for the
first time, apart from the 'expiring hero' passage into which the
development fades. Now, the banishing of the storm is a positive act
instead of a negative exhalation; so the coda theme may become a
thrusting march, one beat a bar:

Ex. 45

Melodically, the rising minor third followed by a falling semitone expands the original undulation, while the bass rises and falls, mostly in fourths, the interval that had launched the first movement's wave-like arpeggios. The eight-bar period is repeated, and answered sequentially in the relative major, with two extra bars to return us, by way of B flat minor, to the tonic minor. A flat major was the key of the abortive lyrical metamorphosis of the theme in the first movement; here, in the last movement's coda, it is, though far from song-like, jubilant: a triumph of the will, muscles stretched, limbs flexed, to withstand threat. Nor is this triumph relinquished when the storm of minor arpeggios with chromatic undulation on top returns, its fury increased because of the speed and the half-bar cross accents. The harmonic sequence, tonic minor, Neapolitan major, dominant seventh, is also restated; and the whole passage is repeated louder, an octave higher. Ultimately we are left with leaping minor triad arpeggios high in the right hand, and pouncing upward fourths and downward fifths in the left. These fourths and fifths, which had initiated the tempest, have become gestures of finality, trumpet-like assertions which preserve potency even during the descending snarls of minor arpeggios and the three tonic triads, separated by silences, with which the sonata concludes.

This is perhaps the *most* conclusive end to Beethoven's Morality of Power which had begun with works such as the Moonlight Sonata, wherein the first movement is a *latent* sonata conflict, the second a dream-like moment of repose, and the finale a full-scale sonata tempest, with long but disruptive coda. The Appassionata follows the same pattern, on a vaster scale, for its first movement is a sonata which fails to resolve its dynamic–lyric oppositions, the slow movement is a point of stillness which at least implies the possibility of a Whole, and the finale is a more ferocious sonata movement which, having the courage to dispense with song, yet wins through. The coda to the Moonlight is wild, and settles nothing, though it starts the process whereby Beethoven was to confront 'fate' and the demons within, seeking reintegration. The coda to the Appassionata, on the other hand, is an affirmation, if not a resolution: after which Beethoven may journey to Jerusalem, the Blakean paradise where the Hidden Song and the Voice of God may sound. The first intimation of this occurs in the great sonata which Beethoven composed contemporaneously with the Appassionata, which is to it both complement and polar opposite.

The Waldstein Sonata is in C major, a key often associated by Beethoven, as by Mozart in the Jupiter Symphony, with power, but also with innocence. It begins innocently enough, with softly pulsing triads of C major, euphoniously spaced, moving in quavers equably repeated through two *allegro con brio* bars of common time. On the fourth beat of the second bar, however, the top line pushes up from E to F *sharp* to G, landing on a G major triad in first inversion; and the melodic line is rounded off with a loop, rising through a major third on the fourth quaver, and descending down the scale back to G. A modulation to the dominant has occurred; so the opening C major triads might be construed as subdominants of G. Though we don't hear them as such, the almost immediate appearance of the rising F sharp does create an ambiguity, which is not entirely cancelled when in the next bar the first inversion G major triad regains its dominant significance. The chord accompanies a near-comic tailpiece to the 'loop', a chromatic acciaccatura to the high D, which trickles down the scale to G; and there is a further surprise in the next bar, for the sharpwards tendency of the first phrase is annulled by its repetition a tone lower, beginning in B flat and moving to F:

Ex. 46

So a sonata in C has, without fully establishing its home tonic, touched on one degree sharpwards and one degree flatwards; and even when the B flat–F major ambiguity irons itself out, it still lands in the wrong, or at least the not quite right, place. For the F major first inversion moves chromatically to A flat as support for the 'tailpiece'; but it proves to be not an F minor tonic, but a subdominant of C *minor*. The bass descends to fluctuate between A flat and G while the right hand, high up and at first still pianissimo, extends the tailpiece into scales that cadence in the tonic minor. An arpeggiated descent, one note to a beat, defines a C minor triad, ending on a sustained dominant G, with pause mark.

The whole of this opening paragraph is, in the modern sense, 'cool', ambivalent. The tailpiece figure might be described as cheeky: yet is also a relaxation since it always descends. Similarly the upwards pushing modulation is always answered by a fall; and the cosily spaced quaver chords move gradually further apart until, by the time we reach the whirling C minor scales in a modest forte, the sonority is almost uncomfortable. All this one might take as a witty introduction to the exposition proper, though the effect is subtler than this, since the music's delaying tactics enlarge the time-scale; as we will see, delay and expectancy are the heart of this sonata. The 'real' exposition also turns out to be irregular, for after a repetition of the first four bars, with the pulsing quavers changed to oscillating semiquavers, Beethoven moves up to the supertonic, instead of descending to the flat seventh. The D minor triads mount by an augmented instead of a major second, carrying us to A minor, C major's relative. This time the tailpiece is twice repeated, first falling from E to A, then from E to A sharp, forming a German sixth with the bass's C naturals, and so moving sharpwards again to E minor. The opening theme had consisted harmonically of alternating tonics and dominant sevenths; for the next eight bars the accompaniment merely rocks between tonics and dominants of E minor, the theme as such having evaporated (bars 23–30). The right hand extends the tailpiece into chromaticized scales which, merely because they *go on*, as contrasted with the fragmentary

twitters of the tàilpiece itself, suggest an approach to lyricism. This
'bridge' ends in descending dominant arpeggios, leading into a two-
part canon in leaping quaver octaves. Each phrase bounds up through
a third, giving melodic manifestation to the harmonic–tonal thrust of
the preludial bars. This time song is attained: for the rising canonic
entries, decreasing in dynamics, establish E major, not minor, and in
this radiant key the second subject unequivocally sings:

Ex. 47

E major is the upper mediant to C. We have commented on many
disturbing mediant relationships in Beethoven's early work and will
later note how significant they become, not merely as periodic
startlements but as substitutes for conventional dominants and
subdominants, in the reborn tonal world of his third period. Mediant
relationships tend to have a liberating effect in that they imply false
relations: in this case between E major's sharps and C major's naturals.
In context, this E major sounds disembodied; but the music, though
sublime is not illusory. It is a new song, as the Psalmist put it, but also a
metamorphosis of the original motive, since it begins with the rising
third inverted, and in its first phrase falls through a perfect fifth, as does
the frivolous tàilpiece. Moreover, although a stepwise-moving
melody, it is richly harmonized, again in alternating tonics and dominant sevenths, with chromatic passing notes. It also involves rapid
modulation between E major and C sharp minor, its relative. The
lyricism, combined with the six-part harmony, gives the music a
hymnic quality, prophetic of the aria in the same key that is the theme
of the variations in opus 109.

It is perhaps the first of Beethoven's hymnic melodies to envisage the Invisible Church, though at this stage it is only a distant mirage. For whereas the aria of opus 109 is a self-contained entity which returns to its source and 'is as it always was', the Waldstein melody is part of a process of Becoming, which in this sonata is not consummated. What happens immediately is that the two-bar phrase, falling in its ripe harmonization through a fifth, is answered by a two-bar phrase rising through a fourth and resolving in a 6–4 cadence. The first two bars are then repeated an octave lower, and the rising third cadences from dominant to tonic. The whole period is then repeated, embellished with flowing, sometimes chromaticized, triplets which enhance lyrical tenderness and textural warmth but lead to no extension, let alone consummation, of the song. Instead, the triplets subside on to oscillating tonics and dominant sevenths (yet again) over a syncopated dominant pedal (bar 50). It is as though the music isn't yet ready either for the hymn's lyrical fulfilment or for the complexity of its harmony: as though, rocking in its repeated phrases between its tonics and dominant sevenths, it is *waiting* for a moment of revelation.

Gradually the triplets quicken to semiquavers, and the hypnotic alternation of E major tonics and dominants is modified by the intrusion of D naturals, carrying us in a descending scale over rocking sixths to a syncopated chugging that denies song (bar 62). Beginning in A major, this presses sequentially through B back to E major, fades to a pianissimo, and leads into eight bars that are purely textural, without any attempt at melodic definition. The nature of this texture is, however, fascinating, for an alternation of semiquavers in the right hand and quavers in the left produces a glittering sonority prophetic of late Beethoven, especially when the written-out semiquavers are metamorphosed into trills. This is not strictly comparable with the celestial trills in opus 109 and 111, but it is strikingly similar to passages in the late Bagatelles opus 119 and 126, and can likewise lead to an at least potential rediscovery of song. Three times 'song' has dispersed in 'texture' based on alternating tonics and dominant sevenths; three times textures have grown gradually more airborne and disembodied. Now, in a codetta, a modified version of the hymn is played by the left hand, which treats the E major triad as a dominant to A minor. Above the left hand's four-part solemnity, the right hand embroiders scales derived from the tailpiece. The four bars are restated an octave lower; a further modified repeat introduces Neapolitan (quasi Phrygian) F naturals which in *their* repeat become modulatory, carrying us through a 6–4 cadence back to C major. So the hymnic song has not been destroyed, neither has it grown, nor achieved self-containment.

This seems the more pointed because, with the exposition's repeat, we hear again the ambiguities of the opening bars. The second time round the 6–4 cadences in E minor and C major are sequentially extended to F, the subdominant, and the development begins pianissimo with the original pulsing quavers, now moving from F to C. The tailpiece answers, however, in C *minor*; and from this point the development relinquishes any attempt at sustained song. Moving sharpwards from C to G minor, Beethoven tosses the looping upward and downward thirds against the tailpiece's falling fifths, which are sometimes perfect, sometimes diminished and tritonal. As the rising and falling thirds change their rhythm from a dotted ♩. ♫♩ to a compressed ♬♩ the mood, far from being hymnic, becomes skittish: but also uneasy, since we do not know what, in this context, skittishness signifies. Gradually the figuration gathers continuity to offset the disintegration of sequential modulations from C to F to B flat minors. Over flowing arpeggios, the rocking thirds seem to be growing into a modest theme, the potentially expressive nature of which is stressed by dissonant appoggiaturas in the bottom line and a momentary Neapolitan intensification in the B flat minor passage. Dynamics stay quiet, apart from an intermittently irreverent squawk on the tailpiece figure; and the hinted-at theme doesn't materialize. When the development returns by way of A flat major to F minor, figuration slows from semiquavers to quaver triplets. Development becomes, in effect, anti-development; for Beethoven brings back those oscillating tonics and dominants, swaying over the syncopated dominant pedal, which we had first heard at the expiration of the hymn-tune in the exposition. The dominants are intensified by being minor ninths as well as sevenths; but though the music moves in sequential modulations it creates an effect of stasis rather than of momentum, drooping from F minor to B flat minor to E flat minor, then through descending mediants to C flat (notated as B) minor:

Ex. 48

This moves down to the tonic G major; which proves to be a dominant to C minor. The effect of this tonal dissolution, allied to the consistent arpeggiated triplet figuration, is weird. Instead of 'developing', we seem again to be *waiting*: lost because we float on the modulations' stream, yet expectant, even hopeful, because the triplets are unbroken, luminous in their keyboard spacing.

Arrived at C minor, the triplet arpeggios enhance the cadential feeling with Neapolitan D flats and G minor diminished sevenths, leading once more to the familiar oscillation between dominant seventh and tonic. The dominant pedal, pianissimo in the bass, becomes a curious revolving cam, descending in semiquavers from C to G; the original tailpiece is transferred from the heights to the depths. It is answered by scales pushing up from D to G, with the Fs sharpened: precisely the ambiguity of the movement's opening. What follows is high comedy. The revolving cam continues to growl in the bass, the fragmented upward scales irregularly to snicker in the treble, the hands growing progressively wider apart:

Ex. 49

When the top line arrives at F natural *in alt* it cancels the sharp Fs of the previous spurtings. The Cs of the cam move up to D, so the figuration can become unsullied embroidery of the dominant seventh of C. The passage winds itself up both metrically and dynamically; having reached a rare double forte, the two hands scurry to meet one another in the middle of the keyboard and to inaugurate, in sudden pianissimo, the recapitulation.

The 'introductory' section is repeated literally, except that the last note of the descending arpeggio of C minor is changed from G to A flat. Five additional modulatory bars move from A flat, serving as Neapolitan to G minor, back to C: a passage that doesn't so much enhance the music's characteristic sense of expectancy as delay progression with almost comic gentility. When eventually it is established, the recapitulation behaves normally. The supertonic repeat of the opening leads to A minor, but stays there instead of moving sharpwards to E. The canonic rising scale octaves are now in A major, leading into the hymn in that submediant key, ripely harmonized as before, but in eight-part homophony. Repeated in the lower octave, the hymn changes tonality from major to minor: or rather to the Aeolian mode, which makes it sound yet more late Beethovenian, and underlines the subtlety of mediant relationships in the piece, since A minor and C major are no longer sharply differentiated. We will meet this equivocation again in opus 101 and opus 106. As before, further repeats are embellished with flowing triplets, until the hymn fades into the 'waiting' alternations of tonics and dominant sevenths. From the return of the hymn, the music is in C major, the home tonic; the chugging syncopation descends to the subdominant, F, pushing up to the tonic again for the glittering semiquavers and trills. Dominant sevenths are superseded by dominant ninths, a chord which gradually acquires greater significance in the sonata. Here the sonority is more than ever prophetic of the late Bagatelles, and even of the glinting ice variation in opus 111's Arietta. The codetta theme, combining the hymn with the tailpiece, moves flatwards to the subdominant instead of sharpwards to the dominant, as in the exposition. Subdominant minor shifts to major; which proves to be a plagal approach to what we imagine will be a resolutory 6–4 cadence in C.

But Beethoven makes the most of his upbeat-approached sequences. Having arrived back at C major, he repeats the phrase in the subdominant, F major (bar 245), so that what we had expected to be the movement's end offers a shock comparable to, though less violent than, that in the exposition's fifth bar, which is in the subdominant of the subdominant. He repeats it in the subdominant's minor, with an interrupted cadence that substitutes D flat major triads for the tonic. This is the beginning of a large-scale coda, in which more happens than in the development itself which, as we saw, was in some ways an anti-development. In the long-range tonal architecture of the sonata these pulsing D flat major triads are Neapolitan flat supertonics to C, though at first we hear them as subdominants to A flat or submediants to F minor. Over the soft quaver chords the loop and tailpiece are impudently bandied around in forte and fortissimo, rapidly modulating from A flat major through B flat, C and F minors and back, with a touch of G minor, to C. The left hand takes over the original theme, with repeated chords pushing up through a third, while the right hand droops in syncopated diatonic scales, which are inverted into rising scales in semiquavers. We may not hear these as thematic relationships, and we certainly cannot foresee the form those descending scales will assume in the finale. None the less, that such affinities exist contributes to our unconscious awareness of unity in multiplicity; certainly the tailpiece now takes on a thematic and dramatic significance we had hardly thought it capable of. Approached by a leaping tenth, the tailpiece gradually gathers energy, losing its ties as the reiterations become more urgent. Above, the right hand's scales fly up liquidly, embellishing the submediant and supertonic triads, arriving at the subdominant chord, intensifying the 6–4 with rising thirds major, minor and diminished, and climaxing on a sustained dominant seventh which is repeated, after a scalic descent, in the lower octave. This leads, with a marvellous sense of arrival (after so much waiting) to the hymn theme in C major, *piano e dolce*. The spacing in the middle of the keyboard warmly envelops; when the phrase is repeated in the higher octave, the sonority glows.

Even so, consummation is not attained; the song does not become an entity. There are intimations of A minor in its chromatic harmonization, and ambiguity deepens when the 6–4 cadence fails to resolve. The rising third from G to B is left suspended, with a pause mark. Back in the lower octave Beethoven attempts the ascent from G to C again, and again fails, more depressively since the A is flattened, to form once more a dominant minor ninth. The flat sixth weighs heavily down, the sharp seventh presses painfully upwards; again there is no resolution, but another pause. So Beethoven tries a third time, an octave lower still, and with a *ritardando*. This time the A is natural again, though dark in sonority, and the B does reach its tonic goal. The concluding eight bars, however, make no pretence of completing the hymn. They simply return to the original pulsing quavers, with their mutually cancelling dominant and subdominant modulations, and to the oscillating thirds and contrary motion scales, and stop, rather than conclude, with suddenly fortissimo dominant and tonic triads. Their disposition is odd: two thumps, then a half-bar's silence; then tonic, dominant, tonic on the beats, which don't balance and so don't sound like an end. Though Beethoven has glimpsed intimations of immortality, this is not the time to encompass them.

As slow movement to the Waldstein Sonata Beethoven originally wrote an *andante favori* in the subdominant, F major, traditionally a pastoral key. It is a large-scale aria in ternary form, highly ornamented and quasi-operatic, yet at the same time rural, even Rousseauistically rural, folk-like. It's a beautiful piece; yet Beethoven was as usual right in coming to see that it was inadequate in the context of a sonata which he knew to be of crucial significance. Placed between the song-seeking allegro and the finale, it was both too long and too elaborate. So he replaced it by what he called an Introduzione to the Rondo finale: a piece which owes its introductory character to the fact that, like the first movement but at a deeper level, it generates expectancy. The tempo is immensely slow: when Beethoven says *adagio molto* he means to be taken seriously. The key is notated as F major, C major's subdominant; but it is a long time, at this slow 6/8 tempo, before F major is established, for this adagio opens, as does the first movement, but on a vaster scale, with delaying tactics. The difference is that, whereas the first movement leaves us in doubt as to what we are waiting for, whether it is comic or tragic, secular or sacred, ridiculous or sublime, we can have no doubt that his introduction portends sublimity, whether or not it arrives.

Beethoven opens on the triad of F, with a low pianissimo octave in the bass, followed by a dotted rhythm on the fifth, reaching up through a sixth, the top A being marked *tenuto*. The gentle thrust of the dotted rhythm and lifting major sixth (conventionally an interval of aspiration) convey a tender yearning: which is enhanced when the low Fs are repeated and the dotted rhythm moves from A through a tritone to D sharp, again marked *tenuto*:

Ex. 50

Grammatically we might construe this, on an equal-tempered piano, as a dominant seventh in B flat; but the tentative rhythm, the groping upward gesture, the hesitant pauses, ensure that we hear the top note not as E flat, but as the D sharp it is: a German sixth seeking resolution on the dominant of A minor. This chord is sounded three times, enclosed within quaver rests which are not inconsiderable at so slow a tempo. The triad of F major has thus behaved not as tonic, but as submediant to A minor; nor is there certitude in this, for after another silence E is substituted for F in the bass, and the rising sixth is repeated, from B to G. This time it is minor instead of major, only to become major again in lifting from C sharp to A sharp, a sharpened approach to the dominant of E minor, which sounds softly in first inversion, again three times, after a far from empty silence. The first inversion triads, compared with the A minor dominant's root position, enhance expectancy; hands open, arms outstretch in supplication. But in bar 5 the bass D sharps are flattened to naturals and then to D flats, while the right hand's dotted rhythm feels up through tritones, F to B, B to F. At last the bass droops to C, and melody *falls* through a sixth to form a dominant seventh of F. The next bar, riddled with silences, has the sixth both rising and falling over a D minor triad; two cadential bars—G minor first inversion, dominant seventh, tonic—return, after more echoing silences, to the sonorous low Fs.

With F major at last a tonic, a song theme emerges; the dotted rhythm and rising sixths (stressed by grace notes) flow into stepwise movement in parallel tenths, with sighing appoggiaturas and resonant sforzandi at the crest of the melody. The cadence on the dominant, at the end of one long bar (bar 10), flowers into threefold canonic embellishment. The answering clause expands the leaping sixth to minor seventh, again with appoggiaturas, sforzandi and threefold canonic embellishment a tone higher, ever the tonic instead of dominant chord. But the operatic flavour of this melody (which is in the same key as the abandoned *andante favori*) is not what Beethoven was seeking in that wondrously expectant opening: so the melody folds in on itself, instead of flowering outwards. The next two bars, inverting the dotted-rhythmed rise into falling fifths or sixths, are curiously telescoped in phrasing. We hear them as though in diminution, crossing the bar lines, and the potential song becomes a middle section that leads back by way of the same II–V–I cadence to an embroidered da capo.

Yet this opening music still sounds 'introductory'. Having assayed and rejected the aria, it looks forward more positively, for its silences are now filled in by triadically oscillating demisemiquavers in the bass, and in the tenor by a move from G sharp to G natural in the dominant chord (bar 18). The bass's demisemiquaver figure survives during the melody's tritonal ascents. The two hands move further apart, until the top line leaps in the dotted rhythm through a freed octave instead of an aspiring sixth, while the bass undulates between A flat and G. Most of this slow moving passage consists of a gradual approach to the dominant seventh, and then ninth, of C. Only seven bars of the Introduction, which is notated with the key signature of F, are unambiguously in that key. For the most part it vacillates between A minor and C major. As the dominant seventh arpeggios simmer down, there is a momentary return to an A minor diminished seventh which adds point to the thematic reminiscence: the quaver triads are sounded three times, as they were at the Introduction's beginning. A solemn VI–II–V cadence dispels ambiguity in favour of C major.

There is no passage in Beethoven's middle-period music more prophetic of his late style than this miraculously exploratory music. The piano texture, at once rich and diaphanous, is comparable with that of the slow movements of the opus 102 cello sonatas, and with the

(also introductory) 'arioso' in the piano sonata opus 101. Through it
Beethoven comes to the threshold of the Hidden Song he had sought
in the rondo finales of those early sonatas we discussed. It is a Song of
Innocence, in Blake's sense, reborn; yet at the same time, being
Beethoven's, it cannot be oblivious of Experience, so that even here,
when the Song has been attained, the later rondo episodes contain
vestiges of sonata conflict, and the end, like the beginning of the
sonata, is ambiguous.

But the tune itself is not. Beginning with an upbeat (distantly
presaged in the quaver rest with which the first movement opens), the
tune smilingly sings, harmonized in those tonics and dominant
sevenths which had obsessed the first allegro:

Ex. 51

Beethoven's pedal markings make it clear that he intends that the first
eight bars should softly sound over a tonic bass, even when the tune
seems to imply dominant harmony; similarly the second eight bars are
consistently over a dominant pedal, even when the tune sings a tonic
triad. Tonics and dominant sevenths, between which this sonata has
veered and tacked, are in European music the central synonym for
temporal progression. In the first movement they had frustrated the
Song's fulfilment; now it seems 'progression' and 'dominance' must
be relinquished as tonics and dominant sevenths are sounded simultaneously. Certainly the song now sings untrammelled; and if one
transposes it a semitone higher, it is not difficult, as Reti has demonstrated, to recognize in it a delightfully liberated version of the first

movement's 'hymn'. It is liberated because it is the hymn theme divested of harmonic complexities, linearly pentatonic, harmonically floating in the bliss of its triadic formations and perfect fifths, over its purring accompaniment of tonic and dominant triads. The semi-quaver figuration recalls the first movement, no less than the tune; it too is relaxed, since the tune is as self-contained as a folksong, apparently freed from direction and intention.

But the relaxation is not and could not be complete. Just before the end of the second eight-bar period, the major thirds in the floating 2/4 allegretto are changed to minor, and fluctuate between major and minor thirds until the tune fades on seven softly repeated dominants. The harmonic effect of the false relations is more wistful than anguished, since the pedalling ensures that the whole passage is bathed in dominant, not tonic, harmony. After the repeated Gs, semiquaver figuration takes over from the tune, and rises through oscillating thirds, as in the 'cadenza' to the first movement. There is a slight crescendo in the ascent; but, arrived in the keyboard's heights, the tune is repeated in pianissimo octaves, with accompanying scales and arpeggios still washed in pedal. This time the repeated Gs become trills which ring beneath the tune, while the scales incorporate liquid demisemiquavers. This is one of the earliest passages in which Beethoven uses trills in the manner of his late music. The trill in eighteenth-century music usually had cadential significance, rounding off a melodic phrase, and was thus temporal. Trills in late Beethoven obliterate temporality and, like the centre of a spinning top, become 'the still point of the turning world'.

Through its trills this ecstatic proliferation of the 'folk' tune rises to fortissimo, and introduces the first episode, which is earthier, if not less innocent. At first, triplet figuration merely spreads tonic and dominant triads, with a few chromatic appoggiaturas, over a syn-copated tonic pedal. A theme defines itself in the bass, in an Aeolian A minor; although metrically restricted, almost clodhopping as compared with the freely swinging first theme, it is not unrelated to the Hidden Song, for it inverts the first movement hymn-tune's scalic fall through a fifth, and obsessively gyrates, like the rondo theme, between tonic and dominant. This tune too is modified, in octaves in the treble, over clattering semiquavers and a sometimes dissonant pedal. It fades into a unisonal recollection of the first theme, in an Aeolian A minor (bar 98) which Beethoven again uses as a bridge to C major. Beethoven's pedalling ensures that we hear the octave unisons as a VI–IV–V–I cadence, carrying us back to a literal repeat of the rondo song, still pianissimo until the octave repeat and haloing trills.

The next episode (bars 175 ff.) is in the tonic minor, and is long enough to do duty as a substitute for sonata development. It opens with broken octaves, again metrically rigid after the flowing song. The linear contour includes both the obsessive progression from tonic to dominant and back, and also the leaping sixths of the slow movement. At first, however, it implies neither aspiration nor lyricism, which the metrical severity precludes. Moreover for the first time the music's innocence is belied by the restless modulations; the C minor motive is sequentially answered in F minor, and shifts to A flat major. Returning abruptly to C minor, the tune appears in spiky octaves, with driving triplets in the left hand. This time sequential modulations extend to B flat minor before moving to A flat major, with the theme in the bass. The figuration remains consistent throughout the modulations, and the effect is frisky rather than fierce: at least until a series of thumping Cs in octaves (which function variously as tonic, dominant and mediant) recall the dominant fade-out to the original song. It is as though the music is trying, wilfully, to summon back that lyricism; after the repeated Cs in decreasing dynamics the song does return, suddenly fortissimo in A flat major, the submediant, harmonized thickly rather than airily, with elided tonics and dominants. In this form the song cannot take wing, cannot aspire beyond its first phrase. It pounces up again, first in F minor, then D flat major (again a flat submediant). At this point the song gets stuck, and the finale re-enacts, in its simpler way, the psychological crisis of the first movement. The music swings softly between tonics and dominants, over a tonic pedal, once more waiting, expectant, unable to take off. Syncopated 'vamping' over a D flat triad wanders into modulations to E flat and F minors, the bass still shifting between tonics and dominants:

Ex. 52

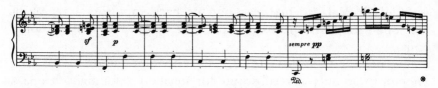

On the dominant of F minor the leaping anacrusis of the rondo's song softly recurs, garlanded in the right hand with arpeggios, with dissonant appoggiaturas. Though the sonority is pearly, the leap cannot release the tune. It merely repeats itself in falling sequences, F to B flat to E flat minors; then wafts to a dominant seventh of D flat: which key acts as a Neapolitan approach to C minor.

But we have still some way to go before the innocent song can smile again. The prancing anacrusis runs into regular alternations of tonic and dominant crotchets, with semiquaver arpeggios on top but with no tune at all. Over soft dominant–tonic pedals, reiterated F sharps and A flats 'stand for' the fade-out Gs of the Song (bars 287 ff.). Dominant arpeggios remain constant for eighteen bars while the bass expands the anacrusis from seventeenth to nineteenth to twenty-first, and gradually ascends to a high F, *sempre pianissimo*. The bass teeters between G and A flat; and the total effect of the eighteen-bar passage, which is pedalled throughout, is of an extended dominant seventh and ninth cadence. This is the most mysterious as well as the longest version of the time-suspended dominant ninth, which has occurred in both the first movement and the adagio.

Having 'marked time' through this mist, the rondo song returns in its octaved form, in suddenly jubilant fortissimo (bar 313). The long episode hasn't really functioned as a sonata development wherein the form would be transformed and rediscovered. It is rather as though the theme—which is a folksong-like entity, almost a god-given revelation—has been lost and has to be blindly (or rather deafly) sought after. One cannot *will* it to come back; but since one knows it exists, there is always a chance of lighting on it. Certainly it affects us now as a sudden blaze of light, as it surges on in its coruscating trills. After that we can hardly regress to another non-development, like the previous lengthy episode, or for that matter like the development of the first movement. Instead, the movement proceeds mirror-wise, for we now have an extended repetition of the first episode, with its broken triplet arpeggios over a syncopated pedal. This time it turns into toccata-like figuration for both hands on dominant and tonic triads, then on a

VI–IV–V–I progression (bars 362–5) that leads to a genuine modulation to G major (bars 367 ff.): the only unequivocal dominant modulation—that prop of classical tonality—in the whole sonata! So
although no theme is audible in this passage, it effects its own harmonic and textural triumph: which is none the less short-lived. For ten
ringing bars dominant sevenths in G alternate with tonics over a low
tonic pedal, emphasized by offbeat sforzandi; then the pedal changes
its meaning to become a dominant to C, the F sharps being intensifying appoggiaturas. The upbeats to the Song are again stretched from
tenth to twelfth to fourteenth to sixteenth, when the A flats screeching
at the top once more create the climactic chord of minor ninth. From
this maximum dynamic point the ninth chord sinks, swaying
pendulum-like to a bar's silence which is not in fact silence, since the
whole passage is sustained by the pedal. Tremulous diminished
sevenths of D and G minors quiver over the pedal. This is the last
occurrence of the dominant seventh and ninth frustration; we wait for
the Song's ultimate metamorphosis:

Ex. 53

The weird and wonderful coda begins with an anacrusis that leaps
from middle C to G *in alt*! The tune rings bell-like, prestissimo in alla
breve notation, at least twice as fast as its allegretto presentation. It
disappears in tingling figuration high on the keyboard, clashing with a

tonic pedal; gathers energy as the figuration moves in chromaticized sixths and tenths; gains momentum with the intrusion of a ludicrously galloping dotted rhythm in the left hand. The song reappears, suddenly *dolce* again, in the subdominant, but soon returns to C in limpidly consonant two-part crotchets. What happens next is a kind of mini-development: A flat, the flat submediant, is substituted for the tonic resolution, and the left hand reiterates the anacrusis against triplet arpeggios, flowing from A flat major to F minor, D flat major to B flat minor, and then vacillating between chords of B flat and F minor, before sinking to a dominant seventh of C (bars 441–57). Explosive contrasts of dynamics render this passage playful as well as gracious; and a suggestion of the *ludus puerorum* remains when, after a Neapolitan A flat and the softest possible G minor diminished seventh, a 6–4 cadence decorated with bell-like octave glissandi arrives at a 'white' C major:

Ex. 54

Contrary motion scales, haloed by pedal, merge into a return of the trills, which are unbroken for thirty-eight bars, while the left hand splits its tonic and dominant triad into floating triplets, and the 'folk' song sings high above. But its innocence is not unadulterated, since it is immediately repeated in the minor, the trill changed from tone to semitone; then in the dreamy flat submediant, A flat; then in F minor, which moves chromatically back to C through a German sixth. These modulations, at so fast a tempo, are whimsical rather than dramatic; at the end of the passage double trills elide tonic and dominant chords. The oscillations of tonics and dominants have become an eternal Now, a chime of bells which identifies fundamental notes with their over-tones (bars 511–14).

In this sonata the Hidden Song, which is the Voice of God, proves to be not the hymn which was potential in the first movement, nor the sublimated aria which had been envisaged in the *adagio molto*, but a tune as melodically and harmonically innocent as a folksong. The consummation of Beethoven's ·'hymn' occurs in the theme of the variations in opus 109, which absorbs pain and pathos into lyricism. A further stage is attained in the Arietta of opus 111, which is simultaneously folk-like and hymnic. Though the bell-like trilling in the last pages of the Waldstein is similar to that in the last pages of the Arietta (involving comparable technical problems in performance), it does not achieve the Arietta's fusion of Innocence and Experience, of child-like song and purgatorial hymn. The Arietta can end in (almost) total joy *because* it is at once innocent and experienced. The innocence of the Waldstein finale is a revelatory moment, but its joy is not total. Innocence and Experience do not fuse in the oneness of song with lyric variation; this is why it is a sonata-rondo, and its coda, glimpsing Eden, yet contains a Fall. After those 'false' relations and illusory modulations the trills disappear, and when the tune returns it is in earthier form, the anacrusis thumped in the bass, the two-bar phrase repeated in echo. Again dominant sevenths are elided with tonic triads, and the effect is hammered home when the four-bar period (two plus two in echo) is repeated with the tune quaver-embellished. From the lower octave the figuration gradually builds up over a tonic pedal, first with tonic and dominant harmonies, then with chords telescoping tonic, dominant and subdominant. In so far as these three norms of progression in European music have become a 'timeless moment', this effect is related to the bell-tolling trills. But it is ambiguous, because the tune has vanished. A big crescendo explodes in tonic triads, bouncing in crotchets, emphasizing the intervals of third and sixth. The last sounds we hear are the first notes of the Song: descending thirds from G to E, separated by silences. Beginning fortissimo, they evaporate to pianissimo, but conclude with the double-forte descent from G to E, followed by forte thumps from E to C. This end is not conclusive, and is far from paradisal, or even Edenic, except in the sense that we may equate the eternal Trickster with Eden's serpent. T. S. Eliot calls the illusory joys of the senses 'the deception of the thrush'. These last bars are the deception of the cuckoo, a notoriously tricksy bird whose cry they utter. The hilarity of this music is synonymous with its blessed humanity; Beethoven, though sublime more often than most, is never portentous.

Beethoven had known through his psychically turbulent middle years that, in the words of Blake, 'the roaring of lions, the howling of wolves, the raging of the stormy sea, and the destructive sword are Portions of Eternity too great for the eye of Man'. Yet he remained, as Wallace Stevens has put it, to play

> on an instrument
> A good agreement between himself and night,
> A chord between the mass of men and himself,
> Far, far beyond the putative canzonas
> Of love and summer.

In the wonderful Waldstein Sonata, a watershed in his creative life, he was learning 'the song with which the frogs praise God', and knew, like Martin Buber, that 'it takes a very long time to learn that song'. For the end of the sonata, Edenic though it may seem, is as equivocal as its beginning; it does not transport us into paradise but rather admits that a reborn innocence, though essential, was not for Beethoven enough. He had discovered that ripeness is all, and was ready for the final stage of his exploration, wherein the Hidden Song becomes an act of faith. One can put this in theological as well as psychological terms, remembering that 'hope that is seen is not hope: for what a man seeth, why doth he yet hope for? But if we hope for that we see not, then do we with patience wait for it' (Rom. 8:24–5). Beethoven had waited, though hardly with patience; as we have seen, the Waldstein might almost be described as a work *about* waiting. Now he is ready to sing the song to 'make all things new' (Rev. 21:5); for 'if any man be in Christ, he is a new creature: old things are passed away; behold, all things are become new' (2 Cor. 5:17). The identity between the theological and the psychological approach has been expressed by Paul Tillich: 'Inasmuch as the Christ is a creation of the divine spirit, so is he who participates in the Christ made into a new creature by the spirit. *The estrangement of his existential from his essential being is conquered*' (italics added). That is what happens in the cycle of Beethoven's last piano sonatas, and is doctrinally manifest in the Solemn Mass he composed contemporaneously.

THE HIDDEN SONG

A study of the late piano sonatas

Who then are they that draw us and whence shall come the Kingdom that is in heaven? The fowls of the air and of the beasts whatever is beneath the earth or upon the earth, and the fishes of the sea, these are they that draw you. And the Kingdom of heaven is within you and whosoever knoweth himself shall find it. And, having found it, ye shall know yourselves that ye are in God and God in you. And ye are the City of God.

The Oxyrhynchus Sayings of Jesus

But what do I love, when I love Thee? not beauty of bodies, nor the fair harmony of time, nor the brightness of the light, so gladsome to our eyes, nor sweet melodies of varied songs, nor the fragrant smell of flowers, and ointments, and spices, not manna and honey, nor limbs acceptable to the embracements of flesh. None of these I love, when I love my God; and yet I love a kind of light, and melody, and fragrance, and meat, and embracement, when I love my God, the light, melody, fragrance, meat, embracement *of my inner man*: where there shineth unto my soul, what space cannot contain, and there soundeth, what time beareth not away, and there smelleth, what breathing disperseth not, and there tasteth, what eating diminisheth not, and there clingeth, what satiety divorceth not.

ST. AUGUSTINE: *Confessions*

Often down here I have entered into a sanctuary; a nunnery; had a religious retreat; of great agony once; and always of some terror; so afraid one is of loneliness; of seeing to the bottom of the vessel. That is one of the experiences I have had here in some Augusts; and got then to a consciousness of what I call 'reality'; a thing I see before me: something abstract; but residing in the downs or sky; besides which nothing matters; in which I shall rest and continue to exist.

VIRGINIA WOOLF: *Diaries*

1. Eros, Dionysus, and Romanticism

Piano sonatas
opus 90 in E minor and major
opus 101 in A major

The Waldstein Sonata is the most prophetic work of Beethoven's middle years, though fulfilment of its prophecy was delayed. Beethoven's next major piano work, the Appassionata Sonata, apparently obliterates the Hidden Song and leads him, in the Seventh Symphony, to the apex of his Morality of Power. It was of the notorious 'revolving cam' in the last movement of the Seventh that Weber, who was a fashionably modern musician rather than an academic fuddy-duddy, made his equally notorious pronouncement: 'Beethoven is now ripe for the madhouse.' He may not have been far off the mark, for so ferocious an assertion of the ego and the will ('I shall seize Fate by the throat, it will never wholly subdue me') would have driven a lesser man crazy, and came near to destroying Beethoven. He went through a second psychological crisis such as we would call a nervous breakdown, and for a period of about five years composed little music. Whether this was due to personal psychological disturbance or to political and economic oppression in these difficult years makes little difference; indeed internal and external causes are hardly separable. What matters is that Beethoven did not go mad, but 'came through'; and what Edmund Burke said in political terms of his (and Beethoven's) society is no less true of the struggle within Beethoven's psyche, the one being a synonym for the other:

> Men are qualified for civil liberty in exact proportion to their disposition to put moral chains upon their own appetites.... Society cannot exist unless a controlling power upon will and appetite be placed somewhere, and the less of it there is within, the more there is without. It is ordained in the eternal constitution of things that men of intemperate minds cannot be free. Their passions forge their fetters.

The 'controlling power' within Beethoven's mind, as contrasted with that rampant in Metternich's Austria, validated his freedom; and when the creative fires were rekindled this freedom was manifest in a radically different kind of music. We commented on some prophetic indications of this in the Waldstein Sonata; there are other hints in the few works Beethoven wrote during his fallow years. It is interesting that one of the most revelatory of these should be a relatively small two-movement sonata of an unusually intimate character. This is the sonata in E minor and major, opus 90, composed in 1814 and dedicated to Count Lichnowsky on the occasion of his marriage.

The first movement, in E minor, is in sonata form, but differs from middle-period Beethoven in its economy. Within its modest dimensions it generates extreme dramatic intensity; yet the music's reticence, its 'controlling power', safeguards it against rhetoric, let alone grandiloquence. Opus 90 is the first sonata for which Beethoven gives tempo indications in German rather than Italian, as though to emphasize the music's intimacy. He says the first movement should be played *Mit Lebhaftigkeit und durchaus mit Empfindung und Ausdruck*, and we may relate the 'liveliness' to the piece's sonata-style urgency, the 'feeling and expression' to its incipient songfulness. The urgency of the first eight-bar clause is evident in the fact that it embraces, within so short a space, two real modulations—to the relative major and dominant minor—and moves in arches, in antiphonally balanced two-bar periods. The first begins forte on an upbeat separated, by the catch-in-the-breath of a quaver rest, from the main beat; moves down the scale in dotted rhythm; lifts through a fourth. Since its last and first beats are both quavers followed by rests, the animation acquires a slight agitation. The answering phrase, moving to the relative major, is soft and discards the rests, so the stepwise movement, both in the tune and the bass, becomes songful. The next four bars, proceeding from relative major to dominant minor, repeat the pattern of loud, soft, broken, smooth; but the ninth bar seems to establish a cantabile line as tonality returns to the relative major:

Ex. 55

Beginning on a tied offbeat, the lyrical tune rises a fourth; descends
through a third and a soft appoggiatura; rises and falls a sixth; then
droops in a chain of thirds. Whereas the first eight bars had (fitfully)
aspired upwards, the second eight bars are a descent, and their relaxation, euphoniously spaced in the middle of the keyboard, is of its
essence song-like. The declension resolves back on the dominant of E
minor, and the final eight bars of the first subject fuse the urgency of
the first period with the lyricism of the second. Perhaps it would be
more accurate to say that urgency is modified into intensity, for legato
line is now unbroken, while lyricism is enriched with widely spaced
tenths, 6–5 chords and chromatic passing notes. Texture and sonority
sound fulfilled, but 'subjectively' so; indeed the piano writing suggests
Schumann, and this is merely the first of several similarly prophetic
passages we will note in this sonata and the next. Romantically, the
tune's arching contour falls of its own weight with a slight ritardando
to the tonic, as though it were the end of a self-contained song in
ternary form, embracing 8 + 8 + 8 bars.

But it isn't; what happens next is a dramatic event. Pianissimo
octaves leap expectantly from dominant to tonic of E minor, the
interval echoing that from the last beat of the second to the first beat of
the third bar. At the end of the octave leaps, however, a sforzando
dominant seventh hurls us abruptly into C major, a flat submediant
modulation such as is to become increasingly potent in the later
sonatas. A sizzling C major scale whirls from the high F to the G below
middle C, and the passage is sequentially repeated in A minor. The
cadential chords are in both cases separated by quaver rests: the agitation latent in the original melody has become patent. But it is also still
mysterious, for the cadence into A minor is immediately followed by a
soft but piercingly dissonant entry of the offbeat rhythm and cascading scale, beginning on B flat:

Ex. 56

The B flats could be explained grammatically as Neapolitans to A minor, but turn out to be a pun, for they change enharmonically into A sharps, part of a dominant ninth leading to B minor. The ninth chord never attains root position, and the cadence, approached by grindingly dissonant chromatic passing notes, is painful. The next six bars reinforce this ferocity, the theme, accompanied by pounding quaver chords, stabbing from first beat to second. Though the rhythm derives from that of the opening clause, the songful quality, lilting from upbeat to strong beat, is demolished. Two bars of 'enhanced' dominant sevenths of F sharp gather to a climax of dissonance in a reiterated dominant minor ninth of B minor, fortissimo. This resolves with subsiding dynamics and slackening tempo into a second subject which, like the second half of the original theme, is a descent, balancing the screwed-up quality of the previous passage. The main line falls offbeat through an inversion and augmentation of the rising fourths and fifths of the potentially song-like first subject. But beneath this spacious descent the left hand rises in arpeggiated semiquavers —spread chords of the tenth, deriving from the sonorous harmonization of the original tune's final bars. Despite the agitation, the harmony moves little, enchained in tonics and dominant sevenths, while the bass's lowest notes form a scale rising through a third, an inversion of the first subject's opening motive. This six-bar clause is repeated with the treble melody broken and rendered more expressive by an offbeat leaping octave, declining in sighs.

A codetta theme, still in the dominant minor, tightens the texture without destroying the memory of song. The bass tramps staccato up a fifth from B to F sharp, which is harmonized as an acutely dissonant suspension within an E minor triad; in fact it resolves on to C major, which becomes a Neapolitan to a minor ninth cadence into the dominant (bars 67–79). Repeated, the minor ninths gradually relinquish their painfulness, partly because dynamics decrease, but more because notes drop out, and harmonic implications are modified. The appoggiatura becomes a gentle droop from the up-beat-prepared first inversion of G major on to B minor; although this is followed by a return of the minor ninth, its resolution is now *upwards*, from G to A sharp to tonic B. The exposition ends with three B minor chords, pianissimo, on the first beat of each bar: stable after the restlessness, yet still a little mysterious because of the silences that separate them.

The development opens with these same three (now tonic) Bs, but no longer as silence-separated chords. They are now single sustained dotted minims, which might be the beginning of a song. And in repeated quavers the Bs remain as a gentle (instead of savage) ostinato, while the first subject reappears above them. Although soft, however, the tune is in its original slightly breathless version with quaver rests, and the music modulates rapidly. Beginning back in E minor, tonality falls to A minor, and veers weirdly to C minor, E flat major and B flat minor, the G flat of which changes enharmonically to F sharp. A G minor diminished seventh then turns into a broken, panting, chromaticized dominant pedal of C minor (bars 100 ff.). Though most of these tonal shifts are too transitory to count as authentic modulations, their effect is disturbing and prevents the song-like tune from establishing itself. It gets no further than reiterations of the dotted rhythm undulations through a semitone, each first beat marked with a sforzando. Yet a ghost of song manages to survive through these broken utterances, even when the melody is widely separated from the chugging bass. Moreover when the texture breaks into rest-separated quavers, moving chromatically in contrary motion and in cross-rhythm, fragmentation unexpectedly leads into the most songful passage in the movement. C minor changes to major, and in this relaxing flat submediant the second phase of the first subject begins on the upbeat, rises a fourth, descends a third and a second, and expands the rise and fall to a sixth. Dynamics remain quiet, metre is unobtrusive

since so many thematic notes are tied across the bars (bars 109 ff.).
Harmonization is at first in two parts only, diaphanously anticipating
textures we will find in the last three sonatas. Chromatic passing notes
give a faintly sensuous flush to the diatonicism: an effect enhanced
when the 'two-part invention' is repeated in tenor and bass register,
with arpeggiated semiquavers in the right hand. This animation is
counteracted by a flatwards modulation to F major, C major's subdominant.

For eighteen bars—a considerable time in so short a movement
remarkable for such textural variety—this figuration remains constant. Yet despite the consistency, the song hinted at in the two-part-
invention passage does not materialize. As the leaping interval in the
left hand oscillates between fourth, fifth and sixth, with increasingly
violent szforzandi on the second beat, we swing back from F major to
A minor and so to the E minor tonic. The leap changes from major
sixth to diminished seventh and thence to an arpeggio, emphasizing
the rising fourth which had originally disrupted the first subject. This
time it creates a strangely elliptical approach to the recapitulation. The
flowing semiquavers turn into high scales reiterated between G and D
sharp; the four-note descent is echoed in canon, first in semiquavers,
then in quavers in stretto, then in crotchets off the beat. It is now
reduced to the original three-note motive G, F sharp, E, in minims tied
across the bars, then gradually increasing back to a quaver pulse, but
with a curious tail-chasing effect as both hands operate canonically
within the same octave:

Ex. 57

Though one can construe this positively as an intrusion of the contrapuntal principle—a canonic many-in-oneness such as is to become

part of Beethoven's rediscovered 'monism'—that is hardly an appropriate description of its effect in context. Here it sounds at least in part ironic, or even deflatory: the development has sought to create a luminous song in unbroken texture; the tail-chasing canon unwinds the song, refragments it in an uneasy giggle: so the recapitulation has no choice but to try again (bar 144).

The three phases of the first subject are unchanged. The leaping octaves are now, however, from G to C, instead of from E to B. The modulation has been accepted; so is the sequential repetition in A minor. But the Neapolitan B flat no longer insinuates itself into the A minor cadence. Instead there is a further surprise: a richly spaced F major triad, moving again from the upbeat to the descending semi-quaver scale (bar 179). It looks as though the F major chord, acquiring D sharps, is to become a German sixth to A minor; in fact the bass inches up chromatically until, in the grinding bridge passage, F major reveals itself as a Neapolitan return to the tonic E minor. The pounding dominant ninths and the second subject are conventionally recapitulated in the tonic; so is the codetta theme, but it is now extended into a coda, the minor ninth appoggiaturas gradually fading out, with each upbeat preparation of the dissonance separated by a silence. The coda slows down and fades away: a romantic dispersion which gives the song a dreamy quality (bars 211–29). The threat of those whirring scales and abrupt modulations has been banished; and when the main theme returns after the disintegrative sighs, the song-phrases have lost the catch-in-the-breath of the quaver rests. The final 8 + 8 bars are quiet yet consummatory, precisely because their binary structure omits the 'middle eight' of the initial ternary structure. No cadential rallentando is called for or necessary; the simple repetition, with the bass doubled in resonant octaves, amounts to a victory for song as convincing in its reticence as the developmental drama had been in its unrhetorical terseness.

What matters is that the victory is enough to justify the second and last movement: a rondo so relaxed that Beethoven can uncharacteristically allow each repetition of his tune to remain almost unchanged by what has happened in the episodes. It is a melody entirely symmetrical, totally unhurried (*nicht zu geschwind*, Beethoven says), and totally songful (*sehr singbar vorzutragen*). The tune is of ineffable tenderness, the harmony simple but rich, the structure regularly periodic, the figuration consistent from start to finish. Beethoven told his recently married patron that the sonata was about love, human

rather than divine; that the first movement concerned divisions
between heart and head, sexual passion and intellect, and the second
concerned the contentment of love fulfilled. The story is unnecessary
to the appreciation of the music, possibly even damaging to it. Schindler says that Beethoven proffered the sonata's 'programme' to the
young prince 'amid peals of laughter'. Though this might indicate
embarrassment on both sides, it doesn't follow that Beethoven
intended his programme facetiously; and the melodic beauty, harmonic equilibrium, formal symmetry and textural consistency of the
music *are* heart-easing. The movement, in healing breaches and attaining rest, behaves like love; if it concerns *eros*, human love rather than
the *agape* of the aria of opus 109, this suggests that for Beethoven the
consummation of human and sexual love was a necessary prelude to
love divine. The religious literatures of all cultures confuse spiritual
and erotic imagery, and Plato's Desire and Pursuit of the Whole did
not exclude sexual union, as is evident in the many sacred rose
metaphors that play upon, rather than deny, the prick of its thorns.
Flora and fauna of paradisal *rosaria* are much the same whether they are
envisaged as mystically transcendent or as sensual bowers of bliss, like
Spenser's. This does not mean that there is no distinction between
erotic and mystical experience, only that they are not antithetical, and
that one may be implicit in the other. This is certainly the case with
Beethoven's two E major airs; to analyse the difference between their
musical effect is inevitably to comment on distinctions between the
sensuous and the spiritual. That these two exquisite song tunes should
be in E major is fascinating but fortuitous, since E major, being the
sharpest key in common use, was—as I have previously had occasion
to point out—traditionally equated with the Baroque notion of
heaven.

Here is the song tune of opus 90:

Ex. 58

How can one categorize it? It's certainly not an operatic aria, for it lacks panache, makes no physical gestures. It's not solemn enough for a hymn, though it might become one, with modifications to the rhythm and figuration. It is not a folksong since, despite its simplicity, it is not monophonic in implication; indeed the second half makes little sense as a monodic tune, divorced from its harmonization. It might be called an air, and has affinities with the simpler type of *Lied*; it's worth noting that another work Beethoven composed during these fallow years was his only song-cycle *An die ferne Geliebte*, love songs addressed to an Eternal Beloved which, in their intimacy, would seem to be concerned with a comparable experience. As a song without words the rondo has been compared to Mendelssohn: which is admissible in so far as the comparison tells us that the mood is domestic, inadmissible if it implies that Beethoven's intimacy is in any sense cosy, and irreconcilable with the spiritual exploration to which he was committed.

It is helpful to consider the rondo melody in relation to the not totally fulfilled song of the first movement. There is no direct thematic parallel; but the first movement begins upbeat with a descending minor third which lifts through a fourth; the rondo begins upbeat with a rising major third which lifts through a minor third and floats down the scale. We respond to this as an *opening out* of the first movement theme. Compared with that tune's restriction, the rondo melody smilingly curves: the more so when the pattern is repeated in quavers, the ascent by step being followed by a further rise through a major third and a dominant–tonic cadence, falling through a fourth, rounding to the mediant. The delicate equilibrium and security of the four-bar period is supported by the warm spacing and level flow of the semiquaver figuration, which maintains a dominant pedal throughout the first eight bars. The bass, scored as though for pizzicato cello, offers the support of rudimentary tonics and dominants, with a touch of subdominant. The style suggests a string quartet, a medium which, however extraordinarily Beethoven had used and was to use it, was currently regarded as domestic: four sensible people—as Goethe put it, using the adjective with both its English and its French connotations—converse together in a room or 'chamber'. According to a publisher's announcement in July 1802, Beethoven deplored the 'unnatural rage' for transcribing piano music for strings, a weakness he succumbed to once only, in his string quartet arrangement of the E major sonata from opus 14. That works agreeably enough, but tells us nothing about the music that isn't evident in the original version: whereas to play the opus 90 rondo on strings reveals the song-like character not only of the melody, but also of the bass and of the apparently subsidiary inner parts. Having heard it on strings, one might play it better on the instrument for which it was sensitively devised.

The four-bar period is repeated with the tune in octaves and the harmony slightly enriched, since the bass moves into Alberti figurations that often flow in tenths with the tune. The bass also introduces a chromatic passing note that effects a momentary modulation to F sharp minor. This time the cadential bar consists of two rising major thirds, reaching up to the tonic, affirming the melody's desire to unfold. The repeated four-bar clause is answered by another four-bar clause, also repeated. This time, however, the tune is itself arpeggiated (as well as arpeggio-accompanied), rather than stepwise-moving. The open melody, rising and falling through a tritone, is expansive, after the previous close movement; its serene equilibrium is now complemented in harmonic and tonal terms, since the ascending tritones of the tune sing over descending *perfect* fifths in the bass, defining sequential modulations to dominant and subdominant. These two plus two bars are balanced by four that form a IV–V–I cadence to the tonic, but incorporate a reference both to the sharpwards modulation (a dominant ninth) and to the flatwards modulation, the chromaticized bass adding a touch of minor to the subdominant chord. The ripely spaced harmony of this section influences the cadence too, for a rising fourth (instead of third) is followed by an appoggiatura A sharp to B, clashing both with the dominant B of the bass and the A natural of the dominant seventh figuration. This sharper edge to the harmony, far from destroying the music's contentment, makes it seem more durable, because more real. When these eight bars are repeated, with the tune in octaves as in the first section, there is one small but subtle change: in the first statement the tune's ascent from B sharp to C sharp is treated as an appoggiatura to the subdominant chord; in the repeat the bass too moves chromatically from G sharp to A. This variant reading does not occur in all editions, but is validated by the autograph. The tiny increase in harmonic momentum makes a point, and is unlikely to be fortuitous.

The repeat of the second section takes us to the twenty-fourth bar. In 4 + 4 further bars Beethoven repeats the opening, now marked *teneramente* and without octave doublings in the bass. The repeat is discreetly embroidered with flowing scales and acciaccaturas. They round off the thirty-two bars of the rondo, the heart-warming effect of which beggars description, though I've tried to describe it! If in the flowing semiquavers and enveloping harmonies we hear cat and kettle purring at and on the hearth, this only enhances our sense of wonder at the music's lyricism. How can such bliss flower from such simple premises? How can a spirit as tormented as Beethoven know such inner quiet? Of course, it is because Beethoven's self-knowledge is uncompromising that his happiness moves us so much; and even within his joy some evidence of the Tree of the Knowledge of Good and Evil must survive. This is why the movement is a rondo, not a self-contained song with the simplest type of variation, such as is to be Beethoven's ultimate musical synonym for paradise. A rondo has episodes, though not sonata-style development. Episodes, merely in being episodic, mean a break in continuity and a possible equivocation of mood. As we shall see, Beethoven manages to restrict both disruption and equivocation to a minimum—far more so than in the celestial-seeking rondo that concludes the Waldstein sonata.

The first episode (bars 32 ff.) takes the dotted rhythm from the second half of the theme, but leaps through a minor sixth instead of tritone, curving back to the perfect fifth. The left hand's arpeggios are somewhat more assertive, since their regular flow is broken by leaping quaver octaves. There is increased energy in the tonality also, since the episode starts in the relative minor and moves to the dominant major. Contrasts of dynamics, carefully notated, add to the urgency, though only during the first eight bars. The second eight-bar period is simply a decoration of the dominant triad of B major (bars 40 ff.). Treble and bass move in contrary motion through a minor third, in parallel thirds and sixths, while a tenor part oscillates between F sharp and G sharp in semiquavers. The phrase is repeated, with the last bar lopped off but with the oscillating semiquavers doubled, in inversion. These trills are too slow to function as 'the still point of the turning world', like the trills in the variations of opus 109 and 111, or even in the finale of the Waldstein. None the less they create a sensuous radiance that has no harmonic movement but generates overtones like a peal of bells. Temporal progression is weakened, if not denied. The lopped-off bar returns in a decorated version of the main theme, in canon, in C sharp minor. Arrived at the dominant, the music flows into a spacious permutation of the episode's scales, augmented to minims and crotchets, accompanied by quaver triplets (bar 60). The songfulness approaches the hymnic, and has something of the relaxed effect of a second subject. After nine bars (compensating for the bar truncated from the previous period), the rondo air recurs in the tonic. This da capo is unmodified; and Beethoven's song proves strong enough to survive not merely the modest disturbance of the first episode but also the more radical adventure of the second.

This is approached (bar 103) by a flattening of the third of the tonic triad, and a minor-keyed extension of the cadential tail-figure of two rising thirds. Modulating to C major, again the flat submediant, the left hand plunges in broken octaves to a widespread dominant seventh, then mounts in diminishing dynamics. The hymn-like falling theme chants remotely in C major, *pianissimo* (bars 114 ff.); shifts to C minor; and then mysteriously to C *sharp* minor. Almost immediately, the 'hymn' resounds in C sharp major, all these slidings between major and minor and between keys a semitone apart being glimpses over the horizon rather than dramatic events:

Ex. 59

So far this modulatory episode has covered twenty-eight bars (103–30). A further ten stabilize the movement, by slowly establishing a dominant seventh decorated with a semiquaver wriggle—a telescoped version of the cadential bars to the original eight-bar clause. Sforzando accents subside as the rondo tune steals in. The restatement of the thirty-two bar rondo tune is again unmodified.

In its modest way, however, the modulatory episode has served some of the functions of a sonata development, for all its material is to reappear with appropriate redisposition of keys. The next episode starts (bar 171) as a strict repeat of the first one, but modulates from its relative minor to the subdominant instead of the dominant. This means that the bell-tolling section in contrary motion, with its written-out slow trills, now reverberates in the tonic major, as does the hymnic motive. Though this resembles a sonata recapitulation, it doesn't suggest a sonata-like beginning, middle and end, for the hymnic theme, analogous to a sonata codetta, modulates from tonic to subdominant, then to its minor and then to C minor. At this point the purring semiquavers cease, and Beethoven appends a pianissimo free canon on the tailpiece figure of rising minor third, falling semitone and fourth. This is augmented to quavers, contrapuntal unity succouring song to carry us safely through a mysterious undulation through C, F and D minors to B flat major-minor, and so to an enharmonic transmutation of the flats to sharps:

Ex. 60

A chord of F sharp major, spread in quavers in the right hand, glows; changes to minor; and leads into a two-part canon embellishing the dominant chord of the E major tonic, and incorporating the thematic third and fourth.

These two canonic passages—the first modulatory, the second static on the dominant seventh of E—recall in microcosm the song's journey, and bring us home, the level semiquavers once more unbroken. So we approach the last full statement of the rondo song, and hear it with slightly different ears. This may be why Beethoven, though he changes neither its melodic contours nor its harmonization, gives it a different registration: the melody is now in the tenor, with semiquaver figuration above it, sometimes with chromatic passing notes (bars 230 ff.). The second half is also melodically centred in tenor register, in two parts simulating viola and cello. Its repeat, however, returns to the original registration, with the theme in octaves in the right hand, and the left hand's figuration unchanged. For this fulfilled song, development is unnecessary or even irrelevant; though Beethoven cannot quite allow this tune the self-sufficiency of the aria of opus 109 or the Arietta of opus 111. He therefore adds a strange and lovely coda, wherein the cadential semitonic dissonance is repeated in varied registrations, modulates fleetingly to F sharp minor, but returns to a 6–4 cadence. The modulation occurs again, more brokenly; and silence is succeeded by another canon on the cadential phrase, its rising minor third sometimes opened to a fifth. This subsides in chromatic sequences over a syncopated dominant pedal.

Any tinge of pain in the music's sensuousness is here absolved, and contrapuntal discipline seems an intellectual means to that emotive end. The final statement of the song can then start to sing in the original scoring, but surprisingly and subtly this is not the conclusion. The cadential motive is inverted and further opened to a rising sixth; after four canonic entries it dissolves, with a small accelerando, into floating semiquavers. The final line flutters in falling thirds and leaping octaves without establishing thematic identity; the last bar reflects the cadential motive in diminution. It would be excessive to describe this coda as 'throwaway', since that would suggest deflation. None the less the end *is* inconclusive, for this song is not yet the mandala-rose for which Beethoven has sought throughout his creative life. This is why his 'third period' was necessary. Opus 90 belongs neither to his middle nor to his late phase. The next sonata, opus 101, is on the threshold, though its promised rebirth is to prove for the moment abortive.

We have observed that there are touches of romanticism in opus 90, a suggestion of Mendelssohn or Schumann. Opus 101 also opens in song-like lyricism and in a sonority that has been likened to the Brahms of the late piano *Intermezzi*, and still more pertinently to Schumann. We know that Schumann loved this sonata, which he rightly considered wayward and fanciful, like his own music; it is evident that he borrowed elements from the lyricism of its first movement and from the nervous energy of its dotted rhythmed march. Before proceeding with our analysis, it might therefore be useful to reflect on the sense in which Beethoven's premonitions of Romanticism—more strongly manifest, interestingly enough, in the few transitional works in which he used German tempo indications than in his 'third period' proper—ally him with later Romantic composers. Except in a crudely chronological sense, and even that may mislead, the terms Classical and Romantic have little critical validity. True, there is some justification for the view that every human psyche seeks an equilibrium between Dionysiac and Apollonian impulses, and that the relation between these impulses conditions the romantic or classical affinities of an artist. One cannot, however, assume that an artist in a society moulded by stable values will tend to classicism, whereas one living in conditions of turbulence will incline to romanticism. Both Beethoven and Schubert, who died within a year of one another, were nurtured in the same classical tradition; both lived in a transitional society. We associate Schubert, but not Beethoven, with the birth-pangs of Romanticism; at least no study of Romanticism could ignore Schubert's mythic status as Wanderer and Outsider. He starts from classical precedents, but inverts them, so that developments become anti-developments, and the *Moment Musical* and the intimate *Lied* are more apposite than the dynamic sonata. Though his greatest works are sonatas, which preserve the traditional tension between the private and the public life, there is a tendency, even in grand, superficially aggressive works such as the posthumous C minor piano sonata, for the *re*gressive and nostalgic dream to become more real than the waking life. This involves, if not a denial, at least a relaxation of progressive 'purposefulness'. Though some of Schubert's friends were intellectually aware and politically active, he himself did not believe that music could, or should, be an instrument of change.

Beethoven, on the other hand, might be called romantic in that he re-creates traditional forms subjectively; yet he does so, especially in his late works, in the interests of an order ever more stringent and coherent. Schubert's dream is in one, not necessarily pejorative, sense an escape. Beethoven's vision is an affirmation; and it is significant that we regard his late works, which had no immediate successors, neither as Classical nor Romantic, but as *sui generis*. Schumann, who borrowed superficial elements from late Beethoven, represents a stage beyond Schubert in the evolution of Romanticism, for in his work the musical 'moment' has ousted the private–public dichotomy of sonata. The Mask and the Dream have taken over from 'reality': Schumann's obsession with cyphers was not merely a game extraneous to his art. In so far as he appeals to Bachian and Beethovenian classical traditions, it is as a bulwark against despair; and the heart of Schumann's romanticism lies in the fact that the bulwark was not strong enough. He literally went mad, whereas Beethoven through his art resolved tensions that today would probably be diagnosed as schizophrenic, or even psychotic. Schumann's lunacy imperilled his creativity and killed him at the age of forty-two. One of his finest and most characteristic works crystallizes madness into art, for *Kreisleriana* is a series of masks and mirrors at once disguising and reflecting the clown-magician of E. T. A. Hoffmann. It is interesting that Hoffmann, a writer who haunted Schumann's imagination, was preoccupied (as *The Tales of Hoffmann* demonstrate) with what we would now call an 'identity crisis', and relevant that he was musically talented. What Hoffmann writes of Beethoven's music is psychologically on the mark, despite the romantic extravagance of its expression:

> Beethoven's instrumental music opens up to us the realm of the monstrous and the immeasurable. Burning flashes of light shoot through the deep night of this realm, and we become aware of giant shadows that surge back and forth, driving us into narrower and narrower confines until they destroy us—but not the pain of that endless longing in which each joy that has climbed aloft in jubilant song sinks back and is swallowed up; and it is only in this pain which consumes love, hope and happiness but does not destroy them, which seeks to burst our breasts with the many-voiced consonance of all the passions, that we live on, enchanted beholders of the supernatural!
>
> Haydn grasps romantically what is human in human life; he is more commensurable, more comprehensible for the majority.
>
> Mozart calls rather for the superhuman, the wondrous element that abides in our inner being.

Beethoven's music sets in motion the lever of fear, of awe, of horror, of suffering.... *Yet the truth is that, as regards self-possession, Beethoven stands quite on a par with Haydn and Mozart, and that, separating his ego from the inner realm of harmony, he rules over it as an absolute monarch.* In Shakespeare our knights of the aesthetic measuring-rod have often bewailed the utter lack of inner unity and continuity, although for those who look more deeply there springs forth, issuing from a single bud, a beautiful tree, with leaves, flowers and fruit: thus with Beethoven it is only after a searching of his instrumental music that the high self-possession inseparable from genius and nourished by the study of art stands revealed (italics added).

We often talk about romantic artists—timidly conventional opinion is apt to include all artists—as being 'neurotic', and in a few cases (for instance Schumann) the adjective fits. Statistically, however, there is little evidence that artists are more neurotic than less creative people; indeed there is some evidence that, clinically speaking, they are less neurotic than business men, politicians, long-distance truck drivers, university professors or even psychiatrists. As Anthony Storr has put it, we are all divided selves, and the term neurotic should be applied only to those whose powers of synthesis have failed: we become neurotic when there is a block to our creativity, whatever its mani-festations, not when it is functioning efficaciously. A 'divine discon-tent' would seem to be basic to the human condition. 'It has its origins in the peculiarities of man's development from birth to maturity and is a necessary consequence of man's adaptation to the world, which is by means of abstraction, conceptual thought and symbolization.' The process of artistic creation, which releases instinct and invents means to control it, is thus closely related to the process of 'growing up'. Dietrich Bonhoeffer has made the same point in theological terms in remarking that 'our coming of age leads us to a true recognition of our situation before God. God would have us know that we live as men who manage our lives without him. The God who is with us is the God who forsakes us (Mark 15:34). The God who lets us live in the world without the working hypothesis of God is the God before whom we stand continually. Before God and with God we live without God.' That is perhaps more directly pertinent to Beethoven than to any other composer; and even in terms of clinical psychiatry we can say that, far from being neurotic, Beethoven discovered a bulwark against chaos not through reference to religious and cultural values outside the self, but rather through a simultaneous re-formation of the self and of tradition. This is why the morphological image applied to Beethoven's art, of which my quotation from Hoffmann provides an early example, is relevant.

Though as a human being Beethoven must have been difficult, his cantankerousness and clumsiness were everyone's human divisiveness writ large, because experienced so much more potently than by most of us. But he not only experienced divisiveness as a man, he also dealt with it as an artist. What he created was and is available to us all, and I cannot believe that his artistic triumph did not reflect on his personality. Even those who found him in one way or another obnoxious were glad to have known him. It must have been a privilege to meet another 'creature of conflict' (in Storr's phrase) who had not only sought for, but found, reconciliation. 'We are all to some extent alienated, and would not be human if we were not so.' Beethoven demonstrates how, in dealing with our alienation, we may become fulfilled. A society that psychiatrically 'treated' Beethoven, as ours might have done, would be a society that, being dominated by fear, did not deserve the privilege of genius. Being fearful, it would not be likely to be offered it.

Since alienation is endemic to the human condition, it must be associated with the artistic process itself. Though it is more manifest in romantic than in classical art, the difference is one of degree, not kind. Certainly shorthand terms like Romantic and Classical are better avoided in discussing Beethoven, and it is interesting that they usually *are* avoided, perhaps more out of puzzlement than from inner comprehension. But if there is a Beethoven sonata that justifies the epithet romantic, in Hoffmann's sense, it is certainly Schumann's favourite, opus 101 in A major, for this is the sonata in which Beethoven's 'self-possession' is most vulnerable. It is the closest he ever came to writing 'neurotic' music; and it may be worth noting that it was composed in 1815–16, when his inner turbulence over his young nephew had reached a crisis of exacerbation. This is not naïvely to claim that the sonata is 'about' that crisis: only that it may have been one contributory strand that triggered off a work that ends with a whiff of lunacy. That lunacy was a springboard for the more apocalyptic struggle of the closely related Hammerklavier Sonata, which Beethoven recognized as a turning point in his spiritual life no less crucial than that of the Eroica Symphony in earlier years.

Even the gentle opening of the sonata breathes a faint unease: for although it begins with lyric song, marked *Etwas lebhaft und mit der innigsten Empfindung*, the vocal fluidity of the theme is subject to recurrent frustrations. Despite its melodic and textural affinities with Schumann, this music is not so much self-contained song as a yearning for songfulness. Those keywords of German romanticism, *innig* and *Empfindung*, are precisely pertinent; and although Beethoven himself described the first movement as 'a sort of dream-like song', that dream is no regression to Eden. Beethoven's dreams, unlike Schumann's or even Schubert's, cannot be indulged in, being stages in a psychic drama. This is why this small movement is not a ternary aria, but a miniature sonata conflict.

The dreamy quality is evident in the first six-bar clause of the flowing (*Etwas lebhaft*) 6/8 tempo:

Ex. 61

The melody steals upon us as though from the depths of sleep; as Tovey points out, it begins on the dominant chord, and even sounds as though it might be *in* the dominant and in the middle of the tune, which floats up the scale from the third and curls down from the high E to D and B. The alto part rocks like a lullaby, the tenor falls chromatically, the bass remains static on a dominant pedal. The fusion of the tenderly arching melody with the warmly spaced harmony makes the song at once sensuous and wistful; and the next two bars sigh in declension, for having leapt an octave from the upbeat, the melody falls in the havering cross-rhythms of the fourth bar. Here the tune is ripely doubled at the tenth by the tenor, while the pedal note, transferred from bass to alto, creates passing dissonances. The bass enters again on the second beat of bar 3, descends lyrically through a sixth, and moves up to the dominant. It serves once more as a dominant pedal while the opening bar and a half are repeated; but this time the chromatic passing notes effect, with a slight ritardando, a modulation to the relative, F sharp minor. So the song's first clause remains unresolved.

The six-bar period is answered by one of ten bars: the metrical irregularity, as compared with the regularity of the opus 90 rondo, contributes to the music's wistfulness. Up to this point the texture has been in four real parts, even more apposite to the medium of string quartet than the movement of opus 90. Now the texture is more pianistic, for the bass is doubled in octaves and the upper parts separate from it. The F sharp minor modulation proves a feint, however, for the second clause starts off again in A major's dominant, E major, and presses to *its* relative, C sharp minor. The tune itself, propelled by this harmonic momentum, gathers energy; instead of arching upwards and then dropping, it extends its rising scale from C sharp to B sharp and resolves after all not on a tonic C sharp minor, but on an A major triad, with the B sharp tied over as dissonant upward appoggiatura (see Ex. 61). The pain of this is reinforced by the wide spacing between the hands: though pain also generates passion as the bass rises chromatically to achieve modulation into the dominant, E major. There has been no tonic resolution on the strong beat; and when the melody does cadence, in the sixteenth bar, a C sharp minor triad is substituted for the expected E major. With its rich passing dominant sevenths and vocally singing appoggiaturas and turns, the music remains too sensuously textured and lyrically sustained for the interrupted cadences to spell frustration. Cadential irresolution none the less contributes to the dreaminess.

What follows is a kind of second subject, though not a contrasted idea. It is a dialogue of speaking voices, again suggesting the medium of string quartet; and the dialogue seems to imply, along with speech, the gestures of caressing hands or opening arms (bars 16–25). The 'cello's' stepwise rise through a third (lightly bowed as two quavers plus one) falls expressively through a seventh, and is answered in free inversion by 'first violin' and 'viola'. This dialogue theme fuses the first bar's stepwise third with the sixth of the bass entry in bar 3; but although it is evolution rather than contrast, it doesn't immediately know where it's going, since it begins in the dominant of the dominant, shifts to the relative minor, and only then cadences into E major. Even so, the triads are unobtrusively in first inversion; the upward floating, appoggiatura-stressed quavers have to be sounded four times before reaching a cadence in root position, moving from the upbeat into the twenty-fifth bar. This unBeethovenian lack of purposefulness is part of the romantic flavour that appealed to Schumann. True, Beethoven compensates for his tonal irresolution with a codetta that at first simply repeats dominant–tonic cadences in E, then telescopes them by sounding dominants and tonics simultaneously over a tonic pedal:

Ex. 62

To do this, however, he sacrifices song, which disappears after the bass has inverted and augmented the opening phrase. Even the tonal affirmation is ambiguous, for the telescoped tonics and dominants, tied across the beats, create both rhythmic and harmonic stasis, fading out until only the third, G sharp to B, remains.

In most editions this exposition covers no more than a page: fifteen bars of first subject, nine of second, ten of codetta theme, if one applies the conventional terminology which is hardly appropriate, and, if it encourages a sectional approach to what is continuous, may even mislead. The development too is constant in texture and figuration; yet although its songfulness is unbroken, tension accrues within it. We begin (bar 35) with the original song-theme arching in the tenor, beneath the G sharp–B third, now sustained. We might still be in E major, or back in the dominant of A; and ambiguity remains when the right hand's syncopated chord acquires an added sixth, and the tenor's tune is repeated at the same pitch but with its initial E sharpened. This takes us to F sharp minor. The original song sings on top, over a double pedal in the syncopated rhythm, with C sharp in the alto, deep octaves on F sharp in the bass. The yearning latent in the melody's arch is intensified because the D naturals at the top of each crest clash with the C sharp pedal, both in the F sharp minor passage, and then in D major when the bass descends to the low E. The melody no longer flows onwards, as in its first presentation; instead, the arches are almost naggingly repeated, with echo dynamics, *forte* alternating with *piano*. Dissonance becomes more acute between a lofty G natural and the pedal's F sharp, as D major merges into B minor, the breathless effect of the syncopated chords being marked by sforzando accents (bars 48–9). Dynamics have risen to forte, tonality sharpwards to C sharp minor. Released from the pedal notes and syncopations, the song descends in free inversion, to close on a first inversion dominant seventh, with pause mark. Pushing up in slightly painful rising sequences from C sharp, we are into the recapitulation before we realize it, especially since recapitulation starts in A minor before the major is re-established. When the music is at last centred on the elusive home tonic (bar 58), the recapitulation behaves normally, though it is shortened and tightened because the long rising scale becomes entirely chromatic, its would-be resolutory appoggiatura being on E sharp instead of B sharp. This puts the second subject, if that's what it is, a fifth lower, and establishes the tonic major for the codetta theme. Its oscillating tonics and dominants over a tonic pedal are, however, extended into dissonant dominant ninths and diminished sevenths, swelling to the movement's only fortissimo in bar 86. The tied-over accents still 'break the time-barrier', and an unstable asymmetry pervades the lyrical coda. Sensuously twining parallel thirds and sixths form a 6–4 cadence; the original arching theme is fused into the rising thirds and leaping sixths. Flow is arrested by the sudden return of the syncopated dominant chord, not loud but thickly scored, on the last quaver of bar 95. After silence, its tonic resolution follows on the last quaver of the next bar. This dubious resolution is repeated, more thinly scored; the movement fades out with the second subject's 'dialogue' phrase in the bass (or 'cello') answered in free inversion in the alto. The hands float apart, to end with an elided dominant–tonic cadence. Again there is softly dissonant pain in the lyricism. Such a 'dream-like song', however beautiful, could not be an end to Beethoven's pilgrimage, nor even to this sonata.

Certainly the second movement at first rejects dreamful song with vigorously corporeal movements. It is a march, in the thrusting dotted rhythm which we have seen to be associated with physical (especially sexual) energy, from the dance music of seventeenth-century Europe to America's barrelhouse boogie. The march's physicality is not, however, unequivocal; though it brings Beethoven down to earth from his dream-like song, it does not exclude intimations of immortal-

ty. The tonal relationship of its key, F major, to A major is that of the
flat submediant, which hardly suggests aggression, and the texture is
lightly linear rather than heavily harmonic:

Ex. 63

The dotted rhythm is notated as quaver, semiquaver rest, and semiquaver, which gives the lines an airy bounce, even during the first
eight-bar period. This balances upward-prancing intervals—octave in
the left hand, major sixth and diminished seventh in the right—against
a bass that falls chromatically, with widely separated two-octave
transpositions. The crests of the right hand ascents are marked by
appoggiaturas, whole tone in the first case, semitone in the second.
These create a momentary modulation to the subdominant minor,
though a dominant cadence, with downward pressing dominant
ninths, soon earths the music again and leads, by way of chromatic
passing notes, to a full dominant modulation. After this section has
been repeated an extra four bars of skittish dialogue between the hands
re-establishes the tonic.

After the double bar the music's airiness becomes overt. With an
abrupt switch to D major, Beethoven embarks on a quasi-canonic
dialogue between widely separated parts, which leap through sixths
and sevenths and droop in appoggiaturas. This 'light' D major turns
out to be a preparation for D minor, and therefore for a not abnormal
modulation to F major's relative (bar 15). But the leaps grow increasingly disembodied as the phrases flicker into trills that end in thin air,
and as the leaps grow wider the appoggiaturas are longer sustained. So
there is tension between melodic levitation and harmonic weight, until
little canonic stretti carry us through G minor to F minor, with
Neapolitan G flats. F minor turns into its flat submediant, D flat major,
when the music floats dreamily in a two-part canon, the originally
declining tail to the phrases now sailing upwards:

Ex. 64

Beethoven directs that the sustaining pedal be held throughout this passage. It doesn't work on twentieth-century pianos, though on Beethoven's instrument the hazy effect is exquisite. In any case the dream does not last. A strange revolving cam, pianissimo in the bass, turns into a triplet-rocking dominant pedal which carries us to a forte in the original tonic, and to a canon in stretto on the tightened-up version of the march theme (bars 40 ff.). Further canons, in contrary motion scales in dotted rhythm, induce a caprine hilarity, though the high inverted entries are subtly marked *dolce*. Any undercurrent of the first movement's wistfulness is banished by a sudden cessation of movement on a loud dominant seventh of B flat (bar 50). The march concludes with a modified repetition of the four cadential bars to its first section.

In so far as it is poised between earth and heaven, there are elements of romantic irresolution in this march, as there were in the 'dream-like song'; we have noticed that it is a prototype for many marches of Schumann in the same rhythm. The trio, however, is quintessentially late Beethoven; and though it evokes a pastoral Eden, as did many trios in Haydn, Mozart and Schubert as well as Beethoven, this Eden marks the distinction between a dream and a vision to which I've already referred. The distinction is not merely subjective to the listener, for the technical features that create the dreaminess of the first movement are not present in the trio. This piece is unromantic in its contrapuntal abstraction, creating from strict canonic writing in two parts a diaphanous texture anticipating the late Bagatelles; there are also affinities with the canons in Bach's *Art of Fugue* and *Musical Offering*. The music's abstraction induces wonder, even a hushed awe:

which does not mean that the trio may not at times be comic. This has repercussions later in the sonata.

Beethoven begins with a gentle oscillation between F and G, which we hear as tonic and supertonic, though they turn out to be the fifth and sixth degrees of the scale, since the trio is in B flat, the subdominant. The F stays as a pedal while the treble and bass complete the B flat triad, oscillating by inversion. After three bars the pedal disappears, leaving a thin two-part canon at the octave, at half a bar's distance. The theme, pervaded by rising thirds and falling tritones, grows increasingly angular as it modulates, after ten bars, to the dominant. After the double bar the canon is at a whole bar's distance, the line still more gawky, with augmented fourths and augmented fifths. Not surprisingly, the texture becomes sharply dissonant, though since the clashes are linearly created they do not have the expressive function they have in most classical and romantic music. A passage such as the following strikingly anticipates the linear counterpoint of such twentieth-century composers as Bartók and Stravinsky:

Ex. 65

Canonic two-in-oneness gives aural reality to the cliché 'beyond Time and Space', for the modulations, or rather the momentary shifts of tonality, are so rapid that they have neither time nor space to establish identity. Eventually the G flats of the diminished seventh of B flat minor pivot back to the major, and restore the original canon under an extended dominant trill; this again suggests the trills in the late Bagatelles (bars 76–8). The next five bars repeat in the scherzo's tonic the canon that had originally appeared in the dominant. They fade on the oscillation, now between tonic and supertonic, which gradually turns into a dominant seventh of F. The oscillations decorate a low pedal C, mirrored by inversion in the treble (bar 87). The texture is still transparent, as the high chords gather energy (D flat over the C pedal, German sixth resolving on to dominant). By this time the march's dotted rhythm has reasserted itself, and a gradual crescendo, over a pedal in rocking triplets, leads to the da capo of the march.

So the first movement has been a 'dream-like song' and the second movement an earthy march that hints at, and in the trio weirdly and wonderfully attains, moments of transcendence. The collocation of the two movements makes it possible for Beethoven to 'start again': for what follows is indeed a song of longing *(langsam und sehnsuchtsvoll* is Beethoven's direction), though the longing is now no romantic dream. Yearning is sublimated into a late Beethoven hymn-aria. At this stage the process of sublimation is not total, but this does not prevent the movement from being 'one of the most pathetic and mysterious things in all music'. The phrase is Tovey's, and its insight, as usual, is precise. The piece is 'pathetic' not only in its intrinsic musical essence, but *because* it is unfulfilled; and it is 'mysterious' because it contains the first visionary gleam—with the possible exception of the comparable slow introduction to the finale of the Waldstein—of Beethoven's ultimate meta-physical serenity, as exemplified in the Lydian adagio of the quartet opus 132 or the Arietta of opus 111.

Beethoven marks it *una corda,* a technical device he had always associated with the super-natural, though not with the specifically mystical implications it has in his late works. The adagio starts, like the first movement, on the dominant, but in A minor instead of major. Bass and alto move darkly in parallel tenths through a third, resolving on the tonic triad. The melody flowers in a written-out turn and an aspiring sixth. Possibly we hear this as a ghostly echo of the yearning sixths of the first movement. Here it is slower, more solemn; and falls through a *diminished* fourth to G sharp, turns back to the tonic A, and lifts through a perfect fifth. Meanwhile the bass octaves rise through another third, then fall, then lift through a sixth to F, to which the melody's E natural forms a dissonant appoggiatura. The resolved dissonance moves up to the high F, modulating to D minor; but the B flat triad on the third quaver acts as a Neapolitan return to A minor, as the hymnic song cadences once more on, not in, the dominant. The G sharp is flattened, and in the next bar plain diatonic concords suggest the modal flavour of the Arietta of opus 111:

Ex. 66

They lead, indeed, to the Arietta's key, C major, by way of a momentary plagal flattening in the bass. Here the hands are widely spaced, but in the next two bars they are in the middle of the keyboard, alternating between dominant sevenths and tonic triads. In this concordant context the rising sixth (from B to G) has lost its yearning.

The next bar returns to the original theme of repeated note, turn and rising sixth, now chanted unisonally in the bass, and in C major (bar 9). The theme is answered canonically in the treble, two octaves higher, while alto and bass return to the pattern of rising third resolving on the tonic. Gradually the resonant four-part texture evaporates, as canonic dialogue between the hands occurs in stretto. The grace notes at the bottom of the left hand's part define a progressive intensification of harmony, which prevents the melodic phrase, despite its vocal lyricism, from flowing on, let alone taking off. It repeats itself seven times, alternating between two octaves, until the static C major triad changes to E minor 6–4, then to a diminished seventh of B minor. From this point the stable diatonicism that had given the song its hymnic quality disintegrates. The a-tonal implications of the neutral diminished seventh, from which derived its horrendous reputation in the eighteenth century, have never been more strangely or more movingly demonstrated. The diminished sevenths descend through a chain of fifths on each half-bar, cyclically falling from B to D minor; then move back to E minor, to approach A minor and the anchorage of a dominant pedal:

Ex. 67

Throughout this disintegration, which remains veiled, remote, unrhetorical, the melody sings its vocal turns with increasingly complex ornamentation, trying to rise phoenix-like from the bass which descends, at first on the initial beat of each bar, then on each alternate beat, down the chromatic scale from a tonic C to the E a sixth below. This E supports the final declension as a dominant pedal; the diminished seventh above it hurts but no longer disrupts, since it resolves on to the fully scored dominant triad. The Song or Hymn has, however, been defeated; or rather has fallen to pieces, since there has been no suggestion of threat from without. The triad dissolves in a cadenza—a slowly spread dominant arpeggio with appoggiaturas (F double sharp to G sharp) that aurally create an effect of false relation.

'Dissolves' in the above sentence is a paradox: for although the mystical hymn is dispersed, the cadenza is to be played *poco a poco tutte le corde*. At this stage Beethoven cannot complete his divine hymn; so the cadenza returns, humanly *tre corde* though still very soft, to the sonata's opening: to a reminiscence of his *humanly* sensuous song of yearning (bar 21). But this dream is relinquished almost before it is under way. There is a pause mark halfway through the second bar, another after the answering phrase. The cross-beat tied rhythm appears stutteringly; mounts to a presto scale on the dominant; turns into long trills on D, D sharp and the dominant E. This launches a vigorous sonata allegro; having aspired, through the scherzo-march and its trio, to the adagio's intimation of the divine, Beethoven cannot make shift with a dream. If need be, the battles of his middle years must be fought again. Inevitably, since so much has happened in his spiritual history, they will be fought with a difference.

Beethoven tells us that this allegro should be played *mit Entschlossenheit*—with determination; it needs it, both technically and experientially. The movement opens as a sonata allegro which calls on contrapuntal resource: for the right hand's theme, emulating the thumping dominant sevenths before the initiatory trills, pounces down a minor third or a second, then shoots up in semiquavers before another plunge through a fifth, perfect or diminished. This is imitated in free canon by the left hand, energetically attaining a sharpwards modulation to the dominant, emphasized by two pauses (bar 12). The pauses might, however, be frustration rather than emphasis: as is suggested when an attempted repeat in double counterpoint, with the right and left hands inverted, runs into trouble. For the pounces become immobilized by repeated tonics, syncopated, and then by a dominant pedal, wavering between E and F natural. The vigorous music has grown almost polite, though the pounces return, marked with sforzando accents, in bars 28–9. It seems that the canonic dialogue is resuming, clearer because there is an extra octave between the parts. When the leaping motive turns into a grittier canon in driving semiquavers, this also gets stuck on reiterated tonics and a four-note scale. The top part attempts to rise to lyrical song, recalling the alternating fifths and sixths prevalent in the first movement and adagio. But the song cannot grow; the effect is on the verge of risibility, like a stylus stuck in a record groove. When the music does define its dominant cadence it sounds, after the obsessive reiteration of tonics, jaunty rather than triumphant; and the second subject proves, in comparison with the grand gestures of the allegro's opening, to be childish in its stepwise-moving dotted rhythm, comic in its canonic entries that make the metrical structure deceptive. We hear the phrases in 2/4 across the bars, so the ultimate dominant–tonic cadence has to be ludicrously squashed into one and a half bars:

Ex. 68

The codetta carries this debunking process a stage further. Thematically it is a permutation of the first subject, leaping down from the upbeat and rising through a semiquaver scale, still presented in vestigial canon. Far from being a tigerish pounce, however, it is now a childish skip, a game of hop-scotch, accompanied by a banal bass of tonic, dominant and subdominant chords (see Ex. 68). It suggests opera buffa, or rather the street songs from which elements of opera buffa were derived. Both song and drama are deflated as they are in a Rossini stretto finale. But this music, unlike Rossini's, doesn't play its own applause; the cadence that ends the exposition in sudden pianissimo is an irony that is witty rather than grotesque. Its rhythmic ambiguities and silences debunk the debunking; and so can justify a return to the optimistic gestures of the opening, when the allegro is repeated.

After the repeat there is a mysterious extension to the codetta, which preserves something of the scherzando mood in that a motive of staccato fourths in quavers, an amiable permutation of the original 'pounce', persists in the tenor. The bass, however, sings in minims, chanting the rising sixths and falling fifths and fourths that figure in most of the work's song-aspiring themes; while the right hand melody, beginning with a *gentle* pounce, mounts gravely up the scale in minims (bars 86–91). Subconsciously, we may be reminded of the ascent up the A major scale in the first movement's first subject. More directly, mood and texture recall the embryonic solemnity of the hymnic introduction to the finale; certainly the spread 6–4 of A minor after the scalewise decline astonishingly reinvokes, as played by Arrau, that incipiently transcendent aria. But the phrase peters out; or rather the 6–4 is never resolved, but is knocked out by a fortissimo return of the descending pounce through a third:

Ex. 69

The recollection of the hymn-aria is not, however, entirely ineffectual, for it prompts Beethoven to assay a development by way of contrapuntal unity—the other basic 'monistic' principle in European music, along with self-contained song. The fugue begins in a whisper, hardly daring to trust its luck. The key is C major, veering to Aeolian A minor; the theme an extension of the original allegro motive (bars 95 ff.). Still very soft, it modulates flatwards to the subdominant, then to its relative, D minor. The groping effect is the more patent because Beethoven ends the fugue theme with a trill and turn that are left suspended, as are those in the march. Gradually, however, the fugue gathers energy, as though Beethoven, gritting his teeth, is attempting a desperate affirmation: 'I will *not* be divided, I *will* be whole'. At the same time textures become acrid and rhythms rigidly metrical, in a manner that anticipates the far more titanic fugue that concludes the next sonata, opus 106. Modulation too grows hectic. After sundry veerings between C major and A minor, F major and D minor, we plunge to G minor and circuitously return to C major, the theme in stretto, with chunky parallel sixths and savagely dissonant passing notes. A wild episode bandies the pounce between varied registers, against leaping octaves, separated by quaver rests, on each beat. Stomping from C major to the modal-flavoured A minor to E minor, the fugue explodes in whirring scales in contrary motion. At bar 180 we arrive back at the original theme, the entries crowding in close stretto, unambiguously in A minor. The trills at the end of the theme are still abandoned in mid-air, and vanish in a hammering of parallel sixths and thirds, also in stretto, with fierce sforzandi. Climax occurs when the bass swoops down to booming chords of the dominant, at the bottom of the keyboard. Within the dominant pedal the fugue subject bells in immense augmentation, with the semiquaver scales spurting on top:

Ex. 70

The figuration then blows up in broken dominant arpeggios; for all its grinding strife, the most the fugue has done is to enable Beethoven to start again, re-enunciating the sonata allegro in what, after the fugal anguish, sounds like A major triumph. Recapitulation can hardly, however, celebrate the Power and the Glory, given the nature of the exposition. Its frustrations may be modified, after the painful and partial affirmation of the fugal development, but not annealed. Once again, after the canonic scales have whirred into a furious organum of 6–3 chords (the only innovation in the recapitulation, bars 220–4), the stylus gets stuck in its groove; the second subject and codetta theme, when they appear in the conventional tonic, remain childish or frivolous, perhaps more so than in the exposition, since the fugue's agony has been so acute. After the codetta Beethoven appends a coda that begins (bar 275) with the rocking fourths and fifths pianissimo, low in the left hand, and in the right hand the tied note and semiquaver figure, amiably without the pounce. An apparently tranquil modulation to the subdominant is cancelled by a fortissimo eruption of the descending third, A to F sharp. Then silence; followed softly by a descending *major* third, A to F natural, a flat submediant triad distantly recalling the march. Another silence: after which the original theme gently dances in F. It is not, however, a real modulation, but a flattened approach to the dominant of A, and a recapitulation of the teetering dominant pedal from the exposition, differing only in that it incorporates the fugue's trill, and at last completes it with a turn and a resolutory note. Momentarily, the music seems almost gracious, certainly playful. There is no finality about this, however. When the fugue's scales return they flicker rather than surge, with the bouncing fourths expanded to fifths, tossed above and below them. The scales cease, the pianissimo fifths spatter down to a low written-out trill between G sharp and A. This continues to growl softly for twelve bars while fragments of the original theme, pared to a falling third and rising scale, twitter above. The music grows softer and slower, running down like a clock. The twiddling semiquaver scale tries twice to rise through the third and fourth, but fails. The deep trills have been rendered yet more sepulchral by the addition of a low E, the same note that had underpinned the fugue's explosion. Here it preserves a certain awfulness as the thematic motives peter out in a gradual ritardando. In the last three bars, however, Beethoven admits to bathos: with a sudden fortissimo he returns to tempo, and thumps seven tonic triads rising through an A major arpeggio, the rhythm rigid, the left hand scoring thick. The crude scoring is of course part of the psychological and physiological effect; it is difficult to credit that quite recent commentators have attributed the passage to Beethoven's faulty hearing! Beethoven was not Mozart, who believed that music ought to sound beautiful even when concerned with unpleasantries. None the less the end of opus 101 *is* grotesquely beautiful in that it is true; the original pounce has become an Olympian shrug of the shoulders, which only a Beethoven could have the courage to make.

Opus 101 begins as a lyrical song that proves to be a dream; continues with a corporeal march which, especially in its trio, glimpses the Word through the Flesh; aspires to an aria–hymn that dissolves in harmonic deliquescence; attempts a sonata conflict which, beginning optimistically, lapses into farce; calls unsuccessfully on fugal unity to restore order; and assays sonata again, which this time flickers out in pathos and bathos. Some very distinguished critics, notably Tovey and Martin Cooper, find the end of this sonata cheerful, even euphoric. This might be a legitimate response to the jaunty fourths and fifths and frisky semiquavers *per se*, but is surely too simple an account of their effect in the context of the sonata. After the energy of the fugue's attempt at unity, after the dissolution of the hymnic adagio into sequential diminished sevenths, even after the yearning of the original song-sonata, we can hardly accept the coda's playfulness at face value. If it is playful, it is so in the same archetypal sense as the *ludus puerorum* which Christ referred to, after the initiatory round dance in the Apochryphal Acts of St. John: 'And if thou wouldst understand that which is I, know this: all that I have said I have uttered playfully.' There is a quality in Beethoven strictly comparable with the teasing zaniness of the Zen masters; nor is it fortuitous that the second subject, codetta theme and much of the coda of the finale in opus 101 should suggest the singing games of children, many of which include a sacrificial scapegoat (often a Fool with a limp or other physical malformation), a mock death, a resurrection, and a round dance to enter the sacred *temenos*. Usually the spell is broken ('Ring a ring o' rosies, pocket full o' posies, a-tishoo, a-tishoo, *we all fall down*'), as it is of course throughout our adult lives, and as it is in opus 101. What Beethoven has done in the sonata is to accept this most basic of human 'failures' and, totally without evasion, to com-pose *out of failure* a *work* which is also an act of *play*. This is his supreme audacity. Only after he had done that could he create the Hammerklavier Sonata, which has all the same elements—harmonic and tonal frustration and clotted textures in wrestling with his humanity; an epical fugue that strives towards unity; parodistic play that deflates and defeats yet also leads to resurrection; a hymn-like aria that glimpses but does not enter paradise—and yet wins through. One might even say that opus 101 was a necessary prelude to the last sonata also, for the allegro of opus 111 opens with the same growling trills with which opus 101 concludes, and metamorphoses the Lion into the Lamb when at last Beethoven *enters* the Ring of Roses to dance the sacred dance, haloed by trills that tinkle like celestial bells. The extreme difficulty of opus 101 for the performer—one might make out a case that it is more difficult to perform convincingly, though not more technically rebarbative, than the Hammerklavier—springs from its enigmatic nature. It rushes in where angels fear to tread; and had to, if in the last three sonatas Beethoven were to be on as familiar terms with angels as he had been, in his tempestuous middle years, with devils.

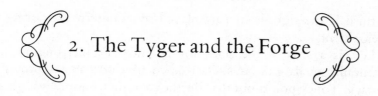

2. The Tyger and the Forge

'Hammerklavier' sonata opus 106 in B flat major

The Divine Presence comprises all worlds, all creatures, good and evil. It is true unity. How then can it contain good and evil which are self-contradictory? But actually there is no contradiction, for evil is the throne of good.

The Ten Rungs of Hasidic Lore trans. MARTIN BUBER

O dreadful is the check—intense the agony
When the ear begins to hear and the eye begins to see;
When the pulse begins to throb, and the brain to think again,
The soul to feel the flesh, and the flesh to feel the chain!

Yet I would lose no sting, would wish no torture less;
The more that anguish racks, the earlier will it bless;
And robed in fires of Hell, or bright with Heavenly shine,
If it but herald Death, the vision is divine!

EMILY BRONTË

Beethoven's opus 106, his biggest and most forbidding sonata, is still, like opus 101, transitional to the ultimate consummation of the trinity of the last three sonatas; but it differs from opus 101 in that it records a (somewhat equivocal) victory rather than a defeat. At first glance or hearing the immense first movement seems to be a climax to the Morality of Power of Beethoven's middle years. It is in his 'power' key of B flat major, and begins with an almost physical gesture of defiance, the clenched fist with which Beethoven confronted a fate that could 'never wholly subdue' him. Three main elements, however, modify this impression and relate the music to Beethoven's final years. The first is the scheme of key relationships, which is rooted in mediants rather than in traditional dominants and subdominants: another is the lyricism of the second subject and its accompanying figurations; and the third is the significant part played by counterpoint during the development.

There is a crux at the start, for Beethoven's metronome mark of 'minim equals 138' is so fast as to preclude any approach to accuracy. Tovey points out that Beethoven's metronome was grossly unreliable, and that he modified the markings for the Ninth Symphony when experience had proved that they were impracticably speedy. Beethoven did not, however, revise the marking for opus 106, and although Czerny describes the given tempo as 'uncommonly quick and fiery', he doesn't say that he (or Beethoven) played it more slowly. Modern virtuosity can just about cope with the tempo; whether it should be encouraged to is another matter. What we can say is that to slow the music down to Weingartner's suggested minim equals 80 is inadmissible, since it radically changes the music in rendering it grandiloquent. There seems little doubt that the movement should be played, if not at Beethoven's tempo, at least as fast as is *musically* feasible, for the music should induce panic, both in the normal meaning and as attributable to Pan. Beethoven wrote to his publisher that 'whatever is difficult, is also beautiful, great and good'; and his attitude to the frailties of the human body, not to mention nerves, was Olympian. Perhaps there was no player, and no piano, equal to the Hammerklavier. In 1824 Beethoven complained that the piano was an inadequate instrument, impossible to play 'with force and effect' without producing a tangle of broken strings 'like a bush in a windstorm'. Such physical imperfections in machines and in the men who operate them would have to be overcome; and they were. Though spiritual imperfections remain, Beethoven's music helps us to conquer them also.

The hammerbeats with which the sonata opens leap titanically from the low B flat to complete the triad, with the third on top, in the middle of the keyboard. The triad is reiterated in dotted rhythm, fully scored and sharpened with a dissonant appoggiatura, and then pounds down from third to tonic. The bass B flat is sustained by Beethoven's pedal mark, not only through this hammer-blow but also through its repetition a third higher. There is a pause over the rest in the second bar, and the hammer-blows are both answered and extended by a potentially lyrical phrase, moving up through a third also, but by step, and then down a second. This motive is repeated a tone higher, and then another tone higher, expanded to incorporate the quaver appoggiatura of the second bar:

Ex. 71

Whereas the hammer-blows had been percussively scored, the answer-ing clause is in three linear parts, with chromatic passing notes that effect momentary modulations to F, to C minor and G minor, and back to a dominant of the tonic. However transitory, these modula-tions hint at the false relations on which the tonal drama is to be founded. Their potential is not, however, immediately fulfilled, for the dominant cadence trails out with a ritardando on the appoggiatura quavers. There is another pause mark; and the stepwise-moving passage is repeated an octave higher. This time the quaver appog-giaturas are extended as the hands move further apart through five bars of continuous crescendo. The cadence into the tonic triad is attained with a sforzando, and the hammer-blow motive of falling third turns into sturdy minims and crotchets on the beat in the right hand, with syncopated quavers in the left (bars 17 ff.). The falling thirds close in from major to minor, to diminished (E flat to C sharp), as the passage modulates to the subdominant, E flat. But since bass octaves on B flat echo throughout, we hear it as the expanded plagal cadence that sweeps through broken octaves hammered between the hands to a reassertion of a dominant–tonic cadence in B flat. The broken octaves pound down the scale stepwise, except for falling minor thirds, B flat to G. When they reach the dominant the triad is still broken, widely spread as dynamics fade. The dissolving triad slows down as it grows quieter, the pedal sustaining a shimmer of overtones between the high and low Fs (bars 31–4). Suddenly and loudly the original hammer-blow motive, at the original pitch, crashes again, as though for a repeat, but changes, on the second beat of the next bar, from B flat major triads to bare octave Ds. On the upbeat these become triads of D major, followed by silence and a pause mark:

Ex. 72

This isn't an end to the punning, for after the pause the bass continues
to leap softly through octave Ds, while the right hand metamorphoses
the D major triad into a G major dominant seventh (bars 40–5). The
key signature changes to G major; and the second subject is initiated.

This is the first of many decisive mediant modulations, triggered by
the motivic thirds; at this point something should be said about their
significance in relation to classical tonality and to the development of
Beethoven's own music. The basic props of classical tonality, as
inherited from the Baroque era, were of course tonic, dominant,
subdominant and relative. Dominant and subdominant define the
norms of progression sharpwards or flatwards, in relation to the tonic.
The relative *is* a mediant relationship, which may imply tonal contrariety and is therefore conventionally restricted to development
sections. In this work Beethoven substitutes mediants, both major and
minor, up and down, for the traditional dominant and subdominant
functions, in exposition and recapitulation no less, indeed rather more,
than in development. This procedure imbues the music with a dis-
quiet, the origin of which we can understand if we consider the link
between mediants and false relation, which had first been manifest in
the music of Europe's Renaissance, and climactically in the seventeenth century. False relation is an analogy for the clash between the
old world of medieval theocracy and the new world of Renaissance
humanism: the concept of harmonic concordance, an auralization of
human solidarity, needs the sharp seventh to produce consummatory
major thirds in cadences; but the sharp seventh conflicts with the flat
sevenths natural to vocal modality. The phenomenon is repeated
centuries later, on a smaller scale, when the 'blue' flat thirds and
sevenths of black African modality clash with the harmonic sharp
thirds and sevenths of the white American march and hymn. The
tension between black and white worlds echoes that between the
medieval and the post-Renaissance worlds; we may yet find that its
consequences are no less momentous.

Just *how* momentous the implications of false relation were in European music was not fully evident until a composer such as Monteverdi wrote his madrigals, in which traditional vocal modality and linear continuity were undermined by the repetition of single notes and of homophonic triads in the rhythms of speech. Frequently these triads alternate in mediant relationships: a single chromatic alteration shifts a B flat major triad to a triad of G major which, with another chromatic alteration, becomes a triad of E major. Compared with the relatively timeless, linear incantation of ecclesiastical polyphony, such devices (usually prompted by words) concentrated attention on the here-and-now of experience, tending towards nervous excitation and fragmentation. Out of this new principles of tonal order, collateral to new principles of social organization, were gradually established, culminating in the tonal hierarchy of the Baroque, based on the cycle of fifths. This survived into the classical era, becoming the cornerstone of the sonata principle. Yet since sonata was a revolutionary process apposite to an incipiently revolutionary society, traditional tonal relationships were, as we have seen in discussing Beethoven's early and middle-period music, more complex and more precarious than they had been in the heyday of the Baroque. Now, in the Hammerklavier Sonata, on the threshold of his 'late' period, Beethoven seeks a new fragmentation, which in turn rediscovers older principles of order, such as canon, fugue and song-variation. Compared with Monteverdi's, Beethoven's fragmentation functions on an immense time-scale; yet it too is an act of liberation—not anarchic, but revolutionary in being re-creative. Though the sonata principle is not subverted, it is reborn; the structural re-creation is synonymous with a rebirth within Beethoven's psyche.

We have an intimation of this immediately the tonality of G major, submediant to B flat, is established: for the sonority of the opening of the second subject material is radiant, flowing mainly in parallel thirds, sixths and tenths (bars 47 ff.). The second subject is not so much a new theme as another 'morphological' permutation of the thirds, both intervallic and scalic, of the first subject group. But whereas the first subject had been dynamic, or at least had alternated force with an aborted lyricism, this G major permutation is continuous, at once songful and euphonious. At first it is an unbroken texture rather than a fully stated theme, the lucent G major being preserved unsullied through sixteen bars. When the music cadences in bar 63 the flowing quavers cease and something like a theme defines itself in the bass: an

inversion of the rising third scale, followed by a fall through a major
third, simultaneous with its inversion as minor sixth. This embryonic
song is answered antiphonally; modulates to the dominant; veers back
to the tonic; and moves through sequential modulations to E minor, D
minor, C major, B minor, A minor and back to G major. Significantly,
in view of the importance of 'falsely' related tonalities throughout the
sonata, the cadential thirds are sometimes ambiguously major or
minor; the autograph and the early editions do not always agree (bars
70–5). In any case, though the modulations render the texture more
acrid, with scrunching passing dissonances, they are hardly 'real'.
They rather serve to gather energy so that the return to G major may
expand in songful spaciousness. Descending arpeggios embellished
with chromatic passing notes flow over ripely spaced dominant
sevenths, which resolve on to first inversions of the tonic triad; the
quaver figuration incorporates the appoggiaturas of the opening bars,
first minor, then major. Repetitions that sound leisurely after the first
subject's flurry bring back a three-part linear texture, absorbing a
motive of rising fourth and falling third within the third-pervaded
figuration. The lines sing, yet maintain tension as the fourths close to
minor, and then diminished, thirds. Momentarily in C major (bar 91),
there is a fortissimo reminiscence of the original, more percussive
version of the scale motive and of the hammer thirds. High in the
treble, syncopated sforzandi prophesy D major, which merely acts as
an 'enhanced dominant' back to G major and the codetta theme (bar
100).

This time the Song seems to be attained. The melody, suddenly
piano, dolce ed espressivo, arches upwards in semibreves and minims,
oscillating once more through minor thirds. Though lyrical, the tune
contains too an element of pathos, since its subdominant triads are
flattened, and its fifth bar hovers between the major and minor third.
The conflict of the hammered thirds in the opening bars has itself
generated the deeper tonal strife between the keys of B flat and G
major, even between the notes B flat and B natural, as will later be
evident. None the less the total effect of the codetta theme is heart-
easing, the more so because a song-like bass line counterpoises the
treble melody, and supports a wave-like figuration of crotchet triplets.
When the theme is restated, the minor subdominant becomes major,
the triplets turn into quavers, and a continuous trill on D, anticipatory
of the trills in the last sonatas, adds bell-like reverberations beneath the
song:

Ex. 73

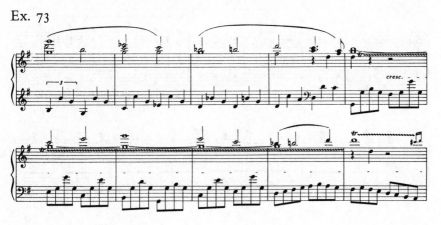

But the 'blue' major–minor alternation remains in the penultimate bar, slightly more agitated because syncopated. With a big crescendo the song disperses, and sundry permutations of the hammer motive reappear in broken octaves. We seem to be thrusting towards an assertive, dominant-enhanced cadence in G; but there is a sudden shock when the rising octaves stab up from G not to the expected B natural, but to B flat. Though we hear this as a minor substitution for the major, it proves to be once more the falsely related *key* of B flat. The octave leap and the hammer rhythm sound twice, separated by silence. When the exposition is repeated, as is essential to the dramatic import as well as the massive proportions of the movement, we know that the Song, though prophetically imagined, is not yet fulfilled.

After the repeat the thrust up from G to B natural is not immediately denied but, prodding up a further third, turns out to be a dominant approach to C minor instead of a tonic resolution:

Ex. 74

In the large-scale exposition the proportion of G major (and of lyrically cantabile music) is more or less commensurate with the home tonic. To balance this, Beethoven launches into the development in a flat C minor, which soon turns into its relative E flat major (which is subdominant to B flat). Yet the customary techniques of motivic sonata development don't suffice: a sforzando thrust up the scalic third stalls on a pause; is echoed softly and hesitantly; and is brusquely answered by the prancing octave leap in dotted rhythm, also repeated, separated by rests though not by silence, since Beethoven's pedalling sustains reverberation. If, as seems probable, 'sonata' has failed as a cohesive agent, Beethoven will assay the fundamental multiplicity-in-unity of counterpoint. The leap from the upbeat is reduced from octave to fourth, and the original dotted rhythm and stepwise undulation are stated softly, but rigidly rhythmed, in canon at the fifth. A momentary modulation to F minor takes us to B flat major, when a third voice enters. By way of further modulations to F and C minors we find our way back to E flat major, and a fourth part enters in the bass, dynamics now having reached a modest forte (bar 56). Although up to this point the fugato has been fairly quiet and constant in its metrical pattern, there has been, in its very rigidity, a hint of desperation. This becomes more overt in the eleven bars following the re-establishment of E flat major, for textures grow spikier, lines more angular, harmonies starker, modulations less stable. Sequences moving through F, G and C minors introduce chromatic passing notes that are explicit false relations, grating dissonantly on those two crucial notes, B flat and B natural. The four-part texture becomes a canon between two parts in parallel thirds, the hammer-blows of the dotted rhythms now aggressive, far removed from the liquid parallel thirds at the opening of the second subject. The stepwise thirds cadence in contrary motion and explode in leaping sixths and octaves. The quaver appoggiaturas splinter (bar 179).

Apparently back in E flat major, a tonic to the fugato section, the music suddenly veers to triads of D major, with the leaping octaves in dotted rhythm. This time, however, the D major chord doesn't act as a dominant to G, but dramatically thunders into diminished sevenths of A and D minor. This is one of the passages for the 'ugliness' of which Beethoven's deafness has been held responsible: as though its texture could be less gruntingly savage without emasculating its function in relation to what is immediately past, and to what is to come. For what happens next is infinitely mysterious, and 'beautiful' on any count. After a ritardando and diminuendo, the D natural octaves change to D sharp, and slide into the songful codetta theme, *piano e cantabile*, in B major, but again with flattened subdominants (bar 201). The strange effect of this, tonally speaking, lies in the fact that we hear B major perhaps as upper mediant to G major, key of the song-aspiring material, but also as lower (flat) mediant to the fugato's E flat, in which case it has become enharmonically identical with C flat. The tonal ambiguities here are so complex that Beethoven landed himself in difficult problems of notation, and in what is possibly the most notorious editorial crux anywhere in his music.

At first he notates the recollection of the codetta theme in two sharps, as though it were in B minor instead of major; he writes in the extra sharps (though in bars 210 and 212 he forgot to sharpen the Gs). I suspect that this notation makes us subconsciously stress the plagal flattening of the subdominant, and also makes the major thirds seem more dreamily illusory; certainly the oscillation between major and minor third becomes, in a decorated repeat, romantically Chopinesque, as the triplet figuration of the accompaniment undulates beneath a haze of quaver appoggiaturas. There is a prophetic hint of the textures of the adagio here; but it is banished by a return of the fugato in stretto, beginning low in the bass with the initial rising thirds which, in imitation, are stretched to fifth and seventh, then contracted to sixth. Beethoven changes the key signature to B major which, enharmonically identical with C flat, is to effect a Neapolitan return to B flat for the recapitulation. It is at this point that the 'crux' occurs:

Ex. 75

The leaping sixths in close stretto are changed from major to minor, as the lower note shifts from G natural to G sharp. Most editions follow this with a further chromatic ascent, changing the interval to a perfect fifth, A to E: which then becomes a sixth, A to F natural, functioning as dominant back to B flat. But Beethoven did not in fact cancel the A sharps of his key signature: so what is actually notated in the last two bars of the development consists of tritones A sharp to E natural, followed by diminished sixths, A sharp to F natural! It is generally assumed that Beethoven forgot to counteract the sharps, and the internal evidence of both autograph and early editions supports that. None the less, one cannot be absolutely certain; the pun on the A sharp and the notated B flat on the final upbeat before the recapitulation would be profoundly Beethovenian. On balance, Tovey is probably right to suggest that Beethoven intended A natural, but that his failure to correct it was an intuitive stroke of genius; his unconscious was wiser than his conscious mind.

In any case the recapitulation begins (bar 227) in apparent triumph, as though the desperate fugato has obliterated even that crazy dubiety. The first bars sound more affirmative then they did in the exposition, because the hammer-blows are continuously supported by the quaver appoggiaturas, without pauses or silences. The answering more lyrical clause is extended in four-part linearity over dominant and tonic pedals, incorporating false relations that create a bitter-sweet intensification of the chromatic passing notes of the exposition. Again there is mediant modulation, but this time to the *flat* submediant, G flat major instead of G major. The lyrical quaver figuration is extended, sounding more dreamy in its flatness. The hammered third section of the first subject, culminating in broken octaves, also starts off in G flat, passing through E flat minor, A flat minor, and something that might be C flat minor standing for B minor. When the D flat chord fades out in wide-flung broken arpeggios, Beethoven mysteriously alchemizes the D flat into C sharp, and adds F sharp below it, with a pause. Since the chord has no third it is tonally ambiguous, major or minor; but it ceases to be so when the movement's climax occurs with a cataclysmic return of the original two bars, now a semitone higher, in B minor:

Ex. 76

The fierce opposition between B flat and B natural, which has dogged the entire movement, attains its apex; after a silence that is indeed pregnant, the leaping tenths in dotted rhythm return pianissimo, gropingly to reveal that the B minor explosion is a Neapolitan approach to the dominant seventh of B flat.

Beethoven's recapitulation has thus proved to be, as so frequently in his mature work, still development; and it continues to be so, even though all the material of the second subject group—the lyrical figuration in flowing quavers, the songful antiphony, the richly spaced dominant sevenths, the explicit song of the codetta theme—is now centred on the tonic major. For after the trill-accompanied repeat of the codetta theme (bars 338–43), the hammered octave passage is considerably extended. Sforzandi vehemently mark the oppositions of B flat and B natural; suddenly and unexpectedly the hammering is succeeded by a version of the codetta song, darkly in E flat minor (bars

362–5), with nostalgically crying passing dissonances, and with trills written out as quaver oscillations between B flat and C flat (equals B natural). Flowing into the major, the song effects an extended plagal cadence, dissolving in (normally notated) octave trills for the two hands. Limpidly flowing scales in parallel thirds (similar to those that conclude the Credo of the *Missa Solemnis*) lead into a coda that stresses the hesitancy, rather than aggression, of the opening measures. The leap and dotted rhythm appear in broken antiphony and contrasted dynamics, moving from B flat major to C minor, from there to D minor, from there to E flat major (bars 377–82). After a silence, there is an imperious dominant cadence: which none the less does not lead to triumphant resolution. Soft written-out trills growl low between F and G flat while fragments of the original motive—dotted rhythm, quaver appoggiatura, descending third—are scattered in different registers and in contradictory dynamics. Tonic and dominant pedals make sharp dissonances with these cadential figures. A movement that had opened heroically ends in suppressed growls and barks or, to vary the metaphor, with a dousing of the flickering flames of the Promethean fire. After a diminuendo to *ppp* an abrupt fortissimo triad and unisonal B flat octaves tell us that Beethoven lives to fight another day; but this Promethean allegro is of its essence a *first* movement which does not, within its length, resolve its contrarieties.

Beethoven had no doubt that the Hammerklavier was not only his biggest but his greatest sonata to date. Like the Eroica Symphony, it was a turning point in his life's work; he even went so far as to say that he was just beginning to learn how to compose! This being so, it is odd that, in communication with publishers and concert impresarios, he seems to have been lax both about the order of the movements and about the necessity for performing the work as a whole. This may have been an unconscious gesture of contempt towards a public that was not 'ready' for the sonata. None the less since the work *is* Beethoven's spiritual history, there can be no question that he cared passionately about its evolutionary totality; and in the light of that there can be no doubt that the normally accepted, though not unchallenged, order of the movements is right. The point of the scherzo as an ironic commentary on the heroic allegro works only if it comes second; complementarily the effect of the immense adagio as the sonata's centre of gravity (in two senses) would be shattered if it were succeeded by the scherzo's prankishness. Moreover, the transitional arioso links the adagio to the fugue.

Charles Rosen, to whose perceptive study any later writer about this work must be indebted, goes so far as to call the scherzo a parody of the first movement: both in the normal sense (a parody guys and renders risible something seriously, even solemnly, intended), and in the technical sense in which the word is used with reference to a Renaissance parody-mass (a tune, ambiguously religious or secular, is reworked and recomposed). I think this is true so long as one does not assume that a parody is necessarily deflatory. Beethoven's scherzo is an ironic reversal, even an anti-climax; but its wit is also positive. The initial motive of the scherzo, like that of the first movement, rocks upwards and downwards in thirds, moving from the upbeat. The figure is stated three times, in periods of 3 + 3 + 1 bars, each statement being a third lower than the previous one, beginning on D, B flat, and G. After this, echoing the second clause of the first movement's first subject, the dotted rhythm pushes up the scale *through* a third, first from G, then B flat, then D, inverting the initial declension:

Ex. 77

The cadence into the dominant is approached chromatically with a B flat minor 6–4; and melodically with a descending fifth. The mood is comic, for the hesitancies of the first movement now have no tinge of desperation. Yet the rapid oscillations of the dotted-rhythm figure between tonics and dominant sevenths have a quality one might call cajoling, while the brevity of the rest-separated, up-and-down phrases combines with their rhythmic ambiguity—we don't always hear them as proceeding from the upbeat, but sometimes in 3/4, phrased across the bar—to suggest unease. Relevant to this unease is the fact that tonality once more vacillates between mediants. The original little phrase in B flat is answered in G minor (not, admittedly, the falsely related major of the first movement); that is answered a third lower in E flat which, after a transitory return to the tonic, becomes a real modulation. Only then does the clause travel towards and resolve in the dominant. A repeat an octave higher emphasizes the dominant modulation by approaching it by way of a German sixth instead of a B flat minor 6–4. Again the dominant is contradicted, for its F acts as a pedal while the dotted-rhythm figure hesitantly veers to C minor. Inevitably, this allows the falsely related B naturals to creep in, as it were, by the back-door, as the third of the C minor dominant seventh. Bars 15–30 consist of puns on the two possible functions of the G major triad, as dominant to C minor and as a major triad 'falsely' related to B flat, in its own right. The upbeat octave B flats (bars 29–30) seem to imply tonal resolution into B flat major, but add a further element of rhythmic ambiguity, since we hear them as a duple metre across the beat. The whole of this passage of tonal and metrical punning is repeated an octave higher in slightly varied registration. The final metrical ambiguity introduces the trio.

The scherzo is all tonal and rhythmic surprise; comparatively the trio is a point of repose, in that it is consistent in figuration and has virtually no harmonic movement. Its effect, though far from funny, is none the less mysterious, since the metrical ambiguity makes the melodic phrases irregular. The tune, which again consists of rocking thirds turning into a spread arpeggio, this time in the tonic minor, begins as 3/4 plus 4/4 plus 3/4, the cross-the-bar phrasing being delineated by the bass's initial soft drum beats (bars 46–54). Though the spreading of the tune's arpeggio suggests a desire to escape from the constriction of the rocking thirds, this is counteracted by the ostinato-like character of the left hand's muffled arpeggiated triplets. At the close of the eight-bar period there is a shift, rather than a modulation, to D flat major, the upper mediant which is also B flat minor's relative. This is immediately cancelled by a return of the ambiguous-rhythmed drum beat, leading to a repeat.

The octave arpeggiated tune is now in the left hand, the flowing

triplets in the right, and the top notes of the triplets are in canon with
the bass tune. Here contrapuntal oneness serves to control any airy
floating in the tune's asymmetry: it is not merely the wide-spaced
texture that sounds hollow, almost forlorn:

Ex. 78

The next eighteen bars repeat the previous section a third higher,
beginning in the upper mediant which is also the relative. But the
music oscillates between D flat major and B flat minor triads, which
sometimes sound like hazy added sixths; is totally concordant; and has
no sense of modulatory direction, let alone progression. Floating with
the tide, the music, like so much in this movement, sounds ambivalent: we do not know whether the experience is pleasurable or scary,
though it would be characteristically human if it were both.

Either way, as trance-inducing pleasure or as titillating fear, it seems
to be dismissed by Beethoven as enervating and potentially dangerous; for at bar 81 he shakes himself out of the trio in a strange
transitional *presto*. The tempo is 2/4, with the minim not far off the
crotchet of the previous 3/4. The theme, first presented in staccato
octaves separated by rests, joins the rising third of the trio theme with
the falling fifth on which it ends. After a scalewise descent it modulates
to the dominant minor, and is repeated in bass octaves, accompanied
by syncopated chords in the right hand. A crescendo throughout this
dominant section leads to a fortissimo repeat of the tune in the tonic,
now accompanied by broken octaves. This releases us from the trio's
hypnosis, and promises more purposefulness than the scherzo itself
had been capable of. So there is another irony: this time the transition
ends not in the dominant but *on* a bell-tolling dominant triad,

sustained by Beethoven's pedalling through five octaves, and then fizzing up in a *prestissimo* scale from the bottom to the top F of Beethoven's instrument. After a brief pause a dominant ninth chord, broken into semiquavers, quivers in the upbeat rhythm of the scherzo theme. The da capo that follows is literal, except that Beethoven makes the point of his mediant relationships more audible by adding bell-like internal pedal notes; the effect is simple but beautiful, and the sketches indicate that Beethoven worked hard to get it just right. This may be why the rocking G major thirds from bar 137 onwards sound more G majorish, less C minorish, than they did in the first statement of the scherzo. Certainly these thirds prepare us for the famous coda, wherein Beethoven puns not merely on the false related triads of B flat and G majors, but also on B natural as enharmonically identical with C flat, and on B flat as enharmonically identical with A sharp:

Ex. 79

The A sharp leads, with a hesitant ritardando, to the third rocking between D and F sharp, which might be part of a B minor triad, but also luminously opens the prospect of D major, the upper mediant that is to become crucial in the adagio and the fugal finale. With a change to *Presto alla breve*, the semibreve more or less equalling the dotted minim of the scherzo, hammered octaves on B natural are translated, without change of notation, into Neapolitan C flats that cut abruptly back into

B flat and to the original tempo. The movement ends with a threefold repetition of the rising and falling thirds, tonic, dominant, tonic, each repeat an octave higher. After the maximum violence of rhythmic and tonal punning, the same contrarieties as were inherent in the first movement here disperse in a throw-away reference to the bowing dominant–tonics of social intercourse. The tiny phrase that initially surprised us in its sequential modulations sounds, in the coda— restricted to its basic chordal progression in three finally regularized bars—at once perfunctory and polite.

It is odd that up to this point the sonata has stated its heroic oppositions and has hinted at transcendent resolutions, yet in total effect its course has been negative, even deflatory. The turning point comes in the sublime adagio, which is unambiguously a song and a sublimation of the humanistic passions of Baroque opera, and is at the same time a hymn. Paradoxically it is also, despite its songfulness, a full-scale sonata movement: a fact significant because it indicates that Beethoven is not yet ready to enter the unsullied 'monism' of air-with-variations such as he explores in the final trinity of sonatas. None the less the movement is hardly recognizable as a sonata, except at a subconscious level, since the tempo is so slow and the melodic span so vast. Moreover, the repeats of the immense themes are decorated in a manner that suggests variation style rather than sonata.

The key is an apparently recondite F sharp minor, a tonality associated by Baroque composers, especially Bach and Couperin, with tragic pathos and purgatorial suffering. Such associations are relevant to this movement, though Beethoven almost certainly decided on this key for internally musical reasons: F sharp enharmonically stands for G flat, which is the flat submediant to B flat; it is also an upper mediant to D, though the point of this will not be fully evident until we reach the end of the work. These up and down mediant relationships reflect the motivic patterns of the whole sonata: in which context the adagio's first bar is especially interesting since it was an afterthought, communicated by Beethoven to his publisher at proof stage. The reason he gave for the addition was that the extra bar would make the thematic relationships between the movements clearer: which proves beyond doubt that by this stage in his life Beethoven was 'aware' of compositional processes that had their source in the unconscious. What the extra bar does here is to complete the pattern of rising and falling thirds; and it does so the more tellingly because it is in octaves. The whole of the first five bars—a long period at so slow a tempo, in which one quaver of the 6/8 pulse takes longer than a minim beat of the first movement—evolves from rising and falling thirds either by leap or step. After the initial undulation up and down, treble melody and cantabile bass move by inversion, so that the spacing of the mainly triadic harmony grows wider until the first inversion of the dominant at the beginning of bar 5. The bass descends through a tritone to a diminished seventh, which is to be a crucial chord throughout the adagio:

Ex. 80

The melody's gravity is hymnic; at the same time it does not evade the physical, for the opening clause suggests, with its gradual ascent in the treble, balanced by the bass's decline, a bodily gesture: arms slowly outstretched, perhaps in prayer. The diminished seventh after the melody's apex, and the stilling of the quaver movement to immobile-seeming dotted crotchets, is a consequence of this corporeality. Tension is created as the limbs are further outstretched; in the next four bars limbs relax as the melody droops down the scale, while the bass rises to level repeated notes that approach a dominant cadence in the middle of the keyboard. The sharpwards modulation balances the falling melody, but is immediately transformed back into a dominant seventh of F sharp minor and then, on the beat, to the scrunch of a dominant ninth. The next four bars, anchored over a dominant pedal, alternate stepwise movement, usually through a minor third, with arpeggiated thirds, building up to a more richly scored dominant ninth. The sonorous registration of the harmonies, the high degree of dissonance that is generated, render the music both sensuous and painful; at the same time this human physicality is at least potentially freed in the long arches of the melody. Beethoven at first attempted to indicate the phrasing of the overlapping arches, but gave up the attempt. Even in this opening clause there is musical evidence that this adagio is concerned with human passion and (in the strict sense) pathos, and with its transcendence. Not for nothing does Beethoven direct that the whole first clause should be played *una corda*; and there is no movement in Beethoven's work that more elaborately exploits transitions between *una corda*, *due corde* and *tre corde*. As we have seen, these technical devices, difficult to reproduce on a modern piano, came to have specific experiential significance in Beethoven's later works. That in this adagio he fluctuates so frequently between *una corda* and *tre corde* itself suggests what the intrinsic musical evidence corroborates: 'Man is an Amphibian' (in Sir Thomas Browne's phrase), living in and between divided worlds, natural and supernatural.

His 'immortal longings' are certainly manifest at the end of the long paragraph over the dominant pedal, for the cadence shifts, by chromatic alteration on the last quaver, into G major. Beethoven notates the last chord in bar 13 as a surprising diminished seventh in D minor instead of F sharp, only to treat the B flat as though it were A sharp, pushing up to the third of G major second inversion. This visionary moment is not a 'real' modulation, but rather a Neapolitan 'elevation' by a semitone of the F sharp minor tonality: thus it complements the relationship between B flat and B natural in the two previous movements. For the two G major bars the texture is smilingly consonant, but it returns to its earlier density to re-establish the tonic and the undulating thirds. The eight bars from the first diminished ninth (bar 10) are then repeated with textural variations that intensify passion: first with flowing inner parts between melody and the bass pedal, and then (in the G major episode) with high octave doublings, richly spaced tenths and sighing appoggiaturas. This time the two resolutory bars make the Neapolitan G major triad explicitly a part of the F sharp minor cadence, emphasizing it by stressing the second quaver of the group of three.

The twenty-six bars of the melody have, at this slow tempo, taken a long time to unfold. Beethoven's directives are *adagio sostenuto*, *appassionato e con molto sentimento*, and fully to reveal the passion and sentiment the pace should be as slow as is consistent with the preservation of line and contour through the immense phrases. This first paragraph sounds like a hymnic aria rather than a sonata first subject; the theme's self-contained nature is emphasized because Beethoven begins to repeat or rather to vary it. Superficially the variation is from the hymnic to the operatic, the music's more terrestrial character being indicated by a change from *una corda* to *tutte le corde*. The first paragraph breaks off on the interval of a diminished fourth, its dominant–tonic cadence incomplete. The bass then embarks on a figuration that sounds like an enriched, immensely slow version of the pizzicato 'guitar' bass of Bellinian opera, with internal pedal notes that palpitate like heart-beats. The melody arches up through its thirds, tenderly embroidered with trills, ties, syncopations and triplets, floating high in the stratosphere:

Ex. 81

This is a pianistic extension of the cantilena of Italianate opera, and one can find precedents for it in the slow movements of Mozart's later piano concertos, and in the piano writing of Clementi, Dussek, Hummel, and Spohr, all of which anticipate the idiom of the nocturnal Chopin. None the less Beethoven's cantilena, though parallel to these examples, is remote from them, largely because his melodic span is so vast. The asymmetrical freedom and continuity of his line break the time-barrier of the bass's heart-beat; yet even as it becomes disembodied, the floating melody creates dissonances (consider the weeping false relations in the thirty-fifth bar) that intensify harmonic stress. The dominant ninths hurt more, at the same time as the decorated line approaches ecstasy.

After eight unbroken bars of this winging cantilena we realize that what is happening is an evolution from, rather than a repetition of, the first paragraph. From bar 36 the syncopated pedal notes grow more obtrusive, while the 'pizzicato' bass rises chromatically and off the main beats from bottom-line A to the A above middle C. Both the syncopations and the chromatics, which quicken as the line rises, induce a crescendo, and also a devious modulation to the relative, A major. Yet the new key is not established. The note A remains as a pedal while a three-part texture flows in chromaticized sequences, the semiquaver figuration still riddled with thirds, both intervallic and stepwise. Though the specifically operatic flavour has gone, the harmony is passionate in its romantic, diminished-seventh-pervaded sequences. When the bass has descended to the A two octaves below the original pedal, the semiquaver figuration has turned into spread dominant ninths of D, in which key the second subject sonorously sings (bars 45 ff.).

Again the key is a flat submediant, which suggests a ripe passivity as compared with the tragic pathos of the F sharp minor melody; the relationship is thus comparable to that existing, in the first movement, between B flat and *its* submediants, G major and (to a lesser degree) G flat major. The theme opens with a tolling of bells. Cavernously deep, the low D, offbeat, falls to A, then down a minor third to F sharp. Meanwhile the lower voice of the left hand undulates up and down through a third, while the semiquaver figuration wavers between thirds and fourths. There is an antiphonal dialogue between the chiming bass and a canonic echo of it three octaves higher; the consonant harmony of tonics and dominants is only slightly clouded by chromatic passing notes when the semiquaver figuration quickens to triplets. Textures begin to glow, as the triplet scales flow in contrary motion and the bass mounts through the D major scale on each dotted crotchet. Having reached C sharp, the bass acquires smaller note values and chromatic passing notes, the harmony being enriched with diminished sevenths. This blissful growing and flowing is suddenly stilled on an E minor dominant seventh; and the *una corda* sign brings

back the hymnic manner of the first subject. This, however, is no more
than a peep over the horizon, for with a return to *tutte le corde*,
arpeggiated diminished sevenths in demisemiquavers mysteriously
dissolve into diminished sevenths of G and then D minors.

Ex. 82

This initiates the codetta, which is also the beginning of a sonata
development; although it lasts less than a tenth of the total duration of
the movement, it is eventful enough to match the song theme's span
and scope.

   Codetta and development are characterized by intermittent shifts
from *una* to *due* to *tre corde*, which are appropriate, as the music is a
wavering between 'natural' and 'supernatural' worlds. Thus the
shimmering sensuality of the diminished sevenths quoted above is
succeeded by an *una corda* passage in simple diatonic concords, swaying from E minor back to D major: a tonality which remains unsullied
through eight bars (63–70). Sixths and thirds swing like a slow pendulum; gradually the concordantly harmonized theme climbs to the
heights, though the bass's flurry of triplets (recalling the earlier
diminished sevenths) promotes a momentary touch of *tre corde*. In bar
69 *una corda* returns, and the rising and falling thirds sing in melodic
spaciousness and harmonic equilibrium. Two bars later serenity is
again disturbed by a transition from D major to B minor, and then
back to the tonic F sharp minor and a direct reference to the first
subject's thirds. Far from inducing stability, this leads to a passage
wherein the disintegrative effect of mediant relationships takes over. F
sharp minor droops to D sharp (notated as E flat) major, and falling

thirds chime downwards, mirrored by inversion in the bass. The
music modulates so rapidly that any anchorage of a tonal centre is lost;
repeatedly the alternating thirds create the harmonic *frisson* of false
relation:

Ex. 83

The passage is prophetic of a-tonal mediant relationships in later
music—especially that of Liszt and Busoni, whose approach to a
'metaphysical' world was probably directly influenced by Beethoven.
    The tonal distances covered by these fluctuating mediants seem the
more extraordinary after the harmonic immobility of the preceding
una corda passage. We are carried on their stream; and the will-lessness
is the point, since relinquishment is a necessary prelude to Beethoven's
approach to paradise. The fluctuations between *una* and *tre corde* continue throughout the tonal deliquescence, as though to emphasize this
development's limbo-like status 'between worlds'. Falling in
crotchet–quaver rhythm in the right hand, rising in semiquavers in the
left, the thirds at last find rest, after ten bars that have seemed like
eternity. Finally they sink to a low dominant pedal of F sharp minor,
above which the 'crucial' chord of dominant ninth reverberates *smor-
zando*. Over a dominant pedal *poco a poco due ed allora tutte le corde*, the
recapitulation crepuscularly emerges (bar 87).
    It is a strict recapitulation in that all the aria themes, first and second
subjects and codetta, are restated in full, or with extensions. It also calls
on variation techniques in that the melodies are at once decorated and
intensified with 'divisions'. At first the harmony is defined by the bass,
which moves in regular quaver chords, like a quietly breathing pulse.
Rising high from its dominant ninth arpeggio, the right hand

embroiders the song with demisemiquavers. The theme, though always present, is hidden in the halo, since it is defined only by irregularly appearing notes in the lower octave, played by a volatile thumb. It is as though after that development or anti-development, wild even in its quietude, the Song is glimpsed through an aqueous mist or through flickering flames. Water and fire metaphors seem appropriate to its liquidity or scintillation, as they will be, yet more manifestly, to the variation-arias of opus 109 and 111. Gradually the heart-beat accompaniment begins gently to pant in syncopation, and at the clause beginning with the dominant ninth the demisemiquavers quiver through minor ninths and octaves. By the time the song unfolds into the Neapolitan G major episode, the demisemiquavers have become consonantly sparkling octaves, with an occasional caressing appoggiatura. The broken octaves are preserved in the return to the tonic, but the repeat of this clause abandons the 'halo', and returns to the linear figuration of its original statement. Inner parts are, however, more active, both melodically and rhythmically: for instance, the octaved upthrusting bass beneath the ninth chord.

During this passage movement gradually slows down, as the lines sink earthward. The cadence is left unresolved, as before; but the operatically ornamented repeat, or extension or transition (it is all these), starts off not in the tonic minor, but in the second subject's flat submediant, D major (bar 113). Over the censer-swinging 'pizzicato' bass, the melody's ties, trills, syncopations and triplets are even more lyrically air-borne than in the exposition; if this cantilena is operatic, it is opera sublimated. When the music modulates to a darker B minor to effect the transition to the second subject, the bass falls diatonically instead of rising chromatically as in the exposition. Tonally, however, we move to C sharp, which proves to be a dominant to the tonic *major*, in which key the bell-tolling second subject radiantly sings (bars 130 ff.). Though this is orthodox in a sonata movement, and though the repeat is literal, the music sounds yet more ecstatic in this 'sharp' manifestation. The low C sharps boom, the triplet scales levitate in aspirational joy. Again there is a sudden *una corda* for the transition to the codetta theme. Beginning in G sharp major resonance, the texture dissolves in the diminished seventh arpeggios, moving to B minor and to F sharp minor. The hymnicly concordant passage opens in D sharp (notated as E flat) major, and swings back to F sharp major for the diaphanously swaying sixths and thirds (bars 145–55). The vacillations between *una corda* and *tutte le corde* recur throughout this modified recapitulation of the codetta; if ever there could be a musical synonym for 'dying into life', this transition, from the dissolving diminished sevenths to the radiant F sharp major diatonicism, is surely it.

This time, of course, there is no dissolution of serenity into the development's tonal and rhythmic mysteries. None the less, there *is* mystery even in apparent resolution, for the final three bars of the transition' move not only between *una* and *tre* corde, but also between the pivotal triads of F sharp and D major. The D major triads, with melodic thirds falling in the treble, rising in the bass, resolve on a third, B to D, which turns out to be not part of a B minor triad, but the third and fifth of a triad on G. It leads into a coda that begins with a full recapitulation of the second subject in this Neapolitan key; what had been, on its first appearance within the song, an effect of colour rather than a modulation, becomes in this coda a moment of enhanced consciousness. Physiologically, it really makes us feel 'high', since it is a semitone above the F sharp major which had seemed to be the music's ultimate goal. But the cross-rhythms of the tolling bells, and the flutter of the passing notes in the triplets, gradually disturb the tranquillity, and carry us, as the bass rises chromatically, to a diminished seventh climax in bar 165, the bells clanging in high syncopation, with Beethoven's *Bebung* effect achieved by shifting fingering. This 'high' episode is, perhaps surprisingly, all *tutte le corde*, a trance achieved in Beethoven's moments of *raptus*. But *una corda* returns with the F sharp minor key signature, and it seems that the movement is to conclude with a reminiscence, or a repetition, of its beginning. The opening clauses are, however, telescoped and subtly modified, since the oscillation between the major and minor triad is explicit in the second bar. At this stage Beethoven cannot totally encompass the transcendence of his F sharp major apotheosis: the rest of his coda is unequivocally tragic. The visionary moment of the G major episode recurs, but in flagging pulse; and the Neapolitan cadence no longer leads to a screwed-up dominant ninth but to a flat dominant seventh of the subdominant (bar 174). As the bass swings between F sharp, A sharp and C sharp, the right hand remotely floats the cantilena's triplets aloft. As before, this passage is *tutte le corde*, humanly aspiring; but it fades into F sharp major triads, poised across the beats while the bass arpeggiates bare fifths, becoming pianissimo (bars 178–80). The sharp major triads never quite surrender the plagal Amen flavour they had when, as dominants of the subdominant B minor, they had first sounded in this last section of the coda. This may be why the end of the movement, 'transcendent' though it is, doesn't sound totally consummatory. The Neapolitan G major in which the coda had enunciated the second subject opened magic casements; coming back to F sharp minor was a return to purgatorial tragedy, which the plagal tendency only underlined. For the rest of the coda we float not only between *una corda* and *tre corde*, but also between intimations of heaven and the pull of the turning earth, manifest in the bass's deep-rotating triplets. The final, infinitely remote statement of the theme vacillates between minor and major third, and also rhythmically between crotchet–quaver and quaver–crotchet. The last of the diminished sevenths, in bar 183, sounds hollowly subterranean: infinitely remote from the major triads, luminously spaced in tenths, with which the movement ends. Curiously, they sound, for all their tranquillity, expectant.

So Beethoven's hymn-aria remains also a sonata movement, rather than a self-contained air with variations like the finales of opus 109 and 111. Its serenity has been painfully achieved, but has to be won again. This is why the adagio cannot be the end of this sonata, as the Arietta is the apotheosis of opus 111. Not only is there more to come: what follows makes sense only in relation to the adagio's final chords. Beethoven changes the *una corda* marking to *tre corde* on the last F sharp major chord. He does not want a complete cessation of the sound before the spread F naturals of the largo introduction to the finale, since the F sharp major triad enharmonically changes its identity to G flat which, echoing the G natural–F sharp relationship of the adagio, then serves as a chromaticized approach to the home tonic. It cannot do so immediately, however, for the point of the largo transition is to accept, however desperately, the disintegrative force of the sonata's obsessive mediants. Hesitantly the bass drops by thirds from F to D flat (a major third), to B flat (a minor third), to G flat, each descent being punctuated by a diatonic triad. The tempo is very slow (Beethoven instructs the player to count four semiquavers throughout the Largo); although the rhythmic breaks are expectant, the silences are unfulfilled. Out of the expectancy Beethoven attempts to rebuild the song that is apparently lost. A freely canonic passage in G flat substitutes rocking fourths for the habitual thirds, contracting them to thirds at the bass entry. Yet this bid for symmetrical unity falters in more descending mediants from G flat major to E flat minor to C flat major, changing enharmonically to B major. Again Beethoven assays contrapuntal unity and continuity: here, the tempo animating, the floating scales in two-part canon recall, a semitone higher, the scales in the coda to the first movement. But Beethoven dismisses this bland canon as too easy and thus, perhaps, not so much serene as complacent. With another descending mediant he bounds (bar 20) into a furious (allegro) two-part invention in G sharp minor, this time with a theme built on *fifths*, expanding to a sixth. Whatever it may be, this canon is not bland; in its savager way it resembles Bach's counterpoint, which we know Beethoven had recently been studying as preparation for his Mass. Yet Beethoven discards this two-in-oneness also, perhaps because, however fiercely driven, it is an archaically Baroque convention, irrelevant to his needs. The invention survives only five bars; then, with a return to Tempo I (Largo), syncopated and broken triads recur, descending by mediants from G sharp minor to E major to C sharp minor to A major. From the descent the octave triplets rise again, over a sustained dissonance of elided tonic and dominant, in a chromatic cantilena, ending with an attempt at rising, cadential trills (bars 29–30). Quasi-operatic recitative proves, however, as impotent as Baroque counterpoint. The descending mediants return in rapider palpitations, hiccuping in a great crescendo from A to F sharp to D to B to G to E to C to A (now minor) to F to D minor: and so in prestissimo frenzy to what might be dominants of D until, slowing down and calming, there is a further drop to F *natural*. This proves at last to be a dominant of B flat, the original tonic. The significance of this aborted attempt to reach D major will be fully revealed only at the movement's climax. Here is the section from the 'recitative' into the allegro:

Ex. 84

Trills ring softly on top, the bass leaps from first to second beat of the 3/4 tempo, through a tenth, a twelve, through two octaves; as the trills descend through semiquaver scales, the *Fuga a tre voci con alcune licenze* is upon us. The adagio's Song had contained within it a dualistic sonata; before Beethoven can encompass the pure monism of unadulterated song he has to tackle on his own terms (not those of Bach) the ultimate contrapuntal unity of fugue. The struggle will be titanic; but this time there will be no ironic evasion, as there had been in the developmental fugue of opus 101. In the fugue theme itself there are two basic constituents. One is the pounce up a tenth from first to second beat, landing on a ferocious trill with turn; the leap is identical with that which released the trigger in the first bar of the first movement, except that it starts *from* the first beat instead of leaping to it. This motive has the elastic spring and muscular power of the Blakean Tyger, whose growl we had heard at the end of the first allegro. The second constituent of the fugue theme is the whirring scale in semiquavers, which incorporates the ubiquitous pattern of descending thirds, at first on each first beat, then on each crotchet. The scales also embrace, as rapid appoggiaturas, the chromatic B natural and E natural, so that even the false relations of the previous movements are inherent in the theme. When once under way, the semiquavers sizzle on for seven bars, as though the tiger's energy has released a fury that cannot be controlled. This seems the more probable when, in the sixteenth bar, the fugal answer occurs with the leaping tenth 'tonally' modified to a tritonal eleventh, carrying us into the dominant. Against the new entry Beethoven fragments the leap, reduced from tenth to octave, perhaps because in this form it is more tractable as the textures

elaborate. Immediately it serves to create a countersubject, which is a
scalic descent with stress on the second beat: so the notion of a pounce,
from quaver plus quaver rest to dotted crotchet, is still patent and
potent:

Ex. 85

The tigerish energy of the two-part texture is reinforced by the fact
that the scales of the countersubject (at first diatonic, then chromatic)
grind against the semiquavers' flickering arpeggios. When, back in the
tonic, the third fugal entry appears in the bass, the grittiness is harsher,
with clinking major sevenths. The surge of semiquavers is remorseless, their chromatic convolutions tight, with the countersubject
fragmented on top.

The first climax comes in a series of stretti on the leaping tenth,
thrusting from F to B flat to G major, the false relations strident (bars
38–42). But the G major tenth becomes a dominant of C minor, and
immediately bounces up to A flat major as dominant of D flat. Though
dynamics are still loud, there is a momentary respite, since the semiquavers shed most of their dusty dissonances; but the countersubject
returns in stretto, sometimes offbeat, with an aggressive tail appended.
There is a touch of wit in this disturbance, since the leaping octaves
(not tenths) become almost playful—cubbish, if we still relate the
music's muscularity to Blake's Tyger. Modulations too tend to in-
stability, vacillating in flat keys as the extended countersubject is phrased,
in chunky parallel thirds or sixths, across the beats. The section ends
darkly in A flat *minor*, which turns into G flat major, and what seems
like a change of mood. Thus although Beethoven's tyger may threaten
loss of control, that never happens: the momentum of the theme has
encompassed an astonishing diversity of contradictory attitudes, and
from them achieves equilibrium. So it does in the next section, if the
term be permitted of a music essentially non-sectional. The G flat
major theme is a more quietly lyrical, filled-in version of the original
leaping tenth. If we cherish any illusions that the tiger is about to purr,

they are soon shattered, for after modulation from G flat to its relative
E flat minor, the semiquaver surge is broken by a vaster pounce, from
the bass D to a D two octaves above, with searing trill (bar 84). What
follows is a free inversion and augmentation of the countersubject,
with an augmentation of the original semiquaver scales pounding in
parallel sixths. Passing dissonances, all marked with sforzandi, are
vicious; the passage is painful to play and painful to listen to. Recalling
Blake's Tyger again, we may well ask what dread anvil forged this
titanic assertion. Through the many-in-oneness of the counterpoint
Beethoven holds on, come what may. That is what Beethoven's
counterpoint is for; it cannot be pre-ordained or god-given except in
the sense that it is hammered out by *his* divine smithy. At the end of
this apocalyptic passage the trills return, screaming or growling
(there's one on the low C!). Far more terrifyingly than the comparable
passage in the fugue of opus 101, this music too yells 'I will *not* be
divided, I *will* be whole'. Apparently of maximum vehemence and
abandon, the passage is also one of the most contrapuntally strict in the
entire score, as the ultimate stretti demonstrate:

Ex. 86

The explosion is severely canonic, the entries interlinked *rectus et inversus* as though in a maze. Again violence earns a respite. The main modulatory points of the fugue have moved with seeming inevitability in descending mediants from B flat to G flat major, to E flat minor, and back up the cycle of fifths to F minor. After the 'explosion', F minor is succeeded by its relative A flat major, in which key the gentler, arpeggiated version of the theme (first heard in the G flat major episode) sings again (bars 120 ff.). Increasingly the music stresses the rise through the third, and although tonality moves flexibly between the major and minor flat keys, a feeling of gaiety, a glow of illumination, takes over from the searing struggle of the 'augmented' episode. The flow of unbroken semiquavers, after the tense-muscled holding-back of the quaver augmentations, is a release, even though passing dissonances are not entirely dispersed. From G flat the music falls to C flat, notated as B, minor. What follows is a critical phase in the fugue's structure; again the pattern of descending mediants is preserved.

Beethoven begins with the left hand playing the original theme inverted and backwards, so that it ends with a trill and *falling* tenth. The right hand plays the countersubject in augmentation, in which form it is song-like but rhythmically tentative, tied across the beats. The backwards version of the theme is also no longer aggressive, but hesitant, as though groping towards the light:

Ex. 87

Even the trills promise lyricism. For some time, however, the music, remaining quiet in dynamics, veering between B minor and its relative D major, is no more than tenderly expectant. As long as the fugue theme goes backwards it sounds lost, directionless, its once aspiring scales dropping through the thematic tenth, while the augmented countersubject, beginning wistfully, grows more plangent in its harmonic suspensions as its contrapuntal stretti increase. Positive direction seems to be discovered as D major is established as tonal centre. As we've already noticed, D major is not only the relative of B minor, but also the upper mediant to B flat, and the lower mediant to the slow movement's F sharp. Between bars 168 and 180 there is virtually no tonal movement, and the texture consists simply of the opening scale of the fugue theme, *rectus et inversus*, in stretto, and in parallel and then contrary motion. The straightforward tonality and the resonant parallel tenths sound 'easy' after the previous acridities, though the rhythms made by the counterpoint are complex, and passing dissonances are not entirely banished. Momentum is maintained when, by way of a chromatic cadential progression (bars 180–85), the theme returns in one of its original forms in the bass, the firm forte of the D major episode now strengthened to fortissimo. The transitional passage is embroidered with Bach-like figurations of tied and dotted notes in the two upper parts.

But however positive the music may seem, Beethoven is no longer concerned with triumphal apotheoses of the type explored in his middle-period works. At bar 195 there is a change of key signature from two sharps to one, and Beethoven demonstrates again how for him fugal unity is always a making and a becoming, by way of variation and metamorphosis. At first tonality is indeterminate, the bass having a sequential version of the countersubject, the treble a version that is rhythmically and wittily transformed; the tenor's semiquavers gather energy through chromatics. Having reached G major, the treble has the theme in inversion, and the other parts bandy snippets of the theme (usually with the octave form of the leaps) between them. Key fluctuates until, as the thematic trills grow louder and more frequent, a clear E flat major is established; this again is a mediant below the last notated tonality. The previous passage, with its teasing entries, though still crazy, is no longer comic, but fearful. The theme, both ways up and in close stretto, blows up in the fugue's third and wildest climax. The prancing tenths, *rectus et inversus*, end in jittery quavers, each second note hissing in an *unresolved* trill. The Tyger spits fire; sparks fly from the smithy.

Compared with the agonized grinding of the earlier explosion in bars 108–15, this climax might be called playful as well as terrifying: it recalls Blake's words 'Energy is Eternal Delight'. So there is a positive element within its disruption; and the 'explosion's' quick-fire sequences from C to G to D minors end in an enormous dominant cadence, approached by a German sixth; then silence:

Ex. 88

Then at last, after the fugue's and indeed the sonata's epical struggle, Beethoven *enters* a D major paradise to sing a three-part fugato, the theme of which is a stepwise undulation, in level crotchets, down and up a third! It is to be played *una corda*, of course, without change in the pianissimo dynamics. Yet although it is haven and heaven (*sempre dolce e cantabile*), it is clearly a distillation of the original fugal subject, as is revealed by placing that theme against it:

Ex. 89

Moreover, the canonic interweaving entails a degree of passing dissonance, including a number of false relations. There is an interesting
crux in bars 250–2, for Beethoven modulates flatward to G in bar 251
but doesn't cancel the C sharps in the next bar. Again, while being
reluctant to disagree with Tovey, I doubt whether this is an error. False
relation plays so significant a part in the work's tonal structure that the
bitter-sweet effect of the suspended sharp seventh and the pang of the
passing C sharp sound exactly right in context; we are surely meant to
feel that this glimpse of heaven is precarious, neither 'here' nor 'there',
tonally and harmonically. Certainly the ambiguous bar prepares us for
the next phase, when the melody moves in arching fourths and fifths as
well as by step, and is harmonically enriched with passing chromatics.
That this fugato, ineffable in its quietude, should yet contain so much
internal dissonance is hardly surprising; the rapid harmonic movement is, retrospectively, the tension of this and the previous movements which has found peace in the equable rhythm of the song-like
theme. This is why Beethoven's peace, like Bach's, 'passes understanding'; the texture is here truly Bachian, though Beethoven's tonality is more fluid. In the first sixteen bars of the fugato the melting
harmonies are not so much modulations as linearly derived transitions, such as both Bach and Beethoven use to effect a synthesis of the
sensual and spiritual. After the fifteenth bar, however, Beethoven's
modulations wander from bar to bar (A major, E major, F sharp
minor, B minor, D major, E minor and so on) with a licence that Bach
would not have allowed himself. Yet Beethoven's licence is not anar-
chy; his heavenly freedom carries him—as the lines float across the
bars—home to earth. The transition from this seraphic D major to the
original power key of B flat is one of the miracles of all music.

There is a tinge of regret as the song-fugue lifts up through a minor third to a diminished seventh in E minor, then to a German sixth of G minor which floats, however, into its relative. The regret is understandable; for as the original fugue theme steals back, while the song-fugue continues, we realize that our hint of heaven, though true, has been momentary. The song tries to cancel the tiger-fugue by stamping in thunderous bass octaves, but is decisively banished as the original fugue returns, *rectus et inversus*, with a flurry of contrary motion scales and the savagest passing dissonances thus far. Though this return serves some of the functions of a sonata recapitulation and coda, it proves, like the first movement's coda, disintegrative rather than affirmative. The trills roar in the bass, the countersubject hammers its syncopated rhythm; but instead of an approach to song, there is a splintering. The hammer-blow climax in bars 321–3, ending with trills yelled on a dominant seventh of F, begins a breakdown, first through a two-part invention with passing dissonances that rise to screeching parallel tenths, then through multiple stretti *rectus et inversus*, the theme left incomplete. Though the tonality remains anchored to B flat and its dominant, neither it nor the desperate unity of the counterpoint can prevent disruption; the dominant–tonic cadence on the *last beat* of bar 356 is grotesque after so much epical striving:

Ex. 90

The coda that follows parallels that to the first movement. In sudden piano the inverted theme leaps through a *diminished* tenth, answered the right way up with a major tenth in the bass. The next inverted entry lands on the low E flat, with a furious trill long sustained, above which seethe arpeggiated diminished sevenths of B flat. Thrusting up, they arrive nowhere. The bass trill changes to a tonic B flat, with the dominant F sepulchrally below it; above, fragments of the theme twitter through E flat minor, ending in choking references to the countersubject, still over the tiger-growling pedal. Finally the trill, within the ritardando, oozes into a G flat triad with a dominant seventh of B flat above it; then inches up to G natural, poco adagio (bar 371). Double trills make a cadence into F and back to B flat, when the fugue's scale reappears pianissimo and *a tempo*. But there is no resurgence of the fugue. The scale swoops down in an immense crescendo and we end with the leaping major tenths and trills, stabbing up the scale in the bass from F to E flat: and so to two muscular dominant–tonic cadences. The leaping tenths, each one a modulation creating a false relation, epitomize the tonal tension that has given impetus to the entire sonata. It sought, but did not finally achieve, consummation in the adagio's hymnic aria, which approached the unity of fugue and glimpsed a heaven wherein song and fugue were indivisible. Not, however, until the final trinity of sonatas does Beethoven encompass that heaven. In the Hammerklavier, vision disintegrates and the fugue's coda returns to the Morality of Power. The sonata ends where it began, being an experience that has to be lived through again and again. Only a Beethoven could have the spiritual, and perhaps physical, stamina to do so. The intellectual rigours of the fugue—and not even Bach wrote a fugue that calls more exhaustively and exhaustingly on contrapuntal device—are necessary precisely because the forces of contradiction within the psyche are so nearly overwhelming; and to this the limb-stretching and mind-boggling 'physicality' of the piano technique is an inevitable complement. Both physical violence and intellectual rigour work in the interests of order; it is remarkable that the fugue, which seems so cataclysmically explosive and so contrapuntally tight, proves to be a balanced structure, the main modulatory points of which move, as does the whole sonata, in descending mediants. J. W. N. Sullivan summed the matter up beautifully, more than fifty years ago: 'Beethoven was a man who experienced all that we can experience, who suffered all that we can suffer. If, at the end, he seems to reach a state "above the battle", we also know that no man ever knew more bitterly what the battle is!'

3. Scapegoat and Fool

Piano sonatas
opus 109 in E major
opus 110 in A flat major

To look back on Beethoven's life's work—as we can more readily then he could himself—is an experience at once fascinating and, in the strict sense, aweful: for with no creator are we more startlingly aware of individual works of art as 'points at which the growth of the mind shows itself'. Beethoven could not have composed *this* work had he not previously created *that*; complementarily, we hear this work with different ears when we know that the other work is embryonic in it. The piano sonatas alone contain a spiritual history of extraordinary depth, height, complexity and comprehensiveness. One might hazard that a near-total humanity was embraced within that sonata-duo of his middle years, the Appassionata and the Waldstein, were it not that the Waldstein hints at realms of experience which, at the time of its composition, Beethoven himself was hardly aware he would be entering. Similarly the strange A major sonata, opus 101, seems not less strange yet entirely inevitable, when considered as a prologue to opus 106. And that epical work is to find fulfilment in the trilogy of the last three sonatas, for the creation of which the Hammerklavier had been, in its turn, essential. Beethoven is the supreme instance in music of our Western 'linear' thinking: which makes it the more moving that the goal of his linearity proves—as we will see—to be the circle.

Compared with the Hammerklavier, the three sonatas opus 109, 110 and 111 are short works, and each sonata is an entity in itself. At the same time it is valid to regard them as three components of one work: and this on interior evidence, not merely because Beethoven claimed to have written them out in one swoop. We will discuss them as the apex of and end to Beethoven's piano sonatas, and also as a prelude to the *Missa Solemnis*, on which Beethoven was working contemporaneously, and which the composer himself believed to be the climactic

point of his achievement. Sketches for the sonatas were found between
the pages of the score of the Mass; musical parallels between the piano
works and the Mass are specific enough for us to regard the sonatas as
an intimate exploration of precisely those physical and metaphysical
themes that the choral and orchestral work states in epical terms. The
sonatas are sonatas, though unconventional ones; to study them as
prelude to the *Missa Solemnis* helps us to understand how Beethoven
approached a large-scale liturgical work which reinterprets Baroque
and even Renaissance techniques in the light of the sonata principle,
though no movement is 'in' sonata form.

If we regard the last three last sonatas as a triptych we will observe
one immediate affinity with the Hammerklavier sonata: their basic
tonalities are E, A flat (equals G sharp) and C; so they stand to one
another in those mediant relationships which had manifested the
Hammerklavier's liberation from traditional tonal bondage. Opus 109
in E major begins with a shortish movement, conspicuous none the
less for the experiential range it covers. Indeed its first page juxtaposes
types of music so apparently contrarious that there was a time when
the movement used to be referred to as a 'free fantasia'. In fact it is a
strict and economical sonata movement, odd only in the fact that its
first and second subjects have attained the maximum contrariety
conceivable: so much so that Beethoven employs for them not merely
different tempo indications, but also different time signatures and
different kinds of notation. It would not be oversimple to say that first
and second subjects are here musical synonyms for the states Blake
called Innocence and Experience: and Beethoven no less than Blake
proves through his art that man achieves wholeness and holiness only
when the two states are reconciled. The one cannot exist without the
other: from Innocence we must grow into Experience; from Experience we have to be Edenicly reborn.

In what, musically, does the innocence of Beethoven's eight-bar
first subject consist?

Ex. 91

Apart from the happy accident of the tonality (we have frequently
pointed out that 'sharp' E major was traditionally a celestial key), we
note that the music flows *Vivace ma non troppo* in regular semiquavers,
the texture as unbroken as a Bach prelude. The regularity itself
suggests continuity, the more positive because the broken arpeggios
which the semiquavers make are all diatonic concords, without even a
passing dissonance, unless one counts dominant sevenths as such.
Moreover, during the first four bars the lower notes of the bass fall
gently down the scale through an octave from E, with only one
substitution of B for F sharp in the penultimate note. During the
second four bars the bass moves down from E to B, then up to F sharp
to effect the simplest modulation to the dominant. Throughout the
eight-bar period the texture is warmly spaced in the middle of the
keyboard, opening up slightly with the bright dominant modulation.
From all these related features the music acquires its innocent contentment; the cat, a creature of immediate sensuous responsiveness,
purrs in the sleek sun. But this quiet happiness is innocent also in the
sense that it is incomplete, for within the music's euphony there is
nothing that one can call a theme. The broken arpeggios of the right
hand define a pattern of rising thirds linked by falling fifths, and
succeeded by a scalewise rise *through* a third. Beethoven inverts some
of the notes' tails, thereby binding the texture together and perhaps
hinting that within this pattern a theme, and specifically a song,
may be latent. In this initial statement, however, song is no more
than potential; it is precisely the song's discovery that the sonata is
'about'.

At this stage in his life Beethoven had no need to prevaricate. He can
admit without fear or favour that light and dark are inseparable; and
there may be evidence of this in the metrical ambiguity of the first
subject itself. For it begins on the upbeat of a 2/4 bar, and is heard
across the bars, leaving an extra half-bar apparently to emphasize
cadential resolution. Then, just when we expect the sharp A to settle
into the dominant B major triad, Beethoven substitutes a broken
diminished seventh, carrying us instead to the relative, C sharp

minor—traditionally a key of purgatorial pain, as was E major of bliss.
He also changes the time signature to 3/4 and the tempo indication to
adagio espressivo; the music is as anguished, in linear-harmonic intensity, as the first subject had been smilingly simple. Whereas the texture
of that first subject had affinities with a Bach arpeggiated prelude, the
second subject recalls Bach's arioso style; that it is arioso—which in
Baroque music is experience in action, as contrasted with aria's con-
templation after the event—is the point:

Ex. 92

The implicit polyphony of the scales in contrary motion creates acute
passing dissonance between G sharp and A and then, in sequence,
between F sharp and G natural. Tension relaxes as we move through
what looks like being a 6–4 cadence into the dominant; but again
resolution is foiled by a diminished seventh substitution. This time the
diminished seventh ripples into demisemiquaver arpeggios covering a
wide range of the keyboard. This liberates the linear-harmonic tension
of the arioso, yet at the same time denies the possibility, at this stage, of
self-contained song. In a sense Experience relapses into Innocence: too
soon for a fusion of contrarieties to have been achieved, yet not too
soon for arpeggiated innocence to be affected by the arioso's shadow.
For the arpeggio slides down to a triad of D sharp (as dominant of G
sharp, itself the enhanced dominant of C sharp, minor), which
chromatically shifts to B major. So the sharp dominant, expected but
frustrated at the close of the first subject, is at last attained; and it is

maintained during a codetta that transforms demisemiquavers into triplets, creating a texture of parallel sixths glinting high on the keyboard. There is still no song, indeed no melody; but the figuration shimmers like a fountain, and the arioso's agony seems to have evaporated into thin air (bar 14). To end the codetta, the sextuplet scales cascade down while rising semiquavers emphasize the cadentially sharp leading note. So there is a positive outcome of the exposition's uncompromising opposition of innocent joy and tragic lament, though as yet there is no synthesis between them.

Some performers, whether thoughtfully or intuitively, seek to establish a mathematical ratio between the tempo of the 3/4 *adagio* and the 2/4 *vivace*. Though this is possible and may be convincing, Tovey is justified in maintaining that all that matters is that the first two bars of the *adagio* should sound longer than the eight and a half bars of the *vivace*, not merely chronometrically, but also because so much happens in them. After the arioso-style bars, the demisemiquavers and triplets will inevitably suggest greater animation and, in the codetta, may well produce a slight increase in pulse. To counteract this, Beethoven writes a ritardando into the last line of the exposition, covering the change of notation back to semiquavers. By the time 2/4 and Tempo I are re-established it will not be far out to take the restored crotchet pulse as equivalent to the adagio's quavers.

The subtle equivocation of the exposition is preserved throughout the brief development which, surprisingly after all those watery scales and arpeggios in the codetta, adheres consistently to the broken figuration of the 'contented' first subject. Yet although the arioso's textures do not appear, their intensity is latent. The thematic rising-scale thirds are now sustained in the left hand; so is the bass's descent down the scale, when we move from the dominant to the relative C sharp minor, the arioso's original key. While the music moves up the cycle of fifths to G sharp and D sharp, sustained notes in the top part expand the descending scale and the thirds (now also falling instead of rising) into a hymnic theme (bars 21 ff.). As Innocence and Experience fuse we become aware at least of the potentiality of song. From the hypnotic consistency of the figuration a promise of ecstasy is generated; sharp minor keys are replaced by dominant and then tonic major; the rising scale of the cadential clause of the first subject ascends higher in the treble, the left hand's broken chords becoming broken octaves. But the Song is still not manifest; we are on the threshold of paradise, not within it, and we cannot follow the celestial call of the reiterated

dominant Bs, through which the broken arpeggios become chiming
bells:

Ex. 93

Within the bell-tolling, the recapitulation is upon us before we realize
what's happening. The first arpeggiated theme is now high on the
keyboard, while the left hand's leaping octaves are low in sonority and
tied across the beat, which turns them into dissonant suspensions.
Levitating ecstasy in the high right hand coexists with an almost
brutish clumping in the low left hand, which Beethoven partially
counteracted in revision by abruptly changing the *forte* dynamic to
piano at the tessitura's highest point. The physical energy of Beethoven
the Activist seems inseparable from the metaphysical bliss of Beethoven the Seer; if the passage makes me think of dolphins leaping out
of turbulent water the metaphor may not be as subjectively fanciful as
it seems.

For dolphins are warm-blooded creatures, of tremendous physical
and even (we are told) intellectual stamina, who live in and leap out of
the watery wastes, for which reason they have often been regarded as
messengers between the physical and the metaphysical. They bear the
souls of the dead across the waters to heaven, and in the mythology of
the Church were confused with their giant relative the whale, who
swallowed Jonah. Thus they became a symbol of resurrection, and
even an emblem for Christ himself. Archetypally, two dolphins
adjoined came to represent the cycle of life and, like the snake biting his
own tail, to stand for eternity. We shall see that such abstruse dolphin-
symbolism may be relevant to the totality of Beethoven's last three
sonatas; in this context, however, as the climax to the development of
opus 109's first movement, they are no more than messengers of
potentiality. Since energy, whether joyous or agonized, is not yet
paradisal, the recapitulation, having counterpoised the dominant
modulation with four bars of tonic, can echo the dualism of the

exposition. Once more resolution is annihilated by the arioso's diminished seventh.

Conventionally enough, the recapitulation of the second subject begins (bar 58) a fifth lower, in F sharp instead of C sharp minor. The sequential repetition is intensified, in the inner part, with demisemiquavers; and the liberation of the arioso's pain into cascading arpeggios brings a shock, since Beethoven substitutes the flat submediant (C major) for what had been the dominant's relative. This crucial modulation by mediant significantly marks the movement's climax and its only double forte. Dramatic forcefulness hints that the fusion of contrarieties that had not occurred in the exposition may be imminent:

Ex. 94

Certainly when the arpeggios pivot back to the tonic major the glittering sextuplets in parallel sixths are extended over four instead of two bars, the descent being by way of alternating (and thematic) thirds instead of straight scales. The bass's semiquaver rise through the sharp seventh, though present, is no longer emphasized. The cloud of fioriture slows down, and fades out, into an ascending tonic arpeggio, trailing at bar 66 into a coda of significant dimensions, in view of the movement's economy.

The tessitura is high and silvery, the broken arpeggios mingling the familiar thirds with seconds. The lower notes of the left hand fall down the scale from A to E, and repeat the pattern, sustained as crotchets. The motive is answered by inversion, the crotchet scale climbing from F sharp to B, first in the right hand, then the left; then truncated to a third, in contrary motion. This emphasis on scale movement, rather than on arpeggios, approaches the Song hidden within the first subject's happiness and the arioso's lament; that the revelation of the Song calls for a fusion of Innocence and Experience is manifest in the next eleven bars. The broken arpeggios cease; the lifting scales remain. At first they are tentative, breathless on the offbeat, separated by rests; then in continuous crotchets, harmonized with precisely those dissonant tensions (diminished sevenths in C sharp and F sharp minor, up-thrusting appoggiatura on E sharp) that had characterized the arioso's initial statement:

Ex. 95

Far from destroying happiness, the dissonances now combine with continuous line and stable rhythm to aspire to a hymn-like song, moving by step through a fourth, or leaping through that interval. The serenity is only enriched by the passing dissonances and by the chromatics in the bass line, until the tune moves scalewise from D sharp to G sharp, and leaps a fourth on the 'enhanced dominant', the C sharp of which is suspended across the bar, to resolve glowingly as a dominant major ninth of E (bar 86). Though this is the end of the first movement's aspiration to the Hidden Song, that dominant ninth is a critical moment, the implication of which will become evident in the finale. What remains of this movement almost literally marks time. The arpeggiated figuration resumes, *legato e piano*, and the disguised thematic tones hover between G sharp and A, F sharp and E, until they droop in appoggiaturas phrased in pairs of crotchets, in place of the previous long slurs. These appoggiaturas, falling from sixth to fifth, are alternately minor and major, pressing wearily down through the semitone, or floating hopefully in an 'added sixth'. The passage remotely anticipates the ewigs at the end of Mahler's *Das Lied von der Erde* and has a comparable psychological effect, given the extreme concision of Beethoven's piece and the expansiveness of Mahler's. But the sharp sixths seem to win the day, and the figuration drifts up in alternating appoggiaturas of C sharp–B, A–G sharp, to attain the stratospheric region of the exposition's codetta. Typically, however, Beethoven ends with an E major triad with doubled third, both hands in the bass register. The sonority would not have been as grumpy on Beethoven's piano as it sounds on ours; none the less the contrast with the immediately previous silvery figuration would have been pointed. A passage from Eliot's *Burnt Norton* seems relevant:

> We move above the moving tree
> In light upon the figured leaf
> And hear upon the sodden floor
> Below, the boarhound and the boar
> Pursue their pattern as before
> But reconciled among the stars.

We cannot yet wing from the earth's mud; and this bears on the fact that the final triad is linked, by Beethoven's pedalling, to the next movement.

This is marked *prestissimo*, an unusual direction in Beethoven, though I think Tovey is right in saying that Beethoven used it to avoid possible misinterpretation, rather than in its own right. It is impossible to play this movement, in which much happens texturally, at anything approaching the *prestissimo* tempo of the finale of the F minor sonata of opus 2. It must sound, as it is, turbulent yet controlled, for the patent discipline is here the point, whereas the point of the apparently relaxed first movement lies in the fact that its discipline is latent. Though both movements are in strict sonata form, the extreme contrast between them extends even to their appearance in score. The dualism of the first movement even entailed different kinds of notation for the two subjects; the textures and figurations of the *prestissimo*, on the other hand, are as consistently unified as those of a Bach binary movement. It was precisely this physicality, this earthiness, that had prevented Beethoven from possessing 'paradise' in the first movement; here the ferocity is realized, projected and at the same time controlled in a sonata movement so tight that it looks, if it doesn't sound, like classical binary style. If this is music of the Blakean Tyger, at an altogether deeper level than the tiger of opus 2's *prestissimo*, Beethoven now rides and is not ridden by him. Though the image has a risible flavour, that is not inappropriate to the music.

The key is the tonic E minor, the rhythm a galloping 6/8, with the suggestion of a lunacy-provoking tarantella. The opening bars indicate that this madness is inherent in the first movement, for the bass is a more melodically organized permutation of the first movement's descending bass scale. Its two segments—E, D, C–A, B: A, G, F sharp–B, E—symmetrically balance: the right hand's upward-bouncing arpeggios give extra punch to the thirds and fifths of the first movement, rounding them off with a tailpiece that again moves up and down through a third and resolves on an appoggiatura:

Ex. 96

These eight bars end in abrupt silence. The next sixteen are over an unremittent dominant pedal, against which scalewise thirds thrust in contrary motion between treble and tenor, sometimes driven into cross-accents of 3/4 against 6/8. After the pedal has shifted to the tonic, tension remains, since the octaves in bars 25–8 combine an inversion of the tailpiece figure with repeated notes grimly reiterated. This inverted tailpiece becomes, without change of figuration, a second subject, at first in the tonic but soon moving to B minor, the orthodox dominant. Whereas the first movement presents the maximum contrast between first and second subjects, here there is no contrast at all, except that of the conventional key relationship. Once in B minor, the anchorage of the pedal is no less stringent than it was during the first subject; as before, it curbs thrusting dissonance and galloping rhythm. After eight bars, however, the pedal note vanishes, the tailpiece figure is splintered in syncopation, and the music threatens to disintegrate:

Ex. 97

The theme fragments to a rocking fourth; but order is restored as the C major sequence turns into a Neapolitan approach back to B minor, in which dominant the exposition ends canonically and in double counterpoint between the hands. Sturdy repeated notes and descending thirds martially discipline upward quaver scales.

Not for a moment in this linearly unified exposition has there been a suggestion that violence might get out of control: the contrast with those earlier and wilder tempests in the Moonlight and the Appassionata sonatas is extreme. Moreover the fact that the codetta's discipline is contrapuntal is significant, preparing us for the development's vestigial attempt to translate sonata dualism into the monism of fugue. Nor is this fugato an epical strife like that in opus 101 and 106; on the contrary, it approaches a hymnic vein, and its theme—a descent down the scale through a third, a fall through the interval of a third, and a scalewise rise through a fifth—is not only identical with the original bass of this movement, but is also allied to the first movement's 'hidden song' (bars 70 ff.).

At first the development's fugued theme is in the bass, with the arpeggiated sonata theme on top. Quaver movement is then restricted to a softly rumbling dominant pedal, while the embryonic song appears in stretto, veering between dominant and tonic, then sliding into C major with plagally flattened As. With the marking *una corda*, which we have seen to be reserved by Beethoven for potentially transcendent moments, quaver movement ceases and stretti grow closer as the theme appears, two dotted crotchets to a bar, *rectus et inversus*. The texture has become not only austerely contrapuntal but also lyrically grave. This contrapuntal many-in-oneness cannot, however, at this stage transmute 'tempest' into 'music', sonata into fugue; the development lasts less than forty bars and is consistently muted in dynamic. Moreover, throughout the contrapuntal symmetries, tonality is in continual flux, sliding from C to A minor, then sequentially sharpwards to E and B minors. At this point the hymn theme (which was also the movement's original bass) is accompanied by itself in

inversion; but far from acting the eternity-serpent that eats its own tail,
the fugato's end denies temporal progression merely in the sense that it
runs down like a clock. Dynamics become softer and softer; dominant
and tonic chords of B minor appear isolated on each first beat of a bar,
separated by silences: until in sudden fortissimo, the mystical *una corda*
banished by *tutte le corde*, the recapitulation bursts on us in the tonic E
minor, the B minor dominants left unresolved:

Ex. 98

At the moment, it would seem, 'religious' affirmation is denied. The
canonic hymn becomes again the sonata's bass, in double counterpoint. The transitional 'tailpiece' begins in C as Neapolitan to B
minor, but lands in the tonic minor after the pseudo-second subject.
The splintered syncopated sequences appear in the same order as in the
exposition, only a fifth lower (bars 144–56). F major therefore
becomes a Neapolitan approach to the stabilizing codetta, with its
repeated notes, martial thirds, and upshooting scales. Beethoven rams
home his affirmation in a coda as economical as is everything in this
sonata. The repeated notes, falling third and scale become, in the bass,
a march, while the right hand asserts the rising thirds and fourths.
Tension may still be manifest in the rigid metre, but the gesture is also
expansive, even triumphant. It is usually played rather grimly, though
it seems legitimate to hear in it, given the context, something like a
defiant guffaw. There is no debunking implication in this. Beethoven
has every right to an assertion of prideful power, even to a flicker of

contempt. The tarantella-spider hasn't driven him crazy; the however
dangerous tiger has been mastered, even though his energy hasn't,
after all, been metamorphosed into linear unity. After this, the dualism
of the first movement's Innocence and Experience can at last become
one. So Beethoven's finale is not only an *aria* rather than an arioso, like
the 'becoming' of the first movement's second subject; it is also a
hymn, and a variation-set on one of the sublimest songs ever created
by man.

The Song (no longer hidden) consists of sixteen bars, divided into
8+8; it must be quoted complete:

Ex. 99

Though the tempo is triple, not duple, and though the theme begins on
the beat, not halfway through the bar, the relation of the aria to the first
movement's *vivace* is immediately obvious. The descending thirds are
still present, emphasized by the sarabande-like rhythm, and now
balanced by the upward thirds moving, unfrustrated, to the dominant.
The second four bars begin with the *vivace*'s falling fifth approached
by a spread arpeggio; incorporate the rising and falling thirds; and
answer the falling fifth with the aspiration of a rising major *sixth*. This
resolves, by way of a tritone, on to, not into, the dominant. Meanwhile, during these first four bars, the bass rises consistently, both
through the interval of a third and through stepwise fifths. It starts in
inversion with the melody; but in bars 3–4 the melody *echoes* the bass.
In bars 5–7 the bass rises from G sharp to E, counterpoising the

melody's descent. In the last two bars the melody's rising sixth and cadential resolution through a tritone and an upwards appoggiatura are balanced against the bass's descending thirds and chromatics. The C natural, pressing down to B, forms a German sixth with the melody's upward thrusting A sharp.

The sublimity of the theme is inherent in its equipoise: both in the rise and fall of melodic stresses, and in the tensions between melodic contours and harmonic bass. This is epitomized in the German sixth cadence to the first half; the appoggiaturas by inversion are sighs that embrace the first movement arioso's *lacrimae rerum*, while at the same time dispensing balm. The second half, after the double bar, consummates the marriage of Innocence and Experience. Momentarily, the theme abandons its thirds and oscillates in sarabande rhythm between notes a tone apart, while the bass rises through a third, offbeat, three times in declining sequences. This carries us from the tonic through F sharp minor to G sharp minor. An F sharp minor triad, prefaced by a spread arpeggio mirroring the one in bar 5, returns us direct from this mediant to the tonic major, the melodic thirds now rising from the second beat instead of falling from the first. The C sharp is repeated at the beginning of the next bar, as top of an arpeggiated dominant ninth. The consummatory effect of this in the context of the whole sonata is extraordinary. Unconsciously we recall the effect of the diminished seventh arpeggio that, at the end of the first movement's *vivace*, had baulked resolution (see Ex. 92); and also the dominant ninth that, in the first movement's coda, had hinted at fulfilment (Ex. 95). Now the chord luminously glows, transfiguring the air's resonance. From it the melody declines, and creates a scalewise rise and fall of a third over a 6–4 cadence. The triple appoggiatura of the final bar is a dissonant hurt, sharper than the chromaticized half-close at the end of the first eight bars, yet for that reason the more healing.

This theme—which Beethoven marks *Gesangvoll mit innigster Empfindung* as well as *Andante molto cantabile ed espressivo*, and every word is justified—is self-contained: so it cannot compromise between variation and sonata, as does the adagio of the Hammerklavier nor, like the finales of the Waldstein and opus 90, between sonata and rondo. Its E major bliss has affinities with the opus 90 rondo, though its mood is hymnic rather than domestic. If it resembles anything, it is Mozart's Masonic music, which we will discuss in more detail in relation to Beethoven's *Missa Solemnis*. For the moment it is more relevant to distinguish this aria theme from the superficially similar rondo-song of opus 90 which, on Beethoven's own admission, also concerns love. But whereas the love celebrated in opus 90 is human and sexual, the love celebrated in opus 109 is, in Beethoven's words, 'the spirit that binds together noble and virtuous souls, *a spirit that Time cannot destroy*' (italics added). We shall understand the force of this rejection of Time when we reach the end of the movement; but in a sense it is already implicit in the fact that Beethoven has created a self-contained theme that remains radically unchanged, however various its variations. That its effect on its first appearance is so much more deeply moving than that of the beautiful opus 90 rondo is due intrinsically to its subtler equipoise of stresses, and also to its consummatory effect in context.

The first two movements had been strict though not conventional sonata movements; the finale is no less strict as a variation-set, and the discipline is inseparable from the fulfilment. Variation I is as lyrical as the Air, though it changes the manner, and to some degree the mood, from the hymnic to the operatic. One could say of this variation, no less than of the adagio of opus 106, that in a strictly technical sense the humanistic passions of Italian opera are here transcended. Though the tempo is unchanged, the harmonic pulse moves more slowly than that of the Air, the first bass note of each bar shaping a rising and falling scale. The sarabande stress on the second beat has also gone, the movement being that of a waltz so slowed down as to suggest immobility. The melody is lyrically open, compared with the hymn. Starting on the fifth, prefaced by a grace note floating through an octave, it falls through a fifth instead of a third, subsiding on a sighing appoggiatura over the dominant seventh harmony of the second bar. Each two bars open melodically with the catch-in-the-breath of the octave lift to the fifth, and descends to an appoggiatura, intensified in bars 3 and 4 because approached by a quasi-vocal turn, and in bars 5 and 6 because it is syncopated. The fourth bar omits the momentary dominant modulation of the Air; perhaps for this reason the cadence in the eighth bar does not need the 'German' flattening in the bass. After the double bar the F sharp minor modulation preserves the lifting grace notes, while chromatic passing notes create more painful dissonance. It may be the increase in pain and passion that makes the return to the tonic air-borne. The grace notes, which had become aspiring sixths after the double bar, are again octaves, wafting in the heights:

Ex. 100

The dotted rhythm caresses and, at the 6–4 cadence, releases two grace notes, one an octave, the other a sixth, on consecutive quavers. It is as though the song soars over and even out of the harmonic anguish when, after the spume of graced quavers, the melody is tied across the beats. There is a harmonic counterpart to this in that the left hand's chord on the second beat of the final bar elides tonic, dominant and subdominant, abolishing temporal progression. Even more than the adagio of the Hammerklavier, this variation distils the operatic ornament of Bellini, and its pianistic transmutation in the nocturnal Chopin, into seraphic grace.

The Song, it would seem, almost dissolves in its airy yearning; indeed in the first eight bars of Variation II melody seems to have evaporated. Still in 3/4 the four-bar period consists simply of broken chord figuration in semiquavers, recalling the opening of the first movement though with even less thematic definition, since its single line of melody is broken, in wide-spaced registration, between the right and left hand. As an effect of colour it is translucent: an intimation of the realms into which the melody itself is to proliferate. The harmony meticulously follows that of the Air in its original statement, returning to the German sixth cadence in the seventh and eighth bars, but with the A sharps notationally alchemized into B flats, so that the passage can be spelled out as a momentary modulation to F major. The repeat is written out because it is a different kind of music, thereby making a double variation. Song returns with the falling third motive rounded off with a 'vocal' trill, turn and slow appoggiatura. This theme enters four times in canon, each entry a note higher. The accompanying chords throb over a dominant pedal, which extends over the next four bars when the figuration pants in broken chords. This compromises with the arpeggio figuration of the first section while preserving the songfulness of the repeat. In their fragmented form the appoggiaturas in the tune become the more expressive; the German sixth cadence returns to its A sharp notation. The second half repeats the double-variation pattern. The eight bars of broken semiquavers ascend to the heights as they dance limpidly through the F sharp and G sharp minor modulations; and glitter with chromatic passing notes in approaching the repeat:

Ex. 101

The second half is intensified by beginning with a dominant minor ninth of F sharp minor, at first mysteriously, presented as octave Ds. In the final four bars the aria-like quality is enhanced because the right hand reduces its broken chords to octaves. The 6–4 cadence, however, is slightly exacerbated by passing diminished sevenths.

Variation III again apparently denies song, while remaining strictly thematic. This is a two-part invention in double counterpoint, the tempo suddenly 2/4 *allegro vivace*. So counterpoint, the other basic 'monistic' principle, has joined song variation in the search for the Whole. Moreover, the counterpoint is of Bachian strictness, and the mirror-like structure denies temporality, despite the animation.

Ex. 102

The first four bars consist of the thirds in contrary motion, moving from tonic to dominant. In the left hand the first note of each beat inverts the right hand's progression, but is filled in with semiquaver scales that also move through a third. Bars 5–8 repeat the first four, with the hands inverted, in double counterpoint; but one chromatic alteration of G sharp to G natural effects, in a flash, the German sixth cadence. The repeat of the first half is written out, because the rising thirds, originally at crotchet pulse, are filled in with quaver scales both diatonic and chromatic; otherwise it is strict. The second half is also in double counterpoint. Semiquavers chatter merrily around the tune's undulations up and down a tone; the F sharp minor and G sharp minor modulations, plus the transient chromatics, explode in an offbeat chord at the end of the fourth bar. In total effect the variation is hilarious, but dangerous: the rigidity of the counterpoint, the mirror-like oneness, check incipient frenzy.

Yet this danger must have been latent too in the interaction of stresses which is the theme, so one cannot regard the variations simply as contrarious 'moods'. Variation IV is seemingly at the opposite pole to Variation III, for it flows songfully in long 9/8 periods. But it too is contrapuntally disciplined, though less severely than the previous variation, being a double canon or, more accurately, a freely canonic piece on a theme divided into two segments. The complete theme consists of semiquavers flowing up through a third, and descending through a fifth, sixth, seventh or octave, the dotted crotchet pulse swinging slightly more slowly than the original theme. The canonic imitations, however, sometimes embrace only the semi-quaver undulations, sometimes only the dotted crotchet tied over to three quavers which, moving through thirds, resolve on an appoggiatura sigh:

Ex. 103

The 'warp and woof' effect of the counterpoint again destroys time, in a manner very different from the two-part invention; the seams do not show and, taking the variation down from dictation, one would be hard pressed to know where to put the bar-lines! During the first eight bars the hands start close together, but gradually separate until there are only two parts, the semiquavers winging aloft, the bass descending in distant octaves. The parts draw together again for the German sixth cadence, which is notated punningly both as a German sixth and as a dominant seventh of F. Morphological metaphors seem appropriate to this half of the variation: the canonic phrases intertwine like tendrils of the vine, separate like a spiral labyrinth, close together like the still heart of a rose. In the words of Marvell's Edenic Garden poem, the parts 'weave the garlands of repose'.

After the double bar, however, the second half is less reposeful, more mysterious. Polyphony disappears, and the dominant ninth that initiates the F sharp minor modulation rocks in trance-inducing semi-quavers, out of which steals a frailly chromatic, spectrally whispering undulation in the higher octave:

Ex. 104

With the G sharp minor modulation the rocking chords reverberate like bells, the overtones' resonance emphasized by cross-accents. At the return to the tonic the scoring is thick, the resonance clanging. We will discuss further, in connection with opus 111, the significance of bell sonorities in Beethoven's late piano style; here we need note only that this 'Chime and Symphony of Nature', to use Henry Vaughan's phrase, contains overtones and undertones of terror as well as of jubilation: which prepares the way for the illumination of the final variation. The texture thins as the undulating scales return, first in parallel tenths, then in wide-flung contrary motion, with unobtrusive grace.

Variation V restores both bodily energy and contrapuntal rigour, being a canonic fugue in quickish *alla breve* time. The main theme is launched by the descending thirds in close stretto, answered in synco-pated inversion:

Ex. 105

The German sixth cadence is spelled as a transitory modulation to F; the repeat fills in many of the thirds with vigorous staccato scales. Texture grows gritty, metallic parallel thirds and sixths being used with much the same effect as they were in the Hammerklavier's fugato passages, except that in this tight structure they never threaten loss of control. The repeat calls on double counterpoint, and a thickening of parts to parallel thirds, in order to enhance power. Then Beethoven introduces his only structural modification to the original Air: he adds a second repeat of the second half, using the identical music, quietened in dynamics. This fugato variation has gathered together the more boisterous, even bluff, energies of the work's second sonata movement, and has submitted them to the oneness-in-multiplicity which is fugue. The sense of almost derisive triumph latent in the coda to the *prestissimo* is in this variation more than a hint. Such abandoned, yet paradoxically rigorous, jubilation would seem to be necessary before the ultimate efflorescence of the song's variations can be attained. Not surprisingly Beethoven feels that, in approaching it, some slight expansion of the time-scale is called for.

In any case the *alla breve* fugato takes us back to the song in its original form, at the original tempo, but with a significant difference: the theme is mirrored by itself in inversion and, in place of the richly sonorous harmony, the four parts are completed by dominant pedal notes, one in the treble, the other in the tenor. The pedals start as crotchets, one to a beat; double their speed to quavers that clash dissonantly with the A sharps in the theme's rising third; turn into triple grouped quavers in 9/8, then semiquaver sextuplets in whole-tone oscillation—that is, in slow notated trills:

Ex. 106

After the German sixth cadence the theme, still in mirror inversion between alto and bass, moves in quavers while the trills are notated as demisemiquavers. By the time we reach the second four bars of the repeat, the trills have speeded sufficiently to be noted in the normal way, chiming in gradually increasing dynamics as the theme, now in quaver triplets, clangs in wild dissonance. At what was originally the double bar the trill suddenly leaps to the low B, and the right hand's demisemiquaver arpeggios surge through the F sharp and G sharp minor modulations:

Ex. 107

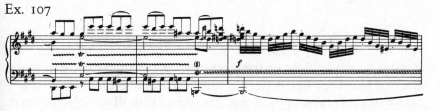

There are more than three octaves between the bass's earth-shaking trills and the tin-foil clattering of the right hand's arpeggios and chromatic passing notes. The effect is more terrible and awe-inspiring than beautiful: in Eliot's phrase, 'the dove descending breaks the air/ With flame of incandescent terror'. But it is a moment of transcendence which is finally consummated when, during the repeat of the second half, 'the dark dove with the flickering tongue' slowly alights. The dominant trill moves up to the high B, and the song theme is picked out, clearly audible though in broken syncopation, above it. Demisemiquaver scales seethe down during the F sharp minor modulation; become rocking arpeggios in the G sharp minor episode; flow in scales again at the return to the tonic. The demisemiquavers fade out, as elided tonics and dominants softly thunder in the bass, once more effacing Time. Beethoven allows himself another slight irregularity: an extra three bars in which the fragmented Song droops *through* the continuous trill and peters out before its completion. (Some idiot editors have inserted the missing notes in nervously apologetic brackets!) Starting as pedals of repeated notes slowly increasing in speed, the trills have been unbroken throughout the variation; as so often in late Beethoven, they have become 'the still point of the turning world': motion so rapid that it ceases to be apprehensible as such. As again Eliot has put it:

> Only by the form, the pattern,
> Can words or music reach
> The stillness, as a Chinese jar still
> Moves perpetually in its stillness.
> Not the stillness of the violin, while the note lasts,
> Not that only, but the co-existence,
> Or say that the end precedes the beginning,
> And the end and the beginning were always there
> Before the beginning and after the end,
> And all is always now.

That, certainly, is what happens at the end of the sonata: for after the trill has, with a gradual decrease in dynamics, alighted from the heights in the middle of the keyboard, while the bass's demisemiquavers become a non-harmonic murmur, it fades on a cadential turn into a strict da capo of the Song. The effect is similar to that of the da capo of the aria in Bach's Goldberg Variations, a work that Beethoven probably knew, for Bach's virtuosic keyboard techniques, especially in the use of trills, seem to be echoed in the exploratory pianism of the opus 109 variations. In any case the da capo of the aria, in both Bach and Beethoven, sounds like a microcosm of the macrocosm, though in Beethoven the process is more psychologically 'inward'.

Hearing the Song again we recognize in it that 'condition of complete simplicity/(Costing not less than everything)', of which Eliot speaks. Though the Song was latent in the first bars of the sonata, though we have heard it in its 'complete simplicity' at the beginning of the variations, we still feel, at the end, that we are hearing it for the first time. So we are, in that it and we, entering the time*less* paradise of the last variation, have been reborn. The Hidden Song has always been there, *since Time was*, waiting for revelation. Now, at 'the end of all our exploring', we

> arrive where we started
> And know the place for the first time.
> Through the unknown, remembered gate
> When the last of earth left to discover
> Is that which was the beginning;
> At the source of the longest river
> The voice of the hidden waterfall
> And the children in the apple-tree
> Not known, because not looked for
> But heard, half-heard, in the stillness
> Between two waves of the sea.
> Quick now, here, now, always—

It might seem that the self-contained song which concludes opus 109, returning circularly to the variations' source, must also be the end of Beethoven's lifelong search. Yet the two sonatas that complete the trilogy with opus 109 are essential to the pattern: for while in opus 109 Beethoven discovered song through sonata, in opus 110 he starts from a song that is also a sonata, and ends with a fugue that is also a song; complementarily, in opus 111 he begins with a fusion of the contrary principles of dualistic sonata and monistic fugue, and ends with a song so unsullied that it can dispense with the opus 109 aria's latent passion and pain—except for one episode that we recognize as retrospective or, in psychological terms, as regressive.

Opus 110 opens with a movement marked *Moderato cantabile, molto espressivo*, once more insisting on the songful expressivity Beethoven sought for in his late works. He also tells us that the opening should be played *con amabilità* and *sanft*, which means gentle in every sense, not merely soft. The key of A flat (enharmonically identical with G sharp) is the upper mediant to opus 109's E major; and A flat is a key with traditionally benign associations, partly because it is the opposite pole to its relative F minor which, as we have noted, was conventionally the key of *chants lugubres* and infernal possession. In classical music—certainly in Beethoven and Schubert, to a lesser degree in Haydn and Mozart, and possibly in Handel and Bach—A flat major's amiability may also owe something to the fact that it is the passive flat submediant to C minor, which to all classical composers, and pre-eminently to Beethoven, was a key of strife.

That the opening theme of opus 110 has affinities with the hidden song of opus 109's first movement and with its consummatory aria is immediately obvious to the ears and senses, if not to the intellect. It too is built on a pattern of falling thirds and rising fourths; but whereas the aria of opus 109 falls and then rises, the arching theme of opus 110 aspires gently up from C to D flat to E flat to F, and so down to the seventh of the dominant:

Ex. 108

Opus 109's sarabande rhythm is replaced by a metrical formula (illustrated in the first two bars of the above example) which carries us forward and is recurrent. The tune is unambiguously a song, gracious in its equilibrium, the more so because the bass line is in inversion with the treble, the two enclosing the inner parts in gentle euphony. The harmony is consonant: tonic and dominant, with a touch of sub-dominant. The first symmetrical clause consists of 2 + 2 bars which falter into a trill on the dominant seventh, and resolve by way of a quasi-vocal turn into a balancing clause. This also consists of 2 + 2 bars, but modifies the original pattern. Bar 5, instead of falling through a third and rising a fourth, ascends through both third and fourth in a rhythm that floats across the beat (6/8 through a 3/4 pulse); the sixth bar descends in the same crotchet–minim rhythm as the second bar, but by way of an appoggiatura sigh, rather than from consonance to consonance. The next two bars again precisely balance the previous two: the theme *falls* through a dominant arpeggio in the 6/8 metre, then rises a fourth. There is a further difference from the first four-bar clause. That had been harmonized in four real, quasi-vocal parts; now the theme is in single notes in the right hand, while the left hand accompanies with a simple pulsation of semiquavers, alternating tonic with dominant seventh chords. The aria of opus 109 fused Blakean Innocence and Experience after having encompassed the turmoil of sonata; the innocence of this initiating song seems, in comparison, not too simple to be true, but at least Edenicly childlike. Its second clause, especially, with its tune floating across the semiquaver pulsation and its soft-sighing appoggiatura, is nostalgic, as though yearning for the presumed simplicities of a childhood unfallen, with dew on the grass. The wistfulness is enhanced during the next three bars, with a momentary flatwards modulation to the subdominant (bar 10). When the right hand's A flat arpeggio has reached its apex it resolves, not in a downward arpeggio, but in a turn that echoes bar 3, an octave higher. Another bar of ornamented resolution re-establishes the tonic. The cadence silverily evokes an antique world of Rococo charm, superficially recalling the music of Mozart's childhood.

For regression does, at least temporarily, seem to create a small haven or heaven: in the last measure of the 2 + 2, 2 + 2 + 4 period (bar 12), the arpeggiated elements of the song break into demisemiquaver divisions, which for seven bars dance through a wide range of the keyboard. The passage is all texture rather than theme, and it glitters like a trill-garlanded variation of opus 109. This sonority, however, is innocently consonant, without the overtone reverberations of opus 109; the effect—to extend the aqueous analogies—is of the twinkling flash of sunlight on *still* water (dew on the grass), or even, since the texture is so bodilessly light, of the flash of dust-motes dancing in sunlit *air*. Yet this translucent bliss is no longer infantile. Though the harmony is still the simplest possible alternation of tonics and dominants moving to the simplest possible dominant modulation, it is none the less defined in the left hand by three regular quaver chords a bar, separated by rests (bar 13). They sound like a soft drum: not ominous, but time-measuring, and thus conscious of mortality. Beethoven tries to reject this from his regressive dream: as the demisemiquaver figuration reaches to the skies, the left hand descends chromatically, taking us back to our tonic home and haven. A delaying passage of broken octaves creates caressing appoggiaturas and melts the time-obsessed metrical pulse (bars 20 ff.). The effect is still more regretfully beautiful in a decorated repeat, the appoggiaturas now overt, and sharply semitonic as well as whole-tone. The hesitant music this time achieves its dominant modulation, though not in root position. E flat tonic first inversion and dominant seventh second inversion oscillate on G and F (derived from the appoggiaturas), with their mirror inversion in the bass. After flirtings with the enhanced dominant B flat, the two hands separate, the bass falling through a chain of trills while the treble stretches up through spread chords of the tenth, off-beat (bars 25–8).

Eventually the trills resolve in a turn, and descend to the E flat triad in root position. The right hand melody jumps from its high B flat through two octaves and a third; and the second subject begins as a counteraction to the first subject's dreamy song, thereby reversing the conventional relationship between first and second subjects:

Ex. 109

The second subject is hardly a theme. True, it is more assertive than the song tune, because built on fragments of ascending scales which stress the dominant's sharp seventh before falling through fourth or fifth from the apex of the ascents. The upward tendency is undermined, however, by the fact that the accompanying figuration consists of pulsing semiquavers, with a bass line descending in contrary motion to the treble. Compared with the liquid sonorities of the movement thus far, the texture is harsh, yet also fragmented. Energy, let alone aggression, cannot be sustained; the scales break off on a 6–5 chord, and the dotted rhythm of the first bar leads to a chromaticized cadence with *fioriture* in demisemiquavers. Tonics and dominants undulate in parallel tenths, and the undulation again denies any dominant assertion, since the rhythm floats across the barlines, and semiquavers veil the triads with a haze of appoggiaturas.

After this irresolute end to the exposition, Beethoven meanders into the development by the most rudimentary means: the pendulum-swaying E flat triad simply droops down a tone to D flat (bar 39), cancelling with one very unfell swoop any vestige of the dominant approach in bars 29–30. A further semitonal descent takes us to F minor, and to a development that needs no more than sixteen bars! Moreover this development could hardly be simpler in its methods. The theme, always clearly on top, is restricted to the falling third and rising fourth, and to the rhythmic formula of the opening bars. It moves sequentially down the scale, instead of up, during the first four bars, the accompaniment consisting of the semiquaver chords typical of the *second* half of the exposition's theme. The music sounds darker in its F minor tonality, though hardly more intense, since melodic, harmonic and rhythmic structure are more rather than less rudimentary, and there are no sharpwards modulations. From bar 44 the accompaniment transforms its chords into semiquaver scales derived from the second subject motive. They sound less innocent, even slightly sinister, in their rises and falls of tension as well as of pitch. None the less they remain continuously lyrical, compared with their fragmented appearances in the exposition. The melodic periods move in two-bar sequences, lapsing into the passive security of D flat major, the flat submediant. Though it soon changes to its relative, B flat minor, this proves to be not a darker permutation of the F minor the development had started from, but an approach to the dominant seventh of A flat.

The beginning of the recapitulation is incorporated at bar 54 within these developmental sequences, so that—as with the recapitulation of opus 109's first movement—we are absorbed in it before we realize what has happened. The song theme is in the right hand at the same pitch, though slightly more thickly scored, and with the undulation of the third bar chromaticized to effect a dominant modulation which is immediately cancelled. The accompaniment transfers the dancing demisemiquavers warmly to the middle of the keyboard, where the song itself appears in the next four bars, with demisemiquaver octaves glinting on top. This time there is a decorated transitional bar modulating to the subdominant for the second clause. D flat major changes enharmonically to C sharp minor, and then to its relative, E major, for the dancing dust-motes or watery sun-flashing episode (bar 70).

Flickering over the soft drum-beat, the demisemiquavers sound yet more luminous in this celestial key which, being enharmonically identical with F flat, is really the flat submediant to the home tonic.

Beethoven adds an extra bar to find his way back, through the parallel thirds and clinging broken octaves, to that tonic. The figuration in tenths creates melting false relations before the second subject reappears, with its contrary motion scales, in A flat. This is conventional enough; but what happens at the end of the veiled cadence is fascinating and profound. The music seems to be fading offbeat into a haze of double appoggiaturas (D flat and B natural to C, F and D natural to E flat). Then, with the right hand floating high, the decorative D naturals suddenly acquire harmonic significance, and are accompanied by dominant seventh chords of E flat in second inversion. It seems that Beethoven is now reluctant to submit to his Edenic dream; even at this moment between sleeping and waking the music tries to aspire sharpwards towards the dominant it had relinquished in the exposition. But in the fourth bar (100) of this 'false' dominant the bass falls again to the flat seventh of the dominant ninth of A flat, and through five bars descending chords subside, haltingly on the second beat, through F minor to a simple dominant–tonic close:

Ex. 110

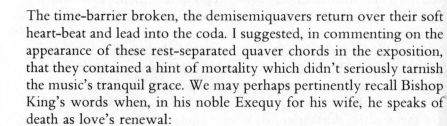

The time-barrier broken, the demisemiquavers return over their soft heart-beat and lead into the coda. I suggested, in commenting on the appearance of these rest-separated quaver chords in the exposition, that they contained a hint of mortality which didn't seriously tarnish the music's tranquil grace. We may perhaps pertinently recall Bishop King's words when, in his noble Exequy for his wife, he speaks of death as love's renewal:

> But hark! My pulse like a soft drum
> Beats my approach, tells thee I come.

Now, in this coda, there is again a synthesis of love and death, and of
Innocence and Experience, in that the song theme is intertwined with
the (sometimes chromaticized) rising scales of the second subject, to
cadence on a dissonant quadruple suspension. The pain of the dissonance is acute; yet the resolution is offbeat, suspended in air. As a
whole the coda might be said to effect, melodically and harmonically,
a 'grown-up' permutation of the wistfulness inherent in the exposition, though Beethoven cannot and would not want to embrace Henry
King's Christian resignation.

   The first movement of opus 109 extravagantly opposes the contrarieties of Innocence and Experience, and hints in its coda at how
they may and must be reconciled. The first movement of opus 110
begins as an innocent song which, being also a sonata, must contain
elements of dubiety; and arrives at a coda that suggests that Experience
may become patent. The scherzo and slow movement are comic and
tragic projections of this incipient grown-upness, which makes possible the consummatory finale; significantly the three movements are
played without a break. In one sense the scherzo is still innocent, for it
is peasant-like, folky, indeed childish in that it begins with a children's
singing game, *Unser Katz had Kaz'lin g'habt*. The tune 'happens' to
consist of a descending minor scale that inverts the hopefully rising
scale of the first movement's second subject, while at the same time
serving, in its inverted form, as bass to the tune. The mood is relatable
to Eliot's description, in *East Coker*, of peasant consciousness:

> joined in circles
> Rustically solemn or in rustic laughter
> Lifting heavy feet in clumsy shoes,
> Earth feet, loam feet, lifted in country mirth

The dark F minor tonality enacts the lumpishness, but is not to be
taken too seriously, especially since the first four bars move forward
on to the dominant, and the next four proceed in contrary-motion
arpeggios instead of scales, cadencing in, not merely on, the dominant,
C major. After the double bar C major becomes the dominant of F
minor again, but presses upwards in syncopation, by way of a dominant of E flat, to the relative major, A flat. The descending scale at

this point turns into another popular song, known in Germany as *Ich bin lüderlich* and in England as *Old John Cobbleham*. It is repeated in the tonic minor; but ends in frustrated cadences, separated by silences:

Ex. 111

The G minor triad gives an irresolutely Dorian touch to F minor, and the comic disruption is enhanced by violent contrasts of dynamics.

This scherzo is clownishly funny but is not, like the scherzo of opus 106, parodistic. Beethoven does not patronize his peasants, for what he is concerned with is the peasant in us all. Tovey convincingly suggests that the potency of the music is in part due to the fact that the curious sforzando on the C major chord in bar 8 implies that the rhythm is that of a gavotte, with bar 1 being preliminary and with the main accents in bars 2 and 4. Although danced in aristocratic circles, the gavotte was low in origin, and Beethoven makes its typical metrical ambiguity a source of *his* low comedy and of unsuspected depths within the psyche: the slip on the banana skin that is endemic to the human predicament. The profounder implications of this become manifest in the extraordinary trio which, once more in the flat submediant (D flat), is a two-part invention with two themes in contrary motion. We now see, or rather hear, that the peasant isn't necessarily earthbound in the loam: for while one theme leaps up in crotchet pulse in thirds and tenths, separated by rests, the other descends in gabbling quavers, alternating thirds and fourths, the generic intervals of the first movement's song:

Ex. 112

The cross-rhythmed, cross-handed effect, with explosive accents and sudden pianos, is crazy; earthiness dissipates, as the flickering quavers take *off* and blow *up*. The music vividly suggests a clown capering around, blipping people and himself with his bladder; and reminds us that a Fool, though clownish, may also be holy. After sixteen bars we have modulated to G flat, then in the next sixteen to its relative, E flat minor. Two extra bars (74 and 75) of dislocated accents point the metrical ambiguity of the tipsy gavotte as they lurch back to D flat, and to a da capo of the first sixteen bars, an octave lower. Four extra bars fade out on the quaver wriggle; that these four bars are marked *una corda* underlines the association of the Fool with divine possession. Certainly we hear the scherzo's da capo with different ears after the trio's lunacy. Its metrical and harmonic ambiguities now sound weird as well as comic: which prepares us for the mystery of the coda. Chords of tonic, dominant first inversion, tonic, subdominant, tonic are separated by bars of silence; the final dominant renders overt the metrical ambiguity of the gavotte, as it serves as upbeat to a tonic *major* triad.

There is a further surprise, and mystery, for this resolutory chord proves to be no such thing. It turns into a dominant to B flat minor and carries us, with no break, from comedy to tragedy. The opening of the adagio is again *una corda*, and is in recitative style, recalling Bach's Passion music. But whereas Bach's Passion can be identified with an event in historical time, the crucifixion of Christ, Beethoven, like Blake, is more introvertly concerned with the crucified Christ within his own psyche, and potentially within that of every man. None the less the movement opens with 'objective' reference to the grandeur of the High Baroque: the screwed-up double-dotted rhythm over a tonic pedal; the A natural of the diminished seventh grinding against the pedal note; the false relation between minor and major third; and a weeping appoggiatura:

Ex. 113

The next bar darkly declines from C flat to A flat minor, cadencing in a
spread dominant seventh: which expands into unaccompanied recitative, alchemizing the accents of the human voice into pianistic terms.
The line is Bachian in that, although monophonic, it is pregnant with
harmonic implications: the weeping appoggiaturas from A flat to G,
from F flat to E flat, from D flat to C flat, the last being in fact
harmonized and carrying us to the flat submediant F flat, enharmonically changed to E major. The rapid shifts of both key and tempo
spring from the music's dramatic enactment. Beethoven evokes a
Christ–Hero's physical presence and, on the repeated A naturals,
invents a new pianistic technique, emulating the clavichord's *Bebung*,
whereby he makes percussively instrumental tones speak 'vocally' in
the tongues of men or of angels. There is a momentary change,
perhaps as God becomes humanly incarnate, from *una corda* to *tutte le
corde*, but *una corda* returns as the recitative cadences from F flat (E

major, by way of two diminished sevenths, to A flat minor. The final unaccompanied cadence-figure, with appoggiatura and expiring fourth, might be a Bachian sigh of the dying Christ on the Cross; one senses the drooping of head, arms and hands as the voice, translated into instrumental terms, breathes its *consummatum est*.

The drama of this wonderful passage may be deeply introspective; none the less it is significant that the conventions it calls on—those of Bach's Passion musics—are operatic. The interior drama of sonata is being reborn, as Beethoven reverses musical history, into the more objective symbolism of the Baroque; personal tragic experience is thus distanced and 'universalized'. When the speaking recitative merges into what Beethoven calls *Arioso dolente* or *Klagender Gesang* this mode of tragic lament is sustained. In the darkest, flattest A flat minor, and in vast bars of 12/16, an accompaniment of pulsing E flats thickens to thirds on C flat, then to A flat minor triads: an immensely slow, gelid permutation of the semiquaver accompaniment to the first movement's song. Indeed the Passion aria that limps from the darkness itself has affinities with the first movement, in that it combines the sighing appoggiatura from strong to weak beat with the second subject's scale, at first always drooping, with no positive upward thrust. The rhythm falters with weariness as accents are tied over the beats (see end of Ex. 113).

But the bass slowly rises to a 6–4 cadence, and the next four-bar phrase irons out the melody's havering into straight dotted crotchets moving *up* the scale. The convolutions return to the line, high up, with a cadence into C flat major. The quiver of life within the wintry darkness serves rather to deepen the pain; semitonal appoggiaturas weep more bitterly as we move through the subdominant, D flat minor, back to the A flat minor tonic. The declining scale in the melody is usually tied draggingly across the beat; insidiously an inner part, wailing in semiquavers, adds to the semitonal dissonance, as one appoggiatura resolves on to another. Though the anguish is acute, it is disciplined in the widely falling arch of the line, in the regularity of the pulse, and in the tonal symmetry. No one but Beethoven could have written this music; if one tries to think of parallels they can only be in Bach's Passion arias (*Es ist vollbracht* from St John), or in some pieces of Mozart (such as Pamina's *Ach, ich fühl's*) which were influenced by his study of Bach.

Beethoven distinguishes this passage from the free, quasi-improvisatory recitative which preludes it by terming it *arioso*, by which Baroque composers meant an idiom halfway between the speaking voice of recitative and the formal lyricism of aria. Though it sounds rather more like aria than arioso, Beethoven's intention was probably to indicate the embryonic nature of its lyricism. Arioso was reserved by Bach and Handel for moments of peculiar significance, when experience was in the making, as heroic people who mattered because of their heroism went mad, fell in love, contemplated murder or suicide. Beethoven's arioso is similarly experience in action, and is certainly heroic, in that life attempts rebirth from a dark night of the soul. The sustained quality of the weary lyricism, the continuity of the figuration, ensure that song survives. The octaval figure with which the arioso ends is to reveal itself later as a backwards inversion of the original theme. Immediately, it allows the arioso to find repose in three repeated, separated A flats, through which the soft drum or heart-beats of the first movement may distantly echo.

There is no doubt that the arioso begins and ends in A flat minor, but Beethoven notates it with six flats, not seven, writing in the F flats as necessary. This is odd, since he had used the seven-flat signature as early as the funeral march of his opus 26, and one would have thought the flatter the better, in this post-crucifixion music of the winter solstice. Perhaps he wished to indicate the 'archaic' tendency of this convention by preserving in the key signature this modal survival, as did composers in the late seventeenth and early eighteenth centuries. In any case the final five notes of the arioso, being in octaves, are ambiguously minor or major: so from their drum beats the transition to the life-affirming fugue, which is again in A flat major, can be spontaneous.

The arioso, we have remarked, is notated in 12/16, recalling, in spite or perhaps because of its enervated valetudinarianism, Bach's association of this time-signature (and the more familiar 12/8) with 'transcendental' melodies of vast span, and with a metrical 'squaring of the circle' in a quaternity of trinities. The fugue, which also looks Bachian in texture, transmutes this very slow 12/16 into a moderate 6/8; and the ear readily accepts this traditionally dancing rhythm as a return to light and life, after the arioso's purgatorial pain. Such light and life is, however, dependent on the arioso's deathly dark, as the fugue's evolution will demonstrate, and as is implicit in the fact that the fugal subject is not a new theme, but the original song of the first movement, shorn of its first note so that it begins with the godly rising fourth, and rhythmically reduced to its simplest terms (see Ex. 108). We have seen that the song has affinities with themes in the arioso and the scherzo. In the first movement the song, though a sonata, was vernally emergent. Then, poised between the poles of comedy (the scherzo) and tragedy (the arioso), it grows up. The innocuous happiness of the first movement's first subject, the dangerous hilarity of the scherzo (especially its trio), and the *pathos* and *agon* of the arioso become one, in attaining the multiplicity-in-unity of a fugue that is vocally conceived. We even have a verbal gloss on the fugue theme's regenerative significance, for its rising fourths and falling thirds are similar to those to which, in the Credo of the exactly contemporary Missa Solemnis, Beethoven set the words *Et expecto resurrectionem mortuorum*. We have seen that the theme is latent in the Aria of opus 109, and patent in its fifth variation.

The opening statement of the fugue subject displays the spacious simplicity of its leaping fourths and falling thirds, the noble arch of the melody, the level rhythm and consistent figuration that give it its Bach-like stability:

Ex. 114

But the flowing quavers of the countersubject, which is directly derived from the arioso's lament (compare the top notes of bar 13 in the arioso with the left hand quavers in bars 24–25 in the fugue), complicate the theme's open quality; and do so the more disturbingly when, from bar 29, the third quaver of each triplet is tied across the beat. The resultant dissonant suspensions do not, however, destroy the music's forward sweep, which carries us through three 'real' entries, from tonic to dominant and back, from tonic to subdominant and back. After a brief sequence in the relative minor, the tonic is restored with a sonorous bass entry in octaves. Chromatic passing notes in the inner parts further increase momentum, incarnating the passion, if not Passion, of Experience. Yet these exacerbations are absolved in the continuously songful texture; and although tonal movement grows wider, Beethoven does not at this point depart from the accepted cyclical modulations of the Baroque age. Tonic, relative, dominant, subdominant and its relative are his tonal props; even when (bars 60–5) the sequences move rapidly, arriving at strifeful C minor, a further affirmation is effected, since the theme enters fortissimo in bass octaves, its first note augmented for stress. Beethoven extends the pattern of rising fourths and falling thirds through a whole octave; and although the countersubject in the upper parts creates sharp dissonances through its tied notes, the spacious, unbroken, up-thrusting music triumphs over the arioso's desolation. The freedom of tonal movement—Beethoven now strays into darker regions such as F and B flat minors—is ballasted by the conformity of the figuration and by the incessant pull of the tonic. In bar 92 this is spelled out as a dominant pedal in tight-stressed cross-rhythm, leading to a fortissimo return of the theme in bass octaves, imitated in stretto. After a chromatic descent in the bass, the motive of rising fourths and falling thirds jubilantly rises. The upwards prances extend beyond their thematic shape, pressing up the scale to a high A flat. A half-close occurs on the dominant, its seventh following a trill and turn which spreads into a quaver arpeggio, down and up, diminuendo:

Ex. 115

Up to this point the fugue, though it has embraced dissonant pain and rhythmic stress within its noble arches, has swept inexorably towards an affirmation which paradoxically owes its sense of liberation to its discipline: thereby demonstrating a theological truth in musical terms.

What happens now, however, is apparent frustration. The D flat of the dominant seventh of A flat changes identity (in implication though not in notation) to C sharp: so the chord becomes a German sixth that resolves on to a 6–4 of G minor. The falling arpeggio is notated in 12–16 semiquavers, slower than the fugue's quavers, indeed at *L'istesso tempo di Arioso*: which is recalled, wonderfully modified. Its tonality, G minor, is a semitone lower than the original A flat minor, and we feel this as almost physically depressive, especially after the A flat major refulgence of the fugue. The scoring of the thudding minor triads sounds viscid, evoking 'the dark time of the year'; and although the arioso has the same drooping contours as before, it is cringingly broken, its appoggiaturas approached by rests that (if one sings the passage to oneself) are literally catches in the breath, so that sighs become sobs, even whimpers.

Ermattet, klagend Beethoven writes on the score; and the music is still exhausted, tired out, in the answering phrase that balances declension with an ascent. For this is no longer in straight dotted crotchets but in a rhythmically tortuous figure that stretches limbs and nerves to breaking point; there is a gasp before each thematic note. Release is promised in the leaps that approach the cadence into the relative; but with a shift to C minor, and then back to G minor, the line sinks dolorously to the earth. Beethoven begins each note of the descent offbeat, notating it as two semiquavers tied but with changing fingering, a doleful permutation of the 'visionary' *Begung* effect in the recitative. The Neapolitan A flat in bar 120 has no counterpart in the original statement; again its weary weight is as physical as Bach's depiction of Christ's suffering on the Cross. Indeed the Arioso as a whole is deeply related to Beethoven's own 'incarnation' of Christs's (and his) physical and spiritual laceration in the Crucifixus of his Missa Solemnis. Significantly, the arioso's physicality, even when *perdendo le forze* in pianissimo, has employed *tutte le corde*. *Una corda* comes only with the arioso's extinction, when its now listlessly lifting fourth is stretched to a minor sixth and the expected minor cadence is translated to a whispered major. The octaval tailpiece is now notated as semiquavers, one on the last of each group of three in 12–16, separated by silences. Though we still feel this rhythmically as a catch in the breath, its thematic import, as a modified backwards inversion of the fugue subject and of the song, its now patent.

The effect of this reminiscence of the arioso is subtle. In context we do not hear it simply, or perhaps at all, as a denial of the fugue, but

rather as a recall of the suffering which made fulfilment possible. The
Baroque classicality of the convention has something to do with this.
Though this Christ figure is Beethoven, and potentially also you and I,
his Passion and passions are objectified in being presented in (however
sublimated) operatic terms. One feels physically the weight of the
downward-tending crucified limbs; one whimpers in the throat, stifles
in the chest, as though one were indeed singing-speaking and crying-
dying. Yet, as in Bach, the physicality of the music proves inseparable
from its metaphysical effects. The tailpiece ends on a G major triad
which, still *una corda*, slowly swells, still syncopated on the third
semiquaver, the chord gradually thickened, then dissolving in a rising
arpeggio. This at last straightens out the dislocated, breathless rhythm,
which should probably quicken its semiquaver–quaver–semiquaver
arpeggio imperceptibly, to bring us back to the original tempo when
the fugue returns in its 6/8 quavers. The swelling G major triads in this
famous passage are often driven by pianists to a frightening fortissimo.
But although Beethoven indicates a crescendo, he does not tell us how
far it should go, nor does he cancel his *una corda* marking. The stifled
effect of *una corda* playing at a strong dynamic is hardly possible on a
modern piano. None the less the effect Beethoven intended is wonderfully appropriate to what is happening in the music. Only if we have
felt the weight of the smothering earth can the rebirth of the
fugue—*nach und nach wieder auflebend*, as Beethoven puts it—be fully
experienced. Here is the transition from the arioso to the fugue's
return:

Ex. 116

Beethoven's control of tonality is here near-miraculous: for whereas
the arioso's G minor had sounded deeply depressive in relation to the

initial A flat minor, these G major triads suggest G's function as upward-tending leading note to A flat. Indeed that is what they prove to be: though not immediately, since the fugue steals back in a transparent G major texture, *sempre una corda*, offering a glimpse of a heaven beyond the horizon. That the fugal theme is in strict inversion, with four entries alternating between the 'fundamental' tones of fifth and tonic, may contribute to this visionary effect, for it sounds, in its glassy scoring, as though from the other side of a mirror. In the Apocryphal Acts of St John, Christ sings 'A mirror am I to thou that perceivest me'; the inverted fugue, now in G major, remote from the basic A flat and associated by Beethoven as by Bach with a state of blessedness, does in context sound like a re-cognition and re-velation: God shows us ourselves, as we truly are in the sight of him. Nor can it be fortuitous that the theme of the fugue inverted proves to be similar to the marvellous phrase to which, in his Mass, Beethoven set the words *Dona nobis pacem* (in the fugue a falling fourth is followed by a rising third; in the *Dona* a falling sixth is succeeded by a rising third). But the *Dona nobis*, Beethoven tells us, was a 'prayer for inner *and outer* peace' (italics added). From his visionary moment of *raptus* he must return to the world, reborn, to die again; and what happens in the rest of the sonata is another miracle which inverts the process whereby, in the St John Passion, Bach alchemized the crown of thorns into a rainbow. With the second fugal entry the translucent diaphony moves to the dominant, garnering softly dissonant suspensions and chromatic passing notes from the countersubject; when the third entry appears it creates not only a subdominant, but also a minor, modulation. The key signature changes from the benedictory G major to G minor, key of the second arioso's desolate lament, the texture drunkenly involving a hierarchy of speeds:

Ex. 117

The original theme, now the right way up, is in the treble, in augmentation; bass and alto have the theme, also the original way up, in diminution and in stretto, with some tonal and rhythmic

modifications, perfect fourths being sometimes diminished, and
entries syncopated across barlines. The metrical excitation grows
crazier as stretti proliferate and tonality strays cyclically through G, C,
F minor, and back to C minor. In this riot of counterpoint, at once
extravagant and controlled, we are irresistibly reminded of the tipsy
clown who had juggled hazardously on his tightrope in the scherzo's
trio. The effect is 'high', but the music stabilizes as the alto sings,
gradually approaching the original speed, an inversion of the theme
with the fourths stretched to fifths, perfect and diminished. We are
returned from a celestial vision (*una corda*) to the world (*tutte le corde*),
though the question as to which is 'real' is left open. Certainly, having
had that vision, we can sing our Song with a difference. The A flat
major key signature is restored; the theme, in its original form at its
original speed, chants in bass octaves with flowing semiquavers on top
(bars 168 ff.). The lower notes of the semiquaver figuration at first
shadowily pick out an inversion of the theme, but such vestiges of
counterpoint are gradually absorbed, until the melody blazes proudly
in the treble, usually doubled in thirds, while the left hand's surging
semiquavers distantly recall the sun-flickering demisemiquavers of
the first movement. (Their tempi will be approximately the same.)
The first movement's dream-song is thus apotheosized as the theme is
grandly expanded, the top note of each crest being augmented before
the scalewise descent. The right hand harmonizes its song with
thickened chords, underlining the basic modulations to dominant and
subdominant; the left hand figuration grows more abandoned, freer
because more widely separated from the right hand's theme. The
ultimate climax begins in bar 194, when the tonic resolution overlaps
with a new thematic statement. The next eight bars pierce the song
with subdominant and dominant passing dissonances high over a
thundering tonic pedal—a positive, affirmative reminiscence of the
titanic Tyger of opus 106:

Ex. 118

The quadruple appoggiatura in bars 201–2 is identical with the painfully *regretful* dissonance in the penultimate bar of the first movement.
That cadence had prophesied the dream's 'adult' fulfilment; in this
cadence fulfilment is attained, here and now, in the flesh, and pain and
joy seem indistinguishable. The Song ends with a threefold repetition
of the downward scale, each sequence rising to counteract the melodic
fall. The climactic dissonant suspension is repeated on B flat to form
the last of the sequences, and so moves up to C: at which point
dissonance dissipates. The sonata flames out in a scintillation of tonic
major arpeggios. The dreamily glittering arpeggios of the first movement are now a crown that has been 'well and truly' earned.

The conclusions of opus 109 and 110 are thus complementary. Opus
109 ends with an Aria that 'reconciles the Eagle', distilling passion and
pain into peace *sub specie aeternitatis.* Opus 110 discovers, in the
inverted recapitulation of the fugue, a moment outside Time, from
which it returns in painful jubilation. The yea-saying of the final pages
contains a note of terror, as does the last variation of opus 109; but in
opus 110 this is not so much in awe of the 'otherness' of God as in
prideful joy at human potentiality. The first movement's dream has
been metamorphosed into a vision, through the agency of man's
peasant earthiness and of a clown who is also a holy Fool. It is
significant that the music should remind us again of that Clown–Fool
when Beethoven, after the G major vision, triumphantly reasserts his
humanity. Opus 109 is the creation, discovery or revelation of the
Aria, and concerns man's need for God; opus 110 musically demonstrates that God, no less, needs his human incarnation. Beethoven
gives more explicit formulation to this discovery in his re-creation, in
his Missa Solemnis, of the traditional doctrines of the Church.

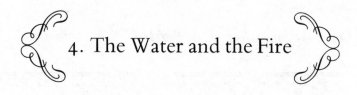

4. The Water and the Fire

Piano sonata opus 111 in C minor and major

Pure olive oil is beaten for the light. We shall be
beaten and bruised, but in order to glow—not to grovel.

The Ten Rungs of Hasidic Lore trans. MARTIN BUBER

Though opus 111 has only two movements, it traverses the total range
of Beethoven's experience, as manifest in the previous sequence of
sonatas. The violence of the maestoso introduction, after the hard-
won serenities and jubilations of opus 109 and 110, is at first a shock.
The sonata opens, as Tovey put it, with an intensity of passion
nowhere greater in Beethoven; and exhibits a discipline and control
equal to it. The initial gesture lurches through the tritonal chord of the
diminished seventh (which for Baroque opera composers was or could
be terrifying), in the double-dotted rhythm of the French overture
(which for Baroque theatre composers was majestically heroic). But
although this reference to the old world of aristocratic autocracy
brings with it a note of regal grandeur, heroic conventions are reinterpreted in subjective terms. Sinews are tightened to defy not merely
any worldly lords and masters but the very gods themselves;
prophetically, we see Beethoven on his death-bed, clenched fist raised
to the thundering heavens:

Ex. 119

The assault is the wilder because it starts in the wrong key: the diminished seventh is in G minor, offbeat. The melodic line descends from E flat to C, resolves in a fierce trill and turn on to B natural, which moves up to C and D in three (initially soft) hammer-blows, changing in the process from a G major triad to a first inversion of the dominant of C minor. The last chord is stressed by being approached through a wide-flung arpeggio. The whole gesture is striking: an appropriate metaphor because this is Beethoven at the Promethean smithy. Yet that the music is different from and more mysterious than middle period Beethoven, even in its mood of defiance, is evident: for although we have arrived *at* what is to be the home tonic, we pass *through* it. The downward pounce is repeated in cyclical sequences that also descend, from G to C to F to B flat minors. At this stage there is nothing to tell our ears that C minor might be a goal.

In these furiously repeated gestures the silences are hardly less momentous than the sounds; if one listens through the rests in bars 2 and 4 one knows what the metaphor means that calls silence 'palpable'. But when we have reached B flat minor (the lowest point in the cyclical descent), there is a rapid diminuendo to a texture now continuously sustained. Although quiet, the music is scarcely less tense, since it is still in the double-dotted rhythm which, instead of being a proud assertion addressed to the world outside (as in the Baroque era), has become an introverted flexing of nerves and muscles. One can almost *see* this on the printed page: for as the dynamics decrease the top line closes in diatonically, in three scalewise descents through a third (inverting the rising third scales of the first 'gesture'), while the bass line rises chromatically to meet it. Eventually, at a further cyclical decline from B flat to E flat minor, the chords huddle in the middle of the keyboard, as though hugging the pain. The effect is the more disturbing because the metrical periods, crossing the barlines, are irregular, vacillating between 3/4 and 4/4.

Rhythm, harmony, texture and spacing in this opening paragraph are directly comparable with the music Beethoven creates, in the Missa Solemnis, for the Crucifixion itself. The parallel is as close as that between the inverted G major version of the fugue in opus 110 and the Mass's *Dona nobis pacem*, and both passages point to the identity between Beethoven's personal experience and his ostensibly public statements; there is something strangely moving in the thought of Beethoven scattering manuscript pages of these intimate sonatas at random within the score of his grand Mass. Moreover opus 111 is to proceed, in its intimate manner, through the same purgatorial pilgrimage as the Mass: as begins to be manifest when the E flat minor diminished seventh, approached by way of a luminous D flat major triad, does not establish itself as a true modulation but shifts, as the bass moves down two octaves, to a 6–4 A flat *major* triad. The bass, still in the screwed-up double-dotted rhythm, creeps up chromatically to E natural and the diminished seventh of F minor. The top line still falls, the bass still rises, from E natural to A flat. Yet the nerves, however stretched, don't reach breaking-point. The bass stabilizes on an F minor triad in first inversion, and changes chromatically into a German sixth on A flat: which at long last resolves on to the dominant of C minor. Beethoven emphasizes this as a point of arrival by abandoning the double-dotted rhythm in favour of level quavers reiterating dominant Gs, with sforzando accents across the beats. The scalewise descent of the bass line from G to C, with percussive passing dissonances, is answered by inversion in the treble, moving through G, A natural, B natural to C. We don't hear this merely as an inversion of the bass stressing the harmonically resolutory sharp seventh; we also hear it as a potential, though as it turns out illusory, completion of the upward three-note motive of the original 'gestures' in bars 2 and 4. Tonal and rhythmic ambiguity seem to be conquered; the four equal crotchets a bar and the pull of the leading note are not seriously compromised by the reminder of the double-dotted rhythm and the original G minor diminished seventh on the last beat of bar 12. Beethoven emphasizes these last three bars' assertion of order by repeating them an octave lower, in which register the sonority is of course darker, the dissonant appoggiaturas of the bass murkier. So order proves equivocal, and the repeated quavers of the dominant pedal grow more obtrusive until they merge into a written-out trill. The violence of the introduction has discovered C minor, and in the low trill has released the growl of the Blakean Tyger. One might almost say that the sonata is 'about' the metempsychosis of the tiger's growl into angels' fluttering wings in the trills of the Arietta. The trills climb from bottom to top of the keyboard; in reference to spiritual experience 'high' and 'low' are metaphors which have a long history in European music.

Even Beethoven never composed music that more vehemently grips one, tiger-like, by the scruff of the neck than this introduction, with its near-schizophrenic duality between downward-thrusting, tonally neutral diminished sevenths, and regular upward scales stabilized with sharp sevenths. Yet the introduction's gripping effect is inseparable from its potency in relation to the whole sonata; this reminds us that for Blake the Tyger is Energy, a force 'beyond' good and evil, yet essential to any act of creation. In August 1812 Beethoven remarked to Bettina Brentano that 'music ought to strike sparks off the heart of a man'; similarly Blake employs the metaphor of the smithy:

> Tyger, tyger, burning bright,
> In the forests of the night,
> What immortal hand or eye
> Could frame thy fearful symmetry?
>
> In what distant deeps or skies
> Burnt the fire of thine eyes?

On what wings dare he aspire?
What the hand dare seize the fire?

What the hammer? What the chain?
In what furnace was thy brain?
What the anvil? What dread grasp
Dare its deadly terrors clasp?

In opus 111 the Tyger as Divine Smith forges a consummatory experience from the sparks hammered off in those initial gestures, the
thematic bases of which may be schematized as follows:

Ex. 120

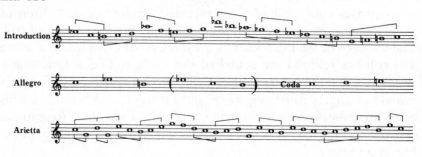

Everything that happens in the sonata may be related to or directly
derived from one or another of these seeds.

What immediately occurs is that the bass trills change from demisemiquavers to semiquavers, their pace rather more than doubled to
Allegro con brio ed appassionato. The basic common time of the *Allegro*
should, indeed, be only slightly faster than twice that of the introduction's common time: which means that the *Maestoso* should not be too
slow to maintain inner momentum. Reference to the traditional relationship in classical music between an introductory *grave* and *allegro*
should not be lost sight of, however 'subjectively' Beethoven may
have transformed it; he hardly allows us to forget it, since he makes the
derivation of the Allegro theme from the introduction unmistakable.
Duplicated in octaves, the introduction's written-out trills end with an
upward thrust through the sharp sixth and seventh to the tonic—the
cadential motive of the introduction in double diminution or, since the
tempo is now twice as quick, in effect in quadruple diminution. After
two and a half beats' 'palpable' silence the main theme enters, also in

octaves; and pianists will know that, probably for physiological reasons, it seems to be easier to play forcefully, as well as more loudly, in octave doublings than with one hand unisonally. Beginning with the thrust up the scale at the same pitch (G to C), the theme moves in crotchets through a rising minor third, followed by a fall through a diminished fourth:

Ex. 121

The pitches are identical with those of the opening 'gesture' of the introduction, though not in the same order; the stress on the diminished fourth jaggedly increases tension. Though derived from the introduction, this theme also harks back some time in Beethoven's life-history, for he first sketched it out in 1802, at the time of the spiritual crisis contemporary with the so-called Heiligenstadt Testament. That crisis was resolved only through the Promethean conflict of the Eroica Symphony, which used the theme of Beethoven's Prometheus Variations for piano as a basis for the symphony's chaconne finale. According to his sketch-book, Beethoven associated the theme that eventually became opus 111's first allegro motive with Prometheus's brother, Atlas. He too was punished by Zeus for insubordination, and was forced to bear on his shoulders the weight of the world. Not surprisingly Beethoven the Insubordinate, who Prometheus-like stole from the gods the gift of fire and power, and who Atlas-like accepted his role as scapegoat for the world's woes, forged this theme in C minor, traditionally a key of strife, and nowhere more impressively so than in his early sonata opus 13 and, in his second period, in the Fifth Symphony, that epical celebration of the will's victory over chaos.

None the less this movement is not an attempt to revive battles which Beethoven had already fought triumphantly; it serves rather to remind us of the distance he had travelled. Despite the theme's aggressiveness, there is a curious hesitancy in its monophonic statement. There is a pause mark over the B natural at the bottom of the diminished fourth: after which Beethoven launches into the Atlas motive again, extending it to leap up a diminished seventh, and down through five quavers followed by four semiquavers of the diatonic scale, thereby inverting two basic motives of the introduction. The descending scale recurs, diminished to semiquavers; holds back in quavers; and surges forward in semiquavers for five and a half bars, at the end of which the four-note have become three-note scales, also diminishing and inverting a motive of the introduction. Leaps of tritone and major sixth separate the three-note descents, each beat marked with a sforzando accent that pounds counter to the scale pattern. These patterns create, within a still monodic texture, spread chords of the diminished seventh of C minor. The attempt at monophonic self-sufficiency—which might have produced a fugue subject—has failed. The would-be assertive line wavers, its rubato being notated. At the end of the monody the semiquavers sizzle ferociously upwards, only to plunge abruptly from the heights.

So Beethoven tries again. The Atlas motive rings on top, accompanied by homophonically pulsing quavers and a quasi-pizzicato bass, in sonata or even symphonic style. Yet sonata too proves abortive. The declining scale of the theme clashes sharply with the dominant pedal notes; its rhythm falters and slackens. Melody drifts into passage-work, with the scales in contrary motion grating against the pedal. The upward cadential scale in bass octaves no longer has the stabilizing force that characterized it in the introduction. It generates a passion that would burst bonds, and the nerves strain to control it. The passage (bars 16–17) calls for elastic muscles if it is to be performed with an appropriately tense exuberance: a collocation of noun and adjective that implies a typically Beethovenian paradox. Not surprisingly, energy again falters. The cadence that follows recalls the approach to C minor resolution in the introduction in that it too moves, *poco ritenente*, from a subdominant first inversion through a chromaticized, relatively emotive German sixth to a trill-embellished C minor 6–4.

After this second 'failure' Beethoven, back in tempo, assays another tack: a texture that embraces counterpoint without being fully fugal. He begins, in bar 19, in the manner of a two-part invention. The Atlas theme, in the right hand, is extended to incorporate the diminished seventh in flowing semiquavers, which also define a series of thematically falling four-note scales. The second voice, in bouncing quavers, is a permutation of the Atlas theme which leaps up through a perfect instead of down through an imperfect (diminished) fourth, and balances this with a descending minor third. As the two related motives interact between the hands they liberate energy, disciplined by both contrapuntal principle and tonal sequence. The main modulation, to the relative, is positive. Having arrived there, the parts proceed in double counterpoint, the Atlas motive (its descending fourth now perfect) in the left hand, the springing quavers in the right. Sequences carry us to F and B flat minors and to A flat major, with something of the harsh vigour of the fugal passages in opus 106. Yet the continuity and regularity of the figuration make the music cumulatively jubilant, until climax comes with the change of key signature to four flats (bar 28). The Atlas motive releases chains of semiquavers that rattle high on the keyboard (a far more scarifying noise on Beethoven's piano than on ours); and as the 'bouncing' sequences touch on B flat minor and D flat major, the lower notes push up chromatically from G to C. If one stresses the first note of each bar, the left hand defines the introduction's cadential scale, with the B flattened. Precisely the original cadential notes are echoed a semitone higher, in the original quaver pulse, at the end of bar 31.

This seems to be a modulation to D flat which stills the attempt at contrapuntal unity. But immense leaps from F *in alt* to the low bass D flat, then up from D natural to the C flat four octaves above, reassert the diminished seventh obsession, and approach a 6–4 cadence into A flat major. What follows is a second subject, in the flat submediant, thereby continuing the pattern of mediant relationships which is pervasive in Beethoven's sonatas after the Hammerklavier. The wild leaps that approach the second subject may hint that all is not well with it, though it seems to be at the opposite pole to the Atlas theme in that it falls through a tonic triad on to a sighing appoggiatura, and seems to be seeking a songfulness comparable with that of the first theme of opus 110, which is in the same key. But it lasts for precisely four and a half bars! Even its first two bars are hesitant, bringing back the dotted rhythm of the introduction, though in gentler form:

Ex. 122

Then the drooping contours dissipate in romantically irregular Chopinesque fioriture (groups of twelve and six) which peter out, *ritardando*, in quintuplet turns. The dominant pedal throughout these four bars changes only on the last semiquaver, to create a momentary touch of F minor; movement stills in an adagio bar that, in dotted upbeat rhythm, promises a lyrical return to A flat major. After an adagio beat and a half's silence, Beethoven smashes this dream of song with a fury of the introduction's diminished sevenths, spattered in *a tempo* semiquavers, in a black E flat minor:

Ex. 123

This outlandish key acts, however, as an enhanced dominant to A flat major, and introduces a codetta theme which is an extended and chromaticized version of the Atlas theme, stomping in the bass. After the familiar rising third–falling fourth motive (with the thirds now potently major and the fourths perfect), the theme stabs upwards, like a sword-thrust, through an A flat arpeggio in dotted rhythm. The frustrated Atlas theme seems to have become an heroic march, imbuing even the 'passive' flat submediant with energy. There is, however, a touch of ferocity in the semiquavers: which is enhanced when the extended Atlas theme is transferred to the top voice, accompanied by quaver chords and by semiquaver wriggles perhaps remotely derived from the quintuplet turns; if so, they are savagely metamorphosed. The arpeggiated sword-thrust is now rounded off with high trills and turns, directly recalling those in the introduction's sequences, but more frantic. Their screams are opposed to growling scales in the bass, as their top notes retrace the introduction's cadential ascent from dominant to tonic, with stressed leading note. Unlike the introduction, however, the exposition then explodes in chromaticized and contracted scales, racked by violent sforzandi: another sonority that would have been more alarming on Beethoven's piano than on ours. As it turns out, these scales, despite their leading notes, lead nowhere, since thumping A flat octaves return, with the exposition's repeat, to the tentative groping of the first bars. Beethoven's repetition of the exposition follows classical precedent, which may seem strange since the exposition has been so inwardly 'morphological'. None the less the repeat is not only necessary to the work's architectural proportions; it is also totally convincing experientially, for it maddeningly underlines the pain of process. Indeed it sounds developmental precisely because we know, the second time round, that growth will be frustrated, aspiration curbed. After the double bar the apparent A flat peroration is again baulked, this time by three beats' silence. Pregnant it certainly is; the more so when it is followed by a single offbeat G and another expectant emptiness. This is suddenly broken by the four-note upward scale with leading note, landing on a dominant first inversion of G. This sforzando initiates a development not the less momentous for being brief.

It starts softly, this time in double octaves, with the extended and chromaticized Atlas motive: the original rising minor third and descending diminished fourth lead into the sword-thrust arpeggio, now in G minor. Monody turns into fugato, the top and bottom voices of a three-part texture having the Atlas theme in augmentation, with the intervals either contracted or expanded: minor third becomes minor second, diminished fourth becomes diminished fifth, and rising fourth becomes rising sixth with cadential trill:

Ex. 124

The middle voice moves at the original tempo, but also has its intervals stretched; the rising diminished seventh recalls the original version of the theme. The texture generates extreme tension which, despite the low dynamic, is at once reinforced and distanced by the many-in-oneness of the counterpoint. Even the semiquaver scales are thematic, since they flow up or down through the introduction's fourths. The modulations defined by the cadential trills' pushing up from leading notes to tonics also follow the pattern of the introduction's cycle of diminished sevenths, falling from G to C to F minors. The same obsessive sequence is repeated when the Bach-like contrapuntal texture is ousted by a loudly syncopated assertion of a G minor diminished seventh, cancelling what had seemed to be an F minor cadence. The Atlas motive reappears in its original and most trenchant form, rising minor third and descending diminished fourth, overlapping in sequences veering between G, C and F minors, each thematic note harmonized with a diminished seventh, while broken arpeggios smoke upwards in the left hand. These arpeggios also establish, probably with the help of the sustaining pedal, a low dominant ostinato on G: so that what appears to be a passage of tritonal dissolution also directs energy towards the recapitulation. As in the first movements of opus 109 and 110, the recapitulation overlaps the development, which is hardly surprising since the whole movement, including the exposition's repeat, is development in the sense that it is life in process.

In bar 75 of the Allegro the descending scale inverts into the crucial approach upwards to the tonic, G, A natural, B natural, C. The shortened recapitulation begins with octaves, but immediately follows them with the chordally accompanied sonata-style version of the theme, with scales in contrary motion. The original passage (bars 16–17) is chromaticized in broken octaves; scatters in a Neapolitan arpeggio of D flat; and cadences in F minor for a repetition of the 'two-part invention', now in the subdominant but descending flatwards to D flat major, B flat minor and E flat minor. The climax is at the top of the keyboard, white hot, shrill with semiquavers in parallel tenths and thirds. The highest notes, marking the return to the tonic, screech the cadential scale from G to C, ending three octaves above middle C. An immense swoop through five octaves and a fifth swings us to the song-like but frustrated second subject, in the tonic major instead of flat submediant (bars 98–100).

In what happens next it is evident that for Beethoven recapitulation is still development: for although it looks as though the drooping second subject will disperse in fioriture yet more dreamily extended than those of the exposition, the adagio phrase, though still halting, this time leads onwards. Radiantly spaced as a dominant major ninth (anticipating, though we cannot know this, the sonority as well as the key of the Arietta), it leads after silence to syncopated diminished sevenths carrying us to F minor. In this key the second subject sings in the left hand, with broken but rising arpeggios in the right. Its mood in this minor version is very different from the almost self-indulgent lassitude of its major-keyed presentation. It still falls, but with a tragic dignity, in the traditional key for tempests, funerals and *chants lugubres*. Meanwhile the right hand's arpeggios now aspire upwards into sextuplet figuration that no longer dissipates its energy, except in a momentary ritardando, so that the quintuplet turns into which the fioriture lead may gather, rather than relinquish, momentum. Pace increases and dynamics intensify as the quintuplets soar higher, through the familiar sequential modulations originally defined by the diminished sevenths of F, C and G minors, now in that reversed order. Far from attempting evasion, or accepting social man's advice to King Lear that he should 'come in out of the storm', the dreamy second subject now leads back into the very teeth of the tempest. The diminished sevenths rage from G to C minor, accepted, even rejoiced in, as inevitable instead of taking us by surprise, as they do in the exposition. When the sword-thrusting codetta theme returns in the tonic minor it sounds more 'real' than it had done in the exposition's A flat major jubilation, just as the second subject's dream-song had been experientially toughened in its F minor metamorphosis.

So although this codetta sounds grimmer than it did in the

exposition, it is less close to the edge of hysteria; and after the chromatic sequences have soared to the heights in a sonority that lacerates,
they land on tonic octaves to launch a coda even briefer, but still more
momentous, than the development:

Ex. 125

The Atlas motive of rising minor third and descending diminished
fourth is enunciated in sturdy crotchets; the entries overlap, since the
last note of each group of three is also the first of the next group. All the
thematic notes are harmonized with diminished sevenths, crashing
from G to C to F minors, the identical chords and cyclical modulations
of the introduction. Each stab is syncopated over a tonic pedal, marked
with a sforzando; one cannot play the passage without tensing the
shoulder-blades—a climax to the physical and nervous tension experienced in playing the same chords, in double-dotted rhythm, during
the introduction. But this time the tension is released: on each offbeat
the sinews and muscles slightly relax, and dynamics decrease until the
last chords of the 6–4 of F become major instead of minor. Changed
back to minor, the bass semiquavers rumble in a stepwise motive that
links a turn to the familiar descent through a fourth. Above this
muttering of a storm that has passed, tonic and dominant chords of
F minor move melodically up through a *major* third, miraculously
freeing the minor thirds of the introduction. When the interval of
rising fourth is balanced by falling fifth, we realize that these F minor

triads are not tonics in their own right, but an extended plagal cadence to C. The resolution, as we might expect, is painfully achieved, for the F minor triad leaps to a crucially dissonant diminished seventh (again!) of C minor, grinding against the bass's F minor arpeggios. But the dissonant diminished seventh does resolve, on to a high C major triad. The mumbling bass changes from F minor to tonic and fifth of C, and spreads warmly to embrace the major tenth. Dissonant thunder has been alchemized into consonant waves, thereby anticipating the last movement's figuration, in addition to the thematic evolution.to be discussed later. The final pianissimo chord rings luminously in first inversion in the right hand, while the left hand adds a cavernous lower octave. There is no middle to the harmony and none is needed, for pedalling and the natural overtones provide an enveloping resonance. Indeed what is left out of the chord as notated is precisely what is to come in the opening triad of the next movement. A simple technical matter here has profound implications: the Whole is *contained within* the reconciliation of opposites which the movement has effected.

It is interesting to consider this movement in relation to the two previous sonatas. Opus 109 begins with the starkest juxtaposition of opposites, and hints that from the union of Innocence and Experience the Whole—for which a musical equivalent is self-contained song—might be attained; that is what happens when, after the second (sonata) movement's triumph over negation, Beethoven creates his Aria with variations. Opus 110 begins with innocence of a different character, in that it is a dream of a song which is innocent because incomplete—not whole. From that partial innocence Beethoven proceeds to a 'projection' of Experience in the scherzo's comic negations and the arioso's tragic lament; then in the fugue to a vision, rather than a dream, of a songful whole; and so to a return to the 'world' in jubilation. Opus 111 plunges *in medias res*, if ever any music did. Its introduction and first movement allegro are experience in the making, totally committed and totally uncompromising. The second subject offers innocence only evasively, in a dream that (unlike the first subject of opus 110) is soon recognized as such, for it peters out. But the whole movement is development, whereby this dream is reborn through the epical conflicts of Experience, which are manifest through a multiplicity of contradictory techniques. Thus the passion released by the introduction's introspectively heroic violence is channelled into the allegro, which tries to define its theme of world and suffering-bearing

Atlas monodically, in sonata style, in fugato and in lyrical song. Each separate attempt fails; each is re-created by what happens in the brief development section; so that in recapitulation they may be not repeated but reborn and, synthesized, may lead into the coda's plagal Amen. This coda gives an affirmative answer to Hopkins's questions: 'Is the shipwreck then a harvest? Does tempest carry the grain?' The Shakespearian Tempest is translated into Music, a 'deep and dreadful organpipe' that may purge us of guilt, and right old wrong. This is what begins to happen as the coda's final widely spaced, softly reverberating C major triad embraces within itself the opening major triad of the second and last movement: which is not only a self-contained song but also a Whole which is a microcosm of Beethoven's lifelong experience.

Chronometrically the movement is long; yet Beethoven calls it not an aria, but an Arietta, or little song. This is not quixotic, for it indicates the kind of song it is. It is not an immense, sublimated operatic aria-sonata like the adagio of opus 106; neither is it a purgatorial hymn like the theme of the variations in opus 109. Though it has some hymnic characteristics, it lacks the harmonic-tonal structure of a chorale, and rather has the simplicity of a folk song. That indicates its self-sufficiency; and although the song is a theme for variation, those variations are of the simplest possible type: divisions on a ground, whereby the theme proliferates into increasingly small note values, with no change in the basic pulse. The movement consists of a song melody, four variations or divisions, a modulatory episode, a repetition of the theme, and an epilogue. All are in one constant tempo and, except possibly in the modulatory episode, there is no hurrying or slackening until the end; the contrast with the waywardness of the first movement is extreme. No less contrasted with the first movement's violence is the Arietta's harmony and tonality. Harmonically, the theme is rooted in diatonic concords; it effects only one modulation, and that is not a point of progression like the conventional movement to the dominant, but an undulation to and from the relative, A minor, which is also the submediant. This may be prompted by the modal implications of the theme; as we shall see, the word 'undulation' is an appropriate metaphor as well as a technical description.

Unlike Bach, whose relationship to creed and dogma was direct, Beethoven was not concerned with number symbolism or with music's magical properties, at least in an overt sense. None the less his last sonata is elemental and even cosmological in scope; and the effect of the Arietta, in context with the first movement, is hardly separable from the trinitarian associations of its metrical proportions. The metres of the introduction and allegro are divisive or multiplicative (two plus two equals four), as befits their linear-progressive nature; the melody of the Arietta we hear as three slow dotted quaver beats a bar, and its consummatory effect is dependent on its 'circular' threefoldness. Though one is sometimes equated with the godhead, one multiplied by one remains one; to become substance it needs the duality of two. But though the potentiality of one has to be released through the duality of two, the opposite poles of divisiveness would destroy themselves in conflict unless there were a synthesizing power to reconcile them. This is the power of three, which in many languages is allied to the word tree, itself a symbol of growth. Unity must pass into duality, and becomes a trinity in the process of becoming manifest. It is not entirely fanciful to say that the Arietta demonstrates this in musical terms no less convincingly than Bach's *Et in unum Dominum* in the B minor Mass demonstrates the Christian doctrine of the Trinity. Beethoven's trinity is Hegelian rather than Christian; but the infinitely slow triple rhythm of the Arietta becomes the unbroken circle that contains all things within itself, active and passive powers, spirit and matter, and their ultimate synthesis.

Nor is this the end of the magical implications of metre in the Arietta: for although we hear it as three very slow beats a bar, Beethoven notates it as 9/16. Nine is a trinitized trinity, and was 'celebrated by the Pythagoreans as flowing round the other numbers within the decad, or ten, like the ocean'. The ocean metaphor, as we shall see, is pertinent, for the Arietta transforms formlessness into bodily creation. Nine was also known as Terpsichore, or the Dancing Muse, 'because of its turning and causing the retrogression and convergency of productive principles to circulate like a dance'. Nine represents this 'perfect balancing of all produced and atomized matter', the alchemical final stage of 'preparation or creation, wherein all things are formed for the change that leads to completion' (quotations from Thomas Taylor).

The tempo direction is *adagio molto semplice e cantabile*. The theme consists of 8+8 bars, beginning on an upbeat though with no apparent stress: a fact which, in conjunction with the extremely slow pace, itself undermines the temporal sense. Each half of the theme is repeated. While one's ears immediately recognize that the simple, open melody is a resolution of the previous movement's rampage, only if one spells

out its thematic contours can one comprehend why. We hear the
serenity of the initial godly falling fourths and fifths (phrased across
the bars) as a release of the plunging diminished sevenths at the
beginning of the sonata. These gentle declensions are balanced by the
smile of a rising major sixth, which then descends through a major
third and a semitone, resolving the Atlas motive in major quietude.
The next phrase extends the same shape, beginning with the Atlas
motive inverted, rising through a major arpeggio and declining to
fourth and second. The last two bars of the first half move up through
a scalewise third (see bar 3 of the introduction), but fall in a peaceful
fifth. The second half begins with the major permutation of the Atlas
motive, expands the rising and falling scale in augmented rhythm,
reaches the fifth as its highest point, and cadences on to the major third.
Here is the complete Arietta theme (its 'skeleton' analysis is given in
Ex. 120):

Ex. 126

While these thematic affinities help us to understand why the Arietta
melody convinces as a resolution of the allegro they cannot, of course,
'explain' its sublimity, its fusion of grandeur with simplicity. Like the
Aria of opus 109, it is a music of Innocence and Experience: though
this Experience, after the purgatorial reconciliations of the first

movement, no longer needs the harmonic and textural complexities of the E major song. Thus during the first eight bars, which incorporate the falling fourth and fifth, the rising sixth, the major version of the Atlas motive, and the rising and falling scale, the harmony consists of rudimentary tonics and dominants, with a passing D minor chord in the approach to the cadence. Spacing and texture are as significant a part of the music's calm, as is the melody itself. Alto and bass lines move warmly in parallel thirds, while the dominant pedal note in the left hand binds tonic and dominant harmonies in stillness, until the fourth bar's 6–4 cadence. During the second four bars the bass descends from G to D, the low octaves reverberating. The climax of the phrase is its highest note G, which is the only note not consonantly harmonized. It is an appoggiatura but, in its wide spacing, tender rather than painful. It prompts the intrusion of a chromatic F sharp in the bass, but this is a momentary cadential heightening rather than a modulation. Immediately the music moves back to the tonic C for the repeat, which is essential to the movement's almost move-less time-scale.

After the double bar the music sidles, rather than modulates, from the upbeat to an A minor triad which we do not at first recognize as a different key. Melody and bass move in parallel thirds (or strictly speaking seventeenths), resolving on a 6–4 A minor cadence to balance the tonic 6–4 in the fourth bar. An internal pedal on the dominant still immobilizes the music; it may be for this reason that the A minor episode hardly registers as a modulation. In any case after the 6–4 cadence the A minor triad becomes a submediant of C again, and moves to plainly sustained concords of dominant, tonic, subdominant and dominant: immensely slow, widely spaced, beneath a melody that is the introduction's stepwise rise through a fourth bereft of, because no longer needing, its forward thrust to a leading note. This melody does not 'lead' because it simply and eternally *is*. The cardinal simplicities of the almost immobile tonics, dominants and subdominants have a faintly modal flavour; we recall that Beethoven had recently been studying, as preparation for his Missa Solemnis, not only Bach but also Palestrina. Yet despite this a-temporality the last two bars of the theme achieve a resolution as subtle as it is simple. The melody rises through the fourth it had originally fallen through, then declines through a third, while the bass echoes the rising fourth as a dominant –tonic cadence. Melodic and harmonic sense are thus identified in a song that is also a dance, at once temporal and a-temporal.

The four variations that follow are rigorous in adhering to the theme's harmonic and tonal structure; nor do they allow us to forget its basic melodic contours. Variation I takes over the slowly lilting quaver–semiquaver rhythm of the opening fourth and lets it flow unbroken in the right hand. The melodic descent fills in the fourths with a third—C, A, G—which is again a smoothed-out permutation of the Atlas motive. The left hand adds a melody in semiquaver triplets, with the third note of each group tied over, at first to maintain the internal dominant pedal. The lowest notes fall on the second semiquaver, thereby creating a latent polyphony in cross-rhythm with the tune. Moreover these low notes are sometimes chromaticized; though this does not change the basic harmony, it makes it more mysterious, because veiled. In the fourth and fifth bars another part, intermittently added in alto register, enhances this effect, tingeing the harmony with passing chromatics on E flat and B flat. The B flat hints at a subdominant modulation and at its relative (D minor) beneath the suspended G. But these are chromatic colourings rather than real modulations that establish a new tonic: the arches of the original C major song are still clearly audible, and its serenity is not disturbed by the undulating cross-rhythms nor by the slightly more volatile harmony. The adjectives 'undulating' and 'volatile' both suggest a fluctuation of the unconscious waters, running far deeper than those we commented on in the Moonlight Sonata. We will see later how potent the water image is in this sonata, since in typically Beethovenian fashion it is simultaneously negative and positive: a dissolution into the inchoate, and at the same time an instrument of purification and rebirth.

After the double-bar the semiquavers in all three parts are occasionally tied over the beat together:

Ex. 127

This produces an odd hiatus: we are poised on a wave or ripple, unsure which way it will fall. The phrase with the augmented rhythm (dotted crotchet followed by dotted quaver) is still spacious, though no longer hieratically still. The bass gently rocks in tied octaves, while the melody yearns through a chromatic passing note, D to D sharp, thereby creating an augmented instead of a plain diatonic triad. The sharpening is, however, immediately counteracted by the flattened B in the next bar. The low, offbeat tones in the bass reverberate; the final two bars are slightly heated by dissonant appoggiaturas caressing the tonic cadence.

One senses the theme as three very slow beats a bar, metrically compromised with duality, because approached on the up-beat. Not until the fourth bar do we feel a stress on the first beat, and it is this, we have suggested, that gives the music its air-borne character. Like the theme, the first variation is in 9/16, with nine level though sometimes disguised semiquavers to a bar. For the second variation Beethoven changes the time signature to 6/16, but this is only a convenience of notation since it is really in 18/32 (twice 9/16), with longs and shorts of half the duration and twice the number of variation I, and with absolutely no change in the basic pulse. Fritz Rothschild, in his *Lost Tradition*, reproves Tovey, who first pointed out these mathematical relationships, on the grounds that Beethoven's time-signature is correct according to the Old Tradition, in that it indicates not the number of units a bar, but where the stresses come. Only it doesn't! Stressed in 6/16, the accents would come on the first and fourth semi-quavers, making nonsense of the melodic phrase. However this may be, at twice the speed the ♫♫ metre becomes a boogie rhythm, rendered seraphic. This is not a joke. This sonata encompasses spiritual purgation, and that purgation includes energies of the body: the Arietta is at once a hymnic song and a ceremonial dance. When Beethoven said 'O God give me the strength to conquer myself, for nothing must bind me to this life', he was referring to an act of transcendence, not evasion; the mystical release of this movement would not be so awe-inspiring if its latent physicality were less strong. In this variation the thematic fourth and fifth are still audible (though marked *dolce*) in the bass, answered in dialogue by the right hand's relatively sensuous parallel sixths. There are more chromatic passing notes to warm the texture (consider the bass in bars 34 and 35), and the chromaticized suggestion of a modulation to D minor is stronger than in variation I. The harmonic scheme is basically unchanged, however; so although the figuration moves at double time (appropriately to use the jazzman's terminology), the pulse is no faster. After the double bar,

indeed, the curious rhythmic stasis that occurred in variation I reappears, more disturbingly. Internal pedal notes rock in the boogie
rhythm above and below the dominant E, and the concords are tied
across the beats at the return to the tonic:

Ex. 128

The water image still applies: the muddy textures of the boogie figure
create an aqueous lulling until, at the tied chords, the waves are
suddenly arrested, as though slapping against a rock. It is pertinent to
note how physical this effect is for the performer, however metaphysical the music's implications. The cadential resolution again has passing
notes that add chromatic richness and even harsh dissonance to the
flowing texture, without changing the basic tempo.

    The enhanced sensuousness of texture and animation of movement
carry us, however, into the next variation, which Beethoven con-
veniently notates in 12/32, though mathematically it should be 36/64
(four times 9/16), with three main beats of four dotted semiquavers,
longs and shorts four times as fast and four times as many as the
original 9/16. The diminutions of the divisions induce ecstasy, while
the unchanging tempo paradoxically negates temporality. Descending
arpeggios in ♪ rhythm are answered in free inversion, and
accompanied by syncopated tied chords that have a similar effect to the
tied-note hiatuses in the previous variations. Though on paper the
figuration looks like surging and crashing waves, at this speed it
sounds more like tongues of fire, which is not surprising if we recall
the analogy between the swell of the unconscious waters and the
crackle of purgatorial fire in the last variation of opus 109. In Paracel-
sian terms fire is life, in that it conquers darkness and purges evil; at the
same time it must feed on life, in order to keep alive. That is why, in
this variation, ecstasy is synonymous with terror. The harmonic
pattern is again unchanged, though the excitation of the passing
chromatics is greater, because marked by sforzandi. The syncopated
dominant pedal in bar 52, with the dissonant diminished seventh and
minor ninth above it, trembles 'on the verge of Being'. In bar 55

chromatic passing notes seem to imply a momentary modulation to B flat, imparting a sense of awe to the elation:

Ex. 129

After the double bar the texture darkens. The syncopated chords hold the breath against the upward-thrusting and downward-quivering arpeggios, which incorporate acridly sharp leading notes into their boogie rhythm. This music surely evokes, even more vividly than the last variation of opus 109, T. S. Eliot's 'dark dove with the flickering tongue'. We might indeed say that in this variation

> The dove descending breaks the air
> With flame of incandescent terror
> Of which the tongues declare
> The one discharge from sin and error.
> The only hope, or else despair
> Lies in the choice of pyre or pyre—
> To be redeemed from fire by fire.

Incandescence intensifies as the leaping chromaticized octaves spring up the bass (bar 59), until at the return to the tonic the scoring is at once glitteringly metallic (in the top register) and viscidly muddy (in the bass chords). 'Garlic and sapphires in the mud/Clot the bedded axle-tree': but only momentarily, since parallel thirds and sixths, thrusting up in this fastest version of the boogie rhythm, end the variation at the apex of the Arietta's ecstasis. A corporeal music has transcended time and the body.

The next variation, which returns to the 9/16 metre since any further 'division' would be impracticable, none the less takes us over the horizon. It is a double variation in the sense that the repetition of each half is a different kind of music. We have spoken metaphorically of water and fire in reference to the previous variations; the elemental pattern is completed if we think of this variation in terms of earth and air, remembering the supernatural music in *Antony and Cleopatra*: the soldiers cannot tell whether it is 'i' the air' or 'under the earth' (Act IV, iii). The first six bars are enveloped in an almost imperceptibly murmuring tonic and dominant pedal, in rocking demisemiquaver triplets. It is a subterranean vibration of the turning earth in the dark time of the year, over which the right hand whispers the harmonies of the theme, always offbeat, gradually encompassing sighing appoggiaturas and chromatic passing notes. The contours of the theme, though hidden, emerge embryonically from that amorphous hum; it is as though the song had gone underground, 'earth to earth, ashes to ashes, dust to dust', smothered in the frozen earth, muffled in the double pedal that telescopes a moment in time. When the upper pedal note eventually moves from G up to A, B and D, and then down over the still reverberating low C, it is to release us from the Earth, our mother. Scales float upwards, *leggieramente*, in parallel sixths, and the repeat (of the harmonic-tonal pattern) occurs in an airy stratosphere, two octaves higher. Perhaps Beethoven's deafness may be said in a positive sense to have made this extraordinary sonority possible; in his mind's ear he heard sounds that were 'not of this world', and his genius transformed a percussion instrument (which he spoke of as inadequate) into a celestial gamelan. No one before had ever created a sonority like this from a piano, nor has it happened again, except for an occasional deliberate emulation, as in the later piano writing of Michael Tippett. The sound is a sibilance, a whisper of 'the breath of God' that can create and re-create life from death. Delicate staccato semiquavers are haloed with demisemiquaver triplets that are not decorative but melodic, an efflorescence of the original song. We recall that the Book of Common Prayer commits the body 'earth to earth . . . in sure and certain hope of the Resurrection to eternal life'. Yet Beethoven's music is beyond doctrinal associations. It rather evokes the earth's perennial rebirth from the winter solstice, or the recurrent archetypal echoes of that rebirth within the human psyche, of which Christian Easter mythology is merely one, supremely potent, instance. Moreover the transition from death to birth is far from easy. Though I have called it an efflorescence (perhaps unconsciously remembering flower-gathering Persephone's descent into the earth, and the immaculate conception of the Eleusinian Mysteries), there would seem to be snowflakes on the flowers, for the temperature of this glinting sonority is ice-cold:

Ex. 130

Again Eliot's *Little Gidding* is relevant:

> Midwinter spring is its own season
> Sempiternal though sodden towards sundown,
> Suspended in time, between pole and tropic.
> When the short day is brightest, with frost and fire,
> The bright sun flames the ice, on pond and ditches,
> In windless cold that is the heart's heat.

> ... no wind but pentecostal fire
> In the dark time of the year. Between melting and freezing
> The soul's sap quivers.

We return to the vibrating earth for the second half, and the sonority seems more sullen after those heights. The pedal now consists of rocking octaves on the dominants and tonics of A minor, then of C major, above which the right hand murmurs its offbeat dissonant appoggiaturas, first in a two-note texture, thickened to double and triple appoggiaturas at the approach to the tonic. This time there are no scales to carry us aloft; Beethoven simply wafts us to the air at the return to A minor. One can pick out the thematic notes from the tinkling demisemiquaver triplets, though they occur irregularly, and hardly ever on the beat. But to 'recognize the theme' would be trivial: what one hears is a continuous cantillation, through which the equal semiquavers of the pedal notes ring like a bell. In bars 94–5 there is a still more disembodied version of the passage in variation III; chromatic passing notes, moving from G up to the tonic by way of B flat as well as B natural, create an effect of levitation. Again, for the performer the sensation is physical: arms feel weightless, head slightly dizzy. Perhaps one must be hypersensitively aware of the body in order to relinquish it.

In any case, levitation justifies the first structural irregularity: Beethoven adds to the eight-bar clause a coda in which Time stops.

The bells continue their distant chiming in demisemiquaver triplets, while the left hand repeats telescoped, pedal-haloed chords of tonic, dominant and subdominant of C. *Leading* notes and *dominants*, those epitomes of 'Western' consciousness, are elided in a timeless moment, just as, more than a century later, they will be in the middle-period music of Stravinsky, with which, it may be, 'Europe' dies, in hope to be reborn:

Ex. 131

After a baptism in the waters, a scorching in the pentecostal fire, and a *conjunctio oppositorum* of earth and air, Beethoven hears this 'gentle sound, for him who secretly hears'; then in a three-bar cadence clause he descends from the heights through tonic, submediant and dominant arpeggios: chords which define the harmonic and tonal structure of the theme, though they are no longer elided. The three bars are repeated, varied in broken arpeggios, and end the sequence of divisions—the proliferation of the melody into increasingly smaller note-values—in bar 105.

The Arietta and its four divisions generate ecstasy, yet, as we have seen, are fundamentally unchanged and unchangeable: states of being, rather than of the becoming with which most of Beethoven's earlier music, including the first movement of this sonata, had been concerned. Though there is, in the theme and divisions, a swing between tonic and relative minor, relatable to the modal flavour of the song and its normally concordant harmonization, one might make out a case that the first 'real' modulation occurs when the repeated cadence-clause dissolves into the famous chain of trills. The original falling fourth of the Arietta rings sonorously in bass octaves, beneath a seemingly endless trill on the dominant's D (bar 106). Sighing falling seconds contract from tone to semitone, and we mysteriously find ourselves in E flat major (the upper mediant), with the falling interval in the bass expanded to the thematic fifth. The trills are now triple, their overtones tremulously resonating over a reiterated B flat. The sonority created by the clashing of the multiple trills with the pedal note startlingly approximates to the tintinnabulation of bells, and reminds us that the bell-sounds in this movement and elsewhere in Beethoven's late work (for instance the variations of opus 109 and intermittently in the *Diabelli Variations*) are far from fortuitous. Of course bells are quite often evoked in classical music, but in Bach, Haydn, Mozart and Schubert they are usually employed onomato-poetically, with a specific dramatic or atmospheric significance (for instance, the bell in the storm-oppressed convent of Schubert's 'Junge Nonne'). Beethoven is unique in evoking the sonority of bells *per se*, with an intuitive apprehension of their symbolism.

Traditionally bells—shaped like the heavenly vault, suspended between earth and sky, reverberating in Nature's harmonic spec-trum—are a summons to spiritual worlds. Even in their association with death they are not usually instruments of foreboding, but serve to disperse evil spirits; they may even allay storm and pestilence. In his fascinating book *The Hidden Face of Music* Herbert Whone points out that the word bell signifies the Being of God (the letter B and el, in Hebrew), and also that being of God inside each separate human creature. 'If [a man] is able to resonate himself he becomes a thing of beauty, as we find indicated in the French *belle*. That thing of beauty, his new being, has the power to banish all forces of error, and it was to banish all devilish forces that was the function of the church bell in the Middle Ages.... If, on the other hand, there is no resonation of that pure being, we have spiritual muteness and all it incurs. There is worldly strife (which we see reflected in the dialectic of the Latin words *bella* and *bellum*, beautiful and war).... The bell begins to ring for joy when a man finds his own way back to pure being!' However fanciful one may find this, there could hardly be a better description of what Beethoven is about in the Arietta; and although in their present context the bells have funereal associations in ringing the death of the terrestrial world, they also herald a rebirth. In their new E flat major tonality, which after so long a stretch of scarcely sullied C major sounds infinitely remote, the right hand's trills climb chromatically until, after the change of key signature, they resolve into the Arietta's upward arpeggios and downward appoggiaturas (bars 5–6 of the theme). They are stratospherically high, while the bass line descends, ringing songfully, to the depths. It is as though the endless trills were released by that moment outside Time at the end of the last variation; the vast distance between treble and bass seems to separate soul from body. Here is the whole passage, with its continuation:

Ex. 132

Incredibly enough, the 'hollow' sonority of this miraculous passage has been ascribed to Beethoven's faulty hearing! Critical imbecility and musical insensitivity could hardly be more absurd in both the literal and the normal sense. What follows is a retrospect of Beethoven's purgatorial pilgrimage: in Eliot's words, true of most of us though not of Beethoven:

> Footfalls echo in the memory
> Down the passage which we did not take
> Towards the door we never opened
> Into the rose-garden. My words echo
> Thus, in your mind.

The thematic contours in bars 120–8 return, with a syncopated, rest-punctuated limp, to the scalewise rising thirds of the introduction to the first movement (see Ex. 120). In its hesitant rhythm the motive has lost its assertiveness, and after its tentative rise, falls through a fifth, extended to a sixth. The phrase gropes in the treble and is echoed in the bass, moving through cyclical modulations from E flat to C minor, to A flat major; then rapidly from G major through a declining cycle of fifths. The final two and a half bars of this modulatory episode pivot from G to C to B flat minor, and so to what looks like A flat major but changes into an inverted German sixth leading back to the original C major tonic (bar 130). All these restless modulations, in a very long piece which up to this point has modulated hardly at all, occur within three lines of music, succeeding one another in ever closer sequence. It is as though Beethoven is looking back at the world from a great height, floating in a crepuscular haze through a recall of passions past. The soft pulsing of the 9/16 semiquavers reminds us of the purgatorial arioso of opus 110; the faltering scale motive from the introduction gradually changes, through the multiple modulations, into permutations of the Atlas theme. At first Atlas's third is diminished, A flat to F sharp; finally it appears at the original pitches but in a different order.

So throughout this retrospective interlude rhythm limps, thematic motives are fragmented, and tonal stability disintegrates; the slow pendulum, the pulse of life itself, swings to rest, in the twilit hush of a *recherche du temps perdu*. There may be Freudian implications in thus harking 'back' to discover what we were and therefore are. In any case retrospection seems to effect Freudian regeneration, since the pulse does not, after all, finally run down. Instead, the bass changes imperceptibly from the broken Atlas motive to a vibration of demisemiquaver triplets: which support a return of the Arietta in its original form (bar 130). The melody itself remains diatonic, while the accompanying figuration, both in the bass and in an undulating inner part, anneals the broken lines of the retrospective episode. The piano sonority shimmers as the accompanying figuration laves the unchanging melody and fundamental harmony. The flow is in full spate: the water metaphor is again appropriate, but with a difference, since the ambivalent implications of water imagery are now simultaneously present. When Thales, the Greek physiologer, said 'everything is water' he was making a pseudo-chemical statement; he was also speaking cosmologically in suggesting that existence is fluid and mobile. But at bottom he was making an ontological assertion that everything is one because it is made of one material. It was only a step from there to Parmenides' theory that the essence of being is one; and it is in this sense that in mythology the waters came to symbolize, in Mercea Eliade's phrase, 'the entire universe of the virtual'.

We are reminded, by the unremittent surge of the accompanying figuration in this recapitulation, of Eliot's words in *The Dry Salvages*:

the sea is all about us;
The sea is the land's edge also, the granite
Into which it reaches, the beaches where it tosses
Its hints of other and earlier creation. . . .

More positively we may recall, from the equilibrium between the surging water figuration and the song that floats above it, the words of Lao-Tse: 'Water never rests, neither by day nor by night. When flowing above it causes rain and dew. When flowing below it causes streams and tides. Water is outstanding in doing good.' In this repetition the two eight-bar periods of the melody sing once only, without repeats; in the second half joyousness is enhanced by the luminous pedal notes in the alto and by a more rapid undulation of the chromatics in the sonorous bass. In the context of the sonata what St John Chrysostom says of the rite of baptism seems pertinent: 'Baptism represents death and entombment, resurrection and life. When we plunge our head into the water, as into a sepulchre, the Old man is immersed, altogether buried; when we come out of the water the New man simultaneously appears.' Similarly Tertullian writes: 'Water was the seat of the divine spirit, who then preferred it to all other elements. . . . It was the water that was first commanded to produce living creatures. In the formation of man himself, God made use of water to consummate his work. As soon as the words are pronounced, the Holy Spirit, coming down from heaven, hovers over the waters, which it sanctifies with its fecundity.' This is a not inaccurate description of the effect as this sublimely simple song 'hovers' over the arpeggiated waves. The freed melody seems at once Creator and Creation, the spirit of God that 'moved upon the face of the waters', from which life 'came forth'. 'Except a man be born of water and of the Spirit, he cannot enter into the kingdom of God.'

Yet this return to the waters, though the goal of Beethoven's elemental sonata, is not quite its end. There remains a coda, generated (bar 146) not by the whole melody but by its last three notes, the descending third G, E, E. Melodically, the descending minor third is the 'natural' pentatonic interval that children and savages spontaneously utter in spells, name-games and incantations as well as song. Harmonically it is an embryonic minor triad which roots us to the earth, and has in European music traditionally been associated with death. Tonally the interval of minor third connects with late Beethoven's preoccupation with mediant relationships which, in their 'false' relations, may imply a *conjunctio oppositorum* of spirit and matter, heaven and earth. The apparent contradiction between these melodic and harmonic-tonal aspects is thus not a contradiction at all; we may recall that the Waldstein Sonata's Song of Innocence ends with this interval at precisely the same pitches, G and E: the 'deception of the cuckoo' in the garden of Eden. Here in the Arietta the third sheds its latent harmonic ambiguities, returning to melodic innocence as the line falls through thirds alternately minor and major: from G to E, E to C, C to A, A to F, harmonized in broken triads that embrace the harmonic complex of the original C major, A minor and D minor chords without departing from the home tonic. Then the flow stabilizes on the dominant seventh, the pedal notes obtrusive in the middle part, and ends with the melodic thirds in inversion. The six-bar passage is repeated with the hands changed over; although the music moves through descending mediants, there is no suggestion of the tonal ambiguity that mediants create in opus 106, 109 and 110. The repeat is extended through two extra bars over a dominant pedal. An open dominant ninth and chromatic passing notes in parallel thirds, in the topmost register, inculcate a Dionysiac frenzy, which merges into near-delirious trills, and a sudden pianissimo. No longer corybantic, the trills continue high on the dominant, transporting us, as prophetically envisaged in the finale of the Waldstein Sonata, into

> the still point of the turning world. Neither flesh nor fleshless;
> Neither from nor towards; at the still point, there the dance is,
> But neither arrest nor movement. . . .

>   Except for the point, the still point,
> There would be no dance, and there is only the dance.

> The inner freedom from the practical desire,
> The release from action and suffering, release from the inner
> And the outer compulsion, yet surrounded
> By a sense of grace, a white light still and moving.

What Eliot, fine poet though he is, can only write 'about', Beethoven *creates* when, beneath or above an accompaniment of the softest demisemiquaver bells, undulating through thirds, fifths, sixths and octaves, the first half of the Song sounds limpidly. The quotation made in reference to the aria of opus 109—'A condition of complete simplicity/

(Costing not less than everything)'—is yet more precisely relevant here, since this Song, unlike that in opus 109, has distilled the burden of harmonic tension into diaphanous grace. To examine Beethoven's manuscript score of these final pages is a strangely moving experience, for the physical, visual materialization of the notes startlingly resembles their sounds. Writing of Beethoven's calligraphy, Georg Schünemann remarks how his script became 'progressively more delicate. The cello sonatas opus 102 show more careful forming and joining of notes, and, in general, lighter pressure on the paper. The stems of the notes are smoothly, almost lovingly drawn and even the spurs and dots of quavers lose their firm, thick, broad up and down cross strokes.... [In the Arietta of opus 111] we can recognize the light penmanship, the fine strokes of the demisemiquavers and the minute heads of the notes, which are sometimes no more than hinted at. The notes suggest the sonority itself, which seems to have passed beyond what is earthly and corporeal, as though the composer's thoughts and visions belonged to another world. The very look of the notes seems to have become the expression of a light, eternal harmony.' (The end of Beethoven's autograph is reproduced on the dust-jacket.)

In this epilogue the first eight-bar period of the theme is not answered by the second. Instead, the trills and arpeggios continue, while echoes of the cadence phrase fade into silence. The falling interval is now God's fifth, instead of the third or fourth; repeated, it is embellished with chromatic appoggiaturas which Thomas Mann's inspired musical pedagogue, Kretschmar (in his lecture on opus 111 incorporated into *Dr Faustus*), described as 'the most conciliatory, pathetically reconciling thing in the world'. As it utters fare-well and go(o)d-bye ('Great God was in us') the trills disperse in pianissimo scales, and the bass's tonic Cs, which have gradually swung to the lower reaches of the keyboard, find silence. The demisemiquaver figuration floats canonically in thirds, creating a sonority reminiscent of the sunlit ice of the fourth variation, though without the metallic tinkle. Perhaps it also distantly recalls the searing scales of the first movement, transfigured to peace.

We don't, however, end in these celestial regions. The canonic demisemiquavers descend, through a crescendo, in parallel sixths, and conclude in the falling fourth and fifth of the Arietta's opening phrase, freely imitated in canon:

Ex. 133

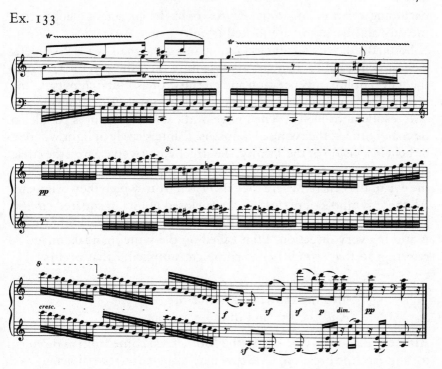

The fourth now begins on the beat instead of on the anacrusis: which makes the last two and two-thirds bars of 9/16 effectually into four bars of 6/16. So the circle is squared or the square circled; duality and trinity are finally identified, as they are also in the (closely related) minuet-epilogue to the Diabelli Variations (see pages 399–403). Moreover there is a melodic complement to this process: for since the fourth is perfect and fifth imperfect, it may not be entirely fanciful to hear in the thematic motive not merely the original alternation of tonic and dominant seventh triads, but also the collocation of God and Devil, Christ and Serpent, which perfect and imperfect fifths have traditionally represented. Here is the deepest musical synonym for 'reconciling the Eagle', a potently ambiguous bird who is a denizen of the life-giving sun and of Yggdrasil, the tree that holds heaven from earth, and who is at the same time a carrier of Zeus's thunderbolts, and the eviscerator of pinioned Prometheus. There is no doubt that Beethoven's music says 'Amen' as the theme's perfect fourth falls, answered by a trinity of rising fourths in the bass, affirming the harmonic relation of dominant to tonic. In an act of benediction melody and harmony are locked in mirror-inversion.

So in Beethoven's trinitarian yea-saying the mandala is complete. The serpent eats its own tail, representing according to the Gnostics the wheel of life, regeneration and eternity; or as Plutarch puts it, 'the serpent feeds on its own body; even so all things spring from God and will resolve into Deity'. The image of the coiled serpent is paralleled by many others: the twinned dolphins; Dante's circle of light wherein he beheld a vision of the Trinity; the street with twelve gates; the circle that enclosed the four arms of the Cross; the petals of the rose that lead the eye to the centre, where they meet and from which they originate. All these symbols of perfection are enclosed points or squared circles: points because they escape definition, circles because they embrace the world in every direction. Eliot called on the same mandala image in referring to that 'condition of complete simplicity' that occurs

> When the tongues of flame are in-folded
> Into the crowned knot of fire
> And the fire and the rose are one.

After the dichotomy of Earth (the Mother we come from and return to) and Air (the breath of God that may disperse terrestrial being), we attain the union of Water with Fire, from which springs (in Dante's words) *la Rosa, in che il Verbo divino carne si fece*. The mandala-rose, red and white, alchemically represents the union of passion and purity, and contains the knot and the labyrinth that in all mythologies symbolize the search for the Whole. The search cannot be completed unless we can submit to the eternally flowing waters, as does Beethoven in his Arietta. Having done so, he enters the paradise garden, the *locus secretus*, the *hortus conclusus*, the *rosarium* wherein in Christian mythology the Virgin Mary becomes again the eternal feminine goddess, the Rose without a Thorn. Not for nothing does the Proper of the Mass for Rosary Sunday describe the Virgin as *'quasi rosa plantata super rivos aquarum'*. In the Garden, Beethoven knows—as did Lady Julian of Norwich, quoted by Eliot—that 'all shall be well and/All manner of thing shall be well'.

There is a sense in which Mann's Kretschmar was justified in saying in his lecture that the final bars of opus 111 are not only the end of this sonata, but also of all Beethoven's sonatas, and even of the sonata principle itself, however many works in 'sonata form' may have been composed subsequently. Schindler, Beethoven's devoted but musically dim-witted Boswell, tells us that he ventured to enquire why Beethoven had not appended a third movement to opus 111, 'appropriate to the character of the first'. The composer gruffly retorted that he had 'no time', and so had extended the second movement beyond normal proportions. Schlesinger *fils*, one of Beethoven's harried publishers, also requested him to add a quick finale. Perhaps that is not totally surprising from a commercially biased, aesthetically unimaginative publisher; but it is almost incredible that Schindler, even after he had got to know the sonata well or at least had heard it many times, still maintained that 'two movements of such sharply differing character' could not possibly produce 'an integrated and satisfying whole'. In any case Beethoven's reply, though a joke, was also, like most of his jokes, intuitively profound. He had 'no time' because, even in the heart of 'Western consciousness', Time was no longer relevant. As Meister Eckhart has put it: 'To talk about the world as being made by God tomorrow, or yesterday, would be talking nonsense. God makes the world and all things in this present now. Time gone a thousand years ago is now as present and as near to God as this very instant. The soul who is in the here and now, in her the Father bears his one-begotten Son and in that same birth the soul is born back into God. It is one birth; as fast as she is reborn into God, the Father begetting his only Son in her.' It follows that 'Now is the minimum of Time. Small though it be, it must go; everything that Time touches must go. The spot that I am standing on is small, but it must go before I can see God.' The rosarium is not a place; to enter it is to spiral out of time, into the labyrinth. In so far as the Arietta effaces time it also obliterates Schindler's inanity: for what could come 'after' Paradise?

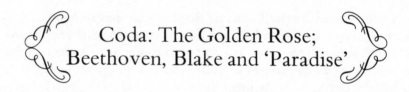

Coda: The Golden Rose;
Beethoven, Blake and 'Paradise'

What does one mean by 'Paradise' in reference to Beethoven's late music? Christian apologists equated Paradise with the Eden we'd fallen from, and even ascribed to it geographical sites (the Fortunate Isles, the Isle of Apples, Atlantis, Avalon, etc.) that might be redis-covered by diligent exploration. Cosmas, in the sixth century, located it east of China, on a continent watered by four rivers, Pison, Guhon, Hiddekel and Euphrates; St Brendan believed it to be in the islands off Japan and claimed to have discovered it on his fabulous voyage; for Sir John Mandeville, a later but no less legendary traveller, it was situated at Alumbo, Polombe, or modern Colombo, in Ceylon, its heart being 'a fair great well that hath odour and savour of all spices . . . the Well of Youth, for they that drink thereat seem always young and live without sickness'. Such magical properties tend to divest paradise of material existence; and although the word, which is of Persian origin, literally means moulded or formed around, and was commonly applied to a walled garden, especially a rose garden, or an enclosed park or orchard, its symbolism plumbs far deeper than the notion of an eternally evasory refuge. From the Sumerian legend of Gilgamesh, through Greek and Hebrew mythology to Europe's Middle Ages and its post-Renaissance reinterpretations in Spenser, Shakespeare and Milton, the paradisal park embraces a number of constant elements. Though it may be heaven or haven, it is not devoid of contradiction, nor even of negative forces, since it is consistently inhabited by a tree, a serpent, and a figure variously described as Trickster, Thief or Winged Messenger. The tree is durable, secure, self-perpetuating, a synonym for tradition, security, 'belonging'—the pastoral community in Shakespeare's *The Winter's Tale* is a good example. The snake is protean, volatile, elusive, personalized, instinctual—as is Shakespeare's Cleopatra. One cannot simply equate these two forces with positive and negative, life and death, good and evil. Each is necessary to the other; only through their mutual interaction can paradise be entered. And the Winged Messenger is the agent (angel) whereby this marriage of Heaven and Hell is consummated. He has had many names, Loki, Hermes, Mercury among them. Blake called him the Human Imagination, and equated him with Christ.

There never was a single work of art that demonstrates this more comprehensively than Beethoven's opus 111. It opens with what is probably the most dramatically rhetorical gesture in Beethoven's music. I use the word 'rhetorical' in its normal, colloquial sense, though something of the strict meaning is relevant too. Rhetoric is a technique of oratory that employs conventional devices to effect acts of persuasion, which means that anything rhetorical must have some of the qualities of a public act. In the first movement of opus 111 Beethoven's rhetoric turns inwards; but he starts with a gesture clearly related to a public and autocratic world; and although the allegro makes strenuous efforts to objectify experience in contrapuntal unities it remains, with its turbulent alternations of mood and tempo, protean, volatile, serpentine, individualized. It is a drama of the personal life wherein Beethoven's physical presence—the clenched fist, blazing eye, unkempt hair and lowering brow—is vehemently manifest.

The concept of objectification is here used in the psychological sense as the opposite pole to narcissism, though of course Beethoven, being a great artist, was never in danger of being in clinical terms a victim of his narcissistic instincts. The processes of his art are, indeed, rational in that they illuminate what is dark, make what is crooked straight: nowhere is this more astonishingly so than in this relatively brief movement. The rhetorical character of the introduction and allegro makes the reconciliation its coda achieves the more impressive; and also makes it possible for Beethoven to create, in the Arietta, the most unrhetorical music conceivable. One might even say that Beethoven illuminates the centrality, rather than abnormality, of psychotic experience in that, to adapt R. D. Laing's words, he doesn't destroy himself with his (serpentine, tigerish, eagle-like) violence, but rather admits, even accepts it, realizing that 'most of us are as deeply afraid to live and love as we are to die'. Because Beethoven was not thus afraid he could say, with Prospero, 'this thing of darkness I/Acknowledge mine', and could create from the admission a tragic music purged by pity and terror. To this Shakespeare again offers the only valid parallel. Although, like King Lear, Beethoven is 'bound upon a wheel of fire, that mine own tears/Do scald like molten lead', he will not, like the craven, 'come in out of the storm' but, like Gloucester, will 'bear/ Affliction till it do cry out itself/"Enough, enough"', and die'. In the coda of the first movement of opus 111, however, he dies, also like

Gloucester, 'Twixt two extremes of passion, joy and grief'; his heart bursts 'smilingly'. After tragic catharsis he enters, in the Arietta, a realm of serenity to which only the transcendental moments in Shakespeare's last plays are comparable: the death of Cleopatra, whose babe-serpent sucks the nurse asleep; Hermione restored ('It is required you do awake your faith ... Music, awake her! ... Bequeath to death your numbness'); the life-giving storm in *Pericles*; the raging thunder that in *The Tempest* becomes musical concord bringing redemption to fallen, desperately stricken men. The tolling bells of the Arietta recall Ariel's sea-knell; it is only after Ferdinand believes that his father has been drowned in the unconscious waters that he finds the pearl without price ('Those are pearls that were his eyes'). The pearl is traditionally a mandala, and the mandala contains an elemental cross:

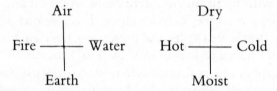

Both Shakespeare and Beethoven live through Hopkins's query, which I quoted in reference to the coda of opus 111's first movement. 'Shipwrack' *is* a harvest, and tempest carries the grain when joy is no longer the opposite of pain, but its transcendence. While Beethoven would not have fully accepted the Christian doctrine of Hopkins's poem, he knew his Shakespeare well, and compared the D minor sonata of opus 31 to *The Tempest*. Opus 111 goes much further than the early sonata, for it telescopes *King Lear* and *The Tempest* into one! What results is a musical act inseparable from, yet independent of, Beethoven's own life, just as the characters in Shakespeare's plays are simultaneously his creatures and their own selves.

We may recall the trenchant words of the *Theologica Germanica* (1497): 'Nothing burneth in hell but self-will. Therefore it hath been said "Put off thine own will, and there will be no hell".' This is an accurate description of what happens in the transition from the first movement of opus 111 to the Arietta, which is a music highly individualized, yet peculiarly impersonal. We have seen that, while nobody but Beethoven could have composed this movement, its melodic and rhythmic equilibrium and its harmonic purity give it a timeless and placeless quality that justify the elemental metaphors we have applied to it. Invoking water, fire, earth and air, like a growing

ree it is seemingly independent of Beethoven's volition, even during
he modulatory retrospect. To it Laing's description of the meaning of
artistic process seems applicable:

> The experience of being the actual medium for a continual process
> of creation takes one past all depression or persecution or vainglory,
> past even choice or emptiness, into the very mystery of that con-
> tinual flip of non-being into being, and can be the occasion of that
> great liberation when one makes the transition from being afraid of
> nothing to the realization that there is nothing to fear. 'There is
> nothing to be afraid of': the ultimate reassurance and the ultimate
> terror.

This 'great liberation' is Beethoven's transcendence, to define which
we may call on Karl Jaspers's adaption of Kierkegaard, whose experi-
mental psychology discovered that 'possibility is the form in which I
permit myself to know what I am not yet, in preparation for being it'.
From one point of view Logos was for Beethoven a reflection of the
essence of Being, as it is in traditional Christian epistemology, and as it
is by implication in William James's statement that religion is what
man does with his solitariness. Yet for Beethoven this meaning could
not be separated from the sense in which the Word also stands for the
possibility of communication and relatedness. Beethoven's word was
no less communication because it was musical, rather than verbal and
intellectually apprehensible. He would have agreed with Jaspers that
communication is the universal condition of man's (as distinct from
the animals') being'. Truth 'does not lie in something already known,
or something finally knowable, nor in an absolute, but rather in what
arises and comes to pass. Truth can only *become*: in its depths it is not
dogmatic but communicative.'

In this sense Beethoven's truth is beyond the truths that have been
developed into philosophical and religious systems. 'If truth for us in
very form remains a limit to the realization of communication',
Jaspers writes, 'every form of truth must be shipwrecked in the world,
and none can substitute itself absolutely for the truth. If therefore there
is truth in this way, then it can only be in the TRANSCENDENCE
which is not some Beyond as a mere second world, nor this world
taken again as a better world. The idea which grasps transcendence
from the unfulfilment of all communication and from the shipwreck-
ing of every form of truth in the world is like a proof of God: from the
unfulfilment of every sense of truth and under the assumption that

truth must be, thought touches transcendence.' Opus 111 is *truth in process*, which is of its nature attempted communication. What the introduction and allegro discover is that to demand fulfilment and salvation *in time* would be to 'cancel the problem of men' who can become themselves only *through* communication. 'In the beginning was the One, the truth as it is inaccessible to us. But it is as though the lost One could be recovered from its dispersion by communication: as though the confusion of the many could resolve into rest through conjunction.' When, exceptionally, moments of transcendence are achieved, as they are in Beethoven's Arietta, they are 'anticipations of possible fulfilled communication, which would at the same time be a completed truth and a timeless unity of the soul and the cosmos. The idea of such an unreality as *a communication that reaches its goal means the elevation of communication into a transcendent perfection where there is no longer any need to communicate*' (italics added). So the Arietta emerges—as Jaspers says of philosophy—'out of its everpresent source in the soul only to awaken the soul and let it participate in a truth that has no purpose and neither serves nor opposes any other truth. . . . It resembles prayer except that it does not have the definite answer of a personal divinity.' Beethoven's prayers are not, like those of Bach, *praeambulae fidei*; the wonder is that none the less his prayers are answered.

In different language Jaspers's point had been made by the ancient Hasidic wisdom which tells us, in Martin Buber's translation, that 'all prayers and hymns are a plea for God's glory to be revealed through-out the world. But if once the whole earth is indeed filled with it, there will be no further need to pray.' In concluding this interludial chapter I would like to turn from the theologians, philosophers and psycho-logists on whose words I have drawn in an attempt to illuminate, though not explain, the extraordinary effect of the Arietta in its context, and briefly to consider two visionary men of genius with whose religious sensibility Beethoven's is intimately in tune. Jakob Boehme was a 'separatist' in the early seventeenth century, as was Beethoven in the early nineteenth; that his conception of God was Beethovenian is implicit in the very fact that he envisaged Godhead as a process rather than as an absolute. God did not create the universe out of his perfection but in order to 'reveal Himself to Himself'. The division of reality into heaven and hell and the earth which is between the two, is itself the divine plan, in which a Fall is both inevitable and freely chosen. God contains both good and evil; man accepts the challenge to participate in, maybe to conquer, multiplicity. Thus 'the life of man is a form of the divine will, and to do the divine will means to become fully god-like and divine, by trying to realize one's highest ideals in thought, words and deeds. God must become man, in order that man may become God.'

Boehme tells us that there are seven phases (qualities or spirits) in God's creative process: desire, motion, anguish, conflagration, light (or love), sound and form. The spirit burgeons in desire, from which it enters into motion: which process itself generates opposition and conflict 'like a rotating wheel which eternally ascends and descends, from which results the greatest disquietude . . . giving rise to horrible anguish'. From this tension bursts forth a mighty conflagration: God's manifestation as a double principle of fire and light, embracing the dark and the light, the good and evil and all the paired dualities of the universe. This lightning flash at once produces and annihilates Time and differentiation: 'God the Father with great ardour and from all eternity yearns to manifest this heart, the centre of the light, and the good and evil generates it with his desiring will through the quality of the fire'. Fulfilment comes through what Boehme calls 'sound' but is really all sensory awareness on all planes of existence; indeed Boehme's 'sound' would seem to be equivalent to the Harmony of the Spheres audible to Adam in paradise. 'Form', the final phase, is paradise reborn. Lucifer was no less a part of God than Adam; 'Christ is effective only when we allow his sacrifice to be operative in us'. Man has it in his power, with God's help, to restore the perfection of Paradise, wherein 'the fire loved the light, receiving from it calmness and beneficence, while the light loved the fire as being its life, in the same sense that God in his quality as Father loves the Son, and the Son the Father'.

The psychological process implicit in this theology clearly parallels that which we have traced in Beethoven's creation, especially the evolving sequence of the last three piano sonatas; we will shortly see that it is no less relevant to the *Missa Solemnis*. If one finds it surprising that Beethoven's religious sensibility should so resemble that of a man who lived two hundred years earlier, in a cultural milieu very different from his own, the fairly obvious answer must be that the essence of religious sensibility is that it overrides temporality and locality, being archetypal. There is at least one link between Beethoven and Boehme in that among Boehme's disciples was another visionary, in this case a poet and painter, who was Beethoven's exact contemporary.

Beethoven did not know of Blake, and it is improbable that Blake knew more of Beethoven than his internationally famous name. None the less the affinity between the two men is profound, and not merely because both were regarded by many 'normal' people of their day as psychoticly disturbed, if not certifiably lunatic. The nature of this affinity is revealed by Northrop Frye's brilliant analysis of Blake's mythology, which equated the cyclical movements of history with a recurrent cycle within the human psyche.

Both cycles exist in four stages, forming a quaternity. The first is the revolutionary birth of Orc, the Son, out of Los's energy, Los being broadly equated with the creative principle. He is a Fall too, as is every artefact once it has been created; his name spells Sol backwards, and contains Loss within its meanings. The second stage is the transference of this instinctual power from Orc to Urizen, who is pictured by Blake as old, armed with ratio, measure and compasses, the 'mind-forged manacles' of Reason, which word is contained within his name. During this stage Orc is enchained and pinioned, more or less equated with Prometheus on his rock, Christ on his tree, and Adonis as Dying God. In the third stage religion is consolidated as something existing 'out there' in Kant's 'starry heavens', associated with preordained moral laws. This is symbolized by Urizen exploring his dens, manu-facturing the Nets of Religion. The verb 'manufacture' implies not merely 'hand-made', but probably also the intervention of machinery and industrialization: to which Blake in part attributes the fourth stage of his cycle, wherein chaos is upon us, symbolized in the crucifixion of Orc and the hanging of the serpent on the dead tree. Blake sees his own age, which is that of Beethoven, as entering this stage, and identifies Locke and Newton with Urizen, whom he later renamed Satan. Newtonian astronomy, according to Blake, reduced God to geometry and human life to a series of behaviouristic reflex actions. 'Single vision and Newton's sleep' substitute abstraction for reality, mathe-matical absolutes for human fallibilities: which is comforting only to men who are on the way to themselves becoming puppets; Franken-stein had invented his monster, Bionic Man was already envisaged. Not surprisingly this age is characterized, as Frye puts it, by scientific technology and complex machinery; by mechanistic wars springing from egoistic tyranny and Empire; and by unimaginative anti-art, in which Blake included most representational painting, such as that of Reynolds.

That Blake's position is extraordinarily close to that of Beethoven is obvious, not the less because Beethoven could articulate his beliefs only in music rather than words. The Boehme-like title of Blake's *The Marriage of Heaven and Hell* is profoundly Beethovenian; and in saying in that book 'Without contraries is no progression. Attraction and Repulsion, Reason and Energy, Love and Hate are necessary to Human Existence', Blake defines the basic polarities of Beethoven's music. There is a political dimension to this, if we think of Orc enchained as mankind enslaved, and relate this to Beethoven's enthusiasm for revolutionary causes, to his dedication of the Eroica to Napoleon, and his later renunciation of that homage. The political dimension, however, is a façade, for at heart Blake's poetry and Beethoven's music are religious: as is evident when Blake continues the aphorisms of *The Marriage of Heaven and Hell* by adding: 'From these Contraries spring what the Religious call Good and Evil. Good is the passive that obeys Reason. Evil is the active springing from Energy. Energy is Eternal Delight.' Blake borrowed his conception of the interrelationship of Heaven and Hell from Boehme and from Swedenborg, who wrote that

> the relation of heaven to hell is like that of two opposites, which act contrary to one another, from whose action and reaction results equilibrium, in which all things subsist. . . . Heaven is a One composed of the most various parts arranged in the most perfect form; for the heavenly form is the most perfect of all forms. . . . How great the delight of heaven is may appear from this circumstance alone, that in the heavens there is a communication of all with each and of each with all. . . . [But] evil viewed in itself, and also sin, is nothing but disjunction from good; hell consists in disunion.

This is close to Jaspers's identification of truth with communication; Beethoven would have agreed with Blake that true can be distinguished from false art because it speaks the language of true as distinct from false religion. Though most art in their day was in Blake's sense false, to distinguish true from false art was possible, though difficult. For whereas in pre-Romantic art grace could descend into the heart only from a heaven 'above', from Blake onwards it could be discovered nowhere but within the mind. For Blake in the Prophetic Books, for Beethoven in the last piano sonatas and the Missa Solemnis (and subsequently in the late string quartets), grace is a still centre where heavenly and hellish manifestations are united. Blake called this still centre Jerusalem, the City of God that Albion or mankind had failed to find only because, as Frye puts it, he had looked in the wrong place. 'Jerusalem is not a place but a condition of mind: which in an unfallen world would be Eden, or England's green and pleasant land, or the lost isle of Atlantis that we may rediscover if only we can drain from our minds "the Sea of Space and Time".'

For Blake the purpose of art, which is synonymous with life, is—to use Yeats's Plotinian terminology—to envisage life as a gyre, simultaneously a cornucopia and a maelstrom. I have employed these metaphors in relation to Beethoven, and will explore their further ramifications in discussing the Missa Solemnis. For the moment, however, I will return to Blake's Tyger, whose tensed muscles, gnashing teeth and flaming eyes are so potently auralized in the opening bars of opus 111. The Tyger is Solar Energy, Blake's Los, and the energy of fire is synonymous with sexual potency. But since sex creates life there is, or need be, no sharp distinction between the sexual and the sacral, as we saw in our discussion of Bach's music in The Dance of God. The Christian Church celebrates the making and blessing of New Fire in a way that parallels fire-producing rites all over the world. The fire-bringer (Beethoven-Prometheus) is the mediator between Earth and Heaven: 'our God is a consuming fire' (Heb. 12:29); and the furnace in the Book of Daniel is also a womb wherein 'I saw four men loose, walking in the midst of the fire . . . and the form of the fourth is like the Son [Sun] of God'. In Isaiah it is said that 'the light of Israel shall be for a fire, and his Holy One for a flame'. The slain Son-Christ is a Sun-Father, whose diurnal rotations are a cycle of births and deaths. Boehme had described the soul as 'a live coal, burned up by God'; medieval alchemists had also used the smithy image, describing how the soul is 'plunged in the fire of divine love', where 'like iron, it first loses its blackness, and then growing to a white heat it becomes like the fire itself. Lastly, growing liquid, it is transmuted into an utterly different quality of being.'

Now Blake's Tyger, whose brightness *burns* in the night, is this 'consuming fire', this 'Eternal Delight'. Yet his energy is also a dark force, inevitable because irrational; and Blake goes on to explore this paradox in a later stanza, when he asks: 'Did He smile His work to see? Did He who made the Lamb make thee?' Blake's question, as Frye points out, is unanswerable, or rather unaskable. Tigers and lambs coexist, and the one can lie down with the other only by denying its nature. In the tiger's world there can be neither good nor bad except that which is discovered by man himself. This is why man is potentially divine but also potentially devilish. Destruction is easier than creation, so it is not surprising that only occasionally may a man such as Blake or Beethoven be courageous enough to embrace the Tyger without denying the Lamb. This becomes the more significant at a time when men find difficulty in accepting a religious creed. Art is not then a substitute for religion; it would be truer to say, as Beethoven himself put it in conversation with Bettina Brentano, that the relationship of men towards art *is* religion.

Certainly it is this simultaneous vision of Tyger and Lamb that Beethoven attains in the collocation of the two movements of opus 111. Blake came close to the visionary heart of this music when he said 'He who sees the Infinite in all things sees God. He who sees the Ratio only sees himself only.' By the Ratio Blake meant the individualizing as well as the rationalizing faculty; it was this individualization that Beethoven had to pass through in order to encompass the Arietta's transcendence. In this movement Beethoven comes as close to seeing God as has been permitted to a creature fallible because fallen, 'sensible of mortality', as Shakespeare put it, yet 'desperately mortal'. To see God means to turn the potential to love and to communicate into fulfilment: to recognize, in Erich Fromm's words, that 'God is I, in as much as I am human'. Though 'these are parts of his ways: but how little a portion is heard of him?' (Job 26:14), this none the less fills us, as we listen to the Arietta, with reverence and awe. Through it, the Word shines and sings.

Beethoven entered paradise in effecting 'a communication that reaches its goal'. That very few are capable of the courage to do that seems to have been and to be accepted by the generality of mankind: It therefore seems pertinent to conclude this chapter with a quotation from Mandeville which admits to the gulf between Beethoven (and Blake and Shakespeare) and Mandeville and you and me, while at the same time asserting the centrality of Beethoven's paradisal experience, its relevance to us all:

> Of Paradys ne can I bot speken propurly, for I was not there. It is far beyonde, and that forthinketh me, and also I was not worthi. But as I have heard seye of wise men beyonde, I schalle telle you with gode wille. Paradys Terrestre, as wise men seye, is the highest place of erthe that is in alle the world, and it is so high that it toucheth nigh to the cercle of the mone, there as the mone maketh hir torn. For sche is so high that the Flode of Noe ne myght not come to hire that

woude have couered all the erthe of the world alle aboute and abouen and benethen, saf Paradys only allone. And this Paradys is enclosed alle aboute with a walle, and men wyte not whereof it is, for the walles ben couered alle ouer with mosse, as it semeth. And it semeth not that the walle is ston of nature ne of none other thing that the walle is. And that walle streccheth fro the south to the north, and it hath not but on entree that is closed with fire brennynge, so that no man that is mortelle ne dar not entren.

And in the most high place of Paradys, euene in the myddel place, is a welle that casteth out the IV flodes that rennen be diuerse londes. . . . And be londe may no man go for wylde bestes that ben in the desertes and for the high mountaynes and grete huge roches that no man may passe by for the derke places that ben there and that manye. And be the riuers may no man go, for the water renneth so rudely and so scharply because that it cometh doun so outrageously from the high places abouen that it renneth in so grete waves that no schipp may not rowe ne seyle agnes it. And the water roreth so and maketh so huge noyse and so gret tempest that no man may here other in the schipp, though he cryede with alle the craft that he coude in the hieste voys that he myghte. Many gret lordes han assayed with gret wille manye times for to passen to be riueres towards Paradys with fulle gret companye, but they myght noe speden in hire viage. And manye dyeden for weryness of rowynge ayenst tho strong wawes. And manye of hem becamen blynde and manye deve for the noyse of the water. And summe weren perisscht and loste within the wawes. So that no mortelle man may approche to that place withouten specyalle grace of God, so that of that place I can seye you no more. And therefore I schalle holde me stille and retornen to that that I have seen.

MANDEVILLE: *Travels*

A summary of the late piano sonatas

Sonata in E minor and major opus 90

1 *Mit Lebhaftigkeit und durchaus mit Empfindung und Ausdruck*
  Short sonata movement with songful potential.

  Key E minor; tempo 3/4

2 *Nicht zu geschwind und sehr singbar vorzutragen*
  Long rondo-song with vestiges of variation technique and of sonata.

  Key E major; tempo 2/4

Sonata in A major opus 101

1 *Etwas lebhaft und mit der innigsten Empfindung*
  Short sonata movement that is also a 'dream-like song'.

  Key A major; tempo 6/8

2 *Lebhalf Marschmässig*
Scherzo-march in dotted rhythm: a serious joke

  Key F major (flat
  submediant); tempo **C**

with canonic trio that hints at mysteries

  Key B flat major; tempo **C**

3 *Langsam und sehnsuchtsvoll*
  Slow interlude, aspiring towards a hymnic aria, but failing to attain
  it.

  Key A minor; tempo 2/4

leading by way of a cadenza into

4 *Zeitmass des ersten Stückes*
  A reminiscence of the dream-song sonata.

  Key A major; tempo 6/8

soon leading into

5 *Geschwind, doch nicht zu sehr, und mit Entschlossenheit*
  Full-scale sonata movement, but with contrapuntal (fugal)
  development and (abortive) coda.

  Key A major; tempo 2/4

Sonata in B flat major für das Hammerklavier opus 106

1 Large-scale sonata *Allegro* (the Morality of Power), but incorporating both song-like elements and fugato, with (abortive) coda.

> Key B flat major, with stress
> on mediant relationships;
> tempo ¢

2 Scherzo. *Assai vivace*
Parodistic of the first Allegro, with partially canonic trio that hints at mysteries.

> Key B flat major; tempo 3/4
> Key B flat minor; tempo 3/4
> but with rhythm dislocated

changing to *Presto* 2/4 for transition to da capo of the Scherzo

3 *Adagio sostenuto*
Aria, both hymnic and operatic, which is also a full-scale sonata movement, and employs variation techniques.

> Key F sharp minor, equated
> with G flat minor (the flat
> submediant of B flat); but D
> major (F sharp's flat
> submediant) also acts as a
> pivotal tonality; tempo 6/8

4 *Largo–Un poco vivace–Tempo I–Allegro–Tempo I–Prestissimo*
Transitional section, experimenting with various kinds of contrapuntal unity at various speeds.

> Key fluctuating rapidly,
> usually through mediants;
> tempo basically **C**

leading into

5 *Allegro risoluto*
Fully developed fugue, incorporating variation techniques with (partially abortive) coda.

> Key B flat major, but
> wide-ranging, and with the
> upper mediant D major
> crucially significant; tempo 3/4

Sonata in E major opus 109

1 *Vivace ma non troppo—Adagio espressivo* (in alternation)
Sonata movement with first and second subjects widely differentiated (Innocence and Experience), each containing a Hidden Song that emerges in an unresolved (but not abortive) coda.

> Key E major; tempo 2/4 (first subject), 3/4 (second subject)

2 *Prestissimo*
Scherzo in sonata form, with first and second subjects closely allied; texture always consistent, development contrapuntal.

> Key E minor; tempo 6/8

3 *Adagio molto cantabile ed espressivo (Gesang mit innigster Empfindung)*
Aria-hymn with five variations and a da capo: Innocence and Experience synthesized

> Key E major; tempo 3/4

Sonata in A flat major opus 110

1 *Moderato cantabile molto espressivo*
Sonata movement that is also a dream-song, with theme related to that of the variations in opus 109.

> Key A flat major; tempo 3/4

2 *Allegro molto*
'Peasant' scherzo, comic but not parodistic.

> Key F minor; tempo 2/4

with 'levitatory' trio metamorphosing the Peasant-Clown into a Holy Fool.

> Key D flat major (flat submediant of F minor); tempo 2/4

leading after da capo of Scherzo into

3 *Adagio ma non troppo –Recitativo–Arioso dolente (Klagender Gesang)*
Baroque-style 'Passion' music, introverted

> Key: *Adagio* begins in B flat minor, *Arioso dolente* in A flat minor; tempo *Recitativo* free, *Arioso dolente* 12/16

linked to

4 Fugue *Allegro non troppo*
A fully developed fugue that is also a song, experientially fulfilling

the sonata dream-song of the first movement: incorporating variation techniques; a reminiscence of
the *Arioso dolente*; an inversion of the fugue; and a return to sonata style for a (triumphant) coda.

> Key A flat major—G minor
> for the reminiscence of the
> *Arioso*—G major for the
> fugue's inversion—returning
> to A flat major; tempo 6/8

Sonata in C minor and major opus 111

1 *Maestoso*
Slow introduction in 'introverted' Baroque style.

> Key free, but establishing C
> minor and

leading into
2 *Allegro con brio ed appassionato*
A reconciliation of the opposite principles of sonata and fugue, with consummatory coda, plagally resolving into the major.

> Key C minor, with prevalent
> mediant relationships; tempo
> **C**

3 Arietta: *Adagio molto semplice e cantabile*
A sixteen-bar Song with four variations (divisions on a ground), virtually unmodulating, with a rapidly modulating retrospective interlude, a repetition of the Song, and an Epilogue.

> Key C major; tempo 9/16 and
> multiples thereof

THE STRONG THIEF

A study of the Missa Solemnis

Every lock has its key, which fits into it and opens it. But there are strong thieves who know how to open locks without keys. They break the lock. God loves the thief who breaks the lock open: I mean, the man who breaks his heart for God.

> *The Ten Rungs of Hasidic Lore* trans. Martin Buber

I have no friends, I must live alone. But well I know that God is nearer to me than to other artists. I associate with him without fear. I have always recognized and understood him and have no fear for my music. Those who understand it must be freed by it from all the miseries of the world.

> BEETHOVEN: letter to Count Ignaz von Gleichenstein 1807/8

What is the price of Experience? Do men buy it for a song?
Or wisdom for a dance in the street? No, it is bought with the price
Of all that a man hath, his house, his wife, his children.
Wisdom is sold in the desolate market where none come to buy.
And in the withered field where the farmer ploughs for bread in vain.

> WILLIAM BLAKE: *Vala:* Night the Second

Men are admitted into Heaven not because they have curb'd and govern'd their Passions or have No Passions, but because they have Cultivated their Understandings. The Treasures of Heaven are not Negations of Passion, but Realities of Intellect, from which all the Passions Emanate Uncurbed in their Eternal Glory....

Thinking as I do that the Creator of this World is a very Cruel Being, & being a Worshipper of Christ, I cannot help saying: 'the Son, O how unlike the Father!' First God Almighty comes with a Thump on the Head. Then Jesus Christ comes with a balm to heal it.

> WILLIAM BLAKE: *The Vision of Judgment*

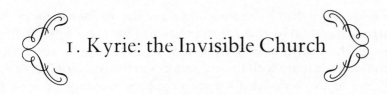 1. Kyrie: the Invisible Church

The instigation of Beethoven's most sublime work was an act of friendship as well as an act of religious conviction. As early as 1818 it was announced that the Archduke Rudolf would be appointed Archbishop of Olmütz on 9 March 1820; Beethoven decided, on his own initiative, that he would compose a High Mass for the occasion. That the Archduke Rudolf must have been a remarkable young man as well as an illustrious musician is testified by the fact that Beethoven had recently dedicated to him the grandest of his piano trios (now known as the Archduke) and the most titanic of his piano sonatas (the Hammerklavier): to which works the Missa Solemnis bears a relationship far profounder than an obsession, common to all three works, with mediant relationships between B flat and D. All three works stretch form, technique and instrumental resources beyond bounds then conceivable. Even though the Mass was originally intended for liturgical use—to which end Beethoven studied Latin declamation, the German text, and ecclesiastical musics of the past—it became a personal testament that was considered beyond the reach of the most accomplished professionals. There is a sense in which contemporary opinion was right: in which the unperformable nature of the Mass, as of the Hammerklavier sonata, is what the music is 'about'. Beethoven paid the Archduke a noble tribute in assuming that he, the dedicatee, would understand, whereas Tom, Dick and Harry, or even the faithful Schindler, wouldn't. Potentially Beethoven pays tribute also to us, his successors, for at the head of the autograph score he wrote 'Von Herzen—möge es wieder—zu Herzen gehen'. He asks for a communication that, to recall Jaspers's phrase, 'reaches its goal'; in so doing he envisages a 'transcendent perfection wherein there is no longer any need to communicate'.

Ultimately the Mass, like opus 111, becomes an act of prayer, a *demonstratio* of Leibniz's aphorism 'summum bonum est cognoscere Deum'. In 1823, the year in which the Mass was finally completed, too late for the Archbishop's ecclesiastical enthronement, Beethoven echoed Leibnitz's words when he wrote to the Archduke: 'There is nothing higher than to approach more nearly to the Godhead than other mortals, and by that contact to spread the rays of the Godhead through the human race.' By this time in his life Beethoven's 'Godhead' had little to do with the orthodoxies of the Roman Church, and still less to do with Kant's deity of ethical morality or with the humanitarian god of the Enlightenment's pietistic theologians. More relevant is the fact that Beethoven himself copied and kept on his desk, engraved and framed, an inscription which, according to Schindler, he came across in J. F. Champollion's *The Paintings of Egypt*: 'I am that which is. I am everything that was and is and shall be. No mortal has raised my veil. HE is himself alone, and to this Only One all things owe their existence.' Into a diary of 1816 Beethoven also copied these words (as he put it) 'from Indian literature': 'God is immaterial and for this reason transcends every conception. Since he is invisible he can have no form. But from what we observe in his work we may conclude that he is eternal, omnipotent, omniscient and omnipresent.' Beethoven's acquaintance with oriental mysticism was of course at second or third hand—probably, Schindler thinks, by way of Schelling and Schlegel; what matters, however, is not the extent or accuracy of his knowledge, but simply the fact that he considered such passages pertinent enough to his own creation to transcribe into his diary, and even to have framed for his desk. He lived and worked in the sight of this invocation to a deity who hardly sounds susceptible to Reason, but rather reminds us of St Augustine's 'word that abideth unchangeably in itself and reneweth all things'; of the Old Testament God of Power who Is what He Is; of Hegel's *Geist* through which all things are manifest and to which all things return; most remarkably he reminds us of Beethoven himself, who was alone by circumstance and by choice and who, cut off from the world by his deafness, became, like Christ, 'a vessel filled with divine conflict'. Psychiatrists have not neglected to relate Beethoven's need for an all-fathering deity to his lifelong battle against temporal authority, and to attribute that in turn to the influence of his drunkenly tyrannical father. Though that may be true enough, the biographical element is a gloss on the psychic struggle of the music, not the other way round. Beethoven did not compose the Missa Solemnis because at the time his paranoia over his nephew had reached its crisis; on the contrary, the crisis in his personal life was precipitated out of the archetypal struggle of his music, wherein he had wrestled—in his own words—with 'the powers of darkness'. Though Beethoven's relationship with Karl ended in failure, his music was a triumph. Schindler tells us that while working on the Missa Solemnis Beethoven's 'whole personality seemed to take on a different form. Never before or after have I seen him in such a condition of oblivion to everything worldly.'

From a superficial aspect Beethoven's partiality for 'oriental' mysticism was part of the Zeitgeist, especially as manifest in the cult of Freemasonry. In its eighteenth-century form Masonry was a paradox. Basically it was the Enlightenment's answer to the 'superstition' of revealed religion and was opposed to, as it was opposed by, the Roman Church. But although it encouraged the toleration of different, even opposed, religious beliefs, it was not atheistical, and was avowedly non-political: the original English Lodge explicitly stated, in 1723, that 'we are resolved against all Politicks', and defined its aims as 'the conciliation of true Friendship among Persons who must otherwise have remained at a perpetual distance'. In France the Masonic programme was parallel to that of the Encyclopaedists: 'all brothers in every country' were to 'unite in collecting materials for a Universal Dictionary of liberal arts and useful sciences (excluding politics and religion)'. In Germany Masonic ideals were more overtly moralistic: G. C. Lessing defined the movement's aims as an 'exercise of Brotherly Love', whereby we are 'taught to regard the whole human species as one family, the high and the low, the rich and the poor, created by one Almighty Being, and sent into the world for the aid, support and protection of each other'. Clearly such aims, being social, could hardly eschew politics: nor did they when, later, the Masons tended to split into two camps, one of which, the Rosicrucians, stressed the mysticism inherent in the cult, while the other, the Illuminati, emphasized rational education as a source of social betterment. By the end of the century the hysteria of the Establishment even maintained that the Illuminati were directly responsible for the French Revolution. The charge was paranoid; even Heinrich Ziegenhagen, the most radical of the Illuminati, who in 1792 published a book on *The Right Relationship to the Works of Nature* wherein he advocated a classless society, maintained that such a community could be peacefully established through education. Katharine Thomson quotes his employment of a musical metaphor: 'As in a concert general harmony can result only if every individual plays his part exactly in time, and discords result if any single person introduces a wrong note, so the happiness of society depends on the correct relationship of the individual, and the happiness of the individual depends on the harmony within society.' No one, not even the Enlightened, took much notice of starry-eyed Ziegenhagen; the rich did not, as he recommended, voluntarily surrender their wealth to the common weal. The disillusioned man committed suicide in 1826.

None the less Freemasonry remained basically an educational movement. Masons went on a pilgrimage, passed through an initiation, in order to see the LIGHT, which could be apprehended only through rational understanding based on a philosophically sound education. This is how Gluck, himself a Mason, reinterprets the story of Orpheus in his opera: Man-Orpheus may himself become god-like in confronting sin, death and the pointless malignancy of fortune with a stoic acceptance born of a 'reasonable' awareness of human limitation. Orpheus sings out his grief—to Nature, not to Society— expressively and intimately, with sighing appoggiaturas but in gently arching, consistently diatonic melodies that are simple, sensuous and passionate, without excess. He comes through the fire and confronts the furies unharmed, because he is as sincere and faithful as a human can hope to be. This is why 'the gods' relent and accept his restoration to his lost Eurydice, which occurs, since it reasserts human fallibility, in the most dramatic, sonata-like music in the opera. The heaven he longs for, as manifest in the music of the Elysian Fields, is simply his own Rousseauistic humanism sublimated, a song played by Dionysus' flute, now rendered pure and innocent, pastoral but no longer in any sense Pan-ic. It is neither an Italian aria nor a French chanson, but something between the two, a rurally presented quasi-folk song of the urban Common but Enlightened Man of the eighteenth century. Both in intention and in technical means the exquisitely orchestrated music is comparable with Beethoven's Pastoral Symphony though, in its unsullied diatonic major, and its ordered but sensuous parallel thirds, it is more dreamily unreal.

The Masonic implications of Gluck's Orphic opera become still more evident in the choral music, which of its nature is communal. The choruses owe something in balance and grace to the legacy of French operatic tragedy from Lully to Rameau, but are simpler, more open, more symmetrically homophonic, with unassertively arching diatonic melodies, harmonized with plain triadic chords, mostly in root position. Haydn, also a Freemason, garnered hints for his own choral writing in The Creation and The Seasons from Gluck's choric homophony; while the fact that there are direct Masonic references in purely instrumental works of Haydn—for instance the E flat major piano sonata no. 59, and the string quartet opus 54—reminds us that the dialectic of the sonata principle was itself a musical synonym for a psychological pilgrimage: a trial or test that might be Masonically interpreted. When Haydn was admitted to the Order, Holzmeister, Grand Master of the Lodge, praised the composer for 'inventing a new order of things in the orchestra.... If every instrument does not considerably diminish its volume, in order not to do damage to the utterance of its companions, the end, which is beauty, would not be attained.' The symphony orchestra, as employed by Haydn, is a musical metaphor, similar to that used by Ziegenhagen, for Masonic democracy, just as sonata, as a principle of composition, is a Masonic initiation and journey.

Haydn did not attend many Masonic meetings, perhaps more because he was old and geographically ill-placed than because he lacked zeal for the cause. None the less the new Emperor Francis II expressed displeasure at what he considered a threat to the composer's devout Catholicism. He had more cause for alarm in the case of Mozart, who had been interested in Masonry for a number of years, and whose entry into the order in December 1784 had precipitated Haydn's entry in February of the following year. Certainly for Mozart the appeal of Masonry was on deeper and more complex levels, for Masonic strands are manifest in most of the greatest works of his maturity. The final trilogy of symphonies is the grandest possible Masonic credo: no. 39 in the Masonic ritual key of E flat major; no. 40 in Mozart's 'tragic' G minor; and no. 41 in 'white' C major representing the triumph of Light, and including a synthesis of homophonic and polyphonic principles. The string quintets, perhaps the greatest of Mozart's chamber works, similarly reinterpret the social aspects of Masonry into psychological terms: the D major and C major in the same spirit as the final symphonies; the G minor as an initiation, an *agon*, and an Edenic rebirth. In the last, E flat major quintet—as in the Clarinet Concerto, and in the cantatas and instrumental works that Mozart wrote, in the last year of his life, specifically for Masonic rites—the composer evolved what amounts to a new idiom: luminously transparent (letting the Light through), seemingly of folk-like innocence, yet fraught with the burden of *lacrimae rerum*. The last piano concerto, K. 595, after many Masonic echoes, ends with a child's ditty, reborn; the tragic pain of the G minor quintet dissolves in a major apotheosis that reminds us of Papageno.

It is Mozart's Masonic opera, *The Magic Flute*, that reveals how the notion of a Masonic initiation could, invoking the Eleusinian Mysteries, reintroduce mystical transcendence into the Enlightenment's humanitarian ethic. Pamina, the central character in the opera, is the object of conflict between the forces of Darkness and of Light. It is she, as feminine intuition, who gives the magic flute to Tamino, who is man striving towards perfection; and it is by means of the flute (with which, like Orpheus, he can woo the wild beasts of the woods) that he can withstand the trials of fire and water. Papageno, man in a state of Nature before Nurture, is also a kind of unregenerate Orpheus, who impudently tootles Dionysus' pipes, and whose bells magically simulate Apollo's lyre. Rousseau's Noble Savage is fused with Nature's bird and with the Innocent Child: which is the point from which regeneration may begin. So Papageno's Edenic music, which we have related to the finales of the G minor quintet and of the last piano concerto, gives a deeper meaning to Gluck's piping in the Elysian Fields, just as the grave symmetry of Sarastro's arias, the spacious homophony of the High Priests' choruses, and the austere Protestant polyphony of the Men in Armour chorale create from the euphony, the regular periodicity and the harmonic sobriety of Gluck a texture and sonority at once enlightenedly civilized and darkly primeval. There are comparable passages in Mozart's last work, the *Requiem*, and in the slow movement of the Clarinet Concerto. Serene, even benign, the dark-hued music is far removed from eighteenth-century opera, yet it is not traditionally ecclesiastical. Perhaps one might say that Mozart's Masonic musics, especially the choruses, are, by way of the German chorale, a cross between hymn, aria and folk-song, though this description is inadequate in that it ignores the high degree of artifice in their lucid part-writing.

The orthodox morality of the Enlightenment adhered of course to the well-illuminated notion of God as master-mechanic, or more specifically as First Architect and Mason. Even though the Mystery within the pilgrimage appealed to the Enlightenment's cult of the Hellenistic, and also, by way of Persian Zoroastrian rites, to its sense of the Exotick, rational man could only blench at the dark irrationalities thus revealed. Nevertheless the truly great artists, those who were 'points at which the growth of the mind shows itself', were such precisely because they did *not* blench. It is not an accident that Mozart's last Masonic works were, despite their light-giving social bias, profoundly death-haunted; nor is it an accident that his Masonic opera explores, alongside the Masonic initiation into Light and Reason, the

Eleusinian death, descent to the dark labyrinth and rebirth, which Gluck's Orphic opera approaches but evades. Though less explicit than Gluck's opera in referring to the lost Eternal Beloved, whom Orpheus as light-giving man-god must woo from the inchoate dark, Mozart's Masonic opera is the more religious, as well as the more psychologically profound work. This is why there is an affinity between *The Magic Flute*, which Beethoven admired most among Mozart's operas, and the Missa Solemnis, which is a personal re-creation of the initiation and rebirth symbolized in the Christian Eucharist.

We do not know precisely what happened in the Mysteries at Eleusis, a name related to Elysium. If we did know, they wouldn't be mysterious; and indeed the word *mysterion* is etymologically connected with that which is mute, and therefore not to be communicated. It would seem, according to the researches of Kerényi and others, that the mysteries began as worship of the corn goddess Demeter or Ge-meter, and embraced the separation by time and mortality of mother from daughter. In the underworld the daughter, Persephone, was raped in becoming the bride of death; was reborn in the spring; only to die again in an eternal cycle. The myth embraces the duality of seasonal process, of Demeter's poppy of oblivion, and of Persephone's pomegranate, the fecund fruit of death. Though the miracle of the Mystery is the rebirth of the seed of corn after its dark sojourn in the earth, the psychological dimension, in relation to individual human beings, is no less significant. What happened to the initiates in the cavernous inner temple seems to have been some kind of vision of blinding light and consuming fire, wherein Persephone, now a goddess of the underworld, gave birth to new life. According to many versions of the myth Persephone was a daughter of Dionysus, passional god of instinct and of the vine; but Dionysus is also said to have been both her seducer *and* the divine son whom she bears in the tomb-womb cave. So the wheel comes full circle and the seasonal sequence is made whole. The Mysteries 'hold the entire human race together', as Pindar put it; 'blessed is he who enters upon the way below the earth: he knows the end of life and its beginning'. On this basis the affinities between the Persephone story, as manifest in the Mysteries, and the Christian Passion are obvious, because archetypal. The metaphor of regenerated and regenerative corn is explicit in the New Testament. St John writes: 'Except a corn of wheat fall into the ground and die, it abideth alone; but if it die, it bringeth forth much fruit.' Similarly from St Paul (I Cor. 15:35–6) we read: 'How are the dead raised up? and with what body do they come? Thou fool, that which thou sowest is not quickened, except it die.' The vision of the *Abgrund des Kerns*, in Goethe's phrase (the atom's abyss), becomes a *visio beatifica* such as is celebrated in the Christian Mass on Easter Sunday with a sudden blaze of light and a purifying fire. By Beethoven's time the relation between High Mass and the Eleusinian Mysteries could be more than instinctive; we know that he was 'consciously' interested in the Mysteries, and spoke of a Mass that would fuse Christian ecstasis with Dionysiac frenzy. In his somewhat dubious dealings with publishers over the Missa Solemnis he mentions two other masses, one in the 'old modes', either *a cappella* or with wind instruments, the other in C sharp minor, a 'transcendent' key (awkward for strings) in Beethoven's music, as is F sharp minor (tricky for tempered keyboards) in Bach's. Such references served to confuse publishers by offering alternative baits, though the Missa Solemnis, when belatedly it reached fruition, seems to have achieved precisely this fusion of techniques. Perhaps the C sharp minor Mass turned into the 'old-fashioned' fugal opening of the C sharp minor string quartet opus 131; certainly if any music carries on from the 'transcendent' polyphony of the Mass, this is it.

Freemasonry, we have seen, involved paradox and contradiction between rational enlightenment and irrational power. Beethoven's Missa Solemnis embraces and reconciles these opposites, starting from the social-spiritual grace that Masonry was consciously aware of. On a sublime scale, the Kyrie begins as though its aim is to inculcate the Masonic virtues of humanity, wisdom and honesty, 'to spread good thoughts and unity among the members so that they may unite in the idea of innocence and joy'. Beethoven's approach is quite different from that of Bach, who treats the Kyries and Christe as three separate movements that form a ternary structure, with thematic and tonal interrelationships. Beethoven inserts the Christe as a middle section within a single symphonic movement. Though it is a ternary form, it contains sonata elements, in that the da capo is developmental. The key is D major, which Beethoven seems to associate here, as in the Hammerklavier Sonata, with the Godhead. The metre has two minims a bar in *alla breve* time; but this doesn't mean that one should count or think in a duple beat, but rather that the four crotchets, felt as a slow duple-swinging pendulum, should be played *cantabile* and *sostenuto*. The fact that the entries occur on the upbeat imparts to the

spacious serenity a sense of elevation: the textures, being architectur-
ally (Masonically) balanced, with strings and wind interwoven, sound
humanely earth-rooted, yet aspirational. Although grand, the mood is
also graciously gentle, both in the sense of being 'honourable, noble,
courteous' (O.E.D.) and also—in view of what is to happen later—in
the technical sense of 'having the right to bear arms'. This Masonic
apatheia and musical decorum are Beethoven's way of beginning, if
not exactly where his society was, at least of beginning where, in terms
of Kantian ethics and Hegelian philosophy, it might reasonably if
ideally have hoped to be. He reinforces the point with his direction *'mit
Andacht'*—with devotion, and seems (how deceptively) to accommo-
date the opening music to his audience's expectations by scoring it for
a normal classical orchestra of double woodwind and trumpets, four
horns and strings. Trombones and timpani are added later, but are
used sparely, though with shattering effect. Organ, used mostly to
support the bass line, is the only extra instrument, and that was of
course not unprecedented in choral and orchestral works.

Bach opens with uplifted arms and hands, as well as voices; Beethoven begins with the wondrous stability of a major triad for strings
and wind, followed by a nobly balanced string melody that falls
through a sixth, rises a fourth, and flows down the scale:

Ex. 134

Solo clarinet, oboe and flute sing through the strings with long-held
tones that droop through a minor third, answered by a diminished
fifth. It is as appropriate as it is fortuitous that the initial melodic
material should be pervaded by falling minor thirds, the basic pentatonic interval from which embryonic melody Edenicly springs; and
by tritones, the harmonically neutral interval traditionally associated
with a Fall. Moreover there is a complement to this in the texture, for
the lines move in lyrical contours of god-like grandeur, while incorporating chromatic passing notes that suggest a humane sensuousness.
This simultaneously earthly and heavenly quality is manifest in the

visual appearance of the score. The arching lines flow with a lucidity one wants to call chaste, the sheer perfection of the part-writing carrying us 'out of this world'; yet balancing this horizontal dimension is the vertical progression of the harmony, which looks as resonant as it sounds, as clear-structured as late Mozart, rooted in but not tethered to the ground. So there is an equilibrium between the physical and the metaphysical, different from, though comparable with, that in the music of Bach. The dialogue between the strings' harmonious concourse and the soloistic entries of the woodwind also suggests an equilibrium between public and private values. There is a concord one may attain in a Kantian communion of 'men of good will'; there are also our individual needs and desires which, even within that communion, cannot be ignored. This dichotomy becomes patent when the voices enter, for Beethoven scores for soprano, alto, tenor and bass soloists, with chorus, in an antiphony parallel to that of woodwind and strings in the ritornello.

There are three entries of the chorus, and three soloistic answers. This is direct Masonic symbolism, for the repetition refers to the threefold knocking by the candidate for initiation on the door of the Lodge, each knock representing one of the trinity of Masonic virtues, Beauty, Strength, and Wisdom. The dotted rhythm on repeated notes also signifies Masonic resolution and fortitude—though the figure tends to have something of that implication in most European music. The offbeat cry of Kyrie on the chorus's D major triad is echoed by tenor solo, whose D is not maintained but relaxed through a minor third, above parallel thirds (another Masonic symbol for harmonious relationship) on clarinets and bassoons (which were by this time established as Masonic instruments). In the second invocatory phrase the chorus's subdominant triad is echoed by the soprano solo, falling through a tritone instead of a minor third: so the first two solo entries more obtrusively repeat those of clarinet and oboe in the opening ritornello. For the third entry the chorus returns to the tonic, the sopranos reiterating high As in a dominant chord over a tonic pedal. The fundamental European norms of progression from dominant to tonic are sounded simultaneously, and the procedure, though dissonant, seems to be reassuring: for though the alto solo's answer still falls, it does so calmly, by step. Throughout these invocations Masonic pairs of clarinets and bassoons, simulating brotherhood, weave in parallel thirds. There is further Masonic symbolism when the string figurations lift through fifths and fourths to create tender appoggiaturas, slurred in fraternal pairs across the beats: an increase in harmonic warmth that promotes a declining chromatic F in the bass, which in turn generates chromatics in the other parts.

Marvellously subtle is the way in which thematic interest shifts between vocal and instrumental elements. At bars 50–5, for instance, melodic argument is entrusted to oboe and horn, then clarinet, while the voices intone the Masonic dotted rhythm. This prepares the way for a sudden piano (bar 59), wherein the chorus embarks on its first (and chromaticized) stretto. Despite the counterpoint, the texture remains open, spacious, even relaxed. There is greater energy at the modulation to the relative minor, when the soprano entry (bar 64), tied across the bar, covers a seventh. Yet what seems to be a further intensification to F sharp minor turns into a dominant to F sharp *major*, which in context glows radiantly (bars 68–77). We have spoken, especially in connection with the Hammerklavier Sonata, of the significance of mediant relationships in Beethoven's later music, both in the sense that they undermine the traditional tonal relationships of eighteenth-century public music, and also in the sense that, involving 'false' relation in the sixteenth-century meaning of the term, they reflect an ambivalence between melodic and harmonic—and perhaps also between metaphysical and physical—worlds. This F sharp major episode is, in relation to D, the first false-related mediant transition in the Missa Solemnis. Later we shall see that the Mass involves an elaborate network of mediant relationships, with some 'allegorical' implications, even though these are not as systematic as is Bach's deployment of traditional Baroque tonal relationships in his Mass in B minor.

On this occasion, however, the false relation of F sharp major changes back to B major and so, by way of a IV–V–I cadence, into the unfalse relative, B minor. Woodwind here take over the broken arpeggios from the strings; Masonically interlocked, their undulating sixths might be pleading hands or wafting wings. With an abrupt crescendo we are carried into the Christe section, which stays in B minor but changes the pulse to 3/2, somewhat faster: probably not far off one bar of the new triple rhythm equalling two beats of the previous tempo. Incarnation in the Christ imparts urgency to the humanely idealized concord of the Kyrie, though the Christe's thematic material is not new. The descending minor third of the tenor's first solo cry becomes more metrically energetic, both in the orchestra and in the entries of the solo voices. A countermotive of rising fourth and falling scale (the 'ecclesiastical cliché' we saw to be pervasive in Bach's Mass) drives forward regularly, even martially; and the *ben marcato* thrusts promote rapid modulation through D and G major, E and A minor, and cyclically up again to B minor. The minim rhythm swings like a pendulum, the falling thirds sometimes being expanded to sonorous octaves. As fugato texture grows complex, Beethoven achieves both intensification and clarity by a consummately skilful mixture of orchestral doublings and octave transpositions; climax is reached when the chorus sings in antiphony with the soloists. Here the music is Bachian in its 'planetary' movement and in the apparent inevitability of its counterpoint, Beethovenian in the wilfulness of its rhythmic impulse. Gradually the Christe sinks to rest: first by way of the bass soloist's descent through an eleventh, then through swings of a fifth that cadence, after a German sixth, in F sharp minor. The sonority of these bars, leading to triple piano but for full chorus, soli and strings, is awe-inspiring, as the chorus returns to the falling thirds, whispered, while the soloists wing the countermotive across the beats. The sopranos' cadential dominant ninth is sweetly painful:

Ex. 135

This leaves us waiting for the da capo which, since it returns abruptly to D major, effects another mediant false relation.

Though this da capo opens strictly, its antiphony of soloists and chorus veers to the subdominant instead of tonic. What follows is more like a sonata development than a recapitulation, for shifts of key and permutation of motive are incessant. The G major subdominant falls to *its* subdominant and hints at D, A and E minors, until chromatic passing notes and overlapping entries of the rising fourth–falling scale motive from the Christe induce a real modulation to the flatness of E flat major. This again is a flat submediant to G, thus far the prevailing key of the da capo. The music wanders back to G and D minors, and undulates through chromatic sequences, during which the choral voices try to hold their own in the dotted rhythm of Masonic fortitude, as though to stabilize the flux. When the orchestral bass settles on a long dominant pedal to the original D major (bars 182–91), it seems to promise triumph. Yet the simplicity of the opening periods is not recaptured. After the dominant pedal has weakened, the restatement of the Kyrie begins in the subdominant again, with a dissonant triple appoggiatura. In bar 170 the coda had stolen in with a mysterious touch of B flat major: which we will understand more fully in the light of later developments. A plagal, subdominant tendency survives through the final bars, as the voices rest on their dotted-rhythmed Ds, while woodwind intertwine in the motive of leaping fourth (or sometimes sixth) and declining scale. In the last two bars the sopranos fall, doubling the tenors, from the fifth to the major third: so the da capo, which has been a revelation of unsuspected depths rather than a recapitulation, disperses on that seminal interval, in its major form. It would seem that concord, whether within the body politic or within the individual psyche, is a state to be sought for, in continual process.

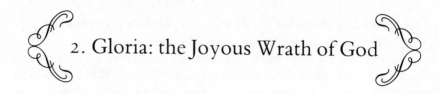

2. Gloria: the Joyous Wrath of God

As though Beethoven were appalled by the inconceivable gulf between the human and the divine, the reality of God shatters the ideality of Man, however Masonicly humane. The Christe had juxtaposed a swinging 3/2 pulse to the architectural balance of Masonic man's duple rhythm, but the two rhythms are counterpoised, not opposed. In the Gloria's fast 3/4 rhythm, however, God rushes in where angels, let alone men, might fear to tread, with a theme of upward surging scales stressing, unlike the plagally flavoured Kyrie, the sharp leading note:

Ex. 136

The choral entries shoot up to high A in the tenors, E in the basses; sustain their altitude; fall once again through a third. No less astonishing are the vast sweep and reiterated bow-strokes of the strings; what must contemporary double-bass players have thought, seeing their parts stomping and skipping through the same immense range as the cellos? The words speak of God in his heaven; if this is D major God-music, it is a God of power, a divine fire. One thinks, as with the Hammerklavier Sonata, of Blake's Los, the holy smith whose name spells Sol backwards. A dominant modulation is emphasized by chromatic passing notes, and the first paragraph ends, on the word *Deo*, with a descent from the high A through a godly fifth, not third. The Byzantine blaze of the music is enhanced by the scoring, with an inverted dominant pedal screaming through seventeen bars on very high flute at one extreme, while at the other bassoons and double-bassoon growl below the tenors and basses.

On the words *Et in terra pax* the music returns to, but does not resolve in, D major. The basses sing softly repeated As, perhaps derived from the 'fortitude' motive of the Kyrie. When the other voices enter they move in 'peaceful' homophony, by step; texture is glued by pedal As on horns. Though the music is hymnic, it is a hymn sung by 'men of good will', here on earth; the repeated notes and pedal notes, the interlocking string arpeggios, the subdominant modulation, recall the Masonic hymn of the Kyrie, and are at the opposite pole to the *in excelsis*'s frenzy. Whereas Bach, in his Gloria, mysteriously inverts the traditional relationship between God and Man, Beethoven adheres to it, though his God, as compared with man's *pax*, seems a disruptive, even destructive, force. The first part of the movement is built on a violent opposition between God's maelstrom and man's attempt at civilized conformity. On the words *Laudamus te* the whirl-wind upward scale recurs and swirls us from D major to B minor; the word *adoramus* is, however, whispered in homophonic repeated notes on the dominant of B, hollowly without the third. *Glorificamus te* returns to D major and to a Godhead yet more impetuous, since the choral voices enter in fugato, with a lurching theme falling through a fifth and leaping an octave, syncopated across the bars. The godly intervals of fifth and octave hardly ennoble the music, however, partly because the syncopated rhythm sounds drunken, partly because the vocal lines are high and strained, reinforced by instrumental parts that move in quavers, creating heterophonic tonal and semitonal clashes. The scoring, with instrumental doublings on high flutes and double-bassoon, covers a range of six octaves. The excitation is brazen. Again there is an interruption of a whispered *adoramus*, this time on a tonic triad in first inversion instead of the hollow fifth of B minor's dominant. The hush is obliterated by a fortissimo resumption of the fugato, which this time modulates flatwards to G, C and A minor. The section ends in a compromise between G major and E minor, and with what looks as though it will be a sustained plagal cadence in G.

The C major triad changes, however, to the minor, and surprisingly effects a transition to B flat major: in which key begins, more slowly and gently, the *gratias agimus*. B flat major is the flat submediant to D major, and the two keys are in false relation, since the F is sharp in the one, natural in the other. This is a 'falser' relationship than that between D major and B minor, mediants which are also relatives; and that Beethoven makes the relationship between D major and B flat major the tonal pivot of his Missa Solemnis bears on the relation between God and Man as manifest in his work. Bach builds his Mass on the axis of mediants that are also relatives; Beethoven exploits the more radical relationship of the flat submediant. Yet though the 'divine conflict' is fiercer in Beethoven, the peace he wins through to may prove yet more awe-inspiring. At this stage in the work—assuming we are approaching it without knowledge of the last three piano sonatas—we have no evidence either way, except for the fact that the Kyrie, though not 'transcendent', has generated a serene content that must, one suspects, have found justification in an individual psyche (Beethoven's). At this moment in the Mass, however, the music claims no more than to be humane as well as human. We give thanks to God, despite the formidable, even terrifying aspect he has assumed in the opening section, in a theme swaying in triple rhythm, at first in a Masonic concourse of woodwind, then sung by solo voices:

Ex. 137

The melody evolves from the basic motive of falling third, but acquires a hint of operatic fervour as the entries entwine in sequences

moving in alternating major and minor, from B flat to C minor, from F major to E flat major. The operatic reference is not fortuitous, since eighteenth-century opera had, after all, been concerned with human relationships in a social context; there is an interesting affinity between the *Gratias* theme and Sarastro's aria *In diesen heil'gen Hallen*. The music's urbane sociability is, however, less solemn, though not less humane, than *The Magic Flute* aria, and may be slightly compromised in that the rhythm is that of a fastish waltz. For although the waltz may have become a relative of the aristocratic minuet, its origins—as we shall see later in reference to the *Diabelli Variations*—were low, and its implications sometimes revolutionary. Certainly if we think of this B flat waltz as a sonata-style second subject to the first theme's thrusting D major scales, it is not merely a passive alternative, as are the brief *et in terra pax* episodes in the first section. Indeed the soloists' lyrical urgency, in stressing quasi-operatically our personal desires, serves to recharge the batteries of Blakean Energy. The subdominant modulation to E flat, which one might expect to create relaxation, in fact brings back (bar 174) the 'whirlwind' theme in that key, which now sounds like, and acts as, the flat supertonic to D major. So God's omnipotence bursts the dykes in a trenchant sonata-style development. On the word *omnipotens* Beethoven for the first time introduces trombones, in a searing dominant seventh of E flat, in a basic G minor. He then silences them for one hundred and fifty-four bars! This savagely underlines the 'otherness' of God. Phrases are treated in opposing keys and in broken antiphony, dichotomy now being between God the Father and God the Son, as a ripe dominant ninth takes us into F major at the citation of Jesus' name. The furious scales battle against 'omnipotently' assertive arpeggios, veering between F major and D minor. The 'divine conflict' within the Two Persons of God rages within Beethoven's mind; but the music cadences, by way of chains of suspensions recalling the *Gratias* waltz, on a gentle dominant seventh of F.

Though what we have just experienced sounds like a sonata development, there is no recapitulation. The larghetto *Qui tollis* serves as a slow movement, and is the most dramatically 'personalized' music thus far in the Mass, as is Bach's *Qui tollis* in his. The theme opens with scalewise-falling thirds and a rising fourth, in Masonic scoring for woodwind. The flavour is, however, very different from that of the Kyrie, because when Beethoven introduces the four solo voices in dialogue and with antiphonal comments from the chorus, their music is operatically projected. They become you and me, individual human creatures pleading for compassion, while the chorus represents Mankind. There may be a parallel with *The Magic Flute* here too, for the pleas of the soloists resemble the Queen of Night's appeal to Tamino to save her daughter. The Christian motive recalls St Thomas à Kempis: 'there is none else under Heaven who can comfort me but only thou ... who bringest me down to Hell and bringest me back again'; if it is true that the Queen of Night began, in Schikaneder's libretto, as a Demeter-like Earth Goddess but turned into a Catholic enemy of Masonic Enlightenment, then the 'we' whom Beethoven's soloists personify embrace both her positive and negative aspects. That the music brings in the mystical as well as social aspects of Freemasonry is suggested by the ambiguous tonality, which hovers between F major and D minor, distantly prophesying the modality of the *Incarnatus*, just as Bach had construed his *Qui tollis* as an Annunciation. At first the voices move in parallel thirds, an interval which Beethoven seems to have associated with the human aspects of Jesus, as well as with merely human brotherhood. With the *miserere* phrase, however, the vocal lines become arpeggiated, with yearning appoggiaturas, angular stretches, and dotted notes and triplets that energize the music into frequent modulations. Even the chorus's interjections grow impassioned, though their severely contrapuntal stretti, apposite to Man as a species as distinct from individually suffering human beings, balance the soloists' declamatory fervour. The reference to *peccata mundi* induces modulations veering between D and B flat major and B minor; sensuously weeping thirds are stabbed with a shiver of tremolando diminished sevenths (Ex. 138).

Such music is of a physical immediacy that anticipates Verdi, though perhaps the only valid parallel to its fusion of passion with spirituality is in Pamina's tragic G minor aria, *Ach, ich fühl's*, in *The Magic Flute*. One can legitimately say that this music combines a Bach-like gravity in its architectural proportions with a Mozartian poignancy in its operatic lyricism, while generating an introspective intensity that is wholly Beethoven's.

The interrelationship between Bach's *Qui tollis*, Beethoven's *Qui tollis*, and Pamina's aria is worth dwelling on. In the case of the Bach and the Mozart there are specific musical parallels. Both themes fall through a fifth, incorporating the third; Mozart rises an octave and returns to the sixth that Bach leaps to. Mozart then falls to the sharp seventh, Bach to the major third and seventh, the chromatic notes in

Ex. 138

each case injecting pain. The flute semiquavers of Bach's *Qui tollis* are matched by Pamina's arpeggiated semiquavers; both themes have a similarly subdued accompaniment. Pamina weeps because she thinks she is unloved, since Tamino, faithful to his Masonic vow of silence, has refused to speak to her. As Brigid Brophy has pointed out, this amalgamates the test by air (which should not be wasted in speech) and the trial of Orpheus who is forbidden to look at Eurydice. After singing her aria, Pamina contemplates suicide, but is saved by three beings who are servants both of the Queen of Night and of the 'white' priest Sarastro. In the Christian no less than in the Orpheus and Persephone stories there is a sojourn in the underworld, where the hero dies as the year dies, and the moon is 'no more' for three days. H. H. Kram has remarked how this myth was adapted to his theology by Luther, who insists that Christ did not merely feel forsaken and condemned by God on the Cross, but really was thus forsaken and condemned. His desolation was identical with Pamina's; for both the only answer to unrequited love and apparent betrayal was death.

The difference is that, whereas for Pamina-Mozart suffering is irremediable except in the transitory moment of its musical incarnation, for Bach-Christ there is a remedy that may be efficacious not merely symbolically in the artefact, but in a life 'beyond'. Pamina is left inconsolable on a minor triad; Bach's *Qui tollis* ends on a *tierce de Picardie* that paradoxically turns into Crucifixion's E minor, which is to prove a gateway to eternal life! 'For as in Adam all die, even so in Christ shall all be made alive' (I Cor. 15:22). In Beethoven's *Qui tollis* there is no direct thematic affinity with Pamina's aria, though the music's fusion of personal desolation with hymnic universality is similar. Moreover there is a further parallel in the strange and sublime canonic quartet in *Fidelio*, wherein the four protagonists distil the *pathos* and *agon* of their interlinked human predicaments into an ostinato-based dialogue that transports them momentarily outside Time (see Appendix B). In this *Qui tollis* the four soloists, enacting their passions and Passion, likewise attain a tranced stillness. The drama in which they are playing is Everyman's, and their theme is the eternal burden of sin and folly.

The parallel with the *Fidelio* quartet becomes still more pointed in the setting of the words *suscipe deprecationem nostram*, for while the voices rise in a human emulation of God's upsurging scales, the orchestral parts become a solemn march, with a chord on each quaver beat, separated by semiquaver rests (bars 257–66). This takes us to B flat, where the chorus enters to depict Christ enthroned at the right hand of God the Father. The music is ceremonially statuesque, with Baroque double-dots, high strained tessitura for sopranos and tenors, and a sepulchral descent for the basses (bar 270). The effect of this, as of the comparable passage in Bach's Mass, is momentarily to separate Christ from suffering Man, who now sings in D major—another mediant relationship. The chorus's *misereres* are in hushed homophony, while the soloists have impassioned syncopated arabesques. The diminished seventh shiver transfers its trembling demisemiquavers to the accompaniment, which quivers through an enharmonic modulation from D flat major to F sharp (equalling G flat) minor (bars 276–8). Unexpectedly this resolves into a radiant G major (bars 279–80); but the unexpectedness is more potent than the radiance, for this slow movement, if that's what it is, ends in duality. The soloists continue their *miserere* implorations, in which the falling sixths and rising fourths relate the motives to the initial germ of the Kyrie, while the chorus utters the *Qui sedes* phrase in grim repeated notes, usually ending with the habitual falling thirds. The chorus itself is gradually involved in the introspective lamentation, until a wild climax occurs with what appears to be a cadence in F major (the key the movement had started from), though it is startlingly succeeded by

a homophonic yell on the 6–4 of F sharp minor. The shock is
emphasized by the return of the long-silent trombones, who reinforce
the climactic fortissimo, affirming the awful mystery of the Godhead.
During the coda, which is mostly in F sharp minor, soloists and chorus
all preface each *miserere* with an exclamatory O. Within a dense orchestral texture the soloists wail chromatically and in descending sixths;
dominant pedal notes, sung by the soloists and by the tenors and basses
of the chorus, are painfully intensified by minor seconds and minor
ninths on oboe and bassoon. The section fades out on a C sharp major
string triad, echoed by woodwind. We are left with God's falling fifth,
with no third. The sound is desolate.

We are hardly comforted when, with an abrupt return to the triple-
rhythmed allegro, timpani introduce a scherzo-like section based on
falling arpeggios in heroically double-dotted rhythm. Both the
screwed-up rhythm and the stark octaves resemble the opening of the
Ninth Symphony:

Ex. 139

Both passages in effect dethrone traditional notions of the heroic. Here
the words—*Quoniam tu solus sanctus, tu solus dominus, tu solus altis-
simus*—depict God in his solitariness; but whereas the God-music at
the opening of the Gloria was a whirlwind ascent, this begins with a
fall, contrarious in rhythm and disjointed in tonality, crashing down
from D to G to C. The lunges of the bass line arpeggios sound

cataclysmic; and although the music swings back to D major, the
screeching high As are desperate rather than victorious, while the
cross-rhythms dislocate rather than affirm. In context the effect
is similar to that of the transitional passage that approaches the
Masonic Hymn to Joy in the Ninth Symphony's finale. Though this
episode is smaller in scale, it is hardly less shattering in impact, for it
sounds, after the passion of those prayerful *misereres*, like the Fall of
God. The sudden diminuendo on the word *Amen* (bars 351–3) chills
the nervous system, like a douche in cold water, as do the subsequent
false related triads of C and A major. The fantastic fugue that forms
this symphonic Gloria's finale hardly puts the Fallen God–Humpty
Dumpty together again, though it certainly exhibits—like the fugal
episodes in opus 101 and 106—all the power that kings, men and
horses could ever hope to muster. It is worth noting that Hegel has
been credited with announcing the Death of God many years before
Nietzsche.

After the *Qui tollis*'s wayward modulations and the *Quoniam*'s metrical dislocations the fugue begins with a rudimentary assertion of
tonal simplicity and metrical rigidity. The Law is defined with a theme
which starts with a tonic semibreve covering a whole bar, leaps a
fourth, and stomps in quavers moving by step. Though the quavers
range through a diminished or perfect fourth and mount to the fifth or
sixth, Beethoven's scoring and dynamics stress the G and E, A and F
sharp, thereby emphasizing the motive of falling third:

Ex. 140

The rising fourth and falling scale, that traditional 'ecclesiastical'
motive, are reinforced by woodwind and trombones. The first four
entries occur conventionally on tonic and dominant in alternation, and
the rhythm remains strict, effecting an assertion of worldly power and
volition, Handelian rather than Bachian. Yet there may be, in so
fanatical an assertion of Law, a desperation that Handel had no need of;
and by the time we reach the Amens the music has become as Beet-

hovenian as it is non-Handelian. *Amen* is shouted in falling semitones and tones, and in tipsily syncopated thirds. We are whirred away from the basic tonics and dominants to E minor and B minor. Through crazily syncopated stretti, declining sequential sevenths sunder tonality; linearly, the stretto-ed Amens erupt across the beat. Modulations whirl through F sharp and B minors, E, A and D majors, C sharp and G sharp minor, each transition occupying a bar or less. Intermittently the original fugue subject tries to re-establish A or D major, but is always defeated. Dominant major succumbs again to F sharp minor (the *upper* mediant); the section dissipates on a choral dominant triad.

This C sharp major triad is immediately succeeded by a return of the fugue in the original tonic (bar 428), sung by the soloists doubled by woodwind, over a slow cantus firmus in the choral bass. Though the entries are in stretto, this attempt at contrapuntal oneness blows up sooner and more devastatingly than the previous attempt, for the syncopated sequences on *Amen* now lead not merely to mad modulation, but to enharmonic puns which the choral cantus firmus is impotent to control. So Beethoven tries yet again, this time ballasting a strict fugal stretto with a dominant pedal in the bass (bar 440). Rhythm is again regular; parallel thirds are enriched into parallel 6–3 chords; climax is built up cumulatively, as are Bach's approaches, via a dominant pedal, to cadential consummation. But whereas in Bach the pedal wins, in Beethoven it doesn't. After modulations to B and E minor *carried through and over* the pedal, the music disintegrates in chromaticized diminished sevenths. When the dominant pedal at last resolves on the tonic, the 'monistic' fugue has become dualistic: for with an excitation of tempo from 4/4 to 2/2 the soloists wildly sing a fugato growing from the syncopated descending thirds of the *Amen*, while the chorus severely reiterates *Quoniam tu solus* in repeated but separated notes that are an 'abstract' formalization of the original Kyrie theme. It is as though Man, rigorously declaiming what he imagines to be God's law, is attempting to curb God's joyous wrath: the Amens are frenzied rather than joyful, while the muttered As on the words *cum sancto spiritu* are minatory as well as forceful. Varied orchestral devices—a prevalence of open-stringed notes, sudden leaps, internal and inverted pedals, displaced octaves—are employed to reinforce power. When the voices and orchestra blaze the original fugue theme in octaves (bar 488), the effect is desperately hopeful rather than jubilant, since it prompts *flatwards* modulations to G and C. At the ultimate climax (bar 513) the sopranos hold their high A for six and a half bars. Again the choral Amens grow tipsily syncopated, even the dynamic accents being inverted, *piano* on the second stressed crotchet, *forte* on the fourth. Upward chromatics induce frantically stuttered Amens, tossed between soloists and chorus, who answer one another with the motivic minor third falling from the high A.

Even that orgy is not the end, for Beethoven again speeds up the tempo to *presto*. Moreover he abandons the Amens—the so-be-its that are our acceptance of God's fearful omnipotence—and returns to the opening triple-rhythmed *Gloria in excelsis* phrase which had incarnated God's majesty *per se*. He returns too to the original rising scale that had emulated the 'mighty wind' that is the Wrath of God. But if God, after his Fall, has re-entered his Kingdom, as it was in the beginning, it would seem that this *mysterium* is, at this stage in our journey, indeed *tremendum, stupiosum et alienum*. As horns *à deux*, transformed into Dionysiac *cors de chasse*, chase one another up God's ladder-scale, there is nothing left of Kant's apprehension of God as perfected moral will; on the contrary, there is the daemonic dread the Book of Job refers to in the phrase 'let not His fear terrify me'. Such wrath is not a negation, since it is the energy that creates life: which is what overwhelms us as the original rising scale, much faster, shoots up from tonic to dominant on the high G sharps and then, with a sudden mediant modulation to F, through A natural, B flat, and B natural! The sopranos' inevitably agonized screeches carry us 'out of ourselves', no doubt; but wherever we've arrived is not paradise. God may be back in his heaven; it doesn't follow, at least in any obvious sense, that 'all's well with the world'. We rather recall the magnificent biblical words: 'It is a fearful thing to fall into the hands of the living God' (Heb. 10:31). 'For who is there of all flesh, that hath heard the voice of the living God speaking out of the midst of the fire, as we have, and lived?' (Deut. 5:26). Beethoven can answer 'I have': though for the moment, in this context of the Missa Solemnis, it seems that the quotation from I Kings 19 is also pertinent: 'And, behold, the Lord passed by, and a great and strong wind rent the mountains, and brake in pieces the rocks before the Lord; but the Lord was not in the wind: and after the wind an earthquake; but the Lord was not in the earthquake: and after the earthquake a fire; but the Lord was not in the fire.'

Having experienced the last three piano sonatas, we know that Beethoven can and will go on to complete this last quotation: 'and after the fire a still small voice'. In this work, the time for the discovery of this 'voice of a thin silence' (how wonderfully that metaphor disembodies time and space!) is not yet: which is why the symphonic finale ends by contradicting the theme's upward sweep with hammered *sub*dominant triads of G and C. We conclude, or rather stop, with no dominant–tonic assertion but with plagal subdominants resolving on the weak second beat, so that they hardly sound like resolutions at all. Finally the chorus, stuttering in its dotted rhythm out of step with the orchestra, cannot even drop from the third to the tonic. *Gloria in excelsis* ends with a hiccup! Has any human creature, except the Shakespeare of *King Lear*, evoked with such uncompromising fortitude not only the tragic destiny of Man but also 'the foolishness of God'?—a foolishness which, as St Paul said, is wiser than men, as his weakness is stronger than our strength. The Dionysiac Beethoven had been, as he himself put it, 'a Bacchus who presses out this glorious wine to make men spiritually drunken', as we are when listening to the finale of the Seventh Symphony. He had also, to modify the metaphor into biblical terms, 'trodden the winepress of the fierceness and wrath of Almighty God' (Rev. 19:15). Here he creates, simply and sublimely, the *mysterium tremendum*, the incomprehensible otherness of God; for as the ancient Hasidic wisdom puts it, the fear of God has little to do with retribution or with the horror of death and corruption: 'God wants you to fear his remoteness'—so that 'you may not fall into sin which removes you from Him'. This is why the Wrath of God is inseparable from his Love. As Jakob Boehme put it:

The foundation of the kingdom of God is pure Yes, as powers of the separable Word. And the foundation of the wrath of God is pure No, whence lies have their origin.... In this question regarding God's love and anger, two kinds of fire are to be understood. First, a love-fire, where there is light only; and this is called God's love or the perceptible unity. And secondly a wrath-fire derived from the receivability of the emanated will, through which the fire of love becomes manifest. This wrath-fire is a principle of the eternal Nature, and in the centre of its inwardness is called an eternal darkness and pain. And yet the two fires form but a single principle.

Quaestiones Theosophicae (1624)

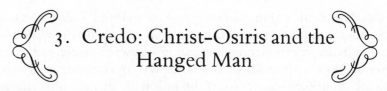

3. Credo: Christ-Osiris and the Hanged Man

This takes us to the heart of Beethoven's religious sense which, like his music, is not an acceptance of or even a search for absolutes, but a process of Becoming. His faith, like Kierkegaard's, is not in universal concepts ('all men are mortal') but in the passion of individual existence ('I too must die'). 'Existence precedes essence'; and just as hope cannot be hope until 'all ground for hope has vanished', so 'without risk there is no faith'. Faith, Kierkegaard continues, is 'precisely the contradiction between the infinite passion of the individual's inwardness and the objective uncertainty'. 'Holy insecurity' is life lived in the face of God. 'If I am capable of grasping God objectively, I do not believe, but precisely because I cannot do this I must believe. If I wish to preserve myself in faith I must constantly be intent on holding fast to objective uncertainty, so as to remain out upon the deep, over seventy thousand fathoms of water, still preserving my faith. ... Faith is an objective uncertainty held fast in an appropriation process of the most passionate inwardness.' So if man's pitiableness reflects 'the foolishness of God', his heroism in seeking to become Christ, even as he teeters over an abyss, complements God's grandeur. This is manifest at the end of the Gloria; for although the music's mighty wind or winepress leaves us, not to mention the performers, breath*less*, yet Beethoven himself, shattered in mind and body, goes on to chant in his own not in traditionally doctrinal terms: CREDO: I BELIEVE.

At this point a backward glance may be helpful. The Kyrie, centred on D major, is a ternary structure, with the Christe, in B minor, as middle section. The repetition of the Kyrie uses the original material, but treats it more as a sonata development than as a recapitulation; the coda is unresolved. The Gloria is an elliptical, telescoped choral symphony. The first movement has two main themes: an upward surging scale in D major, associated with the 'Blakean' Energy that is God; and an undulating waltz-like theme in B flat major, associated with human compassion and brotherhood. A brief but highly dramatic development uses both themes in many permutations. There is no recapitulation, however: merely a transition to a slow movement (the *Qui tollis*) in a cross between F major and D minor, wherein the human elements are intensified by the soloists' quasi-operatic dialogue, while the 'religious' elements are deepened by the chorus's polyphony. Significantly there are here many specific echoes of *The Magic Flute*: in the soloists' Pamina-like arioso, in the melodic obsession with falling thirds (which dominate, too, Sarastro's aria in praise of Isis and Osiris), and in the slow march rhythm that recalls the Armed Men's chorale when they escort Tamino to the rites. But it is not yet time for the rite's consummation. Tonality is unstable, and the movement fades out on the dominant of F sharp, a key which, being enharmonically identical with G flat, stands in mediant relationship to both D and B flat. The larghetto's *misereres* have been an overflow of passion and compassion. A scherzo-like section, again in dotted rhythm and in mediant relationships, substitutes falling arpeggios for God's rising scales. Intervals are gawky, rhythm jagged, tonality uncertain, though with a tendency to plagal flattening and to the false relations consequent upon it (for instance, alternating triads of C and A). After this Fall of God the Gloria concludes with a fugue, at first sturdily Handelian in metre and tonality, but growing gradually more orgiastically uninhibited. The oscillating minor thirds that are the core of the theme are undermined by chromatic sequences and by violent syncopations; textures explode, and Beethoven starts again, twice, attempting to enforce Law first with a cantus firmus bass, then with a dominant pedal. These attempts at order fail: so monistic fugue turns into dualistic double fugue, and then into two codas at increased speed and in operatic rather than contrapuntal stretti. The final broken cadences are not assertively dominant but plagally subdominant.

The Gloria concerns the relationship of God to Man; on the whole from God's point of view, in that his omnipotence remains inapprehensible. The Credo is about the relationship of Man to God; from man's point of view, in that it is a doctrinal statement of what the Church, a humanly created institution, requires us to believe. Though centred on Man's key of B flat major, it opens 'lower' than that, with the subdominant chord of E flat: the plagal pull earthwards which grew so insidious in the latter part of the Gloria. But although we hear the first chord of the Credo as a shocking flat supertonic to the D major that the Gloria had begun and ended in, we immediately shift to the dominant, and then tonic, of B flat. The Credo theme states the motivic descending third not as a cry, but affirmatively, then lifts up a fourth and falls through a stable fifth. The second half of the theme (*in unum Deum*) clinches the assertion with repeated notes and a rising scale in corporeal dotted rhythm:

Ex. 141

Whereas the first Gloria theme bursts banks, leaps hedges, this power-theme is rhythmically defined, metrically controlled, tonally unambiguous. Its force is that of the *dux*, the will-disciplined leader; though it may be significant that its alternation of third, fourth and fifth also relates it to the seminal motive that Beethoven is to associate with the most transcendent moments of the Mass—or for that matter to the sublime fugue theme of opus 110.

The first entry is by the basses; the other parts appear in fugato and stretto, at the fourth or fifth. Though there are momentary transitions to dominant and subdominant, the four voices meet on a resonantly spaced tonic chord, with the third on top. On the word *omnipotentem* the voices climb in octaves to the high B flat; their vigour is hardly compromised by an enharmonic pun between triads of D flat and C sharp minor. None the less there is dubiety here, for after the apparent re-establishment of the subdominant at *factorum coeli*, with the sopranos pushing up sequentially through major and minor thirds, and the dotted rhythm orchestrally augmented, there is a sudden brief hush, prompted by the distance between things 'visible and invisible'. Beethoven brusquely modulates from E flat major to G and D minors, stuttering on the word *et* (bar 30), incapable of conceiving the inconceivable. Though the effect is momentary, it is a premonition of moment*ous* events (bars 179–80).

Immediately, however, hesitancy is swept aside by a fortissimo repeat of the opening fugato, in the original tonic. The invocation of God as Father and Son prompts two statements of the theme, each preceded by a ritornello. At the reference to *filium Dei* we modulate in chromatic sequences, and then, with another abrupt change of dynamics, to C minor and G minor for *ante omnia saecula*, as though the prospect of 'the Sea of Time' induces awe, as well it might. But a very human, physical energy is generated by the reference to *lumen de lumine*. The theme, diminished, assumes a purely triadic form, bouncing down a third and up a fifth between the voices, like rams on the biblical hills, while the orchestral parts skip in dotted rhythm, sometimes through two octaves. The bright C major is shattered by a Neapolitan chord of D flat, leading back to B flat with immense arpeggiated descents by the sopranos. Purposeful order is reaffirmed in an extended fugato which makes a new theme out of the two sections of the original subject: descending thirds are expanded to triads, repeated notes leap through sixths. Tonality stabilizes in the classical certitudes of tonic, dominant and subdominant, but sinks as dynamics quieten (bars 86 ff.). The text has reached the words *Qui propter nos homines*, in a musical texture not surprisingly dominated by Masonic woodwind and horns. The parts move by step, the voices' homophony being low in register, warmly sonorous in its flat-keyed harmony. The effect is suave, almost bland, as compared with the previous rugged energy; it would seem that the text has recalled the ideality of the Kantian Invisible Church, that communion of 'men of good will' evoked in the Kyrie. In this context, after that wild Gloria, the ideal seems more dream-like, floating in the lilt (rather than assertion) of its dotted rhythm, in its flattened remoteness. The dream is brushed aside by the *descendit de coelis* phrase: for the God that comes down, even in order to become and to save mankind, is a God of power. The dotted rhythm is purposeful again. Tonality returns by way of B flat minor to the traditional tonic–dominant–subdominant nexus, ending in a grand octaval descent by all the voices. Sopranos leap through a tenth to the high A and B flat:

Ex. 142

It is revealing to compare this setting of the words with Bach's setting at the comparable point in the liturgy. Bach's God-Christ pictorially descends through arpeggiated thirds but, having landed from heaven on earth, attains resolution in the purgatorial key of G minor, in a sonority low but euphonious, since God's incarnation is Man's redemption (see *The Dance of God*, pp. 215–17). Beethoven's God precipitously topples down an octave in all the vocal parts, only to strain up again on the word *coelis*, through an angular ninth, tenth or twelfth (bars 112–17). Though the genesis of this may also be pictorial, its effect is physical in a manner at once opposite and complementary to Bach's. Beethoven's phrase is unresolved, vocally awkward, even painful. In being such it is typical of Beethoven, whose aspiration was as uncomfortable as it was indefatigable.

What happens next, when God has physically descended, is an Event which calls for and receives a new kind of music. It is also an old kind, being in an austere Dorian polyphony that creates a cross between an aria and a hymn. I have mentioned that Beethoven studied

Palestrinian as well as Bachian and Handelian counterpoint as preparation for his Mass. Since both Czerny and Peters tell us that Beethoven knew Gioseffe Zarlino's famous textbook of 1558, *Istitutioni armoniche*, it is possible that he called on the modes with allegorical as well as musical intentions. Zarlino quotes Cassiodorus' description of the Dorian mode as 'the donor of modesty and preserver of chastity', which seems appropriate to a music concerned with Immaculate Conception: just as the Lydian mode, which Zarlino called 'a remedy for fatigue of the soul and body', was pertinent to the slow movement of the quartet opus 132, described by Beethoven himself as a song of thanksgiving for recovery from sickness, bodily and mental. One cannot be dogmatic about such allegorical interpretations, since sixteenth-century comment on mode (roughly equated with mood) was often contradictory, and usually in conflict with the original Pythagorean terminology (according to which the tritone-infested Lydian mode was regarded as powerfully voluptuous). In a general sense, however, one can say that Beethoven associated modality with the supernatural, if only because the absence of leading notes tended to deny temporal progression. Here in the Incarnatus the manner recalls the initiation ceremonies in *The Magic Flute* which, although not modal, suggest modality through their partiality for concordant mediant and subdominant triads. We have been given a hint of this mystical Masonic flavour in the sudden pianissimos that interspersed the furious fugato. Now Godhead becomes incarnate in a sudden transition from an F major triad to a first inversion of D minor. The hymn melody begins with a whispered *et*, surrounded by silence.

Such repetitions of the word *et* occur in other Viennese masses, but Beethoven transforms a somewhat obvious, even cheap, rhetorical device into magical insight. It is as though in the stammered repetitions and silences, he is *waiting* for the divine light. This may imply doubt as to whether it will come—as the reiterated *ets* later in the Credo certainly do. It also and more significantly suggests that the light Beethoven is waiting for is far beyond that implicit in rational Enlightenment, and even that in the Nicene or any other Creed. Momentarily, dubiety and inapprehensibility stifle the flame of inspiration: so there is a catch in the breath, a faltering of the pulse, before the song steals in, in awe and wonder.

In most editions the opening line is given to tenor solo, though in the autograph it is entrusted to the tenors of the chorus: which has the advantage of rendering the tone more impersonally mysterious, and leaves one fugato entry for each of the soloists; their intimacy then sounds the more moving. After the previous hubbub Yahveh is in his temple: 'Let all the earth keep silence before Him'. The fear of God is still manifest: 'And Moses hid his face, for he was afraid to look upon God' (Exodus 3:6). This awe, incarnate in the stillness of the rhythm and the hush of the purely diatonic harmony, complements the divine wrath at the Gloria's end. The melody itself opens with God's interval of the fifth, and closes its six-bar period with man's familiar falling thirds. Its solemnity is attributable partly to its slow swing between the empty fifth on D and the flat seventh in the A minor and C major triads; its mysteriousness owes something to the subterranean disturbance of the B naturals in the mode:

Ex. 143

At first the song is darkly doubled by violas and supported by diatonically concordant cellos and basses. The solo entries proceed, one a bar, from alto to soprano to bass to tenor, all marked *mezza voce*; they are doubled by reduced numbers of strings, and accompanied by softly repeated semiquaver triads on clarinets and bassoons. The entries are all at the godly fifth, but the rising interval contracts from fifth to fourth to third, relinquishing its modality in the process, so that the tenor entry effects a real modulation from G to C. Over the fugued entries of the voices a solo flute hovers, quivering in slow trills that have the paradisal implications habitual to trills in late Beethoven (bars 135 ff.). Here the trills, which start on the words *de spiritu sancto*, breathe into the Word 'the breath of life'. Through the Virgin Birth man has come to know God in the flesh; yet the veil of the Mother Goddess has never been lifted, nor Danaë's veil that protected her body from the sight of men. The trills also emulate the fluttering wings of the Holy Dove which, at the moment of transubstantiation in the Sanctus and Benedictus, will alight in, and light up, human hearts. Here the dove effects an alchemical transmutation: for when in the seventh and eighth bars of the soloists' fugato the Dorian B naturals turn into a B flat major triad, and then swing to a G major triad, it is as though humanity were divinely illuminated: 'false' relation becomes a glimpse over the horizon, as it occasionally was in the music of the sixteenth and seventeenth centuries.

Witnessing the vision, Mankind, represented by the chorus, intones the words *incarnatus est de spiritu sancto ex Maria virgine* in muttered incantation, over woodwind semiquaver chords that enact 'fear and trembling' (bars 141–4). The section ends on the dominant of D. As the dominant seventh resolves on to a trill on the major third of the tonic, the key signature changes to two sharps; tempo animates to 3/4; and the tenor solo, after another (loud, almost defiant) hesitancy on the word *et*, breaks into *homo factus est*, echoed by the chorus. For the reification of God in man, modality becomes harmonically 'functional' diatonicism, with a humanly recuperative effect comparable with that of the D major episodes in the Lydian slow movement of opus 132. The proudly arching theme rises a second, falls a minor third, oscillates up and down through a major third: a glorious efflorescence of the seeds from which so much of the Mass germinates. The chorus echoes the thirds (descending in the three upper parts, ascending in the bass), reiterating the word *homo*:

Ex. 144

Suddenly the sharps are cancelled and replaced by one flat. While the immediate juxtaposition of *homo factus est* with *crucifixus* is inherent in the liturgical text, no composer before Beethoven has made us so forcefully aware of the abruptness of this transition from Christ's incarnation to his death. *HOMO factus est*; and from the moment he is born in the flesh he is crucified. Though it is improbable that Beethoven believed in the divinity of Christ in strictly doctrinal terms, he accepted him as the Second Adam: 'For as in Adam all die, even so in Christ shall all be made alive' (I Cor. 15:22). He could have found such a concept, indeed, in pagan times, in Seneca's question '*Quid alium est anima, quam Deus in corpore humano hospitans?*', and would certainly have responded to its mystical transmutation in the words of Swedenborg: 'God is Very Man ... and consequently he is God Existing: not existing from Himself, but in Himself. He who has existed in himself is God, from whom all things are.' God incarnate in Christ is every man's potential divinity, his search for the Whole Self. In Blake's sense, Christ *is* the Human Imagination.

We know, from a letter to Breitkopf and Härtel dated 1810, that Beethoven admired the Crucifixus of Bach's B minor Mass, which he described as 'very like ourselves'. It is; but it is also different, for whereas the suffering of Bach's Crucifixus is universalized, presenting Christ's agony operatically but in a kind of cosmic drama, Beethoven's Crucifixus is personalized, theatrically projecting his own suffering. We may recall the relation of Beethoven's biography to his music. Just as his deafness was at once a physical fact and a spiritual allegory, so it is not fortuitous that he was often in extreme physical pain. This is not an explanation of qualities inherent in his art: it would be truer to say that the psychological nature of his experience inevitably involved him in physical discomfort. In his body, as well as in his mind, Beethoven knew what crucifixion felt like: which is why his crucifixion music can be so physical. The heroism of the Baroque rising arpeggio is preserved, along with its proudly double-dotted rhythm; but the short notes, tied to the long, effect metrical dislocations emphasized by the sforzandi, and scrunch on to dissonant suspensions and diminished sevenths, reinforced by shuddering repeated notes and tremolandi. The solo voices wail as it were offstage, against the anguished lament of unnaturally high cellos, bassoons and basses, which jab through a diminished fourth (Ex. 145).

The physical vehemence of this passage involves, too, a minor point of authenticity. Valve horns were available by the time of the Missa Solemnis, and on the whole Beethoven's horn parts sound better on them. Internal evidence suggests, however, that he may have written the parts for natural horns, since he omitted figurations which, though expected in context, would be intractable or impossible on the older instruments. Moreover there are a few passages where the natural horns are still preferable, since Beethoven exploited their imperfections. One of them is the F (written E flat) in bar 161 of the Crucifixus. Here the natural horn, in conjunction with the tangy diminished seventh on clarinets and oboes, would have a snarl appropriate to the music's painfulness, and that this was intentional is suggested by the fact that Beethoven could have obtained the note on the second pair of horns in E flat. Certainly the scoring hammers in nails harder, makes flesh quiver more cringingly, inculcating a physical anguish complementary to the music's mental stress. That these corporeally external events are indeed also internal is manifest in the striking parallel between this passage and the slow introduction to the sonata opus 111 (see page 240–1). The solo voices, also strung across the beats, irregularly incorporate falling perfect along with imperfect (diminished) fifths, those old synonyms for God and Devil which here become, as in the sonata, one in their duality. God in majesty is Man tortured: elevated, but on a Cross. Significantly, the musical idiom is not ecclesiastical but operatic: a wilder version of Mozart's tragic (G minor) manner. It also suggests the trenchant passion of Gluck, whose operas Beethoven did not know well, though their combination of moral grandeur with psychological immediacy would have appealed

Ex. 145

to him. Despite its operatic manner, however, the music is more symphonically introspective, as well as more violent, than Mozart, more complex and concentrated than Gluck. It is also more specific in human terms: in which respect it is relevant to comment on a point in Beethoven's interpretation of the liturgical text.

The punctuation in the Tridentine Mass is in fact as Beethoven treats it:

Crucifixus etiam pro nobis: He was crucified also for us,
sub Pontio Pilato passus   suffered under Pontius Pilate,
et sepultus est.   and was buried.

Traditionally, however, sixteenth-century settings cadence on *Pilato*
and begin anew with *passus*; nor can this have been without authority,
for the Anglican version still reads 'And he was crucified also for us
under Pontius Pilate; he suffered and was buried'. Beethoven's revival
of the original Latin will not allow Pilate the extenuation of being a
well-meaning but unimaginative bureaucrat, but convicts him (and
us, and himself) of a murderous culpability. As the chorus relates
Pilate's part in the story, the orchestra pounds in angular octaves
derived from the opening orchestral motive. When we move from
Pilate's guilt to Christ's suffering, the soloists are reduced to broken
cries on the word *passus*, wailing through those perfect and imperfect
fifths, sometimes stretched to sixths. Meanwhile the orchestra's
figurations grow more tormented: rising thirds or fifths decline
through *diminished* thirds in dotted rhythm, weirdly scored for violins
and bassoons in octaves (bar 167). The phrases seem to hug themselves, in agony, not self-love; their writhings seldom coincide with
the barlines:

Ex. 146

Sometimes the figures create simultaneous false relations, eventually
convoluting themselves in syncopations and diminutions on the
diminished seventh. The key teeters between G and D minors, but
attains what might be rest on a chord of E flat major. The hint of

redemption is momentary, since the new horizon hinted at, if we hear
the E flat triad as a passive flat submediant to G minor, proves illusory.
It seems that the chord is rather to function, as the bass moves
chromatically to A, as a Neapolitan back to D minor: which is again a
feint, for the major is substituted for the minor third in the cadence,
above which the soprano and alto soloists create the sob of a dominant
ninth, once more in G minor. The chorus's fragmented ejaculations of
the word *et* are succeeded by passionately lamenting tritones on the
word *passus* from the upper voices, while the bass soloist rises through
an arpeggiated dominant seventh (bar 182). On the words *sepultus est*,
however, resolution is again denied, for the G minor cadence is interrupted by octave D flats. They might, since they droop to a 6–4 triad
of F minor, be construed as an ungrammatical transition to that key;
but since the F minor triad then descends to a hollow C chord (without
the third, and with the fifth at the bottom), they might also be said to
function as a Neapolitan to C, elusive because the dominant is omitted
(bars 184–7). The panting and sobbing figurations have dissipated.
The scoring is for low strings: grave, at this dark time of the year, yet
still humanly expressive.

   C major is latent, not patent, in this tenebrous cadence; nor is it
immediately explicit in the *Et resurrexit* which proceeds to C only after
six ambiguously modal bars. These bars are surprising, though hardly
in the way we expect. That surprise can be expected is a paradox; yet it
is a matter of liturgical and musical tradition that Christ's (and our)
black burial will blossom into white light. 'And as touching the dead,
that they rise . . . have ye not read . . . He is not the God of the dead, but
the God of the living?' Whether one interprets the words literally or in
psychological terms, they depend on a spiritual innocence as strong as
it is touching: as do also St Paul's words to the Romans (8:11): 'But if
the Spirit of him that raised up Jesus from the dead dwell in you, he
that raised up Christ from the dead shall also quicken your mortal
bodies by his Spirit that dwelleth in you.' Beethoven's music for the *Et
resurrexit*, which is briefly undemonstrative, reflects this holy innocence. Lasting only six bars and calling only for *a cappella* chorus in
archaic Mixolydian homophony, it balances the terseness of God's
arpeggiated Fall with the slain God's scalic rise. Like the Gloria's Fall,
the music is scherzoid in character; but Beethoven employs no vividly
pictorial elements such as Bach develops into corybantic revel. The
tenors' high Gs admittedly sound like a clarion; what follow, however, are pure diatonic concords swaying in false relation between G

and B flat majors, the same sequence of triads that had dominated the Incarnatus. It is man's B flat triad that injects the shock of false relation into the climax. *HOMO factus est*; and as man is reborn, the orchestral 'flesh' is discarded and the *a cappella* voices momentarily chant in childish diatonic concords, after the crucifixion's pain. This may be why the extension of the Resurrexit is, for Beethoven, at first oddly lightweight.

He calls on the traditional imagery of rising scales and piled up triadic entries, but moves from Mixolydian G to diatonic C and F, so that the cycle of falling fifths discounts the linearly upward movement. Moreover the music, though quick, is slightly frantic, certainly not triumphant, for the chorus again stammers out its *et*, as though unable to utter the next clause of dogma. Cyclical modulations and mediant transitions increase the restlessness throughout a chatter of repeated quavers; the 'theme' is reduced to oscillating repeated notes in dotted rhythm. Suddenly, preceding the word *judicare*, one of the trombones enters after their long silence, to emulate the Last Trump. His C flat breaks the regular cycle of modulations, and *arrests* the movement in two senses: the quavers are immobilized, the dotted rhythm is augmented, as we await God's judgement. Traditionally trombones, like trumpets, were solemn and sacred instruments through which spoke, on the Old Testament analogy, the breath of God (Exodus 19:16; Zechariah 9:14). The New Testament handed them to God's minions, the angels, who 'blew a great sound' to 'gather together his elect'. Majesty, splendour, judgement and fear are qualities manifest in the sonorities of trombones throughout the music of European tradition, most notably in the consort that accompanies the visitation of Don Giovanni's Stone Guest. Beethoven's trombones are here directly in this succession: aweful in associating the heavenly throne with the judge's chair, fearful in immediacy of response to the quick and the dead. Imitative entries pile up, as the bass falls from C flat to F, and then to F flat (bars 221–7). If we have been somewhat apprehensively rejoicing, the prospect of judgement has turned uncertainty into terror. But the expected flatwards modulation does not materialize; the bass simply turns back on itself and moves up to G natural on the word *vivos*:

Ex. 147

The mere thought of living cheers us up, for although the syllables of *vi-vos* are stutteringly split, the voices bounce blithely in octaves, and in tonic and dominant triads of C major, separated by rests. The word *mortuos* predictably has the opposite effect: an intrusion of octave C *sharps*, over low strings supported by grisly double-bassoon, moves to a dead chord without the third; and so back to D major for *cujus regni non erit finis*. The music is now almost jaunty, the chatter of quavers being restored, the fugued motive a simple version of the falling thirds, major and minor. Modulation is rapid (D major, G minor, B flat major, C major, D minor), and false relations are prevalent, emphasized by sforzando accents. It would seem that while the *incarnatus* and *crucifixus* are parts of the Creed that Beethoven himself experienced, he cannot accept the psychological, let alone physical, fact of resurrection as unequivocally. Or at least the *resurrexit*'s experience of being new-born ('Except ye become as little children') is only one step towards the transcendence that must grow from, not shuffle off, the 'mortal coil' of agony and death. It is certainly remarkable that Beethoven concludes this section by isolating the word *non* from the phrase *cujus regni non erit finis* and by sounding it three times, in short sharp barks. The sense of the words is inverted; that of the music, confirmed.

This must be why Beethoven then unliturgically repeats the opening music of the Credo for the words *credo in unum spiritum sanctum*,

thereby completing the threefold invocation of God as Father, Son and
Holy Ghost. But this invocation is more hastily introduced by the
orchestra, compared with those in the exposition; and although the
music is the same as at the beginning of the Credo, it is in a different
key. Beethoven attempts affirmation afresh, the more wilfully because
in the dominant. Since the original music opened with a subdominant
triad, he now begins with a triad of B flat, the 'real' tonic, though it
doesn't here serve a tonic function. The apparent da capo proves to
be neither a recapitulation nor exactly a development. At first only the
two lower voices have the original Credo theme of falling third,
rising fourth and falling fifth, in canon at the seventh. The other two
voices have a countersubject in short repeated notes, a perfunctory,
even trivial permutation of the repeated note theme that had been
evolved in the exposition. This has point, in that by means of it
Beethoven rattles through the doctrinal sections of the Credo
(*credo in unam sanctam catholicam et apostolicam ecclesiam*, etc.) in which
he doesn't feel deeply involved: words are gabbled, notes gobbled,
with near-ironic effect. Meanwhile one, then two, then three
parts bellow the unchanged Credo theme as best they may. They
have a hard time of it, for the orchestra develops an elaborately
polyphonic and harmonically sequential texture based on a diminution of the theme's dotted rhythm. Excitement is increased by the
rapid modulations, one every two bars; so is the threat to stability.
Eventually Beethoven takes expectation by the scruff of the neck.
Everyone yells *Et expecto resurrectionem* fortissimo, in octaves and in B
flat, with the dotted rhythm mounting through the bass. Sopranos
attain their high B flat (bar 294) and sustain it; but for the word
mortuorum there is a sudden break, a change of dynamics and of key (to
G minor). The *vitam venturi* is approached with more fragmented *ets*,
though boisterously.

   The energy is, however, for the moment illusory; having modulated to F, the dominant, the music shifts back to B flat, over rising
scales in the bass that will later be seraphically transformed. For the
Credo ends with a consummatory fugue, the theme of which recreates
the 'perfunctory' repeated notes of the countersubject to the Credo's
da capo, once more revealing their potential nobility. The process
happens stealthily, since at first the scoring is for low flutes, clarinets,
bassoons, horns, violas, cellos and basses, the top frequencies cut off; it
is as though the melody were floating through closed doors. The
thematic repeated notes are now allegretto in 3/2; the last of them

droops a third, then another third. Thematically the material is thus basic; so is the key, which is Man's B flat major. Interestingly enough, Beethoven wrote on the sketch for the *Et vitam venturi* fugue the words 'Applaudite amici', and it seems that the unity he is here seeking is man-made; like Kant's Invisible Church and Moral Law, it leaves the Starry Heavens to themselves. The ingenuity of the counterpoint doesn't destroy the music's gracefulness, which is potential grace; it sounds, at first, like a hymnic minuet. The texture's complexity does remind us, however, that a communion of 'men of good will' is an ideal difficult to attain. For one thing, this proves to be a *double* fugue, in which the repeated note theme is counterpointed against a flowing upward scale in crotchets, ending with a descending sixth on *Amen*; for another, the texture is in almost continuous modulation. The main subject appears in increasingly close stretti; textures elaborate until there is four octaves' distance between flutes and oboes and cellos and basses. The sopranos have a notorious entry on a high B flat (bar 328), which Beethoven refused to alter in the interest of fallible performers. He was right, of course, for the jubilation the music gradually generates—as the closed doors open and we enter into *communion*, perhaps with God as well as with men—depends on its arduousness. Certainly Masonic community begins to 'take off': the countersubject introduces sinuous syncopations and tied notes across the beats; the repeated note theme, in being inverted, acquires an aspirational lilt. Tonal movement is prevailingly flatwards, to A flat, D flat, G flat majors and E flat minor; but both subjects increasingly move *upward*: consider the bass entry in G flat, with its sequentially rising sixths. The music's spiritual-social grace springs from this equilibrium. B flat minor provides a transition back to the tonic, and the section ends with the main theme in stretto, the sopranos entering on the high B flats, though in more practicable fortissimo. Instead of a final cadence in B flat there is a sequence of modally related concords: triads of G, A and D in hemiola rhythm.

Tempo speeds to allegro con moto and the fugue is renewed, in G minor. The original main theme, in the orchestral bass, is accompanied by itself in diminution. The diminished version becomes the main theme; movement is agile, both in scalic quavers and in leaping sixths in crotchets, derived directly from the end of the first fugato countersubject, though they are also motivic if we think of them as thirds inverted. At first the sixths prance in the tenors, then altos, then sopranos, in each part more frequently and more exuberantly. Grace

gives way to joy as the music modulates sharpwards from E flat to
B flat to F. The upward thrust grows ever more potent, until the
sopranos' threefold leaping sixths are answered by five leaps in the
bass, the last one expanded to an octave:

Ex. 148

The basses sustain a long pedal F, the function of which is more
complex than that of a dominant pedal. Over it permutations of the
original minim theme appear, preserving the repeated notes but
changing the falling third to a rising fourth, diminished in the tenors,
perfect in the sopranos. Each note of this augmented theme—
augmented, that is, in the context of the allegro con moto section of the
fugue—has a sforzando accent; fragments of the crotchet version of
the theme flicker fiercely in other parts. The F pedal in the orchestral
bass changes into a dominant seventh of C minor, only to resolve in E
flat. Amens are chanted to descending thirds, harmonized with
diatonic triads; a fugal stretto turns into an octaval statement of the
main theme, in minims, and in B flat. Again there is a strong plagal pull
to the cadence; after which the jubilation stabilizes, with grandly
Masonic sobriety, in a *grave* coda.

But after so much, this cannot be a return to the Masonic mode of
the Kyrie. When the motivic thirds fall in the chorus from the high B
flat, the solo voices enter smoothly, mingling wide-spanned arpeggios
with rising scales. The chorus recites Amens on soft repeated notes or
seconds, the two syllables hesitantly separated by rests; scales from the
soloists and the violins and flute rise longer and higher, sometimes tied
floatingly across the bars. Soli and chorus meet on a sustained B flat
major triad; the solo flute reaches high F, which it repeats three times,

both as Masonic symbolism and, more significantly, as a 'sublimation' of the *Et vitam venturi* theme (bar 461). It stays aloft, without descent through the third, and suddenly the chorus interjects four repeated major triads, fortissimo and staccato, as though wilfully asserting the worldly and temporal order, however Masonically orientated, from which the fugue had sprung. But that worldly order is no longer an adequate truth; so the barking chords simply cease, and the spirit again floats upwards on gentle woodwind scales, while the Holy Ghost calmly descends on strings:

Ex. 149

The intrusion of the flat seventh in the falling phrase restores the plagal feeling and establishes a subdominant triad. At the top of the scales a 6–4 chord on flutes and oboe wonderfully anticipates the sonority that, in the Benedictus, will initiate the descent of the Holy Ghost to the individual spirit, rather than, as here, to the corporate identity of the Church. Now the chord releases upward scales in diminution (semiquavers instead of quavers) on pianissimo strings: which resolve from subdominant to tonic without dominant intervention. After this plagal Amen, the orchestra ends with repeated Fs, which remain stationary on flute and first violins, but fall through thirds in the string basses and trombones; the music evaporates on the offbeat. If this recalls the human-spiritual order of the Invisible Church, it is distantly. The effect of this dissolving coda can be fully apprehended only in relation to the fugue that had concluded the Gloria, and to the Sanctus and Benedictus that are to come. The Gloria's fugue began as an attempt metrically and tonally to control, and in that sense to humanize, the God of Power, but proved impotent to do so; the coda to that tremendous piece exploded in upward scales that, bursting bonds, gave audible manifestation to the Joyous Wrath of God. The double fugue at the end of the Credo, which purports to state the doctrine of the Church, starts from an audible synonym for social order that may become spiritual grace, and concludes dreamily with the recognition that ultimately grace is not of this world. The last two bars' reference to what I called the 'hymnic minuet' seems to sum up what man, as a social-religious being, might legitimately hope for, on this earth: the spiralling scales, fading into that 6–4 on oboe and flutes, tell us that only in terms of an individualized vision can the *incarnatus* be fulfilled. This is what happens in the Sanctus and Benedictus. After the scales' aspiration towards the Godhead we achieve, musically and liturgically, an act of transcendence.

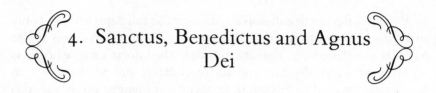

4. Sanctus, Benedictus and Agnus Dei

Persephone Restored; 'a prayer for inner and outer peace'

Beethoven's incarnation of the *numen* in his Sanctus is closer to the vision of Isaiah than is Bach's; whereas Bach evokes the *majestas* of God's holiness and the glorious glitter of angels' haloes that are suns, Beethoven evokes the wonder that caused the seraphim to cover their faces with their wings. The scoring, for low strings and woodwind, with soft interjections from a trinity of trombones, creates a solemn awe, and reminds us of the traditional associations of German *Turm-musik* not merely with civic pride, but with the holy: as Kuhnau put it, 'we know from experience that when our city pipers in the festive season play a religious song with nothing but trombones from the Tower, then we are greatly moved, and imagine we hear the angels singing'. Beethoven himself made a contribution to this long and honourable tradition in his three *Equali* for four trombones, written for the Towermaster of Linz for the All Souls' Day ceremonies of 1812. There is a memory of that tradition in the opening of the Sanctus, though the music is more deeply introverted. Perhaps one might say that tower-music has been refashioned in the light of the initiatory music from *The Magic Flute*, with the mystery enhanced by the ambiguous modality. Certainly Beethoven's Sanctus relates back to his Incarnatus: which is appropriate, since the Sanctus is the point in the liturgy at which the divine event, annunciated in the incarnation of God in Christ, is supposed to be manifest in *us*.

Significantly, the opening notes of the Sanctus theme are identical with the *homo factus est* phrase; in a slow 2/4 the melody rises a tone, falls a minor third, rises a fourth. The arching contour recalls, more remotely, the opening of the Incarnatus, as does the scoring for low strings and bassoons. Three entries in fugato generate an awe-ful hush, perhaps because, since each answer is 'real', there is a Lydian tritone in the second bar, and a false relation between the D natural of the second bar and the D sharp of the third. Again the falsity of false relation is a recognition that, in Sir Thomas Browne's phrase, 'man is an Amphibian', capable of living simultaneously in physical and metaphysical worlds. This is another passage in which 'authentic' orchestration may have musical point, for the stopped notes on the D and E horns (especially the seventh harmonic, which was considerably sharper than the tempered pitch) would have deepened the sense of wonder, not less because the notes' utterance was fraught with an element of danger.

In any case, the tonality of the opening bars is mysterious because illusory: for though the key signature has two sharps, the music is never in B minor. It begins in B Lydian, modulates smoothly to E minor and G major, cadences in D major. A solemnity of trombones returns us to a B minor triad, and to the thematic thirds, though there is no dominant–tonic cadence. When the solo voices enter, the rhythm regularized and the falling third expanded to a serene fifth, the passage is repeated, but the D major cadence is not resolved. Its dominant is chromatically altered to become an A minor triad, and the vocal fugato resumes more flowingly, since there is more quaver movement, but a tone lower, doubled by clarinets and horns:

Ex. 150

We arrive at C instead of D major; perhaps because C is the modal flat seventh, the mystery seems the holier. Back in D, by way of A and B minor, the voices whisper *Sanctus*, while the orchestra throbs an inverted dominant seventh, intensified by a minor ninth. The tremolandos here may have a theological justification, for a sixth-century Bishop of Arles tells us that the seraphim exclaimed *Sanctus* 'with simultaneous trembling and rejoicing'. From this whisper the *Pleni*

sunt coeli somewhat surprisingly explodes in D major mirth, using the word both in the modern sense of merriment and in the medieval sense of physical and spiritual well-being.

Compared with the mystery in which we have just participated, the Pleni seems, and is, an extrovert celebration of the fullness of life, or at least of the life we might live, being reborn, here on earth. The D major animation springs from the arpeggiated vigour of the vocal lines, with their bounding leaps and cross-accents, and from the strings' cascading scales. The style is heroically High Baroque, Bachian; modulation too is restricted to the classical fundaments of tonic, dominant and subdominant. As so often in the Mass, the subdominant proves stronger than the dominant, pulling towards, though not yet attaining, the 'blessedness' of G major. The Osanna, changing to a presto 3/4 (probably slightly faster than dotted crotchet equals crotchet of the Pleni), is the same kind of music, but in strict fugato, the four entries proceeding from soprano downwards. The words *in excelsis* provoke a recollection of the sizzling scales to which the phrase was first set in the Gloria. The effect, however, in Beethoven's re-created Baroque idiom, is very different, being no longer fear-ful but joyous. This is understandable, because the omnipotent Godhead no longer needs to be 'understood', since in the moment of transubstantiation he has become incarnate in us. This being so, it is important that the Pleni and Osanna should be sung, as Beethoven directs, by the soloists, not the chorus. This joy is a prelude to and consequence of our individual experience of the numinous. At this moment it is we—Beethoven, you and I—who enact the rite, and it is we as individual creatures who may be permitted to rejoice. God, as St Augustine puts it, has 'accepted the tribute of the human voice, and wishes us to take joy in praising him'. It is interesting that contemporary opinion was surprised, perhaps outraged, at Beethoven's attribution of these parts to the soloists, and Schindler argued lengthily with the composer, stressing the impracticability of the procedure, given the stamina of soloists and the size of the modern orchestra. Beethoven remained adamant. Unfortunately Schindler doesn't recapitulate Beethoven's reasons for sticking to his guns. My explanation is of course speculative; but at least we now know that on the matter of practicability Beethoven was right. A sensitive conductor can even follow Beethoven's direction of *allegro pesante* (which refers to phrasing and accentuation rather than to dynamics), and the soloists will still be audible. Twentieth-century singers who perform the Mass are usually of high quality, but probably no better than the great and great-voiced singers for whom Beethoven composed expressly. Schindler's advice that the Pleni and Osanna should 'always be performed with full chorus' is both presumptuous and unnecessary. Nowadays we usually have the courage to trust (even deaf) Beethoven, who proves justified here no less than in the taxing tessitura of the choral parts in the Gloria and Credo.

At first the Osanna betrays a strong dominant assertiveness. Its energy is reinforced, as was that of the triple-rhythmed fugato in the Gloria, by heterophonic doublings of the voices by woodwind and strings, the latter filling in the crotchet movement with (often dissonant) quaver passing notes. But the last paragraph veers towards the subdominant; and for the first time in the Mass one sharp becomes the key signature of a movement. Interestingly, the jubilation of the Pleni and Osanna has been brief: hardly more than a passing reference to the externalized 'benefits' that may accrue from the Sanctus' inner grace. One might say that here—as often in the genuine 'monumental Baroque', with its ebullient trumpets and drums, its pridefully arpeggiated but harmonically earth-rooted themes—man is playing at being God. But though Beethoven pays this deference to Man's vainglorious folly, he leaves us in no doubt, when he proceeds to the Praeludium of the Benedictus, that ego-boosting games and external benefits, however acceptable and even delightful, are no substitute for a blessedness within the psyche. Perhaps the briefly mundane rejoicing is there precisely to testify to its insignificance, as compared with the numinousness which an individual man may, in his solitariness, now and again encompass.

There is a liturgical precedent for Beethoven's Praeludium, which corresponds to the improvised or composed organ music that was traditionally played 'with a rather grave and sweet sound', as a seven-teenth-century authority put it, during the mystical moment of the Elevation of the Host. Such music, as created by Frescobaldi, or by the French organ school from de Grigny to Couperin, was slow, polyphonic, close-textured, chromatic: so is Beethoven's Praeludium, which is probably the most sublime instance of introversion in Euro-pean music. It deepens the holy silence created by the Sanctus, so that silence becomes 'palpable'. Karl Barth has suggested that though 'creation is grace and God does not grudge the existence of the reality distinct from Himself', he yet 'remains hidden from us even in His revelation: God who, in disclosing Himself, conceals Himself; who in coming near to us, yet remains far from us; who in being kind to us, remains holy'. Indeed it is the 'hiddenness' of God that conditions *The Idea of the Holy*, of which Rudolf Otto has written:

> In neither the sublime nor the magical, effective as they are, has art more than an indirect means of representing the numinous. Of directer methods our Western art has only two and they are, in a noteworthy way, negative: viz. darkness and silence. The darkness is such as is made all the more perceptible by contrast with some last vestige of brightness which it is, as it were, on the point of extinguishing; hence the 'mystical' effect begins with semi-darkness. The impression is rendered complete if the factor of the 'sublime' comes to unite with it and supplement it. The semi-darkness that glimmers in vaulted halls, or beneath the branches of a lofty forest glade, strangely quickened and stirred by a mysterious play of half-lights, has always spoken eloquently to the soul, and builders of mosques, temples and churches have made full use of it.

So has Beethoven in this Praeludium. The theme of rising second, rising fourth and descending scale, presented in a slow-swinging triple pulse and in hushed fugato, sounds embryonic, newly emergent; though it harks back to the themes of the Kyrie and Sanctus, it looks forward to the Benedictus and Dona nobis. The scoring is for low flutes, interlocked with violas, bassoons, divided cellos and double-basses (which descend to a low C sharp that didn't exist on the instrument in Beethoven's day; this may be why he reinforces the line with very soft organ pedal). The sonority itself evokes the half-lights of a forest, while the many-in-oneness of the fugued song suggests, in its exploration of horizontal and vertical dimensions, a Gothic cathedral which is itself a stylization of a 'lofty forest glade'. Nor is it fortuitous that the overlapping figurations should recall the Masonic Gratias, but should transmute it into mystical terms, in the sense suggested by Otto. Here the dark texture is *labyrinthine*, miraculously evoking an Eleusinian descent below consciousness and the earth. After five bars of unsullied G major, tonality dissolves, flowing in twelve bars through a multiplicity of keys. When at last the music earths itself on long dominant and tonic pedals, dominant ninths and diminished sevenths throb over the immobile bass:

Ex. 151

Beethoven himself had anticipated this visionary moment in the prelude to the quartet in *Fidelio*, for there too the music 'introspects itself' in convoluted chromatics as the four characters enter a canonic trance, wherein they see and know themselves (rather than one another) for a 'first time' that is time*less*. It is still more significant that this extra-ordinary moment in Beethoven's Mass should be prophetic not so much of early Romanticism as of its end. The ninths and sevenths, the enveloping texture, the scoring, most of all the incessant modulations which, far from being dramatic events, are a dissolution: all these are strikingly similar to Wagner's *Tristan*, and still more to *Parsifal* and to the Adagietto of Mahler's Fifth Symphony. Wagner, high priest of the Romantic ego, was to discover a universe within the mind, and was conversely to learn that the only way to find the Self is to lose it. Complementarily, Mahler's life-work was to be balanced between Experience of man's inevitable crucifixion, and Innocence which is the memory of an undivided Whole. All this and more is latent within Beethoven's Missa Solemnis. He really was Blake's Bard who 'Present, Past and Future sees'; his ears had heard 'the Holy Word that walked among the ancient trees'. Beethoven thought of himself as a Seer, the Bard who heard Jehovah speaking to Adam in the Garden. In his Mass especially he called upon the 'lapsed soul' to regain control of his world, surrendered when man adopted Reason ('the starry pole')

in place of Imagination. Earth, which is fallen man, will arise from the 'slumbrous mass' when the Human Imagination reanimates the 'starry floor' of Reason, the 'dewy grass' of sense impressions, and the 'wat'ry shore' of material reality. Beethoven, like Blake, exhorts us not to 'turn away'. If we don't, we may escape the coils of materiality, and 'fallen, fallen light' will shine again.

The metaphor of coils reminds us that we have spoken of the chromatically enfolding fugato of the Praeludium as 'labyrinthine'. The original Cretan labyrinth, devised by Daedalus to cabin and confine the instinctually monstrous Minotaur, symbolized in the Eleusinian Mysteries the descent beneath the earth and 'below' consciousness, from which new life may spring, the 'spring of the year' being identified with a psychic rebirth. Taken over by Christianity, labyrinths were designed to decorate the floors of churches (there is a famous one at Chartres), where they symbolize both the delusions of time and space and the redemptive power of grace. We have evidence (recounted by Hugo Rahner in his book *Man at Play*) that throughout the Middle Ages and almost up to the seventeenth century it was common, at the New Year and at the Feast of the Holy Innocents, for bishops, clergy and choirboys to proceed, almost ceremonially to dance, through the convolutions of the labyrinth on the church floor, playing with a ball that was an image for Christ the Sun, who alone may lead us through the misty confusions of the world. It is improbable that Beethoven knew of this practice, but certain that the effect of the transition from the Praeludium's labyrinthine darkness into the Benedictus is like a shaft of *sunlight*. The literal meaning of the word Praeludium is 'before play'; from the murky delusions of the maze floats the dancing play of angels.

A high G major triad in first inversion shines on two flutes and solo violin. Inevitably we recall the second inversion of an E flat major triad, at the same pitch, in a similar flute-haloed sonority, at the end of the Credo. Then it had been hopeful prophecy; now it is revealed truth: for the solo violin as Holy Ghost—or as the Jewish Messenger of Peace, or the Arabian Rohmat Allah—floats down from the heights in a swinging 12/8. This slow declension answers the 'aspirational' upward scales at the end of the Credo; we cannot miss the parallel because Beethoven releases the Holy Dove with a chord and sonority so similar, though in a different key, to that on which the Credo's soaring prayer had ended. There is a further and profounder point in that the calmly falling 12/8 scale is an inversion of the wildly upsweep-

ing scales that, in the Gloria, had given aural 'flesh' to the Wrath of
God. Having reached the low C and B, the solo violin soars into a long
arching cantilena of a type which Beethoven had anticipated in the
slow movement of the quartet opus 59 no. 2. There too the solo violin
wings in the heights in a 12/8 pulse, with a softly throbbing accompaniment. Czerny tells us that Beethoven conceived this movement while
regarding the 'starry heavens' and reflecting on the Music of the
Spheres. In the Benedictus this celestial song is vastly expanded. The
unearthly serenity derives partly from the 12/8 pulse which here, as so
often in Bach, represents a quaternity of trinities or a squaring of the
circle: the melody flows in time and space while seeming, since its span
is immense, to annihilate them. Similarly, though a gently breathing
pulse animates the stepwise-moving quavers, accents dissolve because
the falling scales are recurrently tied across the beats. Similarly again,
harmony is euphonious, even rich, yet sounds disembodied because
the high triads are in first inversion rather than in root position; the
scoring, with solo violin poised over interweaving woodwind, is
diaphanous:

Ex. 152

Sometimes the polyphonies are supported by pizzicato strings (an echo of Orpheus's plucked lyre?) and by soft trombones (an echo of the sacral brass of the dead?). In the Praeludium the polyphony has veiled the chromatic harmony, just as Eleusinian (and in emulation Masonic) initiates were veiled before their descent into the underworld. Now, in the heights, the veiling figurations are translucent. Light filters through, as the horns enter on a dominant pedal and the choral basses softly intone the opening phrase of the plainsong Benedictus, now fully born from the prophecy of it in the Praeludium's rising second. The sacred Word has sprouted in the dark earth; it is worth noting that in several languages the words for speech, sprout, sperm and sprinkle are interrelated.

Though this music has Christian connotations, in that it quotes plainsong and flows in imitative polyphony, its atmosphere is again more Hellenistic than Christian. Persephone, restored to light and life, sings not even in an Invisible Church, but in the Elysian Fields that had been musically depicted by Gluck. But Beethoven has freed the music from the 'Sea of Space and Time' in which Gluck's Orpheus and Eurydice were happy to be reunited, and his flutes are here once more magical rather than rationally enlightened. We saw in our discussion of Bach's St. John Passion that the flute was often substituted for Orpheus's lute (equivalent to the lyre), and was in Christian eras often associated with Christ as shepherd (see *The Dance of God* pp. 118–20). Here the exfoliating melody for solo violin, haloed by flutes, is at once spiritual, enacting in its apparently endless convolutions the winging of the Holy Dove; and also physical, embodying the sensual loveliness of Persephone, 'gathering flowers, from gloomy Dis restored'. Here the violin fulfils much the same function as it serves when Bach employs it as an obbligato instrument in, for instance, the heaven-aspiring 'lark' music of the Laudamus te in the B minor Mass. The violin is quintessentially expressive, in human terms, yet capable of supernatural grace. Some such synthesis was undoubtedly the goal of the new kind of *'cantique ecclésiastique'* that Beethoven hoped to create in the 'choric ode on the victory of the Cross' which he spoke of not long before his death. If in the Gloria of the Missa Solemnis he had created a 'Bacchic Festival', in the Benedictus he transforms liturgical ritual into a personal, and sensuous, communion with God. Beethoven as Seer addresses 'the Almighty One of the Woods' where—as he scribbled on a sheet of manuscript paper in 1812—'every tree speaks through Thee. O God! What glory in the Woodland! In the heights is Peace—Peace to serve Him!'

Man alone with God, in the world of Nature, is 'naturally' released from temporality. We have noted that one source of this timelessness is the vast, often overlapping, span of the melodic phrases; other sources are the harmony's frequent elisions of tonic, dominant and subdominant triads, those props of European harmonic 'progression'; the prevalence of drones and pedal notes within the texture; and what one might call the long-term range of the structure. For though subtly balanced, the Benedictus is devoid of Beethovenian developmental momentum. Thus the first eight bars (the violin's descent of the Holy Ghost and the plainsong intonation) serve as introduction. The first section proper of this aria-concerto-fugue begins in bar 119 with the violin solo, drooping in caressing appoggiaturas, then lifting upwards, supported by the throb of trombones, with trumpets and timpani. Any hint of pain in the appoggiaturas is dissipated in the euphony and in the violin's equilibrium between stepwise movement and immense 'open' leaps. In the fifteenth bar of this solo, which ends in a high trill (bar 133), the solo alto enters, followed by the tenor in canon at the seventh, their theme being a simple undulating scale derived from the violin melody. Since both the Praeludium and the plainsong intonation open with a rising second, there may be thematic point in the fact that the canonic entries, until the coda, always occur on the second or seventh. During the following fifteen bars the canon is between soprano and tenor, who effect the first real modulation, to the dominant. The canon is now supported in resonant tenths by the two other voices. This completes what we may call the A section, since with the modulation comes new, or newly transmuted, material.

The solo violin now flows upwards (bar 149), mingling semi-quavers with quavers; its animation inspires more expansively lyrical phrases from the soloists. If we think of the solo violin as an angelic messenger, we may say that the human solo voices are always aspiring towards, though they can never attain, its liberated ecstasy. This dominant section, which we will call B, ends after another eight bars in an interrupted cadence, substituting a B minor for a D major triad (bar 156). The next four bars, which form a brief C section, are the closest the Benedictus comes to climax: the four voices intone the words *In nomine Domini* fairly loudly, in repeated thirds, effecting a dramatic extension of the plainsong intonation, while the solo violin cascades down through arpeggios of B minor, of a dominant major ninth and then, calming, of a G major tonic. During a codetta-like section, which we may label D, violin and woodwind rise imitatively through quaver scales; solo voices weave a canonic dialogue on the words *qui venit*, the canon perhaps mirroring how man, in a state of blessedness, follows in God's footsteps. The theme, with rising second and falling third, is the same as the Sanctus motive, though it begins on the upbeat.

After further intonations of the *In nomine* a second real modulation occurs (bar 168). Being to the subdominant, it balances the first dominant modulation, and lasts about as long. Beethoven accords it a change of key signature, which he had not considered necessary for the dominant modulation. One might think that the double-bar suggests that he regards this modulation as the inauguration of a development; but this is not what happens. For a while there may be a hint of dubiety, and therefore of potential drama: the syllables of the word *benedictus* are oddly split, and the word *qui* is homophonically uttered three times, each with a sforzando accent, twice followed by a silence, as though the identity, or even the existence, of this 'who' were being called into question. The effect is no more than transitory, however; with the entry of the soloists this E section floats in ever longer periods through balancing octave oscillations on the violin; moves slowly through tonic to dominant; but then fades in brief cadenzas for soprano and alto. The 'middle' has not developed, and is succeeded by an even more ecstatic permutation of section B, wherein the soprano rises to high C, the closest the voices attain to the violin-angel's celestial altitudes (bar 195). Section C is then repeated, a fifth lower than its first statement; the codetta theme (D) also reappears, now in the subdominant, but flowing back to the tonic, to end with the violin's long cadential trill. So although the structure has a mirror-like symmetry— A B C D E B C D A—it is non-sectional in effect. There are no seams, only a continuous stream of melody: the Hidden Song revealed.

The Benedictus has virtually no beginning or middle, but it has an end. Beethoven embraces the second Osanna within the Benedictus since, having attained blessedness, he cannot bathetically return to mundane mirth. So the second Osanna forms a canonic coda to the Benedictus, the theme being a simple rising fourth that then declines down the scale in the lilting 12/8 rhythm. The consummatory feeling of this springs partly from metrical considerations: the entries of the theme, which is a distillation of some of the basic motives of the Mass, appear symmetrically at a bar's distance, moving from bass upwards (bar 213), and thus balancing the first Osanna, wherein the entries moved from top to bottom. Moreover, entries are now at the traditional fifth or fourth instead of second or seventh, thereby emphasizing harmonic stability along with melodic unity. After briefly complementary modulations to dominant and subdominant, the canon concludes in a rare fortissimo, but on first inversion of the dominant of G; this sounds less cadential than the chord would in root position. During the last twelve bars the solo violin resumes its soaring song, the voices their plainsong intonation. There is, however, a crucial difference, for the intonation now merges into a phrase rising through a minor third from B to D, and pressing up through the leading note to the tonic. The motive is an inversion of the original cry of falling third, which is now resolved harmonically as well as melodically. It is sung four times in canon, no longer at the fourth or fifth, let alone second or seventh, but in ultimate unison or octaves. This is the Mass's *consummatum est*, reminding us that the word 'sacrifice' itself means a making holy.

Looking back on the sequence of the Credo, Sanctus and Benedictus we can see how Beethoven has embraced the double symbolism of the Cross, no less than Bach; but whereas Bach receives the symbolism as doctrine which, because it concerns mankind, concerns himself, Beethoven arrives at the archetype through a process of self-discovery. What he experiences in the Crucifixus is the fact of human suffering, born of duality, the Tree of Calvary being the Tree of Knowledge of Good *and* Evil. Only after having eaten of the fruit of that tree could Adam stretch out his hand to pluck of the fruit of the Tree of Life, which flourished in pre-lapsarian Eden, and which Beethoven, in his Benedictus, equates with the creative force inherent in Nature herself. 'Nature', of course, includes Beethoven's own nature, as well as the natural (rather than man-made) world in which he exists. When Beethoven says 'It is as though every tree in the countryside said Holy, Holy, Holy! Ecstasy is in the Woods', he is close to what Blake meant in saying 'Everything that lives is holy'. There is a parallel, too, between Beethoven's and Goethe's Hellenism and Nature-worship; between the landscape and soundscape of the Benedictus, and the primeval woods and druidical forests within which Goethe's Faust and Helen disport themselves. Beethoven and Goethe are, in their respective arts of music and poetry, the supreme masters of their time; and for both, joy is the obverse of suffering and its necessary complement. In the representation of the earthly paradise in the second chapter of Genesis four great rivers spring from the root of the Tree of Life and flow towards the four cardinal points, thus tracing a cross on the surface of the terrestrial world. These can be related to the quaternity of elements which issue from a single source, corresponding to the primeval ether (Genesis 2:9–17). So Beethoven's crucifix is the agony of antagonism, the crossroads of possibilities and impossibilities, of construction and destruction, which man has made from his Fall. Momentarily, in the Benedictus' bliss, the Tree of Knowledge becomes the Tree of Life, in the 'sweet stillness of the forest'. For Beethoven the Cross is thus a symbol of totality; in Jung's words, 'as an instrument of torture it expresses the suffering on earth of the incarnate God, and as a quaternity it expresses the universe'.

Yet although Beethoven has experienced Paradise Regained, and the Benedictus' final cadence is another plagal Amen, through which the solo violin wings in a subdominant arpeggio over almost motionless concords, this can be only a moment of personal illumination within Time's context. Grace may descend as ecstasy ascends, and Time may seem to be effaced. But the last movement, Agnus Dei, must bring us back to fallen Earth, where we once more exhort the Lamb of God to purge our sins. Having been where we have been, knowing what we know, our cry is more fraught with pity and terror than it was when, from the communion of the Kantian Invisible Church, we first uttered those declining thirds in the Kyrie. Beethoven has justified his sublime statement that 'whoever understands my music will henceforth be free of the misery of the world'. This does not, however, mean that the misery no longer exists: as Beethoven makes manifest by beginning the Agnus as an aria for bass solo, the darkest of human voices. He also writes the aria in B minor, which he called 'a dark key', and which we have seen to be Bach's key of purgatorial suffering; it suits Beethoven's purposes the better in being an upper mediant to G and a lower mediant to D major. The latent modality of the Sanctus is abandoned in favour of a sonorously scored, humanly passionate diatonicism; complementarily, the fluid rhythm of the Benedictus gives way to a time-dominated pulse, like a slowly thudding heart. The melody is impelled by the simplest possible cry of the motivic thirds; appoggiaturas and chromatic embellishments render them operatic, the more so when the male voices of the chorus respond to the soloists' ululations:

Ex. 153

Yet the manner is hymnic as well as operatic, with bassoon-pervaded Masonic scoring; and despite the passion—still more evident after alto and tenor have taken over from the bass soloist—there is only one real modulation. Though it is a subdominant modulation to E minor, it paradoxically increases vehemence. Falling thirds are stretched into arpeggios; rhythm is agitated by pulsing quavers. The tonic is regained by way of a brief 'enhanced dominant', and leads not so much to a da capo as to a development. The four soloists weave a ripely harmonic polyphony, no longer obsessed by the falling thirds, though they are still present. Dissonant passing notes are stabilized by a dominant pedal; a sudden pianissimo tremor of Neapolitan C major screws up the approach to the final section, wherein the voices quieten to crotchets and minims. Meanwhile strings and woodwind writhe in quaver figuration that combines drooping appoggiaturas with lifting thirds, fourths and fifths: 'our' operatically projected suffering sounds like a simpler, more overt permutation of the agony of lacerated Christ-Beethoven in the Crucifixus. Pain is alleviated by a *tierce de Picardie*, which functions, however, as the dominant of the subdominant and, as the chorus breathes *Agnus Dei* in dotted rhythm, unexpectedly resolves on to the dominant of D.

The Dona nobis pacem, which Beethoven calls 'a prayer for inner and outer peace', is introduced by the soloists, who sing a spacious theme beginning with the motivic third, which then expands into a falling arpeggio and is fused with the lilting rhythm of the Benedictus. This is notated, however, not in the Benedictus' winging 12/8 but in a more earthily dancing 6/8: which suggests that the Dona nobis is concerned with the effect of our incursion into the numinous on our life in the world. But although the music does not induce anything like the Benedictus' metaphysical ecstasy, it achieves more than the Kyrie's social-spiritual grace. When the chorus enter, their flowing melodies are freely canonic, the strings' seniquavers a liberated delight. The consummatory phrase is unaccompanied:

Ex. 154

The Kyrie hymn seems to be fulfilled in the falling sixths and *rising* thirds, at first in homophonic euphony, then, orchestrally accompanied, in canon. Sustained parallel thirds between male and female voices suggest amity, while woodwind and strings recall the Benedictus' rising and falling quaver scales, in a delicate dance rather than in vocal suavity. The pastoral flavour of this music has point since, as we

have seen, Nature seemed to Beethoven to offer the possibility of
communion with God. The link with the Benedictus becomes explicit
when the canonic theme changes to rising fourth and falling scale,
thereby being identical with the Benedictus' canonic coda. Throughout, the key gravitates around D major, with intermittent sharpenings
to the dominant; the Mass's plagal tendency seems to be annulled.

   None the less, though Beethoven has been utterly 'changed . . . in
the twinkling of an eye', and God's grace has spilled through his art on
to the world, the World as such remains unredeemable. The section
ends with the chorus uttering pugnacious sforzandi, repeating the
word *pacem* in an almost hectoring tone (bars 150 ff.). If man is trying
to bully God, he pays the price of his human imperfection and pre-
sumption, for the dominant triads are succeeded by three unison
dominant As which become an unexpected transition to a mediant F
major triad, pianissimo. This proves to be a dominant of B flat, man's
key as opposed to the godly D major in which we have been lyrically
singing and liltingly dancing. The belligerence that follows is all too
human; timpani and distant trumpets evoke a martial music, alternating open fifths with the clenched fist of a dominant ninth:

Ex. 155

There is an allegorical appropriateness in the fact that the screwed-up
human imperfection of the ninth counteracts, if it does not demolish,
the perfection of the godly fifths; yet the impact of the passage lies
most in its frightening realism. It summons up present actualities; we
must remember that Beethoven had known war at first hand and,
according to Ferdinand Ries, had spent the night of 11 May 1809 in
'great fear' in his brother's cellar, as the city was bombarded by French

artillery. 'Frightful and terrible is the sound of the trumpet, when it announces the advance of the enemy'; even deaf Beethoven heard it, and quailed, during one of the two occupations of Vienna by Napoleon's troops. Yet paradoxically it is the very naturalism of the passage that makes it, in the context of Beethoven's Mass, significantly insignificant; through it we become aware that 'inner peace' is ultimately independent of the outer kind. Beethoven suggests this by having the solo voices declaim *miserere 'timidamente'*, in operatically falling thirds. Though their rhetoric is not 'insincere', their theatrical projection, even melodrama, implies that the contagion of the world's wars, their physical and emotional deprivations and bestialities, is ephemeral. This anti-liturgical naturalism deeply disturbed contemporary opinion. Even Schindler recommended that the passage be omitted, at least if the work were performed in church. We don't have the right to be condescending to Schindler, for the audacity of Beethoven's conception is breath-taking. It is only by hindsight, more than a hundred and fifty years after the event, that we can fully apprehend his synthesis of inner and outer experience. In this context the point is that, though the trumpet's loud clamour swells to fortissimo, the Song survives.

The wailing thirds (which, however operatic, hark back to the original cry of *Kyrie*) cohere again into the 6/8 hymn; and do so by way of a modulatory passage that implies development. Tonal movement is rapid, from C to F to B flat, then through G, C, A, D, B and G in alternating minor and major. The more agitated movement, prompted by 'outer' war even within the inner life of the hymn, makes the restatement of the *a cappella* hymn-phrase even more benign than it was on its first appearance. This time it is expanded into a noble fugato, beginning with *two* falling sixths and a rising fourth. The key is the Benedictus' G major, though with veerings towards its dominant. The texture is canonic; but contrapuntal discipline seems to encourage freedom, since the intervals gradually expand until the bass immensely leaps down an octave, up an eleventh, down a sixth. With D major affirmed, we hear again the quaver and semiquaver scales (typical of both the Credo and the Benedictus) the sustained thirds on the voices, and the simplest form of the rising fourth canon. As linear movement rises and tonality lifts sequentially, the music induces a joyous content.

Unlike the Benedictus, however, this is not a state of blessedness outside Time, so it is subject to the accidents inherent in mortality. Tranquillity is brushed aside, not by martial bellicosity but rather by mundane triviality; it is not beyond the scope of Beethoven's imagination to imply that there may be a connection between the two. However this may be, a presto scherzo-like orchestral interlude is built from a frisky permutation of the falling third motive, perkily rounded off by a trill through the (temporal and worldly) leading note; a countersubject is not unrelated to the scale movement and leaping fourths of the Benedictus, which is thereby blasphemously, though momentarily, debunked:

Ex. 156

The interlude begins where we were, in D major; but modulates through G major, C major and C minor, and crazily dissipates through rapid sequences around the 'mundanely' orientated B flat. Piercingly orchestrated, the scatty hubbub anticipates Mahler's symphonic evocations of the world's tawdry turmoil. Though the parallel thirds and sixths in contrary motion, as the music reaches such remoter regions as A flat and D flat, are merry rather than scary, the merriment would seem to be inane, since it leads (bar 326) into a fierce recurrence of the minatory march in B flat, drums blatant, trumpets raucous. Beethoven lights on a profound psychological insight in thus defining the relationship between inanity and evil.

Yet once more the Song prevails. Solo soprano screams *dona* on a high A flat, which falls through a tritone instead of the habitual third. This takes us from B flat to the subdominant. When the other soloists enter, the A flat changes enharmonically to G sharp, and the devilish tritone becomes a godly perfect fifth. The enharmonic modulation cadences in A major, which is again mutated into a dominant of D. The hymnic song sounds again, violins embellishing the dancing semiquavers with a frisson of demisemiquaver turns, similar in effect to Beethoven's paradisal trills, but less completely fulfilled because discontinuous. Over sustained dominants on horns, the soloists undulate in rising and falling scales derived from the Benedictus; the chorus interject chordal antiphonies. Through this long lyrical paragraph there is virtually no modulation. Contentment is almost absolute, but not quite, because the semiquaver figuration recalls the mundane hurly-burly of the orchestral interlude. We are not altogether surprised, therefore, when the chorus, after dominant octave As on horns similar to those preceding the martial episode, barks cadential *pa-cems* in a I–IV–I–V progression, the syllables splintered, and the orchestra glitters in high parallel thirds and sixths. The chorus then yells the word on sforzando *tonic* triads, with the third on top. The effect is ambiguous, for although bellicose, we can also take it as triumphant (bars 380 ff.). Equivocation remains when voices and orchestra calm to stepwise movement, with sustained internal pedal notes. We seem to have reached a haven in a simple homophonic restatement of the hymnic phrase which, once having been discovered, significantly does not change its identity. None the less distant war-drums sound again on B flat (bar 406), sundering the D major bliss, fading into a cadence on *pacem*. Then again muffled drums reverberate: an effect of dissolution which Beethoven laboured so hard to achieve that his pen wore a hole in the manuscript paper (bars 412–14). Again the B flats, extraneous to the D major tonality, are effaced in a cadence that stills to peace, the melody twice descending by step through the seminal interval of a minor third, while the harmony moves from dominant to tonic by way of the subdominant, maintaining plagal relaxation. Unobtrusively the dancing upward scales resume, and the chorus repeats its benedictory phrase once more, fairly, but not very, loud. The final choral phrase omits the specific reference to us ('Nobis'), and merely says, non-committally and perhaps not very hopefully, 'dona pacem'.

Throughout this coda the scoring is oddly insubstantial, divided between strings and wind, with staccato articulation, so that bassoons, usually sombre in this Mass, become clownishly skittish. The contrast between such delicate 'foolishess' and the melodic radiance and harmonic euphony of the hymn-phrase is a distillation of the *conjunctio oppositorum* inherent in the whole Mass and, indeed, in life itself. This is why, in the sprightly figurations of the Mass's final pages, there is still a hint of sprites and minor demons, if not of the daemonic fiends Beethoven had confronted during his and Christ's Passion. True, the last two tonic triads fall through God's fifth instead of the germinal third; but they are far from final, being tossed off, with a stress on the offbeat, if anywhere.

So 'concludes' is too strong a word to use of the Missa Solemnis. The Agnus had rooted us again in the world we must live in, conscious of human fallibility and mortality. After the transcendent experience of the Sanctus and Benedictus, Beethoven can, however, effect a fusion of the social-religious manner of the Kyrie with the Benedictus' *ecstasis*. The visionary moment can be only personal, not communal. What the final version of the hymnic song offers is a hint of what life within the Invisible Church might be like. But its serenity remains ideal rather than real. It cannot be impervious to the frenzies of the world, whose trumpery trumpetings and feckless follies will recur, since God's Kingdom is 'not of this world'. Beethoven was unambiguous about this. It is evident from the letter he wrote to Archduke Rudolf in August 1823, after the Mass was at last completed, that he was convinced that in his moments of *raptus* he, unlike the generality of men, was able to enter God's Kingdom and therefrom to offer 'intimations of immortality', 'bright shootes of Everlastingnesse'. He was an instrument, he said, through whom 'divine rays' might be 'disseminated among mankind'. Beethoven had the right to believe not so much that the disseminated 'rays' of his music made people 'better', as that they helped them truly to live. Though the Blake-like 'terrifying honesty' which is the heart of his art sometimes makes us quake, it is precisely this courage that makes us recognize in his work the supreme achievement of modern man.

When we look back on the structure of the Missa Solemnis as a whole it almost seems that the power of Beethoven's musical 'mind' must have been superhuman. Such complexities of interrelationship and of transformation, carried through on so vast a time-scale and all demonstrably functioning, suggest that intellect and intuition were coexistent. Despite what he learned from earlier composers—and we have seen that he studied the counterpoint of Palestrina, Handel and Bach, and the monody of plainchant, as a preparation for his Mass—what is most remarkable is Beethoven's uncompromising originality. The influence of Bach is more evident here than that of his revered Handel (it is interesting that in 1823, the year of the Mass's completion, Beethoven was contemplating a 'well-fugued' work on the B.A.C.H. theme); but Beethoven's Bach is as totally recreated as is the modality he acquired from plainsong and Palestrina. For a Beethoven, musical techniques are not learned from models, however august; they are minted in a divine smithy, so that even liturgical tradition becomes a personal apotheosis. Only in the light of such creative incandescence can we appreciate the complex yet logical relationship of parts to whole. Let us recall this total architecture, which is also psychological evolution.

I KYRIE and CHRISTE: a symphonic ternary movement consisting of

Kyrie I   Tempo 2/2 *Assai sostenuto*   *Mit Andacht*
         Key D major
         Characteristics: the cry of the descending third
                      the dotted rhythm of fortitude
                      a texture of homogeneous polyphony
                      antiphony between the soloists (as individual souls) and the chorus (as the Masonic Church).

Christe   Tempo 3/2 *Andante assai ben marcato*
         Key B minor
         Characteristics: double fugato, one theme derived from the falling thirds, the other a rising fourth and flowing scale.

Kyrie II   Tempo I
         Key D major
         Characteristics: a developing recapitulation, with plagal-tending coda.

II GLORIA: an encapsulated choral symphony consisting of
First movement
   First 'subject': *Gloria in excelsis*
      Tempo 3/4 *Allegro vivace*
      Key D major
      Characteristics: fugato on rising scale and descending third, alternating with stepwise-moving homophony; 'The Joyous Wrath of God'.
   Second 'subject': *Gratias agimus*
      Tempo 3/4 *Meno allegro*
      Key B flat major
      Characteristics: a Masonic waltz-hymn and a

> quasi-operatic aria in harmonic
> polyphony;
> 'Man in the Invisible Church'.

Conflict and development of both subjects.
No recapitulation.

Slow movement: *Qui tollis peccata mundi*
>> Tempo 2/4 *Larghetto*
>> Key F major–D minor
>> Characteristics: freely modulating, tense
>>> equilibrium between operatic
>>> dialogue of soloists and
>>> 'ecclesiastical' polyphony of chorus.

Scherzo: *Quoniam tu solus*
>> Tempo 3/4 *Allegro maestoso*
>> Key ambiguous
>> Characteristics: tonal instability and rhythmic
>>> equivocation
>>> falling arpeggios and double dots;
>>> 'The Fall of God'.

Finale: *In Gloria Dei Patris*
>> Tempo 4/4 *Allegro ma non troppo e ben marcato;*
>> Codas 3/4 *Presto*
>> Key D major
>> Characteristics: a fugue, at first metrically and
>>> tonally rigid, then disintegrating.
>>> Three attempts at contrapuntal
>>> order, all frustrated: leading to two
>>> codas, one on *Amen*, the other on
>>> *Gloria in excelsis*, this being a
>>> permutation of Gloria I.
>>> Plagal-tending cadences.

III CREDO: also an encapsulated choral symphony, but more
complex in structure
First movement: *Credo in unum Deum*
>> Tempo 4/4 *Allegro ma non troppo*
>> Key B flat major
>> Characteristics: a developing fugato, the theme a
>>> 'positive' recreation of the falling
>>> third and rising fourth; the second

motive transforms this theme into
assertive repeated notes and rising
fourth.

Slow movement: *Et incarnatus*
    Tempo 4/4 *Adagio*
    Key Dorian D minor
    Characteristics: a modal hymn–aria–fugue with
                paradisal trills
Homo factus est changes to
    3/4 *Andante*
    (diatonic) D major, with theme related to Kyrie I
Crucifixus changes to
    3/4 *Adagio*
    D minor
    Characteristics: freely modulating, rhythmically
                unstable, acutely dissonant and
                'physical': dichotomy between
                quasi-operatic soloists and chorus, as
                in Qui tollis.

Scherzo: *Et resurrexit*
    Tempo 4/4 *Allegro*
    Key Mixolydian G, then F major, freely modulating
    Characteristics: at first *a cappella*, simple, concordant:
                then disintegrating, leading to da
                capo. Counterpoise to the 'Fall of
                God' in the Gloria.
    Developing recapitulation leads into

Finale: *Et vitam venturi*
    Tempo 3/2 *Allegretto ma non troppo*
    Key B flat major
    Characteristics: double fugue with both subjects
                related to first Kyrie, as well as to
                subsequent material. Speeds to
                Allegro con moto with theme in
                diminution and leads into
                Coda: *Grave*: ends softly, with the
                rising scales of 'the Wrath of God'

transformed into human prayer, the
spirit aspiring;
'The Invisible Church on earth', after
the divine event of Incarnation.

IV SANCTUS: a hymn–aria–fugue
> Tempo 2/4 *Adagio   Mit Andacht*
> Key Lydian B minor–D major
> Characteristics: thematically a distillation of previous
> material, from Kyrie I onwards.
> 'Mystical' modality, with sacral
> trombones and four solo voices.

Pleni sunt coeli and *Osanna*
> Tempo 4/4 *Allegro pesante*
> 3/4 *Presto*
> Key D major
> Characteristics: a sudden return to 'Baroque Power
> and Glory': the mundane 'benefits' of
> the transcendent vision still scored
> for solo voices, with full orchestra.

V BENEDICTUS:
Praeludium: an orchestral interlude, thematically related to Kyrie
I and to Sanctus
> Tempo 3/4 *Sostenuto ma non troppo*
> Key G major, but very chromatic
> Characteristics: 'veiled' scoring, harmonic
> polyphony; chromaticism prophetic
> of late Romantic music;
> 'The descent into the Dark
> Labyrinth'.

Benedictus: a large-scale aria–concerto–fugue
> Tempo 12/8 *Andante molto cantabile e non troppo mosso*
> Key G major
> Characteristics: level movement, canonic
> counterpoint ('many-in-oneness'),
> plainsong intonation; the solo violin
> as Dove or angelic messenger; soli
> and chorus interfused, rather than
> antiphonal; an inversion of the end of

the Credo, as the Holy Ghost
descends.

The Benedictus key of G major is
subdominant to God's D major, and
has here itself a pronounced plagal
tendency.

VI AGNUS DEI: a hymnic aria
　　　　　　Tempo 4/4 *Adagio*
　　　　　　Key B minor
　　　　　　Characteristics: a 'dark' key and a dark voice,
　　　　　　　　　　　　　　beginning as bass solo but gradually
　　　　　　　　　　　　　　involving the other soloists and the
　　　　　　　　　　　　　　chorus. Thematic falling thirds
　　　　　　　　　　　　　　pervasive; rhythm relatively
　　　　　　　　　　　　　　metrical, after the Time-dissolving
　　　　　　　　　　　　　　Benedictus. Soloists and chorus in
　　　　　　　　　　　　　　antiphony again because, after the
　　　　　　　　　　　　　　transcendent vision, we are now on
　　　　　　　　　　　　　　earth, asking for God's mercy.
　　　　　　Leads into

VII DONA NOBIS PACEM: a fugued dance
　　　　　　Tempo 6/8 *Allegretto vivace*
　　　　　　Key D major
　　　　　　Characteristics: the fugued material fuses Kyrie I
　　　　　　　　　　　　　　with the Benedictus—the Invisible
　　　　　　　　　　　　　　Church with a personal vision;
　　　　　　　　　　　　　　the dance-song is disturbed by
　　　　　　　　　　　　　　martial and mundane interludes in
　　　　　4/4 and 2/2 *Presto* centred around
　　　　　B flat major and minor, but tonally free.
　　　　　Coda recreates the Kyrie in choral homophony, with
　　　　　pronounced plagal feeling;
　　　　　no finality, since God's Kingdom is 'not of this
　　　　　world'.

Thus the Gloria and Credo are large-scale choral-symphonic movements related to one another both thematically and structurally: as one
might expect, since the words of the Gloria prefigure those of the

Credo. The Dona nobis pacem relates back to the Kyrie, but reinterprets its material in the light of the Gloria and Credo, and still more through the liturgical heart of the Mass, the Sanctus, Benedictus and Agnus Dei. These relationships are reflected in the key-scheme, which is less hieratic than that of Bach's dogmatically ordered faith, but hardly less spiritually allegoric. Whereas Bach's tonal scheme is based traditionally on (godly) fifths, Beethoven's is founded, like so much of his late music, on mediants and the false relations they entail. The main keys are D major, which tends to be God's key, and B flat major, which tends to be Man's, but of course the two overlap. In the first and last movements D major symbolically becomes the Church Invisible, while in the Pleni and Osanna it is physically human again, in the High Baroque manner: men playing at being God. Similarly B flat may gravitate from man *per se* into a music of the Masonic Church.

The 'goal' of the Mass, tonally, is G major, which for Beethoven as for Bach is the key of blessedness. It is a lower mediant to B flat; and a flat submediant to B minor, which is D major's relative. B minor, for Beethoven as for Bach, is a key of suffering, whereby a synthesis between God's D major and Man's B flat major occurs and, 'for the time being', finds haven in G major's benediction. This can happen because of ambiguities in Beethoven's tonality. D major-minor, B minor and G major acquire modal characteristics (Dorian, Lydian, Mixolydian) which may be inherent in the mediant relationships, and which transmute the 'illusory' element in false relation into the 'transcendental'. Of course Beethoven's modulatory range is wider than Bach's; in the Missa Solemnis almost every key is touched on, even if but fleetingly. None the less the scheme outlined carries the burden of the work; it is worth noting that the only other keys which have structural importance, F major and F sharp minor, also stand in mediant relationship to D and B flat (F sharp being enharmonically identical with G flat).

So complex a structure, on so grand a scale, combined with the elaborate interrelationships of theme, motive, rhythm and harmony which our analysis has revealed, surely argues for a compositional process beyond rational understanding. It is interesting that Einstein, a scientist as great in his field as Beethoven in music, has maintained that 'the mystical is the sower of all true art and science. To know that what is impenetrable to us really exists, manifesting itself as the highest wisdom and most radiant beauty, which our dull faculties can comprehend only in their most primitive forms—this knowledge, this feeling, is at the centre of true religiousness' (quoted by Philipp Frank). In the light of this, Beethoven's statement that he wrote out the last three piano sonatas without pause, in between working on movements of the Missa Solemnis, does not seem totally nonsensical, though in another sense it took him a lifetime to create the sonatas. Similarly he toiled for four years on the Mass, yet the complexities of formal evolution and the precision of experiential logic are such that one can only imagine that the actual composition was achieved in the state Beethoven called 'raptus'. There is some evidence that this was so. Schindler tells us that towards the end of August 1819

> I arrived at the master's house in Mödling. It was four o'clock in the afternoon. As soon as we entered we learned that in the morning both servants had gone away, and that there had been a quarrel after midnight which had disturbed all the neighbours, because as a consequence of a long vigil both had gone to sleep and the food which had been prepared had become unpalatable. In the living room, behind a locked door, we heard the master singing parts of the fugue of the Credo—singing, howling, stamping. After we had been listening for a long time to this almost awful scene, and were about to go away, the door opened and Beethoven stood before us with distorted features, calculated to excite fear. He looked as if he had been in mortal combat with the whole army of contrapuntists, his everlasting enemies.

About the mortal combat there can be no question, though contrapuntists were not Beethoven's unworthy adversaries. The fight was rather that between Yahveh and Moses, 'waylaid by night'; between Jacob and the God with whom he 'wrestled until the break of day'; between Jesus as the Human Imagination and Lucifer as fallen angel and *mysterium horrendum*, the savage beast in whose belly the soul may—according to St John of the Cross must—be buried. The distraught Beethoven, emerging from closeted conflict into the light of day, seems a personification of what Goethe meant by the Daemonic Man, from whom 'an incredible force goes forth, and who exercises an incredible power over all creatures, perhaps even over the elements. And who can say how far such an influence may not extend?' This power, Goethe continues, can be defined only in antitheses. It is neither human nor divine, neither angelic nor devilish; it is 'like chance, for it points to no consequence; like providence, for it indicates connection and unity. All that hems us in seems penetrable to it; it seems to dispose at will of the inevitable elements of our being, contracting time and expanding space.... It fashions a power which, if not opposed to the moral world order, yet intersects it in such a way that one might take one for the warp, the other for the woof.'

This power that takes over the entire being is the basic meaning of the Greek word *daimon*, which was corrupted into daemon or even demon, for medieval Christianity, distrustful of sensual possession, tended to reduce demons to hobgoblins, near-comic emanations of our lower natures that threaten our divine potential. But Beethoven, like Goethe and Rilke, had come to see that 'if my devils are to leave me, I am afraid that my angels will take flight as well': to recognize that if daemonic possession is a madness, it may also be the sublimest sanity, since only in embracing the destructive along with the constructive forces in the psyche can we hope to attain the Whole. According to Aristotle, happiness is *eudaimonism*, 'being blessed with a good genius'. The word genius itself, the Latin equivalent for the Greek *daimon*, is derived from the verb *genere*, to generate or beget: so Eros is a daimon, and Nature, like Blake's Tyger, is herself dynamic and daemonic. To deny the daimon therefore, as Rollo May has put it, 'makes us accomplices on the side of the destructive principle', and leads to atrocities such as those perpetrated, in the death-camps of Hitler and Stalin and the racial persecutions of the immediate present, by our ostensibly enlightened century. Goethe explicitly described Beethoven as 'one possessed by a daimon, and it is all the same whether he speaks from feeling or knowledge, for here the gods are at work and scatter the seeds far, and we must wish that they proceed to an undisturbed development. His genius lights the way for him and often illumines him with a lightning stroke, while we sit in darkness and scarcely suspect from which side day will break.' Oddly enough Goethe, who had been a daimon himself, and who admitted in 1812, after the meeting at Teplitz, that he had never met a man or artist with more formidable inner force than Beethoven, was in old age as scared of Beethoven as he would presumably have been of his own Faust. He considered the Fifth Symphony a work subversive enough to threaten civilization, and would have been appalled by the spiritual as well as physical ferocity of the Missa Solemnis, especially its Gloria. For the venerable Goethe, Beethoven's reprimand to those negligent servants who slept, instead of feeding him, while he was locked in mortal combat, would have been a blasphemy: the more so because Beethoven's question, 'Could you not watch with me one hour?' involved a lie, since the one hour was actually five or six! Yet if, with Blake, we equate Christ with the Human Imagination, Beethoven's question was not blasphemous at all; in the Hammerklavier Sonata and the Missa Solemnis he had experienced Calvary and had cried 'My God, my God, why hast thou forsaken me?' Beethoven's apprehension of God was in this sense identical with his apprehension of the creative act; as Robert Duncan has written in *The Truth and Life of Myth*:

> The immovable God of Jehovah declares himself a God of Jealousy, Vengeance and Wrath. Reason falters, but our mythic and deepest poetic sense recognizes and greets as truth the proclamation that the Son brings that just this Wrathful Father is the First Person of Form. And the Poet too, in this myth of Love and Form, must go deep into the reality of his own nature, in the Fathering Chaos or Wrath, to suffer his own Nature. In this mystery of art, the Son's cry to the Father might be too the cry of the artist to the Form he obeys.

The daemonic element in Beethoven is thus the personally psychological complement to the archetypal Marriage of Heaven and Hell which I commented on in the last piano sonata opus III, and to the mythological and theological identification of the Two Trees, of Knowledge and of Life, to which I referred in the analysis of the Missa Solemnis. Certainly Beethoven's personality, no less than his music, was a *conjunctio oppositorum*: if we recall Schindler's portrait of the daemon Beethoven in the throes of his Credo, we cannot deny that it induces awe and terror, but has also a quality that it is difficult not to call grotesque, even farcical. It is illuminating to place beside this story the several accounts of disasters resulting from deaf Beethoven's conducting, of which the most hilarious is Spohr's description of Beethoven's performance of his 'new piano concerto' (no. 4 or 5) in 1808:

> Beethoven was playing a new piano concerto of his, but already at the first tutti, forgetting that he was the soloist, he jumped up and began to conduct in his own peculiar fashion. At the first sforzando he threw out his arms so wide that he knocked over both the lamps from the music-stand of the piano. The audience laughed and Beethoven was so beside himself over this disturbance that he stopped the orchestra and made them start again. Seyfried, worried for fear that this would happen again in the same place, took the precaution of ordering two choirboys to stand next to Beethoven

and to hold the lamps in their hands. One of them innocently stepped closer and followed the music from the piano part. But when the fatal sforzando burst forth the poor boy received from Beethoven's right hand such a sharp slap in the face that, terrified, he dropped the lamp on the floor. The other, more wary boy, who had been anxiously following Beethoven's movements, succeeded in avoiding the blow by ducking in time. If the audience had laughed the first time, they now indulged in a truly bacchanalian riot. Beethoven broke out in such a fury that when he struck the first chord of the solo he broke six strings. Every effort of the true music lovers to restore calm and attention remained unavailing for some time; thus the first Allegro of the Concerto was completely lost to the audience. After this incident Beethoven wanted to give no more concerts.

Thayer says that this story cannot be true of the public concert, at which Spohr was not himself present, though he does not explain why he considers Seyfried's evidence untrustworthy, and he admits that, on Ries's evidence, it bears some resemblance to an incident at a rehearsal. That there is a general measure of veracity in it is supported by several similar and better authenticated stories. Certainly the Credo anecdote and this one are revealingly complementary: in the former, awe invites the nervous titter; in the latter, the farcical savagery of the events tempers risibility with dismay, for the condition that occasioned these antics, Beethoven's deafness, is no cause for mirth. Looking back, we recognize that the supreme greatness of Beethoven's work is attributable precisely to this risky equilibrium between the sublime and the ridiculous, the tragic and the bizarre. The comedy of the opus 22 piano sonata and the ironies of the fourth and eighth symphonies, not to mention an overtly funny piece like the early trio for clarinet, cello and piano, have undertones often mysterious, sometimes sinister; Harlequin-Fool capers in the midst of the *pathos* and *ecstasis* of opus 110; the grandeur of the Missa Solemnis can find place, in the Gloria, for 'the foolishness of God' and, in the Agnus Dei, for man's desperate vainglory and idiot fribble. Again the only valid comparison is with Shakespeare's *King Lear*, whose tragedy encompasses, along with pity and terror, pathos that is near to bathos ('Thou'lt come no more,/Never, never, never, never, never./Pray you, undo this button'), and savage farce (Gloucester's self-precipitation off the non-existent cliff).

'We finite ones with infinite souls are born only for sorrows and joys and it might almost be said that the best of us receive joy through sorrow', Beethoven wrote to the Countess Erdödy in 1815; in the following year he added 'man cannot avoid suffering and his strength must be to stand the test. He must endure without complaining, know his own nobleness, and so again believe in his own perfection: which perfection the Almighty will then bestow on him'. It may not be fortuitous that Beethoven wrote such moving letters to the Countess Erdödy, a woman of exceptional beauty and intelligence who, at her first confinement at the age of seventeen, contracted a painful disease. Though Reichardt, in commenting on her association with Beethoven, exaggerates and perhaps sentimentalizes her distresses, there can be no doubt that she suffered—from ill-health, from the sudden death of her son, and from the state's disapprobation. In 1819 she was exiled from Austria for her liberal opinions and perhaps actions: so like Beethoven (who Schindler hints was her lover), she was a sufferer and an outcast. She bore affliction with tranquillity, even gaiety, of mind; and perhaps discovered, as did Beethoven through his music and through the Missa Solemnis in particular, that suffering may be the gateway to self-knowledge, and ultimately to joy. In 1816 Beethoven had written to Fanny Giannatasio that 'he is a base man who does not know how to die; I knew it as a boy of fifteen'. Though there is no evidence that Beethoven was ever near death in his youth, we cannot doubt the truth of this assertion. We have seen that in his music he died many times, to be reborn; when the fact of his physical dissolution was irrefutable he expired in a manner worthy of King Lear, of his own life, and even of his music.

Dr Wawruch's medical report tells us that shortly after Beethoven had received the last sacraments he quietly quoted the words 'Plaudite, amici, comoedia finita est'. This has been interpreted as a jokey shrug of the shoulders, even as a dismissal of the Church's mumbo-jumbo, though neither account is probable since the word comoedia does not imply that the play is funny. It does, however, suggest that Beethoven, who had been a player of instruments mediatory between himself, man and God, momentarily saw his life as theatre: a simulacrum of the reality revealed in his music. Anselm Hüttenbrenner's much-quoted account of the moment of death will bear repetition:

During Beethoven's last moments there was no one present in the death chamber but Frau van Beethoven and myself. Beethoven lay in the final agony, unconscious and with the death-rattle in his throat, from 3 o'clock, when I arrived, until 5 o'clock; then there was suddenly a loud clap of thunder accompanied by a bolt of lightning which illuminated the death-chamber with a harsh light (there was snow in front of Beethoven's house). After this unexpected natural phenomenon, which had shaken me greatly, Beethoven opened his eyes, raised his right hand and, his fist clenched, looked upwards for several seconds with a very grave, threatening countenance, as though to say 'I defy you, powers of evil! Away! God is with me.' It also seemed as though he were calling like a valiant commander to his faint-hearted troops: 'Courage, men, forward! Trust in me. The victory is ours.'

As he let his hand sink down on the bed again, his eyes half closed. My right hand lay under his head, my left hand rested on his breast. There was no more breathing, no more heart-beat. The great composer's spirit fled from this world of deception into the kingdom of truth.

Those abnormal weather conditions have been confirmed by the investigation of meterological records: so perhaps Goethe was right in suggesting that supremely daemonic genius may have 'an incredible power over all creatures, perhaps even over the elements'. Zuckerkandl's view, quoted in my introductory chapter, that in music man 'invents himself', proves to be true of Beethoven in a startlingly literal as well as philosophical sense. 'The closest analogy to the functioning of a musical composition is the functioning of a human life.... A man's death might be compared to the moment when a melody ceases to 'grow' and enters actual existence.' If we think of Beethoven's life's work as one evolving composition, which it is, we can hardly deny that his last minutes on earth and his death in a whitely snow-besprent world, accompanied by Promethean thunder and illuminated by Goethe's 'lightning stroke', re-enact his music's story, from the earliest years to the end.

There is a passage in Grillparzer's noble funeral oration that epitomizes our awareness of Beethoven as an instrument of cosmic forces, of the Energy which is God:

He was an artist, and who shall stand beside him? As the Behemoth sweeps through the seas, he swept across the boundaries of his art. From the cooing of the dove to the thunder's roll, from the subtlest weaving of wilful artifices to that awesome point at which the fabric passes over into the lawlessness of clashing natural forces—he traversed all, he comprehended everything. He who follows him cannot continue; he must begin anew, for his predecessor ended only where art ends.

It says much for Grillparzer that he had the intelligence and courage to see and say that, and it says much for the society that Beethoven lived in that Grillparzer was not speaking as a member of a cultured élite, for an élite. Some twenty thousand people 'of all classes and vocations' attended Beethoven's funeral; had we a Beethoven among us, would we so recognize and honour him? At least we honour the historical Beethoven now, since he is still present, and may even be the most deeply significant composer of *our* time, since no man has approached with more unflinching honesty and fortitude the psychic turmoils of his and our divided and distracted age. Indeed Beethoven's ultimate revolution, achieved in his final works, was not so much a reaction against malformations and hypocrisies in the world that made him, as a reappraisal, however unconscious, of many values that had made post-Renaissance civilization possible. The Arietta of opus 111, the slow movement of opus 132, the Benedictus of the Missa Solemnis are, in their escape from temporal progression, the beginnings of that process whereby music, through the sequence of late Wagner, Debussy, Stravinsky, free atonal Schoenberg, Webern, Messiaen, Ives, Varèse, Stockhausen, Cage, at least envisaged the possibility of a society freed from the bondage of our linear thinking, quantificated knowledge and progressive science. And Beethoven had done that, unlike his successors, without surrendering a tittle of the human power that stemmed from the 'Western consciousness' that he supremely embodies.

It may be significant that Beethoven's discovery of the Whole in his Missa Solemnis is at once a communion with God and with Nature. The segregation of a God 'up there' from Nature 'here around' us is abolished; to find God, which is to find the Self, is also to heal the breach between Man and Nature, wherein God *must* be manifest. Such seems to be the import of Grillparzer's reference in the quotation above to Beethoven as cooing dove, rolling thunder and clashing natural forces. Beethoven indeed 'traversed all' and 'comprehended everything'. Grillparzer speaks for us today, as he spoke for the mourners of 1827:

You who have followed our escort to this place, hold your sorrow

in sway. You have not lost him but have won him. No living man
enters the halls of immortality. The body must die before the grave
is opened. He whom you mourn is now among the greatest men of
all time, unassailable for ever. Return to your homes, then, distres-
sed but composed. And whenever, during your lives, the power of
his works overcomes you like a coming storm; when his rapture
pours out in the midst of a generation as yet unborn: then remember
this hour and think: we were there when they buried him, and when
he died we wept.

IV

POSTLUDE

To see a World in a Grain of Sand
And Heaven in a Wild Flower,
Hold Infinity in the palm of your hand
And Eternity in an hour.

WILLIAM BLAKE: *Auguries of Innocence*

He who binds to himself a joy
Does the winged life destroy;
But he who kisses the joy as it flies
Lives in eternity's sunrise.

WILLIAM BLAKE: *Miscellaneous Poems and Fragments*

All things began in Order, so shall they end, and so shall they begin again;
according to the Ordainer of order and the mysticall Mathematicks of the
City of Heaven.

SIR THOMAS BROWNE: *The Garden of Cyrus*

PRELUDE

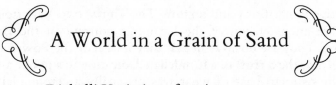

A World in a Grain of Sand

Diabelli Variations for piano opus 120

According to Thayer, the composition of the Missa Solemnis covered a period of five years. The Kyrie was begun in 1818, shortly after the Archduke's ecclesiastical appointment was announced. The sketch of the Gloria was completed in 1819, that of the Credo in 1820. The remainder of the work was sketched out by 1822; the full score was finished by the middle of 1823. The last three piano sonatas were composed, we have noted, while Beethoven was working on the Mass, to which they are affiliated experientially and in specific details of theme, motive and tonal relationship. For this reason it is valid to regard them as a trinity which is also a single work, though Schindler cannot be correct in saying that they were written out in 1820 'in a single breath'. The sketchbooks indicate that opus 109 was composed in 1820, in between work on the Mass's Credo, Benedictus and Agnus Dei. Sketches for opus 110 follow those for the Agnus, and Beethoven himself gives 25 December 1821 as completion date for the sonata. According to Beethoven opus 111 was completed on 13 January 1822; sketches for this work are also found amongst those for the Agnus.

Beethoven's last three piano sonatas were not, however, his last music for the instrument. There remain one major work, the Diabelli Variations, and several minor pieces in the form of Bagatelles and folk-song variations. That these works are either small, self-contained movements, or in variation form rather than in the evolutionary style of sonata, is significant. We have seen that for Beethoven, as a composer trained in the Viennese classical tradition, variation was the static and 'monistic' principle, opposed to the 'dualistic' dynamism of sonata. In his early years Beethoven often used the simple song lyric in this way, though his first-period variations—for instance the first movement of opus 26—usually contain elements of disruptive wit more violent than was habitual in classical tradition. During his middle years Beethoven developed variation towards drama, either because he used the static, lyric type as a negative contrast to the dynamic energy of sonata, as in the slow movement of the Appassionata, or because he made variation itself into development, cumulative in harmony and texture. The Thirty-two Variations in C minor are an extension of the harmonic concept of the Baroque chaconne. They are positive in that they incarnate the Power and the Glory (if also the terror) of a Handelian dedication to a public assumption. The ostinato bass of what was originally a ceremonial dance imposes monistic order, against tremendous odds, on chaos: as is evident in the two supreme examples of the genre, Bach's C minor Passacaglia, and Couperin's B minor Passacaille which, being a chaconne-rondeau, uses a slightly different convention to the same ends. In Beethoven's chaconne-variations the metrical and harmonic ostinato feels even more rigid and obsessional than those in Bach or Couperin: partly because the violence that is being curbed is more extreme, partly because there is less alleviation in melodic terms.

Still more significant, however, are the Fifteen Variations opus 35, wherein Beethoven as democratic Prometheus takes over from the spiritual though not titular aristocrat who made the Variations in the sonata opus 26. For the opus 35 Promethean theme admits to its harmonic and non-lyrical nature. The fulfilment of this arpeggiated motive is to occur in the chaconne-finale of that crucially Beethovenian work, the Eroica Symphony, where it becomes a resolution of sonata conflict fully meaningful only in relation to the first three movements. So Beethoven-Prometheus is an intermediary between man and the gods; the gift of fire he steals may include material power, but is also the divine spark which can be lit in man only through suffering. In the transition from Beethoven's second to his third period this kindling happens: Prometheus on his rock becomes Christ on his Tree, in a purgatorial process out of which, in the final movements of opus 109, 110 and 111, song is reborn. The Diabelli Variations, Beethoven's longest piano work, represent a further stage, in that variation is no longer a consummation of sonata, but is a cosmos in itself.

The story of the work's origin is well known, though confusing. Diabelli, a composer as well as publisher, commissioned most of the fashionable composers of his day to write one variation each on a theme of his own creation; the proceeds of the publication were to go to succour 'the widows of the late wars'. According to Schindler, this was in 1822. The fifty-one composers invited, mostly forgotten, include some who have survived time's tarnish. Among them we may perhaps (just) include the once-fêted Hummel; certainly Weber; and supremely Schubert (who transformed Diabelli's tune into a nostalgic

Viennese *Ländler*); Liszt (then an eleven-year-old prodigy whose variation is as elegant as it is precocious); and Beethoven himself, who at
first grumpily declined Diabelli's request, but later offered Diabelli a
complete set of variations instead of a single contribution. Diabelli
accepted, requesting six or seven variations, and terms were agreed on.
Ultimately Beethoven produced thirty-three variations. That is
Schindler's story. Lenz, however, on the authority of Holz who knew
Beethoven well in these years, tells us that Diabelli, having received
thirty-two variations from the fifty-one composers he had
approached, asked Beethoven for his one variation; and was met with
the retort that he would cap their thirty-two variations with thirty-
three of his own. Thayer thinks this story improbable, since it is
unlikely that Diabelli would ask Beethoven for a variation he had
already bluntly refused to write. That point is unimportant: what
matters is that Diabelli made the offer—according to Schindler in
1822, according to Thayer in 1821, and according to recently
unearthed evidence in the form of sketches for some of the variations,
possibly as early as 1818, the year in which Beethoven embarked on
the mammoth undertakings of the Hammerklavier Sonata and the
Missa Solemnis. Whenever he started the variations, he abandoned
work on them, whether in contempt of Diabelli's stunt and his 'cobbler's patch' (*Schusterfleck*) of a tune, or under pressure of weightier
matters, and didn't seriously tackle them again until the Mass was
nearly completed. The variation-set finally reached the publisher in
1823; and one has to admit that Diabelli, who was no genius, was also
no fool. He described the variations as being 'of no ordinary type, but a
great and important masterpiece.... The most original structure and
ideas, the boldest musical idioms and harmonies are here exhausted;
every piano effect based on a solid technique is employed, and the
work is the more interesting from the fact that it is elicited from a
theme which no one would otherwise have supposed capable of such a
working-out.... All these variations, through the novelty of their
ideas, care in working out, and beauty in the most artful of their
transitions, will entitle the work to a place beside Sebastian Bach's
masterpiece in the same form.' That, though a publisher's puff, is
exceptionally perspicacious; and it must have been a heartfelt tribute
to the music's quality, since Diabelli must have known that so long
and in every sense difficult a piece could not be a commercial
proposition.

Wherever it ended up, the origins of Beethoven's variation-set were low and 'common', and that is part of the point. The waltz, the most popular dance of the day, sprang from demotic roots; country dances of *Ländler* type, perhaps the round dances of Alpine mountain folk, evolved into a potentially 'polite' triple-rhythmed dance, based on the movement of the swing. The waltz's folk origins are important. It was unabashedly a couple dance, and unashamedly based on the circularity of ternary rhythm, which had been threatened by the duple, incipiently linear and martial rhythms that became fashionable during the High Renaissance. The minuet was the most significant dance of the late eighteenth century precisely because it combined triple with duple metre: the dance steps are both 'straight' in 3/4, and in persistent hemiola, spread across *two* bars. From this came the minuet's equilibrium between courtship and courtliness; it wasn't merely an entertainment, but also an apotheosis of a civilized ideal. By Beethoven's day, however, the minuet was in decline, as was the aristocracy who danced it. Voltaire ridiculed it when he compared the abstract metaphysicians of his day to dancers who, 'most elegantly adorned, bow a few times, mince daintily across the room exhibiting all their charms, move without progressing a single step, and end up on the very spot where they started'. It was time for a breath of fresh air. With the advance of democracy, waltzing winds from Austria ruffled complacency. Minuets speeded up, and the *Ländler* waltz of the beer-gardens was enclosed as trio within the minuet and its da capo, as is evident in the chamber and orchestral music of Haydn, Mozart, Schubert and Beethoven himself. In the second half of the century the waltz was established in its own right as a dance of 'wild fury', in which 'the girls look mad and half ready to swoon'. In 1787 the mandarin Dr Burney splutters in condemning the waltz's lasciviousness: 'the word *waltzen* implies to roll, wallow, welter, tumble down, and roll in the dirt of the mire'. By this time the waltz is not only emotionally barbarous and sexually permissive, but also politically subversive. Something of this reputation survived throughout the nineteenth century, despite Chopin's decorous transmutation of the waltz into a music for Parisian salons. Harridans whirlingly waltzed around the Bastille; waltzes were danced by Schumann's often frantic lovers and by Liszt's Mephistos; and although Beethoven composed amiably social waltzes for commercial reasons, waltz rhythms in his 'serious' works often suggest revolutionary fervour, or at least unrest.

Diabelli's fatuous little waltz tune is neither licentious nor

revolutionary, but it is certainly low in tone and would be common-
place, were it not that its first clause betrays an astonishing resemblance to the sublime Arietta theme with which Beethoven concludes
his last sonata. We cannot be sure which came first, for although the
Diabelli Variations were published later than opus 111, we have seen
that there is confusion as to the year in which Beethoven first sketched
out the variations. The order of precedence is immaterial; either way,
Beethoven must surely have noticed the similarity (falling fourth
expanded to falling fifth, over a simple alternation of tonic and dominant harmony: see Ex. 157 below), and on that basis must have been
encouraged to explore—at what unexpected length and complexity—the theme's implications. It is as though he were saying: 'Very
well then; I'll start not with a divine aria such as I arrived at, after so
arduous a struggle, at the end of my last sonata, but with the everyday
frippery of this cobbler's patch. But I'll see the world in a grain of sand;
the inner form of this work will metamorphose this trumpery waltz
into a celestial, not merely aristocratic, minuet.' Thus the waltz
becomes revolutionary in a sense Diabelli cannot have dreamed of; it
turns into a minuet ideally danced in that 'small court' which Beethoven envisaged, which is not of this world, but is a *temenos* within the
mind. The parallel with Bach's Goldberg Variations is close. Both
works are in equilibrium between Being and Becoming, Bach stressing the former, Beethoven the latter; the relationship between the two
sets of variations complements that between the B minor Mass and the
Missa Solemnis.

Here is Diabelli's tune:

Ex. 157

It opens on an upbeat with a written-out inverted mordent, perkily decorated with an acciaccatura. It is divided between the hands, since after its treble descent through a fourth, the right hand simply reiterates tonic triads, while the bass answers the treble tune with rocking fourths and a tailpiece in quavers, moving by step from third to fifth and down through a tonic arpeggio. The four-bar clause is echoed a tone higher over dominant seventh harmony, the descent in the right hand being expanded to a fifth. This sounds like bourgeois street-music, tritely jaunty as compared with the heroic sarabande that initiates Bach's Goldberg Variations. The gamin-like impudence is emphasized when the symmetrical four-bar phrases are followed by diminutions into two-bar sequences, first flatwards to the subdominant, then sharpwards to the dominant. The sforzando motive of semitone rise followed by major third is mirrored by inversion in the bass. The final four bars of the sixteen-bar period modulate to the relative minor, again with treble and bass mirrored in contrary motion; but cadence in the dominant. The dominant–tonic cadence makes its rudimentary harmonic point, but is also thematic, comically inverting the bass line's opening.

It will be observed that, despite their melodic poverty, these sixteen bars contain quite complex harmonic and tonal implications; this must have been another reason, in addition to the tune's resemblance to the Arietta, that prompted Beethoven to use Diabelli's waltz as impetus to a large-scale work. The second sixteen bars, after the halfway house, immediately change the new G major tonic to a dominant seventh of C, expanding the left hand tune into an arpeggio, and the quaver tailpiece into a falling scale. Sequential repetition a fifth lower this time effects a real subdominant modulation. Then the perky two-bar sequences switch from subdominant to dominant; and the final four bars repeat the cadence of bars 12–16, unambiguously in the tonic major, wide-spaced and double forte. Throughout these sequences the sforzandi on the upbeats are scrupulously indicated, giving the music a cheery aggression and 'push'. The tone is common as well as comic.

It is this tone that gives Beethoven the cue for the irony of his first variation, which is unexpectedly remote from the theme, though it preserves, as do almost all the variations, its tonal structure intact. The time signature is changed from that of a fast waltz to a *marcia maestoso*. The dotted rhythm recalls the heroic overture, while both rhythm and melody are prophetic of the overture to Wagner's *Die Meistersinger!*

Ex. 158

Old-world aristocratic nobility and the romantic actor's rhetoric are juxtaposed with Diabelli's cobblers' or shopkeepers' music. The thematic root of falling fourth expanded to falling fifth is maintained, as is the stepwise movement, derived from the theme's cadential bars, in the bass. In the two-bar sequences the sforzandi are carefully marked, somewhat undermining the grandeur, as do the chromatics in the bass, which provoke passing modulations to the subdominant of the subdominant and to the relative minor. In the second half the dominant seventh similarly turns into a modulation to the supertonic minor, and there are abrupt changes of register as well as of dynamics. So although the first variation's quasi-heroic panache sounds like an ironic comment on the theme's lowness, it isn't simply that, since its nobility is subject, at least until the diatonic resolution of the last four bars, to distortions of phrasing, dynamics, rhythm and key. Wagnerian public solemnity has become, for Beethoven, as much an 'act', an illusion, as the social frivol of Diabelli's waltz. True heroism, wherever it may be, is not there; it is not portentous, though it may portend the Hidden Song that makes us whole.

This search is conducted in the first twelve of the Diabelli Variations through three groups of four variations, as distinct from the trinities of the Goldberg Variations. (See *The Dance of God*, chapter IV.) Each member of Beethoven's quaternities tends to grow more lyrically song-like or contrapuntal, or both. Thus the second variation of this first group abandons the public manner, whether in Diabelli's popular vein or in Beethoven's equivocally noble transformation of it. We return to triple time, with Diabelli's repeated tonic and dominant triads pulsing lightly in the left hand. The right hand, syncopated off the beat, decorates the theme with softly dissonant appoggiaturas; quaver chords, divided between the hands, create a texture both melodically and harmonically veiled. There is no continuous song, neither is there a pompous public gesture, so the variation begins a process of involution—especially in the delicately sensuous chromaticizing of the two-bar sequences and in the double appoggiaturas after the double bar. With no variation of the *leggiermente* dynamics, melody, harmony and rhythm are disguised. A mystery is hinted at, though not revealed.

In variation 3 Diabelli's *tune* begins to flower into Beethoven's *song*. The appoggiaturas of variation 2 are absorbed into lyrical line— melodically in the B natural on the upbeat, harmonically in the dissonant Bs in bars 3 and 4. The fifth and fourth of the bass are tied across the bars, dispersing the theme's body-rhythm; the answering clause is over a motionless dominant pedal, the appoggiatura on the upbeat contracted to a diminished third. The two-bar sequences are again chromaticized; though still phrased across the bars, they have no sforzandi. Throughout the texture is *dolce*, the tempo unchanged from the previous variation. After the double bar, however, canonic entries on the upbeat quavers aspire upwards to unity, only to dissolve oddly at the subdominant modulation into a static revolving cam, pianissimo in the bass:

Ex. 159

The two-bar sequences are also chromaticized with diminished thirds and confused by ties across the bars; if song is envisaged, it is not fulfilled.

Variation 4, still *dolce* and lyrical, calls also on counterpoint in its search for the Whole, for Beethoven's metamorphosed version of the theme enters on the upbeat in threefold canon. The rising and falling fourths are filled in with thirds and, in the answering dominant seventh clause, are embellished with chromatic passing notes. The A minor modulation, though present, scarcely establishes itself in the haze of chromatics, though the dominant cadence at the end of the first half is assertive enough. At the beginning of the second half Beethoven returns to three-fold canonic texture, with the theme in free inversion. Wide-spaced entries overlap, and the subdominant modulation has a mysterious touch of dominant ninth. E minor is substituted for the complementary dominant modulation, this displacement of G major by its relative being the first departure from Diabelli's tonal scheme. Its effect is proportionate to its irregularity; because of this, the re-establishment of C major, after its mediant minor, sounds a note of triumph, not final but potential. Song and counterpoint offer a distant prospect of metamorphosis:

Ex. 160

The promise seems to be short-lived, for variation 5, appears to abandon not only sustained song, but even the tune. It's content with Diabelli's opening tag of descending fourth, now followed by descending thirds to form an arpeggiated triad, and sometimes extended to a sixth. The inverted mordent turns into two cheeky repeated notes. The two-bar sequences are telescoped by sforzandi accents in 2/4 against the basic 3/4; Beethoven makes a joke—instead of a lyrical-dramatic climax—out of the previous variations' tonal irregularity, for he ends the first half in E minor, substituted for G major. The second half inverts the fourths, beginning in E minor; shifts to the dominant minor ninth of F for the subdominant sequence, and baldly replaces the dominant with the flat supertonic, D flat:

Ex. 161

The final throw-away cadence harks back to the E minor anomaly, since the dominant seventh changes on the third beat to a mediant first inversion. Grammatically the E may be an unresolved appoggiatura; none the less its effect in context is that of a raised eyebrow.

Beethoven marks variation 6 *allegro ma non troppo e serioso*. Though it is certainly more serious than the gaffe-like fifth variation, its effect is once more equivocal, as though the 'serioso' were in inverted commas. It begins loudly as a canonic two-part invention, the theme being a trill and turn leading into a cascading arpeggio. Diabelli's four-bar pattern of tonic and dominant seventh is adhered to. Although the motive is explosive, like the fugato writing in the first movement of opus 111, the contrapuntal control sounds severe, almost schoolmasterly. During the subdominant and dominant sequences the mood changes, partly because the semiquaver figuration is ambiguously major-minor, partly because the trills and turns lift expectantly through a sixth. They become comically urgent as they chase one another's tail through the sequential modulations, the minims diminished to crotchets. By the time the semiquavers reach the dominant modulation at the double bar their sonority has become *dolce*, prophetic of later metamorphoses; the variation *is* serious, but in a sense different from expectations aroused by the canonic opening. The second half adheres strictly to Diabelli's harmonic pattern but begins with contrapuntal inversion: trills, turns and arpeggios surge upwards, emphasizing the fifth. The subdominant and dominant sequences cover the keyboard; the return to the tonic is approached with a shiver of minor. This time the strettoed trills don't arch through a sixth, but press up by step to a high resolution which, without cadential finality, simply ceases. The texture here is the first tentative anticipation of the celestial regions of the final minuet.

Variation 7 is also based on wide-flung arpeggios, but in dotted rhythm, somewhat agitatedly mixed with triplets. While the bass line masks Diabelli's harmony by descending through two octaves of tonic and dominant, the right hand exuberantly springs in a rhythmic complexity enhanced by tied notes across the bars. Moreover, the dominant seventh *chord* becomes a modulation to the dominant key; complementarily, the modulation to the relative is intensified by touches of the enhanced dominant, E minor. After the double bar the motives are modified as in variation 6. The bass rises through two octaves, the dominant seventh turns into a dominant minor ninth. The two-bar sequences are again ambiguously major-minor; the bass rocks between fourths that are perfect or diminished. Though not songful, this variation's energy is, in figuration, rhythm and harmony liberated, as compared with the previous variation; and so can lead into the songfulness of variation 8, wherein upwards pushing figuration subsides to the bass, tonic and fifth being approached *sempre ligato* by semitone appoggiaturas. Meanwhile the right hand melody sings in dotted minims, moving warmly by step in parallel thirds. The second four-bar clause doesn't radically alter the harmony, though it might be construed—owing to its C sharp appoggiaturas—as a momentary modulation to the supertonic. After the double bar the *dolce e teneramente* dotted minim theme is inverted and widely separated from the surging quaver bass. The variation is balanced between serenity (the stepwise-moving theme) and unease (the undulating bass). Its song is still veiled: more so, indeed, than the last two variations of the first 'quaternity'. So we are not surprised when it is banished by a return to low comedy—and by the first shift from the tonic C major to its minor.

Beethoven also changes the tempo to 4/4, launching the variation from Diabelli's acciaccatura and inverted mordent. He marks it *allegro pesante e risoluto*, and the music, galumphing in imitation between the hands, is bucolically peasant-like as well as *pesante*. It is also metrically contrarious, since we hear the heavily accented upbeat as a first beat, so that the imitations stride the bar-lines. For the subdominant and dominant sequences Beethoven substitutes rising chromatic sequences on diminished sevenths of G, D and C minors; each begins on the fourth beat, which sounds like the first. The ambiguity is 'corrected' only in the V–I cadence of the sixteenth bar. After the double bar Beethoven chromatically substitutes A flat and D flat for G and C. The unresolved appoggiaturas 'stand for' the key a semitone below; a device anticipatory of Bartók:

Ex. 162

Enharmonic puns proliferate in chromatic sequences, bandying the inverted mordent between the hands; clodhopping rustic mirth has hinted at wonders, as it does in the scherzo of opus 110.

There is a suggestion of opus 110 in the rapidly flickering tenth variation also, not specifically in theme or motive, but because the figuration recalls that Holy Fool with his bladderstick. Theme becomes a presto shimmer óf tonic and dominant seventh quavers, over a lightly dancing descending crotchet scale; the two-bar sequences are gossamer. The repeat is varied, since the scale now descends in the right hand in 6–3 chords, occasionally chromaticized with double appoggiaturas, over a long low trill on the dominant. There is a crescendo through the trill, culminating in cross-beat sforzandi. Though there is no double bar, the second half inverts the first. Suddenly pianissimo, the left hand scale rises through dominant seventh and subdominant minor ninth, and in the written-out repeat the 6–3 chords now dance upwards over dominant, and then tonic, trills. The low trills in this variation aren't seraphic, like those in the finales of opus 109 and 111, nor are they growling tigers like those in the Hammerklavier and the first movement of opus 111. They at once grow out of, and support, the music's slightly dippy ecstasy:

Ex. 163

They are a rustle of wind, evoking perhaps the great god Pan.

On the whole, variation 10 is positive in impetus, to lead to two variations which, though not freely lyrical, are song-like in moving by step. Variation 11 has the texture of a string quartet movement, and variation 12 that of a string trio; we are reminded that after this, his last major piano work, Beethoven turned to equal voiced strings as the medium for his profoundest utterances. Variation 11 has a consistent figure of a triplet turn on the upbeat, woven into a texture of consonant chords in a gentle allegretto. The previous presto variation had returned to 3/4, but at a tempo too rapid to have any connection with a waltz; this variation could be in waltz time, but has lost any suggestion of a waltz's corporeality. There is no change to Diabelli's harmonic scheme, except for the now familiar substitution of E minor for G major in the two-bar sequences, which move in 3/4 phrases across the bar-lines. After the double bar, sonorous triads are again built up from the interlocking triplets, on dominant sevenths of C and dominant ninths of F. On the way back to the tonic the triplet turns create false relations that please, rather than hurt. The final cadence unfinally effaces itself.

Variation 12 has the same texture, enriched to parallel 6–3 chords. The phrasing is still ambiguously across the bars, the tempo slightly more animated. Chromatic appoggiaturas give a discreet pathos to the two-bar sequences, and after the double bar the 6–3 chords float high, tinged with false relations; the sequences oscillate chromatically over a low revolving cam, a more cavernous version of the cam in variation 3:

Ex. 164

The effect of the continuous rhythmic dislocation and the static bass is weird, potentially other-worldly. Despite the stepwise movement, the song remains hidden, perhaps because it runs so deep.

One might almost say that in the Diabelli Variations 'development' is essentially introverted: Beethoven doesn't work *out* a conflict in sonata style, but through each quaternity of variations penetrates more deeply into the heart of Being. In the next twelve variations he abandons the pattern of a gradual approach to song. Variation 13 is again comically disruptive: more so than any previous variation, since it begins off-key, or at least with an A minor instead of C major triad, and makes a jittery use both of silence and of contrasted dynamics. The original tonal sequence is telescoped, the two-bar sequences being absorbed into the silences. The joke lies in the contrast between the fully scored dotted rhythm and the laconically soft crotchet thirds. The dotted rhythm is in stretto at the dominant modulation: an effect more startling than funny. After the double bar Beethoven again substitutes Bartókian unresolved appoggiaturas for the harmony note (B flat equals A sharp, standing for B natural):

Ex. 165

Here the tonal progressions are sometimes only implicit in the silences, much as syntax is elided in some modern poetry (for instance early Auden, or cummings).

Not surprisingly, Beethoven follows this wittiest and most hermetic of the variations with one which is very serious, even solemn. Tempo changes to a *grave* 4/4; texture is as thick as that of variation 13 was skeletonic. The double-dotted rhythm of the heroic overture is used consistently, and the sombrely arching turn of the theme is imitated in quasi-canon. The original harmonies are resonantly spaced in the left hand's chords. At this slow tempo we don't hear the upbeat as such, but rather respond to the tonic–dominant progression as two groups of seven crotchets each. The two-bar sequences, still in double-dotted rhythm, are painfully enriched with double appoggiaturas both up and down:

Ex. 166

Again E minor is substituted for the dominant modulation. The music's ceremonial grandeur coexists with an inner tension that stretches both muscles and nerves, recalling the maestoso introduction to opus 111. Though the first half ends in E minor instead of G major, the second half begins with an expansion of the original dominant seventh, the turn unfolding in gradually thickening registration. The same happens with the sequences, which climax in a diminished seventh of D minor, widely separated from reverberating octave Fs low in the bass. This variation is a turning-point in that, although grand, it is not public music. Its germ was in Diabelli's giddy waltz, yet in becoming heroic it has no tang of rhetoric or Prize Song. For the first time in this work Beethoven evokes the Invisible Church.

It has vanished again in variation 15, a presto scherzando in 2/4: far from sublime, yet still mysterious. The first 4 + 4 bars are consistent in their rhythmic formula, phrased as usual across the beat, and modify Diabelli's tonic–dominant formula only with a few chromatic passing notes. The two-bar sequences and relative minor modulation turn, however, into a strange chromatic undulation, mirrored in the bass by inversion. It is as though the chromatic cam of variation 12 has pervaded all the parts, so that dancing grace becomes a dissolution. The same happens in the second half, except that by the time the chromaticized scales have returned to the tonic major the hands are separated at the extremes of the keyboard. We never quite return to earth; the playfulness of the music again contains a suggestion of Beethoven's *ludus puerorum*.

Variation 16 is related to variation 6 in that it is launched by a trill, and dominated by a fast moto perpetuo of semiquavers, this time in broken octaves with chromatic appoggiaturas. The tempo is 4/4, and the military dotted rhythm makes a bid for stability, but cannot win against the dissonantly clattering octaves. After the double bar the figuration is inverted, as in variation 6. There is an enharmonic pun when the appoggiatura G sharp in the broken octaves momentarily turns into A flat, in a sudden pianissimo, at the return to C major. Variation 17 extends the previous one. There is no change of tempo, and the theme in the bass becomes military, with Diabelli's repeated notes comically insistent. The variation's relationship to Diabelli's original is—except for the fact that it is a march instead of a a waltz—obvious, even crude: as though Beethoven wishes to remind us, after so many glimpses over so many horizons, that all that has happened is contained within that original 'grain of sand'. Moreover, although the thematic aspect of this variation is simple, its total effect is not, for the right hand decorates the bass theme with a continuous clatter of high semiquavers. Basically, these are broken chords embellishing Diabelli's sequence; yet the harmony notes are all intensified with chromatic appoggiaturas, so that the texture sounds almost polytonal. Again there is an affinity with early Bartók, who substitutes a note a semitone distant from the note to which it 'ought' to resolve. There is a particularly odd passage in the second half, when Beethoven returns to C major by way of what seems to be a dominant of B minor:

Ex. 167

Enharmonically, we *hear* this as a fusion of a complex of chords: A sharp equals B flat which stands for B natural; F sharp represents itself but also G natural, and G flat as appoggiatura to F natural as the dominant seventh of C. Though Diabelli's little waltz has become an assertive march, there is a whiff of threat in its buoyancy.

Variation 18 returns to song, but with a curious hesitancy. The time signature is again 3/4, but all the phrases flow across the bar, the broken melody moving by step in contrary motion between treble and bass. Tempo is moderate, the sonority *dolce*, which is none the less mysterious when the sequences of the second eight bars sing in tenuous octaves, the now unbroken line embracing the chromatic appoggiaturas:

Ex. 168

After the double bar the undulation is in parallel tenths, but this warmth is counteracted by the augmentation of the rhythm at the ends of the phrases. In the subdominant section the appoggiaturas are again octaval and the rhythm equivocates between 3/4 and 6/8. The texture manages to be both spare and complex; the final four bars are silvery in high flowing quavers, now rhythmically 'straight'. There is not so much a cadence as a cessation on octave Cs.

Variation 19 relates to variation 7, as variation 16 had harked back to variation 6. The Fool returns, capering with his bladderstick; although Diabelli's harmony is undisguised in the first eight bars, the music is both melodically and rhythmically dizzy, since it is a canon beginning on the upbeat, answered on the first beat. So the bar lines have little formal significance; indeed the bouncing arpeggiated phrases in canon *cannon* off one another, like billiard balls; there is a pyrotechnic element both in the presto pianism and in the dangerously prestidigitous counterpoint. This clown is a virtuoso juggler who keeps the balls moving even when they have bounced to the middle of the keyboard, for the two-bar sequences rise in chromatic excitation. After the double bar the canon is as usual inverted, and the sequences that follow the subdominant modulation are again chromaticized, in sudden pianissimo. Energy in this work is never a simple positive, unless one considers Diabelli's own waltz to be such. Beethoven veers between energy and mystery, since it is the identity, or at least the interdependence, of flesh and spirit that the work celebrates. Nothing could reveal this more profoundly than the twentieth variation which, transporting us from the at least superficially ridiculous to the sublime, prophesies the ultimate vision. Moving *andante* in dotted minims in 6/4, it opens low in sonority with a fugato on Diabelli's falling fourth. The original tonic–dominant harmony pervades the first four bars, veiled in chromatic passing notes which, in the two-bar sequences, ghostlily undulate between G minor with flat seventh and the first inversion of an A minor dominant seventh:

Ex. 169

Similarly the dominant modulation is approached by a strange enharmonic shift, A sharp equalling B flat as it moves through a diminished third. In the second half this technique of chromatic and enharmonic substitution is weirdly extended. The dominant seventh is approached in the bass by a tritonal aspiration and, in the subdominant modulation, by an augmented third. There are multiple enharmonic puns (C sharp becoming D flat, F flat turning to E natural) and tonality-neutralizing whole-tone progressions, until the final resolution is approached by acute dissonant suspensions over a low tonic pedal. This variation is one of the most mysterious passages not only in Beethoven, but in all music, comparable only with the 'descent into the labyrinth' in the Praeludium to the Benedictus of the Missa Solemnis. Like that Praeludium, it is a music of introversion, solemnly hieratic; through the painfully slow harmonic and rhythmic ambiguities, we are as much baffled as awed by the *mysterium tremendum*. The holistic song is heard 'in the mind's ear', but is not revealed. Interestingly, this variation has been compared to the accompaniment to a religious song of Hugo Wolf. Certainly the music is more mysterious than anything in nineteenth-century Romanticism *before* Wolf, mostly because its tonal implications are so elliptical. Beethoven, unlike Wagner, asks us to fill in the blanks, and makes music in that sense as 'modern' as any that has been created subsequently.

The strangest miracle is that this visionary music should have evolved from the seed of Diabelli's footling waltz. Beethoven himself seems a little appalled, so the next three variations are in different ways deflatory. Variation 21 opens in common time, allegro con brio, with the familiar trill and turn on the upbeat followed by octave leaps, with a chugging of thirds in the left hand. Four of Beethoven's bars here are equivalent to Diabelli's first eight, and are hardly less perfunctory. But Beethoven changes the time-signature back to 3/4, meno allegro, and the sequences are hesitantly song-like, phrased across the bar lines in contrary motion. The second half follows the same pattern, but inverts the leaping octaves. Variation 22 carries deflation to the point of derision. Having noticed that Diabelli's tag of falling fourth and falling fifth is identical with the beginning of Leporello's 'Notte e giorno faticar' in Don Giovanni, Beethoven quotes Mozart, and in octaves, with the harmony no more than implied! He misses out the subdominant and dominant sequences, but cadences to the eighth bar in a stretto on Mozart's upward triplets, in A, D and G—a doubly enhanced dominant. After the double bar the fourths start off pianissimo, but in A flat instead of G: again a Bartókian displacement of the basic key by unresolved appoggiaturas. A flat is succeeded immediately by E, substituted for G major, and there is an uproarious crescendo through the rising triplets, fluctuating between the flat and sharp cadential seventh. (Beethoven had anticipated this in the approach to the recapitulation in the first movement of the Waldstein Sonata.) The hesitancy adds two bars to the second half, which concludes, however, with Leporello's and Diabelli's fourths inverted. There is little left of song in this variation, for even Leporello's street-song doesn't get beyond its introductory motive. There is no harmony either, except what is *implied* in the octave passages. But there are extravagant tonal adventures, such as the flat submediant relationship of C to A flat to E (equals F flat). This reminds us that although Leporello is a common man, he is a different kettle of fish from Diabelli. He's not a man for ghostly visitations, but he's aware that they sometimes happen to superior people. Beethoven catches in microcosm, through his sparse texture and elliptical modulations, the essence of Leporello's nervosity. In so far as he's a Common Man, his timidity becomes ours in response to the awe-ful and baffling solemnity of variation 20.

Variation 23 also attempts release, this time in an extrovert mirth that might become hysterical were it not controlled by a strict return to Diabelli's harmonic formula. The structural chords—tonic, dominant seventh, dominant seventh of subdominant—are vigorously marked on the first beat of alternate bars of 4/4, filled in with scurrying semiquaver scales in contrary motion. During the modulating sequences the semiquavers are broken in toccata style between the hands. The second half repeats the pattern, approaching the subdominant with a touch of D minor. Yet if these last three variations are a shoulder-shrugging evasion of the holiness promised in variation 20, they are not destructive, but are rather a momentary relaxation before Beethoven encompasses his vision. Variation 24 suggests a 'higher' and 'deeper' plane of consciousness, harking back to variations 3 and 4 in being both song-like and contrapuntal. Beethoven calls it a 'little fugue', marking it *una corda* and *sempre legato*. It absorbs Diabelli's falling fourth and fifth into an equable song, fugally imitated in four parts, with tonal rather than real answers, which suggests that the texture is at once linear and harmonic. The concourse of smoothly flowing quasi-vocal lines creates a harmony at once euphonious and, in its lucidly spaced suspensions, pathetic; significantly there is more harmonic movement within the linear texture than there is in Diabelli's theme. For the first time Beethoven has abandoned Diabelli's sequence of tonic and dominant seventh, replacing it by four fugal entries *on* the tonic but ending *in* the dominant, with tender double suspensions:

Ex. 170

The first entry falls in tranquil crotchets through the C major arpeggio C, G, E; curls back to the fourth; resolves through D to E. We can hear it either as tonic followed by dominant seventh, or simply as an embellished version of the tonic; the tonal answer falls through a godly fifth, then furls back from the sharp seventh to the tonic, so the harmonically resolutory feeling is stronger than in the first statement. Each entry is slightly modified. The modulation to the relative is approached by way of D minor, with greater tension in passing notes; yet harmonic pain brings lyrical release, until the last entry, effecting the dominant modulation, starts with a falling fifth, and leaps with calm expansiveness to the octave (bars 14–15). Beethoven is concerned more with the contours of his theme than with its precise pitches; its shape is remade by what harmonically and tonally happens to it. In this he differs from Bach as a fugal composer. None the less this fughetta is profoundly Bachian in its equilibrium between lyrical serenity and harmonic pathos, fused within rhythms that are regular, yet at the same time, by way of tied notes, suspensions and syncopations, individually flexible.

After the double bar the theme is inverted so that, instead of drooping, it rises in tender wonder. Moreover, during the first eight bars, movement is upwards tonally as well as melodically, since fugal entries move in sequence through D, A and E minors, each underlined with a diminished seventh. The music's calm is not, however, radically disturbed; the remaining eight bars move, with the theme again *rectus*, back through the same tonal sequence in reverse. The return to C is by way of an exquisitely painful double suspension, and the final cadence is an apotheosis: a triple suspension that falls chromatically, through a plagally flattened 6–4, to a sighfully suspended fourth. Throughout, it is the clarity of the part-writing that anneals suffering: the harmonies' dissonance is absorbed in a concourse of singing voices, in the middle register of the keyboard. The Bachian flavour of the music to which I referred is more than a generalization: there is a specific parallel with, say, the texture of Bach's last chorale prelude (see *The Dance of God*, pp. 299–305). More importantly, there are precedents in Beethoven's own music, most pointedly in the D major episode in the Hammerklavier's fugue. The psychological effect of the twenty-fourth Diabelli variation in the context of the whole work is not strictly comparable with the effect of the D major fugue in the Hammerklavier's sonata-strife. None the less the Fughetta *is* a climax: a state of Being which is part of a process of Becoming. Like the D major episode in the Hammerklavier fugue, which is also to be played *una corda*, it offers a glimpse of paradise, but cannot enter the sacred garden. So it is succeeded by four variations that are scherzo-like but not disruptive. Variation 25 opens with the simplest recapitulation of Diabelli's harmonic scheme, in a 3/8 too fast to be recognized as waltz-like. There is no lyricism, and the left hand consistently uses the revolving cam motive that figured in variations 3 and 12. There the cam had been negative, in that it stifled melodic growth; here it is playful, almost kittenish. The first half begins with Diabelli's chord sequence, but ends with a modulation to the relative instead of dominant; in the second half the subdominant modulation extends scattily into the flat supertonic, to make a Neapolitan return to C.

Variation 26, like variations 7 and 19, keeps the arpeggiated figurations simple harmonically and texturally, yet phrases them across the bar lines. The two-bar sequences also run counter to the bars, but in scale form in contrary motion. The second half repeats the patterns in textures that grow diaphanous. Variation 27 also uses broken arpeggios in its first eight-bar clause, and contrary motion scales in bars 9–16. But the broken chords are now decorated with semitone appoggiaturas, creating a tinglingly metallic quality. The effect, reinforced by abrupt changes of dynamics and of register, is wild, compared with the earlier variations (7, 16 and 17) that have used similar techniques. Variation 28 shifts to 2/4 time, allegro, phrased across the beats. There is no lyrical element; the appoggiatura motive, chromaticized and with fierce cross-accents, ceases to be the decorative device it was in the previous variation, and becomes a mainspring of energy. After the double bar the texture consists starkly of appoggiaturas in octaves, climaxing in a triple appoggiatura in bar 24, to create the subdominant modulation. Both the chord and the spacing are identical with the mysterious sonority in bar 5 of variation 14: the work's first (however introverted) intimation of the heroic mode. This may not be fortuitous, for what follows is a sequence of three variations, all slow and in the tonic minor, and all recalling classical Baroque tradition. The tragic implications of variations 14 and 24 have become overt.

Variation 29 is in a slow 3/4 wherein the first six bars are equivalent to Diabelli's eight. The harmonic pattern is modified in that a bar of tonic is followed by a bar of dominant, both repeated. There is no subdominant–dominant sequence or relative modulation, but the dominant modulation at the end of the first half is at first to the minor, which changes to major on a double suspension. Melodically the variation is a ceremonial lament exploiting Baroque dotted rhythm, with demisemiquaver portamentos on to the beats. After the halfway house the theme is transferred to the bass for the subdominant modulation, then lifted to the treble at a modulation to the supertonic (D flat), substituted for the dominant. The return is by way of a chromatically approached German sixth. The manner is grandly pathetic; both the melodic gestures and the harmonic conventions (especially the Neapolitan supertonic) suggests a sublimation of Baroque opera. We think of Gluck rather than of Handel, for Beethoven is concerned not with public absolutes, but with moral values he himself has won.

This becomes more profoundly evident in the next variation, which is a four-part fugato also beginning with a dotted rhythm. Tonally the first bar is ambiguous; it could be E flat major, but turns out to be C minor. The lines flow gravely by step, in a solemnly processional four-pulse which we come to feel as eight quavers, since the music becomes harmonically eventful. The texture is vocal, again *una corda* and *sempre legato*, so we are not surprised that the fugal polyphony proves to be more meditatively withdrawn than conventional Baroque counterpoint. Yet although Diabelli's street-tune seems to have been engulfed in the Invisible Church, the variation is structurally regular, except for the (by now familiar) substitution of the flat supertonic for the dominant. The two-bar sequences are chromaticized, darkly wavering; and the first half fades from the supertonic to its dominant A flat through a triple appoggiatura. This relates rather to the quasi-E flat major opening than to C minor. The second half begins with a free inversion of the first motive, embracing rising fifth and sixth into the step movement. Tonality moves from E flat (or rather the dominant of A flat) major to its subdominant D flat major. Sequences again wander across the bars, dispersing in a German sixth. In the last four bars an inverted stretched-out version of the motive floats upwards through tritones and minor thirds, see-saw-like:

Ex. 171

That only these four bars are repeated makes them seem the stranger: tranced, time-annihilating, 'out of this world'. The formality of Baroque counterpoint has been translated into a spiritual no-man's-land, 'on the edge of Being'.

Vision seems imminent in variation 31, a *largo* aria in which one bar of Beethoven's 9/8 is equivalent to four bars of Diabelli's 3/4. The immense melody links vocally arching contours (a written-out turn, a scale descending in slow siciliano rhythm, a dissonant upward appoggiatura) to level repeated quaver Gs—a sublime evolution from Diabelli's idiot repeated notes:

Ex. 172

Compared with Diabelli's time and body-obsessed little waltz, the time-scale of Beethoven's aria seems vast; its manner is grandly Baroque—somewhere between or beyond a Bach Passion aria and the tragic G minor lament of Mozart's Pamina. The answering clause on the dominant seventh is embellished with quasi-vocal roulades; the bass pulses like a slow pendulum. Instead of the two-bar sequences, Beethoven repeats his opening clause with more elaborate ornamentation, modulating to the relative major. This replaces Diabelli's passing modulation to the relative minor, and leads into the dominant modulation at the end of the first half. Beethoven's dominant modulation is to G *minor*; throughout the long cadence fioriture grow increasingly rapid, spattering from demisemiquavers to sextuplets to hemidemisemiquavers, with a plethora of chromatic passing notes. We can relate these coruscations to Bach at his most Baroque, and prophetically to Bellini and Chopin. Yet the effect is far from sensual; the figuration is frailly air-borne, and the faster it becomes, the more its convolutions destroy the bar lines, effacing the swing of the pendulum, which is also the slow ticking of Time's clock. It is as though the tragic aria-lament of variation 29 had sprouted wings.

The first half is repeated, and the coruscations of the final bar are changed, to modulate back from G minor to E flat major—its flat submediant, and C minor's relative. After the double bar Beethoven for the first time departs radically from Diabelli's formula. He returns to his aria, in E flat, immediately modulating to its subdominant A flat, and then flatwards again to D flat major. Though the sonority, in the middle of the keyboard, is at first hymnic, by the time we have reached D flat the music is again air-borne. The fluttering chromatic ornamentation is still more Chopinesque and, as tonality mounts sequentially through an (implicit) A flat to E flat major, F and C minor, fioriture dissolve in trills. Time's pendulum is not re-established; the trills evaporate in the stratosphere. The vast final 'bar recapitulates the pattern of the G minor conclusion to the first half, in the tonic minor. Beethoven repeats this second half too, and the repeats are important because they affect the time-scale. This aria lasts a very long time in comparison with Diabelli's street-tune; indeed in context the duration seems endless, and therefore a-temporal. At the end of his repeat Beethoven surprisingly duplicates his feint at the end of the first half: the fioriture tail off in hemidemisemiquavers that create a dominant seventh of E flat major. This leads, the divine aria having dissipated into thin air, into the only variation centred on a key other than the tonic major or minor:

Ex. 173

Variation 32 is a full-scale double fugue, beginning in E flat major. The main theme consists of Diabelli's falling fourth, hammered repeated notes, and upward and downward scale, transmuted into a Handelian, or perhaps Haydnesque, fugue subject, briskly affirmative though hardly heroic. The second theme is a cliché of Baroque counterpoint, not far off an inversion of the B.A.C.H. motive; descending thirds rise a semitone, chromaticized to define tonality. This double fugue is a paradox. After the three minor, tragic variations have ended in a Beethovenian synonym for eternity, the double fugue reasserts the Morality of Power, the human will that Beethoven has seemingly relinquished. It is fast, metrically rigid in allegro alla breve, and in that sense time-obsessed; moreover, compared with any of the variations, not merely the climactic *largo*, it is in continuous tonal momentum. It thus has more of the qualities of a sonata than any other section of the work; yet it is in fact a fugue, and a double one, imposing unity on contradiction. Its effect in context is thus complex. Its sheer exuberance and assertiveness make it a liberating climax, beginning in the key which, in middle-period works such as the Eroica Symphony and Emperor Concerto, Beethoven associated with heroic power. Yet in so far as it incorporates elements of sonata it is retrospective, harking back to the struggle Beethoven had undergone in order to arrive at the threshold of paradise. Given the difference in scope and concept, it does for the Diabelli Variations what the retrospectively modulatory episode does for the Arietta of opus 111.

The first twenty-eight bars drive irresistibly onwards, modulating sequentially every other bar, but held together by the unremittent metre and by the harmonic 'glue' of the chromatic second motive. In bar 28 the main theme is expanded from falling fourth to fifth, as is Diabelli's tag, first in E flat, then fiercely in the bass, in C minor. The emphasis on C minor reminds us of the work's basic tonality, but doesn't quell tonal enterprise. Sequential modulations now gravitate around C, G and F minors; the theme is inverted, furiously pounding in fortissimo bass octaves. The counter-theme generates more chromatic passing notes and sequential sevenths until the effect would be febrile, were not the rhythm stable. Climax comes as the inverted and extended theme thumps from the bass, incessantly modulating until it cadences on a widely spaced diminished seventh of E flat. Suddenly pianissimo, the main theme is now modified because its repeated notes are tied, bouncing across the bar lines; the counter-subject turns into a chattering of quavers. The modulations, mostly to a conventional dominant or subdominant, are less hectic, though the low-pitched registration tends to growl. After a long crescendo the original version of both fugal themes returns with the running quavers as countersubject; in the context of the work as a whole, the double fugue is a large-scale variation which incorporates variations on the variations. Repeated notes hammer fortissimo, until there is a broken cadence on a diminished seventh over a tonic pedal. That Beethoven calls on this diminished seventh half-close twice recalls the similarly repeated 'feint' in the previous variation, wherein both halves end on a dominant (not diminished) seventh of E flat. Chronometrically these two variations are by far the longest in the work; each ends in limbo. From the mystical heights of variation 30 we are abruptly swept to the

fugue's mundane power and glory, from which world we are in turn
transported by the alchemy of an enharmonic pun.

For Beethoven spreads his diminished seventh arpeggio into a
cadenza, bar-less and metreless after so much remorseless motor
rhythm:

Ex. 174

He changes the time signature from *alla breve to* **c**, *poco adagio*; the
diminished seventh resolves normally on to its E flat tonic, moving
from strong to weak beat. Then he adds a C flat appoggiatura to the E
flat triad, resolving on E flat first inversion. The C flat is metamorphosed into B natural, the E flat into D sharp, which resolves upwards
on to a first inversion of E minor! It is as though, after the fugue's
will-dominated turmoil, Beethoven is waiting, expectant, listening
for the Hidden Song he has had intimations of throughout the work,
notably in variations 20, 24, 30 and 31. This time the miracle occurs:
what we hear, in the thirty-third and last variation, is Diabelli's tune
purged of dross, as it might sound in paradise.

Diabelli's theme is a low waltz; Beethoven's ultimate metamorphosis of it is a minuet, a dance also in triple time but originally, as we
have noted, aristocratic. We also commented on the fact that in its
heyday the minuet was at once a dance and an ideal of civilization,
wherein the circularity of triple rhythm was, in the dance steps,
counterpointed against the linearity of duple rhythm. Throughout the
sequence of variations Beethoven has repeatedly explored the possibilities of duple phrasing within a triple beat; in the final minuet he
attains the equilibrium in purely musical terms. It is significant that the
Arietta of opus 111 explores precisely the same ambiguous identity

between triple and duple metre, concluding 'circularly' with an ellipsis of three into two (see page 271). Both in the Arietta's epilogue and in the final Minuet of the Diabelli Variations an eighteenth-century ideal thus becomes a universal: an Orphic equation between the Dionysiac and Apollonian, pertinent not merely to a phase of civilization at a specific time, but to the human psyche at any time. Beethoven's minuet is not aristocratically heroic, but celestial: a godly dance which is also a Song no longer Hidden. It is at once complex and simple; melodically almost folk-like, as is the Arietta of opus 111, yet elaborate in ornamentation. It reasserts Diabelli's harmonic and tonal scheme in a manner that is readily recognizable, yet with no suspicion of the waltz's tawdry tarnish. The dotted rhythm descent through the fourth is indeed *grazioso e dolce*, and the repeated notes are exquisitely garlanded with acciaccaturaed semiquavers in parallel tenths. The two-bar subdominant and dominant sequences, wherein the linear duple within the circular triple rhythm is manifest, are likewise embroidered. The modulation to the relative wafts in broken octaves; the resolution to the dominant flows into parallel 6–3 chords. Sonority shines; after the initial upbeat Cs there are almost no notes in the bass clef. It is strange that the decoration does not compromise the music's simplicity: it is as though the folk-song-minuet glows with an inner light, so that even the acciaccatura figure—which superficially recalls eighteenth-century *politesse*—reflects spiritual grace rather than, or as well as, good manners. These are the manners that 'maketh man', so we may suspect that the effect has something to do with that equilibrium between triple and duple rhythm, which is still more pervasive after the double-bar. The theme is now discreetly inverted, with an appoggiatura tenderly feeling up through a tritone, in a manner similar to the epilogic phrase in opus 111's Arietta. The subdominant modulation embraces delicately imitative part-writing, and the dominant modulation, on the way back to the tonic, is heightened by a Neapolitan shift to the flat supertonic. These abstruse modulations have a very different effect from the restless modulations in the fugue. They reveal secrets within, but do not obliterate, the theme's basic simplicities, whereas the fugue's modulations were abortively purposeful. On the return to the tonic, the broken octaves quiver into demisemiquavers, and the cadential bar in triplets decorates them with chromatic appoggiaturas. By this time we recognize that the minuet's techniques of ornamentation embrace most of the figurations—broken arpeggios with or without appoggiaturas, contrary motion scales, parallel 6–3

chords—that have been explored during the work. This is another
sense in which the last variation is consummatory.

Each 'half' consists of twelve bars, as compared with Diabelli's
sixteen. After the repeat of the second half Beethoven appends a
ten-bar episode. At first he creates a dialogue from the semiquaver
figure of bar 2, over a low tonic pedal, beginning in the subdominant,
rising to the tonic. Semiquaver scales in contrary motion float to an
enhanced dominant reassertion of the tonic, with Diabelli's fourths
and fifths inverted in the silvery heights of the keyboard, accompanied
by syncopated suspensions derived from the theme's descending scale.
This leads to a pianissimo shortened and simplified repeat of the
minuet, now in unbroken quavers, haloed with floating demisemiquavers. The passage is comparable with the da capo of the arietta in
opus 111, the demisemiquavers fulfilling the same function as the
eternal-seeming trills of the Arietta; even Diabelli's repeated notes,
gently breathing, are absorbed into song;

Ex. 175

The glittering figuration descends in waves to the keyboard's depths,
tingling with chromatic embellishments.

This da capo returns to Diabelli's eight-bar period, now disposed as
two bars of tonic, two of dominant, and four bars each reiterating the
subdominant–dominant–tonic sequence. The modulation to the relative is omitted, probably because Beethoven wishes the repeat to have
the consummatory effect of a coda. Indeed, the recapitulation is no
longer a minuet; the courtly gestures of the original figure—dotted
rhythm quavers separated by rests, semiquaver turn—have vanished
in unbroken figuration that sounds like supernal bells, and evokes the

light that 'never was' on land or sea. What is still to come is another eight-bar period that is specifically a coda. It begins with a canonic imitation of the original falling fourth, filled in with a third, so that melodically it assumes an 'innocent' pentatonicism. There is an entry on each beat of the 3/4 pulse, moving on the last crotchet from tonic to dominant seventh. At the end of the work the music is pared to this basic succession; both the figuration and the canonic treatment are strikingly similar to the end of opus 111. And Beethoven repeats this fundamental verity no fewer than six times. The first repeat is in semiquavers, the second in semiquaver triplets, the third in high demisemiquavers, with a crescendo to a modest forte. Two more repeats swirl the demisemiquavers into the lower reaches of the keyboard, while the right hand lifts in unobtrusive syncopation through broken arpeggios. In the penultimate bar the left hand's demisemiquavers float up a slightly chromaticized C major scale; the right hand descends to meet it, then fades in reiterated triplets and semiquavers on Diabelli's original tooting Gs. The left hand's chromatic wriggles, as they approach the upward scale, may distantly recall the revolving cams of previous variations; if so, what had been disruptive has become a spontaneous brook-like babbling.

The final bar, however, is odd, for after the scales and repeated Gs have vaporized in pianissimo, Beethoven appends on the second beat a single C major triad, *forte*, widely spaced, as at the minuet's beginning. To call the effect comic would be to overstate; none the less it makes the Minuet more equivocal, as an end, than is the Arietta of opus 111; this points to a more general distinction between the last three sonatas and the Diabelli Variations. The sonatas, because they *are* sonatas of however unique a kind, have a goal to which they win through: their ends may be implicit in their beginnings, but when we have arrived there we 'know the place for the first time'. The Diabelli Variations, on the other hand, are a circular rather than linear work. True, they metamorphose Diabelli's worldly waltz into an other-worldly minuet, but not by an evolving process of self-discovery. Like Bach's Goldberg Variations, and despite the difference between the two composers' approach, they rather see 'a world in a grain of sand', making us aware that experience is a totality in which the trivial and the sublime coexist. The macrocosm is within every microcosm: Diabelli's waltz is Beethoven's minuet to those who have ears to hear. In his Sermon XC Meister Eckhart remarks that three things prevent man from knowing God: 'the first is time, the second corporeality, and the third is multiplicity or number. . . . These things must go out for God to come in, except thou have them in a higher, better way; if multiplicity has become one in thee, then the more of multiplicity the more there is of unity, for the one is changed into the other.' This is as relevant to the Diabelli Variations as it is to Bach's Goldberg Variations wherein, as we noted in *The Dance of God*, the translation of line into circle and of multiplicity into canonic unity is more explicit.

We saw that the multiplicity-in-oneness of the Goldberg Variations of its nature implied irony, the recognition of other—even of apparently contradictory—modes of experience. The same is true of the Diabelli Variations, in which irony is more pervasive than it is in the last three sonatas, though they are certainly not ignorant of it. One might go so far as to suggest that irony conditions the Diabelli Variations' total structure. While it would be misguided systematically to chart the sequence of variations, it is helpful retrospectively to consider their interplay. Thus the first twelve variations divide, we have noted, into three groups of four, each of which tends to be more song-like than the previous number. In each case the transition to the first of a quaternity has a disruptive, sometimes deflatory, effect. The next set of variations abandons this pattern, and begins by opposing the craziest joke thus far (variation 13) to the first intimation of a new kind of grandeur: Baroque heroism reborn in the Invisible Church (variation 14). Song is then submerged in this group of variations, though the scherzo type grows zanier and therefore potentially ecstatic. Such lunacy seems to be a condition of divine illumination, for it carries us, in the twentieth variation, within the portals of the Invisible Church, where we hear echoes of a Hidden Song that remains, however, unuttered. After three more scherzoid-schizoid variations, fulfilment seems at hand in the fughetta (variation 24), for song melody and diaphanous counterpoint promise a Bachian synthesis of the physical and the metaphysical. Yet the fughetta is not in itself an end; it rather enables Beethoven to objectify, in the psychological sense, the contrarieties of experience. A set of (profoundly comic) scherzo-toccata variations recalls in sublimated form earlier variations (7, 16, 17, 19), and is succeeded by three overtly tragic variations in the minor, culminating in a *largo* aria which one may call, with a fair degree of technical and psychological accuracy, transcendental. Yet even this is not a point of no return, for it leads into the double fugue which, although a fugue, carries us back to the hurly-burly of the world and the pressures of the Will. The ultimate irony occurs in the weird transition from the fugue to the minuet; again it is not so much an evolution from–to, as a coexistence of will and transcendence. That final mild bump on the C major triad on the second beat of the last bar discreetly reminds us of this ambiguity, which makes the Diabelli Variations so curiously difficult, and so twentieth-century, a work. Its prophetic qualities induce both startlement and awe.

I have spoken of the Diabelli Variations as a work which, like Bach's Goldberg Variations, sees 'a World in a grain of sand'. The subtle interrelationship of even the minutest parts to the whole makes it music which destroys the notion of temporal progression, and perhaps even that of linear thinking. I have suggested that in the last three sonatas and the Missa Solemnis compositional process would seem, for all the throes and birthpangs Beethoven went through, to have been in a sense instantaneous: as was—according to his famous letter—the act of composition to Mozart at the height of his powers. Here, no less than in the specifically doctrinal Missa Solemnis, we touch on the heart of Beethoven's experience as a 'religious' composer, and may recall the Platonic origin of such instantaneity. Before the universe was created, Plato tells us in the *Timaeus*, 'there were no months and years and days and nights, but in bringing the universe into being God brought these into being too. They are all parts of time, and WAS and SHALL BE are created forms of time too, though we thoughtlessly and mistakenly ascribe them to the Eternal Essence. For we say that it WAS, that it IS, that it SHALL BE, whereas in truth IS alone applies to it.' Medieval philosophers moulded by Greek thought wrote in comparable terms: thus Boethius in the *Consolation of Philosophy* defined eternity as '*Interminabilis vitae tota simul et perfecta possessio*', while St Augustine, in the *Confessions*, remarks of Eternal Wisdom that 'to have been and to *be about to be* are not in her, but only to *be*, seeing she is eternal'. In his treatise *De Trinitate* Augustine writes of mystical experience in terms that would serve precisely as an account of the compositional act as described by Mozart, and manifest in these late works of Beethoven: 'Mayhap when "we shall be like him" our thoughts will no more go from one thing to another, but in a single perception we shall see all we know at one and the same time.'

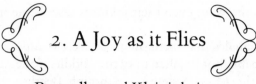

2. A Joy as it Flies

Bagatelles and Kleinigkeiten

In writing of the Diabelli Variations, Philip Barford has suggested that what inspired Beethoven was 'not Diabelli's trivial waltz, but the spiritual force of *Ursatz* embodied in it'. The word *Ursatz*, which means primary movement or initiating principle, was much used by Schenker in his analyses, for he believed that behind any sequence of musical events, however complex, there was a simple process, an aural organism, on which the composer's sensibility worked. This *Ursatz*, Barford says, 'must have a hidden, universal expressive potential and, because universal, objective. It can have as many particular applications as the composer can draw out of it; but what he draws out of it will depend on the depth of imaginative-conceptual penetration of the universal form.' There is an analogy with Jungian archetypes, and it is in this sense that it is legitimate to speak of Beethoven's late music as the artistic equivalent of 'religious meditation on a symbol no more complex than a circle, cross or triangle. Beethoven's belief, reported to Goethe by Bettina von Arnim, that music mediates between the spiritual and the sensuous, reveals a clear insight into the principle involved. In this case the spiritual is the universal principle, the sensuous the particular modification in tone. The art of musical variation, in particular, can thus be understood as a creative meditation on a universal form.'

Throughout his life Beethoven sought for the Hidden Song, the Voice of God that is *Ursatz* fulfilled. Its spiritual simplicity was to be discovered only through long-range forms that reconcile opposites, as do the sonata opus 111 and the Diabelli Variations. But it is interesting that at the end of his life Beethoven composed some small aphoristic piano pieces that do not need development because they are *Ursatz* incarnate. Though he called them Bagatelles, they are not, like Diabelli's waltz, trifling. On the contrary, they are profoundly mysterious; their mystery lies in the fact that *Ursatz* and fulfilment are here identified. There is no 'process' from, towards; it is as though the jottings in Beethoven's sketchbooks have become the consummated work. This is why the Bagatelles, though not as 'great' as the Arietta of opus 111 or the quasi-folksong that concludes opus 135, seem timeless in much the same way; even their jokiness reveals the 'playfulness of God'.

The six Bagatelles that form opus 126 were composed late in 1823, and were probably not finished until the middle of 1824. They were an aftermath of the Missa Solemnis; although Beethoven called them 'Kleinigkeiten' he worked hard on them, making many preliminary sketches, and declared them to be 'the best of this kind which I have written'. They were clearly planned as a set, with the mediant relationships typical of the music of Beethoven's third period. Nos. 1 and 2 are in G major and minor respectively; no. 3 is in E flat major; no. 4 in B (equals C flat) minor; no. 5 in G major again; and no. 6 in E flat major. No. 1 is a remarkable example of *Ursatz* fulfilled in song; though it is only a page long, the process whereby song is revealed is manifest latently and retrospectively. The opening eight-bar clause has a simple, folk-like melody (*cantabile e compiacevole*) flowing in triple time by step, expanding into a rising fourth and sixth, subsiding in gently dissonant appoggiaturas tied across the bars. The two last bars form a little codetta: beginning with a rest and upbeat quaver, they fill in the rising sixth and declining appoggiatura. The left hand, supporting the melody, sustains a dominant pedal during the first three bars, then moves scalewise and in warm parallel thirds canonically to echo the tune. Though F natural appears twice as a chromatic passing note, there is no real modulation in this eight-bar clause, which is repeated delicately ornamented with trills and flowing quavers:

Ex. 176

If it were really a folk or popular song, these sixteen bars would be complete in themselves. What happens after the double bar is strange, however; for although Beethoven starts with four bars of modulation to the dominant—conventionally enough but slightly abrasive in semitonic dissonance—he then changes the time signature from 3/4 to 2/4, without altering the pulse, and teeters on the dominant triad first inversion. The cadential phrase of rising fourth and falling scale vacillates between fourth, fifth and third, fragmented; quickens to triplets and then to semiquavers, and coalesces again in flowing figuration like that at the end of the original eight-bar clause, but twice as quick:

Ex. 177

A trill-garlanded 6–4 cadence returns to a dominant seventh of G, expanding into a cadenza (*grazioso, non troppo presto*) of rising and falling scales. This ends on a D minor diminished seventh, which subsides back to G major, with the original song resonant in bass octaves. The texture of the upper voices, supported by the song's bass, is thicker and darker than anything thus far in the piece, but soon clears to a luminous diatonicism, comparable with that of the opus 111 Arietta. Spacing between the hands is wide, and the tune does not reappear in completion. Its scales are instead translated into little canons by contrary motion, with sharp passing dissonances. This 'many in oneness' sounds simple but isn't, for the second half of the piece is a microcosm, an elliptical retrospect, of the 'process' whereby the heart-easing song was discovered. Beethoven directs that the second half should be repeated, which is feasible since it is an inverted development, 'emotion recollected in tranquillity'.

No. 2 in G minor at first offers no hint of a song, hidden or otherwise. It is a miniature scherzo, on a semiquaver motive of rising arpeggios—first G, B flat, G, D, then stretched to G, B flat, G, E flat, which anticipates the flat submediant relationship which is to be a structural point of the set. We may sense an affinity with the 'teetering' motive that threatens the simple song in no. 1, though the intervals are not identical. Certainly Beethoven starts here with rapid disruption, counterpoised by flowing quaver scales with chromatics, and modulates, in the second 'eight', to the relative major. The F major pedal in the bass then effects a curious hiatus, both in the aggressive semiquaver arpeggios and in the lilting quaver scales. An extra ten bars slow the movement to crotchets, the bass line augmenting and inverting the original upward-flowing quaver scale. After the double bar Beethoven marks the melody *cantabile*: it is turning into a song-like, possibly folky tune, with a gently pulsing accompaniment. Unlike the song in no. 1, however, this tune modulates, first back to G minor, then to C minor, at which point it brusquely breaks off and the fierce semiquaver figure returns, its upward leap expanded to a minor sixth. The figure is now repeated, separated by silences; oscillates between the rising sixth and fifth; appears to find its way back to G minor by way of a German sixth; but then wavers in enharmonic puns. What sounds like a wide-spaced F sharp minor triad turns into a diminished seventh of G minor, with C sharp as passing note; what sounds like a second inversion triad of D flat major proves to be a decorated cadence into C minor, the D flat being notated as C sharp, which moves to D natural. Four flowing bars apparently in A flat major are a Neapolitan return to G, which in the coda toys with the major before reaccepting its minor tonality. The savage arpeggiated figure does not rear its head in the penultimate bar of the first section. Yet the Neapolitan passage is a consequence of the initial savagery, since the contours of its sustained crotchets songfully echo the line stabbed out by the top notes of those semiquavers:

Ex. 178

In this sense there is progression in the piece, which none the less seems timeless, since everything happens 'in the twinkling of an eye'.

No. 3 drops to the flat submediant and is unadulterated song: indeed a Masonic-style folk-hymn to which the E flat tonality is appropriate. Again Beethoven marks it *cantabile ed espressivo*; the movement is a level 3/8, the texture darkly rich, at first over a tonic pedal. The melody is arch-shaped, moving in the first four bars through falling third and rising sixth, then declining down the scale. In the second four bars the intervals are stretched to fourth and seventh, and the arch comes to rest in a 6–4 cadence. So the tune has a gentle nobility and a healing grace, enhanced by the mellow texture when it is repeated an octave higher. For seven bars the music is still on a dominant pedal, the spacing now wide; but what seems to be a modulation to the dominant is contradicted by cadenzas on the dominant seventh and tonic of E flat, poetically haloed by pedal. Caressing chromatic passing notes droop into a long trill over a repetition of the tune in the left hand, disguised in broken semiquavers which pick out the theme in their top notes, asymmetrically. At the end of the trill the right hand takes over the tune and, mounting to the heights, dissolves in demisemiquaver filigree, glittering with chromatic passing notes, as in the final Minuet of the Diabelli Variations. The left hand's rocking semiquavers remain thematic until a four-bar coda balances the dominant pedal bridge passage that had started at bar 17. The tonic pedal, beginning in bar 48, is sustained beneath rising thirds and sixths. The swaying dotted rhythm is new, and strange; it suggests the running down of a clock. Time must have a stop; and does so the more because Beethoven's pedalling sustains the dominant *through* the tonic chord.

The fourth Bagatelle, which descends again to the flat submediant, notated as B minor, is longer than the others and structurally more conventional, in that it is a scherzo and trio. It would not, however, function effectively as a scherzo in a sonata; and the point lies in the fact that its trio is not an episode 'within' the scherzo. The Bagatelle begins fiercely in a three-voices texture, *presto alla breve*, the figuration is arpeggiated, the rhythm metrical, and the bass line freely inverts the treble. Surprisingly the first eight bars modulate not to dominant or relative, but again to the flat submediant, G major. After the double bar the arpeggio theme starts off in G major's relative, E minor, moving to *its* flat submediant, C major, then back to G. Contrasts of dynamics and syncopated accents are violent; sudden silences point the ambiguity of another C major modulation which threatens to behave as a Neapolitan to B minor. Momentarily it does so: but then turns into a tootling tune in E minor with arpeggiated accompaniment. Back in B minor the scherzo ends with the arpeggiated motive in stark octaves.

This scherzo is all dynamic action and kinetic energy, extravagant in modulation, vigorous in cross-accents; it has no suggestion of song. In contrast the trio is harmonically and tonally almost motionless, since the left hand reiterates a bagpipe drone on the bare fifth; and it is at least the ghost of a song, in that the right hand weaves broken but stepwise-moving strands of a tune in the tonic major. It ascends to blissful heights; disappears in a still passage of pianissimo tritones in semibreves; and is repeated, frailly wandering. As the tune floats into the upper air, the bagpipe drone is slightly darkened by a touch of subdominant; returned to middle register, the tune peters out, after hesitant silences. The scherzo sounds da capo, and in the original sketch was followed by a short coda referring to the trio. At a very late stage, almost in proof, Beethoven erased this coda and wrote out the trio again in full. So we end, if the word is valid, with its whimpering pastoral dream, discounting the scherzo's energy. It is as though Beethoven is deflating his earlier will-dominated self, seeing the Promethean ego as comic, though not necessarily ridiculous. In such moments one realizes that Beethoven's laughter is the surest safeguard of his sublimity.

Bagatelle no. 5, descending a major third again, arrives back at G major. The mood too is similar to that of no. 1, in that texture is limpid, flowing in equable 6/8 quavers. The movement suggests a pastoral dance as well as a song, the treble melody being supported and also answered by two lower voices moving in contrary motion through parallel thirds. The original rising figure—G, B, C, D—openly smiles, but cadences in a soft sigh, first in a minor, then a diminished, third, with momentary modulations to relative minor and subdominant. The second eight bars start as a decorated repeat, yet are more than that, for chromatic alterations, notably the unexpected D sharp in bar 10, imbue the tranquil melody with a question mark. The ties across the bar lines, as the melody rises higher, create tender appoggiaturas. The first section ends in E minor which, after a double bar, switches yet again to a flat submediant—C major. The melody wooingly undulates in parallel thirds; the bass is immobilized on a tonic pedal, but the broken arpeggios add a countermelody in tenor register, on offbeat quavers. In the ninth bar of this 'middle' we return to the G major tonic, the parts winging away from one another. After the 'middle' has been repeated there is a two-bar bridge to a repetition of the first eight bars, an octave higher, with two slight but poignant modifications to the tune: the chromatic D sharp and the high E in bars 36 and 37, and the decorated appoggiaturas in the two final bars.

This is the simplest and most self-contained song of the set, which may be why it precedes the sixth bagatelle, which is by far the most mysterious. It opens with a *presto alla breve* prelude which consists of a tonic pedal with rocking tonic triads, and dominant sevenths clattering loudly over it, while the right hand chitters in Rococo scales, ending with a staccato tonic triad four times sounded (see end of Ex. 179). Nothing could be further from any kind of song; the inane racket seems to have no connection with the tune enunciated, after a slightly stunned silence, in an *andante amabile* 3/8. The key is again E flat major, another descent to a mediant, but if we think this Masonic key promises another hymnic song, we are to be disappointed. For the initial solemnity of the quietly swaying tonic pedal is belied by the hesitancies on the last quaver of each bar, and by the seductive parallel thirds in dotted rhythm. There is a suggestion of Austrian beer-garden rather than of Masonic temple, though even in '*Kleinigkleiten*' such as this, Beethoven's bacchanalian mood may have a touch of divine frenzy. An abnormality is inherent in the fact that Beethoven conceives the piece in what he called *ritmo di tre battute*, with which he had recently been experimenting in the Missa Solemnis and Ninth Symphony. The first section consists of five symmetrical three-bar phrases, modulating from E flat major to its relative C minor and back, and then to the dominant B flat. In this key Beethoven embarks on three more three-bar phrases decorating the beer-garden-type tune he has reached at the end of the first section, and modulating back to C minor. Two, not three pivotal bars then modulate to C minor's flat submediant, A flat major, the triplets of the beer-garden tune having become a hazy drone in the bass. We probably hear the A flat tonality both as subdominant to the initial E flat, and as submediant to C. Either way, there is a tonal deepening and darkening as, in A flat major, the original song emerges again, even more hesitantly than before. Stepwise parallel thirds and sixths glow over the harmonically unmoving bass, which, however, touches on F minor when the tune sings in its arching fourth and fifth. Sequentially Beethoven moves back to E flat and to the perky triplets over the broken bass, completing seven symmetrical three-bar periods since the A flat episode, by the time he reaches the next double bar. Finally he gives us five three-bar periods, exactly balancing the first section, only with the material in reverse order; the impudent triplets ascend to the heights, fall by way of chromatic passing notes in parallel thirds and contrary motion, and land on their original hesitancies, with pause marks over the third quavers, over a dominant instead of tonic pedal.

The structure of the piece is thus mirror-like in three-bar phrases, with two extra pivot bars in the middle of the middle; its circularity is capped by a literal repetition of the *presto alla breve* at the end:

Ex. 179

It is this extraordinarily subtle non-progressive structure that gives the piece its disembodied feeling. Coming from the greatest of all composers normally concerned with process and progression, this little bagatelle may count as Beethoven's most prophetic utterance. When we hear the exact recapitulation of the inane prelude as postlude, it is as though Beethoven is *shuffling off* this mortal coil—the Rococo racket within which most of us live for most of the time. The nervous cackle does not deny the 'still centre' of a song that is part sacred, though more than half profane. Only Beethoven, at the end of his life, could have carried it off, convincing us that total veracity to experience may redeem man's *almost* irremediable triviality.

The other late set of Bagatelles, opus 119, was written at various times between 1821 and 1823. The pieces don't form a whole, as does opus 126, and some of the earlier ones refashion material dating back to the early years of the century. It seems probable, however, that the last five were written out together; sketches for them occur among those for the sonata opus 109 and for the Credo and Benedictus of the Missa Solemnis. These pieces are even tinier than the Bagatelles of opus 126, yet they too may become *Ursatz* incarnate. Especially remarkable is no. 7, in a four-part texture which begins like a string quartet, with trills and interior polyphonies, and ends with an ascent to heaven in gradually increasing speed values, over a continuous trill on low C. There is a parallel with the Diabelli Variations here, as there is with the next member of the set, which embraces chromatic polyphony and vocally biased false relations within a similar four-part texture. The last member of the set, no. 11 in B flat, unambiguously reveals the Hidden Song which is also a hymn. Beethoven marks it *innocentemente e cantabile*, and lives up to his prescription. The tune, balancing falling thirds with rising fourths, is serene, over a level crotchet pulse. After four unmodulating bars, it moves in the next four to the dominant and relative, and apparently to a diminished seventh of D minor: which turns, however, into a miniature cadenza on the dominant seventh of F, changing to that of B flat. A modified version of the song an octave higher sings *molto cantabile* over pizzicato-like chords. These four bars are repeated at the original pitch in an exquisitely cool, string-quartet-like polyphony:

Ex. 180

The final four bars are homophonic and hymnic: simply concordant, yet briefly and mysteriously recalling the false relations inherent in the F major–G minor modulation of bars 5 to 8. It is worth noting that transcendental moments may occur in the earlier members of the set: consider the transmutation of the perky triplet turns of no. 2 into the twinkle and tinkle of the concluding bars: a child's version, for musical-box, of the conclusions of the Diabelli Variations and of opus 111.

Schindler tells us that malicious gossip bruited it abroad that sick Beethoven's invention was exhausted, so that he had turned to the production of trifles and folk-song arrangements, like Haydn in old age: to which Beethoven retorted 'Wait a while; you'll soon learn differently', and wrote out the last three sonatas and the Missa Solemnis. Clearly it was not commercial motives that prompted him to write the Bagatelles: their smallness and unpretentiousness is their essence ('small is beautiful'), complementing the scope and complexity of the Ninth Symphony and the Missa Solemnis. They could have been composed at no other time in Beethoven's life: which goes too for the folk-song arrangements which he himself called *Brodarbeit*. Haydn, arranging Scottish folk songs, dresses them up in elegant eighteenth-century perukes, making them amenable to the drawing room. Beethoven, in his late sets, does not civilize them in that socially acceptable sense, but translates them into the visionary Eden implicit in his late music. The folk's song becomes identified with the Hidden Song that is the heart's core; as well it might, given that the 'folk' should possess a heart-wholeness which modern man has surrendered for the difficult benefits of being conscious of being conscious.

Purely on a technical level, in keeping the piano writing negotiable by amateurs, Beethoven creates a touching purgation of the pianism of his final years. Consider the first *air écossais* of opus 105, *Das Hirtenmädchen* (The Shepherdess). The sixteen-bar tune is dominated by a falling arpeggio, is symmetrical in rhythm, and unambiguously diatonic. Beethoven harmonizes it without modulation, in a simple texture pervaded by pedal notes. The lift through the third from the tonic in bar 2 is the only obviously folk-like feature, unless one counts the snappy dotted rhythm as such. Yet although the first variation looks on paper elegantly Rococo, it sounds like folk music sublimated in late Beethovenian terms. The melody is broken into syncopations and arabesques; the originally rudimentary harmony acquires chromatic passing notes, and in the second half a modulation to the subdominant.

Yet the Rococo-style ornaments speak intimately, in an interiorized version of the Scotch snap; even the miniature cadenza suggests the spontaneous improvisation of a folk fiddler, rather than operatic sophistication. Variation 2 returns to harmonic simplicities, consisting of broken chord triplets, punctuated by offbeat accents. The wit lies in the dislocation of those accents to the third semiquavers: a tipsy effect which leads into the Edenic sound of variation 3, in which the tune dissolves in arpeggiated semiquavers, floating to the top reaches of the keyboard. This musical-box sonority we noted in the Bagatelles also; here Beethoven counterpoises it against a variation in the tonic minor, beginning in severe fugato. But the Scotch lift in the tune banishes gravity and destroys the counterpoint, so that the variation fades out on dominant sevenths and ninths, separated by silences. A little chromatic cadenza leads to a coda stating the tune in the major over a tonic pedal, yet now embracing both the subdominant modulation and the diminished seventh approach to the cadence. Innocence and Experience are here allied in a manner as typical of late Beethoven as it is atypical of the eighteenth century.

The second *air écossais, Von edlem Geschlecht war Schinken*, is scarcely less subtle, though without the pathos of no. 1. In C minor, it reminds us of the scherzo-like pieces from the Diabelli Variations, and is conceived as a dialogue between soprano and tenor voice. The fun is inseparable from the simplicity: consider the rudimentary E flat major modulation and the return of the 'tenor' part from it. Variation 1 fills out the tune in quaver movement, comically exploiting the leaping octaves; variation 2 balances leaps in dotted rhythm against shooting scales, the texture lean. Variation 3, however, changes to the major, and unexpectedly hints at the luminous sonorities of opus 111's Arietta, with comparable internal pedal notes and gentle appoggiaturas. Recurrently the four-part texture thins into monody; key returns to the minor, and we end with a statement of the tune at the original speed. Now it is played by the left hand in tenor register, while the right hand trills continuously on the high G. The long trill is interesting, after the Arietta-like third variation, and its irony is touching and profound. The 'wholeness' of folk song, compared with that which Beethoven attained, after a life-time's experience, in his Arietta, is put in its place, firmly, but without condescension.

There is a similar quality in the variations on *The last rose of summer*. Again the statement of the lovely tune is remote from eighteenth-century convention; the snapped notes and grace notes of folk tradition are preserved, while the intermittent doublings in thirds and sixths emulate a folk fiddle. The single notes of the bass mostly alternate between tonic and dominant, and although there is an unfolk-like modulation from the tonic E flat to its relative C minor, this is immediately cancelled. The tune exists, and is not expatiated on. Nor is it in the variations. In no. 1 the melody flows into triplets, in two parts in parallel tenths or sixths, the lilt only momentarily disturbed by chromatic passing notes. In variation 2 the tune appears intensified in the left hand, again with doublings in thirds and sixths, while the right hand's filigree of semiquavers 'takes off'. In the third and last variation the tune has left the earth, being hidden in a flutter of triplets and demisemiquavers broken between the hands: a texture typical of the late sonatas, of the Diabelli Variations and the Bagatelles. Finally this figuration dissolves into a triad of the flat submediant C flat: in which key begins a small postlude, restating the original tune and veering from the C flat triad to a 6–4 cadence in the E flat major tonic:

Ex. 181

This, after the dancing sunlight of the third variation, sounds like a recollection of Eden: of a day when song, heart-whole, was also unhidden. It is not surprising that Beethoven found something in Scots and other folk songs that eighteenth-century rational man was not looking for. In child-like form it offered him the *Geist*, the *Ursatz*, the Voice of God that was the object of his lifelong search, though his own song, rediscovered, was immeasurably more mysterious and more sublime.

Occasionally this note of sublimity echoes through the folk-song variations themselves. The variations on another famous tune, *O du nur bist mein Herzebub* ('O thou art the lad of my heart, Willy'), begin almost as simply as *The last rose*, and proceed in variation 1 through delicately misplaced accents and chromatic alterations. In variation 2 a bagpipe drone accompanies a chromaticized countermelody in the tenor; in variation 3 triplet figurations are broken, with surprising harmonic consequences, between the hands. Variation 4, however, in the minor, is hymnic in its gait and mysterious in its enharmony, with a modulation to C flat that sounds like B and E majors. The reversal of the triple rhythm from long–short to short–long, combined with the *tierce de Picardie*, gives the two final bars a quality that is indeed extra-ordinary; something of this remains when the merrily floating triplets of the final variation dissolve, over a bagpipe drone, into a twilit dream. This is another instance of Beethoven's personal re-creation of folk 'innocence', to which most modern men cannot attain, and which many don't want, or think they don't need. For Beethoven, we have seen, it was the pearl without price. It is not fortuitous that one of his variation sets—this time on an Austrian, not Scottish, tune, *A Schüsserl und a Reindel*—should include a variation which, in its use of diatonic concords moving very slowly in false relations, reminds us of those most visionary moments in his music, the twentieth of the Diabelli Variations, and the Praeludium to the Benedictus of the Missa Solemnis:

Ex. 182

Such affinities between Beethoven's *Kleinigkeiten* and his most pro-found music are not fortuitous, but are the condition of his wholeness. We have repeatedly noted that Beethoven, the most overtly tragic of the European masters, also creates (as does Shakespeare, with whom I've frequently allied him) art that is often wildly comic and sometimes uproariously hilarious. We have compared aspects of Beethoven's humour—in for instance the last movement of opus 101—to the *ludus puerorum*; and we may recall that throughout history children's games, participated in with simultaneous gravity and joy, have served as an image of the paradise we have lost but would recover: a dance of the spirit at last allied in perfection with the flesh, uncontaminated by ulterior motives, existing in a present that is, or seems to be, also eternity. (That real children, even in play, may often be motivated by jealousy, greed, spite and other post-lapsarian qualities does not affect the ideality of the image.) According to Clement of Alexandria, the infant Dionysus played 'with tops of different kinds and dolls with moving limbs, apples too, the beautiful golden ones of the clear-voiced daughters of Hesperus'. More than a thousand years later the myth is still active in Goethe's Faust who, dying into life, is transubstantiated among a 'blessed choir of boys', where *hervortritt erste Jugendkraft*'. Boehme tells us, in the fourth of his Theosophical Questions, that before the angels and the world of creation existed God 'sported with himself'; and the Divine Wisdom is said to have created the entire universe in the spirit of a game: 'Iucundabar ante faciem eius in omni tempore, cum laetaretur urbe perfecto.' In Christian mysticism the Logos, according to Meister Eckhart, is at once a god of power and a naked boy, who tosses in his hands the ball of the world. God asked Mechtild of Magdeburg to lay her soul in his holy arms, that he might 'play with it'; the Venerable Bede speaks of 'the playing of grace' in reference to Christian liturgy:

> En ludus est credentium
> tuis frui complexibus
> quam tanta gignis gaudia
> pandis polique ianuas.

Even the *putti* that gambol over Baroque tombs and churches are a dancing image of paradise as well as the plump fruits of a life dedicated to sensuality.

Throughout the centuries, and in many religions, the playing child has thus been an image of man redeemed. As Jung has put it, 'the child is all that is abandoned and exposed, and at the same time divinely powerful: the insignificant, dubious beginning, and the triumphant end. The "eternal child" in man is an indescribable experience, and incongruity, a disadvantage, and a divine prerogative.' It must be this archetypal value that makes Beethoven's *ludi puerorum* pertinent even in the context of his greatest and most complex works. We have noted how in the Missa Solemnis itself the dark *Prae-ludium* initiates a dancing *play* of angels who, though not little children, are ourselves as we might be, Edenicly in paradise: for 'the divine dance', as Lucian puts it in his *De Saltatione*, 'brings the souls of men into the right rhythm and shows forth in visible fashion what the inner beauty of the soul has in common with the outer beauty of the body, because it makes manifest the point where the two flow into one another'. This is a valid description of the effect of the holy game and divine dance of

Beethoven's Benedictus; and there is a sense in which it is relevant too
to those bagatelles and *Kleinigkeiten* of his final years, wherein the *ludus*
exists in and for itself, in a magical moment which is Now. Only
Mozart among European composers, in some of the music of his final
years, such as the last piano concerto K.595 and the E flat major string
quintet K.614, enters the same magic circle and exerts the same spell;
and Beethoven's ultimate *ludi* are smaller in scope, apparently still
simpler in texture. Listening to his Variations on *The last rose of
summer*, to the tiny B flat Bagatelle from opus 119, or to the 'circular' E
flat Bagatelle that ends opus 126, we begin fully to understand the
famous words from St Matthew (18:3): 'Except ye . . . become as little
children, ye shall not enter into the kingdom of heaven'. The myth of
the child-king is world-wide and ageless; Ecclesiastes tells us: 'Better is
a poor and a wise child than an old and foolish king' (4:13); and the
Ancient of Days proclaims: *'Ite et ludete.'*

Coda

I know of no other Christianity and of no other Gospel than
the liberty of both body and mind to exercise the Divine
Arts of Imagination, Imagination, the real & eternal World
of which this Vegetable Universe is but a faint shadow, & in
which we shall live in our Eternal and Imaginative Bodies
when these Vegetable Mortal Bodies are no more.

WILLIAM BLAKE

The two books, *Bach and the Dance of God* and *Beethoven and the Voice of
God*, grew from an attempt to examine Bach's B minor Mass and
Beethoven's Missa Solemnis as distinct but complementary affirma-
tions. It seemed necessary to ballast Bach's quasi-Catholic Mass with a
detailed study of his most representatively Protestant work; and useful
to preface it with an investigation of the nature of Bach's musical
idiom as exemplified in cello suites and in preludes and fugues for
keyboard. A chapter on the 'abstract' works of Bach's final years
served as postlude. In the Beethoven book the central chapter on the
Missa Solemnis is supported by detailed analysis of the last piano
sonatas, which are closely related to the Mass and were composed
during the period of its gestation. Commentary on earlier sonatas
serves to define Beethoven's place in European history. It might be
argued that the late string quartets complement the abstract works of
Bach's final years, and that my last chapter should have concerned
them. The parallel is not exact, however, for the late quartets can
hardly be considered an appendix. They are a new exploration, insti-
gated by the religious preoccupations of the Mass and of the sonatas
contemporary with it. Justice could be done them, if at all, only in a
separate book.

Certain late piano works, again exactly contemporary with the
Mass, can however be construed as appendices, and it is to them I have
devoted my final chapter. The last four sonatas are an experience
collateral to the Mass: in their purely instrumental terms they follow
the same purgatorial path. The Diabelli Variations, the opus 126
Bagatelles and some of the late folk-song variations are an aftermath, in

that they stand, in their 'circularity', beyond that experience, so that the implicit comparison with the quasi-mathematical certitudes of late Bach is exact. The mirror-circle of the last Bagatelle of opus 126 is Beethoven's non-contrapuntal complement to Bach's canons that emulate the serpent who swallows his own tail; that Beethoven achieved this from such apparently common material is endemic to his genius. So my final chapter appropriately brings the wheel full *circle*, in that the Bach book, *The Dance of God*, started from a consideration of music as magic in primitive societies, explored the growth of 'consciousness' in European music, and found Bach's *crucial* significance in his equilibrium between unity and duality, interpreted in terms both of musical technique and of metaphysics. Of all European composers of consciousness and duality Beethoven plumbed deepest and soared highest. Having courted the relatively broad masses in his revolutionary symphonies, he arrived at a transcendent religious experience that was individualized rather than communal, and that became yet more intimately so in the medium of string quartet. We have noted that this dichotomy between the public and the private life is, however, more apparent than real, for if modern man seeks transcendence through the solitary psyche, what he discovers, on the rare occasions when transcendence occurs, is not personal but archetypal, and in that sense universal. Modern Man, of whom Beethoven is the supreme exemplar, seeks a rebirth; and that the last page of Beethoven's last quartet should be a sublimated folk song is deeply revealing. The Self returns to the Not-Self; the Folk become synonymous with the Child; the Child with a pre-dualistic phase of consciousness; and that with the Oneness which is God. It may therefore be that when I referred to the *Kleinigkeiten* as being magical I may not have been speaking metaphorically: the brief coda to *The last rose of summer* variations sounds magical because magic is precisely what it invokes, in the same sense as does some ritual ululation of the 'primitive' tribesman referred to at the beginning of *The Dance of God*. The magical coda is wistful, as the cry of the tribesman does not overtly need to be, because such recovered bliss must for modern man inevitably be precarious. But if unworldly, it is not unreal; and is the more to be valued because modern man has known more, suffered more, than child, peasant or 'savage'.

So Bach and Beethoven, though at opposite poles as composers of religious affirmation, are also interdependent, as is manifest in the public and private aspects of their belief. Bach respected

Establishment—unequivocally that of his Church, equivocally that of the state—and drew reverently though not slavishly on precedents religious, occult, social, philosophical and mathematical. He thereby became a *revealer* of truth in Spinoza's sense: 'he who has a true idea knows that he has a true idea and cannot doubt the truth of the thing perceived. Truth is its own standard. Even as the light displays both itself and darkness, so is truth a standard both of itself and of falsity.' This means that negative impulses, however fiercely undergone, may be resisted. Presumably Bach, as a good Lutheran, believed in hell-fire and eternal damnation; but although his music is permeated by consciousness of mortality, even at times by what we would call a death-wish, I can recall no passage in his work that enacts hell's torments. This could be because hell, in post-Renaissance (and Bachian) cosmology, is of its nature anti-musical: Macbeth's witches can only utter doggerel in what we may hazard is more a croak than a song. Mostly, however, it is because Bach's acceptance of doctrine and dogma is positive enough to conquer destructiveness.

Beethoven, on the other hand, was no respecter of Establishment, and often called on precedents only in order to refute them: '*My* morality is here and here', pointing to his head and heart; 'then *I* permit them', of 'forbidden' parallel fifths. We have seen that there are many passages in Beethoven's music, especially in the Hammerklavier Sonata and in the Missa Solemnis, which prove that he had experienced hell, even if he didn't, in Bach's sense, believe in it. He knew, with Jürgen Moltmann, that 'the field of destructive and constructive possibilities is laid out. . . . Peace with God means conflict in the world because the good of the promised future stabs into the flesh of the unfulfilled present. Everything that is is created out of nothing. . . . A creation out of nothingness is nevertheless simultaneously a creation within a sea of nothingness. A creation out of chaos is an order of life within chaos. Therefore every creation is an open creation, open for its own destruction as well as for its redemption and new creation.'

In the tenth of his *Theosophical Questions* of 1624 Boehme asks: 'What was it the devil desired, with a view to which he turned aside from God's love?' and replies: 'He desired to be an Artist. He saw the creation and understood the foundation of it. Whereupon he wished to be a God, and rule with the central fire-power in all things.' It is in this sense that Beethoven, like Lucifer, became a *discoverer* of truth; and just as Bach's revelation of God turns out to be also a discovery of the Self, so Beethoven's discovery of the Self turns out to be also a revelation of God. Boehme further said that 'The Yes is divine, and the No is the selfness of Nature, that is the perceptibility of the desire. This desire of perceptibility has become a product or work, namely angels. These are nothing else than God's thoughts, according to Love or Anger. . . . The more inwardly anyone can enter into the power of a thing, the nearer he comes to the Deity. . . . in which the two central fires [of Love and Wrath] lie in one ground.' This dual identity, which medieval alchemists called *unus mundus*, is at once a pre-existent pattern and the goal of man's seeking: which is symbolized—as we have noted in reference to Bach's St John Passion and B minor Mass, and to Beethoven's last sonatas and Missa Solemnis—in the double image of the Tree and the Cross. This is found in Druidic rites, in Thor's hammer, on coins and urns of ancient Corinth, Chalcedon, Etruria and Syracuse, and in magic ceremonies in Iceland and Scandinavia, long before its Christianized version asserted the interdependence of Hell, Purgatory and Heaven. In countless manifestations through innumerable ages it has appeared, in dreams and visions and artefacts, as the figure of the mandala wherein, we saw, four corners framing a central point construct, in the form of a cross, an archetype of the Self made whole. Despite the deep distinctions between Bach's Mass and Beethoven's, between the Goldberg Variations and the Diabelli Variations, each carries us to the heart of the same mandala. 'If I know my relation to myself and the external world', said Goethe, 'I call that Truth. And thus every man can have his own truth, and yet Truth is still one.' Bach and Beethoven enfold us in one truth 'By the purification of the motive/In the ground of our beseeching', to call on Eliot's words yet again. Bach purified his motive of the dross of publicly attested guilt; Beethoven purged his of the distortions of privately engendered self-will. Both men testify to the truth defined by Bonhoeffer in his *Letters and Papers from Prison*:

> To be a Christian does not mean to be religious in a particular way, to make something of oneself (a sinner, a penitent or a saint) on the basis of some method or other, but to be a man—not a type of man, but the man that Christ creates in us. It is not the religious act that makes the Christian but participation in the sufferings of God in the secular life. The 'religious' act is always something partial; 'faith' is something whole, involving the whole of one's life. Jesus calls men not to a new religion, but to life.

Both men could have said, with Berdyaev:

> I can see no solution of the betrayal of the world by Christians or of the betrayal of Christianity by the world until history is ended. Only beyond history is there victory for the Kingdom of God and of man.

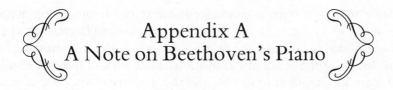

Appendix A
A Note on Beethoven's Piano

'Broadly speaking, Beethoven and the piano arrived in the world together.' So writes Bernard Roberts in his introductory comments to his fine recording of the complete piano sonatas. He percipiently expands this remark by pointing out that, whereas wind and stringed instruments are extensions to man's breathing and limb movements, the piano, a man-made mechanical contrivance, 'is at first an obstacle to flowing musicality'. It is, however, 'earthy, dynamic, and egoistic', and can 'simulate legato, and thus be deeply expressive. It can also suggest things far beyond its nature, and therefore be visionary. Take these descriptions of the piano—firmly on the earth, self-sufficient, egoistic, dynamic, deeply expressive and visionary—and you have a fair characterization of Beethoven himself.' It is not therefore surprising that Beethoven started off as an improvising/composing pianist, and that he should have written for the instrument throughout his life. It was his first musical love, though not his last; and although in his final years he described it as an inadequate instrument, or at least as one less adequate to his visionary explorations than the string quartet, he had, within the pilgrimage of the thirty-two sonatas, embraced the total range of his experience, physical and metaphysical.

Nowadays Beethoven's piano music is usually played on large concert grands, and no one feels this needs justification, since the modern piano is regarded as the fulfilment of Beethoven's pianistic aspirations. There is a sense in which it is true that the Hammerklavier Sonata encouraged the development of an instrument capable of supporting its level of dynamic intensity; one cannot on the other hand assume that the instrument appropriate to mature Liszt and later nineteenth-century composers is the instrument Beethoven envisaged, and there is some reason to think that the fortepianos of Beethoven's day, however inadequate to the idealities of sound in Beethoven's head, approximate to those idealities more closely than do modern instruments.

Twentieth-century editors often admit this in reference to the early sonatas, pointing out, for instance, that the 'muddy' texture in the C major sonata of opus 2 would be more tractable on a fortepiano of around 1800. Editors further inform us that some of Beethoven's pedal effects—we've commented on the *una corda* in the first movement of the Moonlight Sonata, the transitions between *una corda*, *due* and *tre corde* in the adagio of opus 106, and the 'visionary' *una corda* effects in opus 110 and 111—are impossible on a modern instrument. One can now put this to the test, because Paul Badura-Skoda and Jörg Demus have recorded a number of the more significant sonatas on instruments contemporary with the music. Badura-Skoda plays the Moonlight on a Broadwood of 1815, similar to an instrument Beethoven owned. In his performance the preludial adagio sounds less veiled, perhaps less sensuous than on a modern piano, but also far more mysterious, because we hear the sounds on three different planes: the sustained cantabile bass, the rocking triplet arpeggios, and the 'distant horn' melody on top. The colours are distinct, yet intermittently merge, aided by the *una corda* device; this enhances the hallucinatory quality of the music, the hint of depths beneath the waters, lights beyond the horizon: effects which, on a modern grand, tend to be enveloped in a warmly romantic haze. The allegretto comes out as much sharper than on a modern piano. If this makes its dream-like quality less evident, it emphasizes its Edenic innocence; the bagpipe drone of the first half of the trio sounds more bucolic, contrasting with the suavity of the dominant seventh sequences in the second half. But the presto finale provides, on the Broadwood, the biggest surprise, for it sounds far more tempestuously terrifying than on any modern instrument, even though its dynamic level may be lower. Survivals of harpsichord-like sonority, in clattering arpeggios and flickering semiquavers over the dominant pedal, bubble and sizzle in a manner that simultaneously suggests water and fire; the turbulent waters have indeed burst their banks, thunder reverberates and lightning flashes—especially in the shooting scales that follow the barking Neapolitan chords in the approach to the codetta. Here the sound thrills—remembering that the word derives from the Old English *thirl*, which the *O.E.D.* defines as 'to pierce, to run through a body as a sharp instrument does', thereby adding a sexual threat to the note of daemonic, or even demonic, possession. On the fortepiano it seems inevitable that the movement should blow up in its extended coda; the diminished seventh climax in bars 164–6 comes out as a scream. Proportionately, the movement's iron control is the more impressive.

Even more electrifying is Badura-Skoda's performance of the

Appassionata Sonata on a Viennese piano of a slightly later date. Beethoven owned a Graf similar to this 1823 model; only after I had heard this recording did I realize how startling to contemporary audiences the work must have been. Moreover, on this instrument it startles us today, as though we were hearing it for the first time: the deep arpeggios are more cavernous, the hammer-beats more minatory, the thickly syncopated chords more shattering, the arpeggios more lacerating, than on a modern grand, the big, rich tone of which rounds off the corners, sacrificing bite and edge to volume. My first hearing of the slow movement on the Graf, moreover, modified to a degree the account I have given of its nature and function. I think I am right to describe it as song-variations on a tune which, by the standards of the arias in opus 109 or 111, is not remarkably beautiful; none the less the pearly sonority the Graf creates as the divisions flow on suggests, as a modern piano does not, that the Hidden Song, the Voice of God, is latent beneath the apparently rudimentary music. Aria is not consummated, as it is in the late sonatas, but one knows that it is waiting to be born. This makes the shattering of expectancy, in the diminished seventh approach to the finale, the more devastating; and the whirlwind of this movement, sweeping irresistibly to its presto coda, sounds immeasurably more dangerous, and therefore frightening, than it can on a more mellowly even-toned grand. The ghostly pedalling in what Tovey calls 'the death of a hero' passage is inimitable on a modern piano: as are the dissolving pedal effects which are crucial to the last movement of the companion sonata, the Waldstein. That great sonata benefits almost unreservedly from performance on an early nineteenth-century instrument. The accompanying quaver chords of the first movement which, on modern instruments, aggressively chug, on a fortepiano excitedly dance, generating the sense of expectancy which, we saw, was the heart of the work. The mysterious interlude between the first and last movement profits from the fortepiano's tonal variety; and if the rondo tune does not sing with the dreamy ease which is germane to it, the ravishment of the pedal effects provides compensation.

Jörg Demus gives us a rather different but related revelation in his performance of the F sharp major sonata opus 78, on an 1825 Graf now located in the Beethoven house at Bonn. This beautiful transitional sonata, to which Beethoven was justifiably partial, is a lyrical work in only two movements, both fairly fast. The Graf cannot make the cantabile melody of the first movement sing with the radiance to

which we've become accustomed; what it can do more adequately
than a modern instrument is to reveal the dramatic tensions beneath
the apparently unruffled surface. The development, however brief,
thus sounds eventful, as it is; when the dotted rhythm motive enters in
abrupt forte, one realizes how crucial, and accurate, Beethoven's
dynamic markings are. Wonderfully effective too is the contrast
between the broken version of the song-theme in the coda, the darkening of the semiquaver accompaniment as the harmony is chromaticized, and the brightness of the final F sharp major triads. Similarly in
the scherzo-like second movement, dynamic contrasts are more
strongly characterized by the Graf. The alternating-hand semiquavers
glitter like sunlight on water (there is a parallel with the 'leaping
dolphin' passage in the first movement of opus 109); yet they become
mysteriously darkened by what seem to be slight harmonic modifications. Consider, for instance, the sonority the Graf gives to the
alternating semiquavers when, in bars 110–16, they fall instead of rise.
Such darkenings prepare us for the momentary cessation of movement in bars 175–6 of the coda. The dis-ease of the chromaticized
chord survives, after the luminous dominant seventh arpeggio, into
the final statement *a tempo*; the C and A naturals carry, on the Graf, a
distant threat that makes their resolution into F sharp major the more
delight-ful. Beethoven's light is dependent on its awareness of
shadows on the grass: which the 'early' instrument reveals more
subtly than the beautiful but enveloping modern grand.

It was with reference to the sonatas of his third period that Beethoven described the piano as an unsatisfactory instrument. I have
suggested that there is a sense in which any mechanical contrivance
must be inadequate to such music; none the less, now that we can hear
these works played on well-restored or newly created fortepianos it is
becoming clear that 'period' instruments are truer to this music's
heart, as well as to that of the early sonatas. Consider Badura-Skoda's
performance of that difficult transitional sonata opus 101, on a Graf
dated 1823, more or less contemporary with the music. The first
movement sounds less romantically Schumannesque than on a modern
piano; but so of course would Schumann's own music, which was
composed for just such an instrument. Badura-Skoda takes the
movement at a fairly brisk tempo, and sonorities blend less hazily than
on a modern grand, so that it sounds less like the 'sort of dream-like
song' that Beethoven described it as. Yet the music's subtleties are
more telling because the spacing of the parts, in their widely separated

registers, is clearer; the leaping sixths, sevenths and tritones in the
tenor and alto range 'speak' like human voices (listen to bars 16–25), so
the music's romantic intimacy is enhanced. Similarly the dissonances
created by the appoggiaturas in the passage over the subdominant
pedal (bars 38–50) are sharper, so the pain within what might be
mistaken for sensuous indulgence is more acute; the climax on thickly
scored offbeat dissonànces in bars 85–7 sounds almost savage. This
makes the release of the song-phrase into the high register during the
final bars flow with an airy grace. In short, if the romanticism of the
movement is less explicit on the Graf than on a modern piano, its
human substance is more evident. Beethovenian expressivity is the
heart of the matter; what was and remains new in the music is more
accurately manifest on a then contemporary instrument.

The rest of the sonata reveals this more directly. The scherzoid
march comes out spikier, so that the unease beneath its virility is
always manifest. The D flat major passage at bar 30 and the weird
revolving cam in the bass of bars 33–5 sound, in this context, the more
'out of this world', their pedal-haloed sonority contrasting with the
metallic precision of the canonic return at bars 40–5, and the bass's
upsurging scales. The Graf delineates the two-part texture of the trio
with a glassy clarity; it is not exactly ghostly (again Badura-Skoda
takes it very briskly), but it is far from comfortable, holding a precarious balance between the march's contradictory moods of dreaminess
and aggression. The adagio interlude uses the fortepiano's *una corda*
device to glimpse supernatural worlds and, through the cadenza, to
return, *poco a poco tutte le corde*, from the gravelly diminished seventh
over a dominant pedal to the restatement of the 'dream-like song'
which the first movement had started from. This, however, is a dream
from within our earthbound state: which is swept aside by the finale, a
sonata movement crossed with a fugue. Here the Graf is an unqualified
asset. The quasi-contrapuntal textures are cleanly defined, and the
effects of high comedy are complementarily more hilarious. The
'stylus stuck in the record groove' passage (bars 36 ff.) is grotesque; the
cross-bar rhythms of the child-like tune in bars 53–63 are more
gawkily emphasized by the sharp contrasts of dynamics; the *opera buffa*
codetta-tune bubbles over its percussive accompaniment, which the
fortepiano, unlike the modern grand, doesn't iron out. The Graf also
reveals the movement's darker undercurrents: the clotted texture of
canonic parallel thirds and sixths, with sforzando cross-accents,
explodes in a tremendous climax at bars 195 ff., with the thematic

motive tolling thunderously in the deep bass, and splintering in dominant arpeggios. If this makes the transition to the recapitulation at bar 204 more triumphant, it is only momentarily so, for the recapitulation re-enacts its hesitancies, and the coda disperses in fragmentation that fuses the light with the dark elements of this extraordinary movement. On the Graf its ambiguously complex nature is, though far from easy, more intelligible that it is on a modern instrument, which muffles its contrariousness. Surely no one, hearing the last two pages on the Graf, could plausibly maintain that the music's effect is merely merry.

I suggested that the problematical opus 101 was a necessary stage in the approach to the next sonata, opus 106, the climactic work in Beethoven's career as a composer for piano. Badura-Skoda says he blenched at the thought of tackling this work on the kind of instrument which the modern piano, partly because of Beethoven's apocalyptic invention in the Hammerklavier, had been designed to supersede. We can understand his caution, especially since Beethoven himself, hammering at keyboards in an attempt to auralize earlier works considerably less mind and ear-boggling, was apt to leave them looking like birds-nests after a violent thunderstorm. Still, by this time Beethoven was deaf, and never heard what a Graf might have been capable of, if sympathetically handled; listening to Badura-Skoda's performance of the Hammerklavier on this 1824 instrument, we can but gratefully share his surprise at its success. For much of the time it is not merely a success, but also a revelation.

To begin with, the relatively shallow keyboard makes it possible for Badura-Skoda to take the first movement, if not at Beethoven's notorious metronome mark, at least considerably faster than we usually hear it; and to do so accurately, as contrasted with Schnabel's at-tempo version, which is both gabbled and garbled. The pedalling reveals Beethoven's disintegrative textures, which complement the metrical precision of the initial martial motive. The G major textures of the second subject glow, as they flow into the trill-garlanded codetta theme. Perhaps a modern Steinway can make this sound more beautiful; but it cannot approach the Graf in attaining a luminosity that exactly balances the music's darker aspects. This becomes manifest in the development, when the instrument extracts remarkable sonorous variety from the pedalled parallel thirds in dotted rhythm, interspersing the gritty fugato, which is defined with savage precision. That savagery may be precise sounds paradoxical; but we have repeatedly noted that Beethoven is a paradoxical creature, and the phrase seems accurate when, at bar 201, the codetta theme sings in B major-minor through a haze of triplets and quavers, only to be snarlingly rebuffed by the reappearance of the dotted rhythm motive, very loud and very low. Modern instruments cannot emulate these violent contrasts, not merely of dynamics, but also of timbre, since mechanical 'improvements' have been designed specifically to even out the tone-colour. On the Graf we understand why this altercation justifies the notorious enharmonic puns in the approach to the recapitulation. In the coda the contrasts between the silvery flowing scales and the homophonic, dotted rhythmed eruptions are no less pointed. The low trills from bar 385 to the end become awe-ful, a growling of the Tyger, rather than a cavernous reverberation.

The scherzo profits less from the 'authentic' instrument, though its audacious cross-rhythms are more audible, because more precise. The quasi-timpani beats at the beginning of the trio sound more threatening than we are accustomed to, and the prestissimo scale at the trio's end screeches like a knife on glass. The adagio is more problematical. A player on a modern piano can take it more slowly than Badura-Skoda does, and can still preserve a cantabile line, and an even rich sonority in the unfolding harmonies. The music calls for such spaciousness, being simultaneously eventful and apparently immobile. None the less the Graf offers compensations, especially the variety of timbre which can be effected by transitions between *una corda* and *due* and *tre corde*. These transitions are, as we saw in our analysis, clearly indicated in the score; and no modern instrument can compete with the Graf in, for instance, making the transference from the ripe resonance of the D major second subject, powerfully ringing in the bass at bars 45 ff., through the contrary-motion scales beginning at bar 53, to the sudden *una corda* homophony in bar 57, to the *tutte le corde* on a diminished seventh. The enharmonically related mediants in the development (bars 76 ff.), and again in the approach to the coda (bars 145–55), are no less inimitable. The final F sharp major triads sound the more radiant because the Graf has offered so rich a variety of timbres.

The fugue, which we would expect to be most rebarbative on what used erroneously to be considered a primitive instrument, comes off best of all. This is probably because the Graf makes us so vividly aware of the violence of the experiential contradictions on which Beethoven seeks to impose the unity of fugue. Certainly Badura-Skoda encompasses an astonishing variety of timbres and textures in the preludial passage wherein Beethoven 'tries out' different potential answers to the mediant dissolutions that threaten the sonata. The canonic scales sound pearly; the quasi-Baroque two-part invention furiously clatters (bars 20–5); the quasi-operatic cantilena soars over earthy bass dissonances (bars 29–30). The fugue itself Badura-Skoda takes at a frantic pace, yet he delineates it more clearly than is customary on modern instruments. This is partly because the keyboard action speaks more readily, but more because the sonorities can be defined on separate planes. The extreme complexity of the counterpoint, which creates incessant cross-rhythms and metrical interlacings, can be *heard*, though it never sounds easy, because it never is. Throughout, one is thus aware of the uncompromising integrity of Beethoven's acceptance of opposition and contradiction, while simultaneously hearing how his discipline is equal to his violence. The occasional flowing lyricisms (for instance the G flat major episode at bar 75) co-exist with the most savage truculence (for instance the augmented and syncopated theme against sforzando parallel sixths in bars 86–100). Similarly the spitting leaps to the thematic trills complement the wayward hesitancies of the fragmented version of the theme inverted; and the ultimate splintering of the leaping tenths and trills at the climax in bars 230–8 is precisely counterbalanced by the celestial *una corda* episode that follows. The Graf cannot make this sing with the mellifluence we've come to expect from a Steinway or Bösendorfer, and I suspect that the sound we get misrepresents Beethoven's *ideal* intention. On the other hand the return of the original fugue subject, within this lyrical texture, and the gradual destruction of that songfulness, works magnificently, as does the final quivery disintegration over the tiger-growling trills, and the dominant–tonic reaffirmation of the end that is also a beginning. On a modern piano so much variety, complexity and intractability is deadened by the sheer volume of the sonority; on the Graf, because differences may be distinguished, they may also jell. The clotted textures make sense because we can hear them. Though that sense is often terrifying, we know what we are being terrified of, instead of being mowed down by a musical bulldozer.

So the Hammerklavier Sonata, which one might expect to be most inimical to delicate mechanism, and which was certainly one of the reasons why the iron-framed piano was developed, proves a triumphant vindication of the old wooden-framed instrument. With the final triptych of sonatas, profit and loss are more difficult to estimate,

probably because these works enter the 'ideal' world of the late Beethoven's aural imagination, rather than merely storming its portals.
The Hidden Song for which, I have maintained, Beethoven's late
music, perhaps all his music, seeks must, of its essence, *sing*. We know
from his and his friends' comments that even in his early days Beethoven encouraged a cantabile style to a degree at variance with Classical, and behind them Baroque, precedents. By the time he reaches the
hymn-aria that concludes opus 109, the sonata-song that opens opus
110, and the Arietta of opus 111, a singing line with evenly sustained
tone is not merely desirable, but necessary. Having heard these
melodies blooming on a modern Steinway or Bösendorfer, under the
fingers of a Kempff, a Solomon, an Arrau or a Pollini, we are likely to
jib at the unevenness of tone and the intermittent creaks a Graf will
produce in these contexts, and may suspect that Beethoven's im-
patience with the piano in his later years was justifiable.

   Familiarity with the sound of these sonatas on these instruments
will, however, somewhat modify this impression; or at least we'll
come to doubt whether the realization of the sound Beethoven
'ideally' heard for these song melodies is worth the sacrifice of so many
other qualities pertinent to the Beethovenian experience as a whole.
Badura-Skoda has recorded opus 109 on the same 1824 Graf on which
he plays the Hammerklavier. The first movement reveals its contrarieties of Innocence and Experience far more vividly than on a
modern instrument, and this is not merely because the pianist plays it
faster than is customary. The simple harmonies of the first subject's
broken chords shine lucently; complementarily the polyphonic–harmonic intensities of the second subject are more acute. The development, though still at a brisk pace, profoundly fuses 'light' figuration
with 'dark' harmony, so that the 'leaping dolphin' passage at the start
of the recapitulation sounds more dangerous, more electrical (to use
Beethoven's own word), than it does on a modern instrument. Much
the same is true of the coda's tentative approach to a hymnic song,
though here I find Badura-Skoda's tempo too hurried for full effect.
The prestissimo second movement sounds much savager than we are
accustomed to; even though its dynamic level cannot be as great as that
offered by a modern grand, we are more nervously aware of a threat
only just held at bay by the rigour of the form. This is the more pointed
because the *una corda* in the fugato development hints at other worlds
of feeling, the sonority of which, along with the thematic and harmonic substance, is brusquely dismissed at the recapitulation, *tutte le*

corde. The metrical aggression of the stamping coda brilliantly exploits the instrument's percussive qualities.

In the last movement the Graf cannot do justice to the first statement of the sublime song, nor to the *bel canto* of the first variation; and Badura-Skoda's tempo seems to me slightly too hurried, as though he were suspicious of the instrument's powers of sostenuto. The broken arpeggio variations are, however, more limpid than on a modern instrument, and the two-part invention of variation 3 and the miniature fugue of variation 5 sound spikily exciting, with the Beethovenian sense of startlement which later pianos tend to dampen. The whimpering ghost in the second half of variation 4 is weirdly other-worldly; in the final variation the gradual return of the aria, haloed with trills, is an illumination. The sound of the low dominant trill, piercing rather than supporting the treble's sizzling demisemiquavers, is quintessentially Beethovenian. It's like the wrath of God as well as 'the fury and the mire of human veins'. Only when we have been through this purgatorial fire can we deserve the lofty line's slow descent, brokenly limping through the coruscating trills, to the aria da capo. And if that recapitulation does not sound as seraphic as we hope it might, we can this time almost hear it as such in the mind's ear, as did deaf Beethoven. One of the virtues of the early piano is that its variety of timbre stimulates the aural imagination.

Demus has also recorded this sonata on a Graf: the famous instrument of 1825, which is now housed in the Beethoven house at Bonn. This fortepiano was built by the maker especially for the composer, and was presented to him. It was equipped with four instead of three strings, in the hope that Beethoven would be able to hear it. In fact it does not sound louder than the 1824 Graf Badura-Skoda plays, but more confused, and for this reason I find Demus's version less rewarding. Discounting this, however, his approach seems to me sometimes more musically 'inward'. His tempo for the first movement is less hurried than Badura-Skoda's, so that he is able to suggest the embryonic emergence of the 'hymn' in the coda; his prestissimo is not so fast as Badura-Skoda's, but (given the instrument's jangling sonorities) more furious. In the last movement the Song doesn't approach the bloom we now expect of it, though I like Demus's slightly slower tempo better than Badura-Skoda's. The tolling bells and the 'flames of incandescent terror' are still more awe-inspiring on this instrument than they are on Badura-Skoda's; Demus handles the return to the Aria with as close an approach to perfection as we are ever likely to hear, outside the paradise which this music aurally incarnates. It sounds like fluttering feathers on the wings of the Dove; this is a tribute partly to Demus's art, partly to the qualities of the instrument, which can encompass such magical evanescences.

Demus also plays opus 110 on this Graf. The song-like first subject of the first movement sounds more tinklingly Rococo and less idealistically dreamy than I suspect Beethoven would have wished; the demisemiquavers' 'dust-motes in sunlight' are also fiercer than we are accustomed to, though the overlapping figurations that begin at bar 21 glint with a *painful* radiance that is exactly appropriate. There is more pain, too, in the chugging semiquaver bass to the second subject than we hear from a modern instrument: Beethoven's 'thick' bass textures may sound less muddy on a contemporary fortepiano, but are not necessarily less nasty, and here their snarl is the point. The rising and falling semiquavers in the bass of the development also sound slightly sinister on the Graf, especially in contrast with the right hand's guilelessly unchanged repetitions of the opening phrase of the sonata-song: which in context sounds wistful, even forlorn, as though the song hasn't much chance of establishing itself, let alone of growing to full flower. In a sense this is apposite, since the consummation of song is delayed until the coda of the final fugue. Again, the sonorous variety of the fortepiano is attuned to Beethoven's poetic paradoxes, and so tells us something about the music that modern performers often miss. The Graf is not, however, adequate to the movement's lyricism; the haze of enhanced dominants before the coda, and the offbeat return to the tonic in bars 98–105, call for a melting luminosity of which it is incapable, though Demus phrases impeccably.

The scherzo sounds gruffer and bluffer than on a modern piano, the crazy trio more inspired in its tipsiness. The adagio arioso, beautifully paced and spaced by Demus, achieves through pedalling a variety of tone and an intimacy of articulation which cannot be realized on a modern instrument. The arioso line, drooping over the thick semiquaver triplets, loses some of the bloom of song which is latent in it and patent on a Steinway, but compensatorily reveals the pathos of melody which, on Beethoven's own description, is not yet consummated in song, but, as arioso, is halfway between recitative and aria. The songful fugue again needs greater sostenuto and a more cantabile tone than the Graf can give it. On the other hand its relapse back into arioso therefore convinces the more, while the re-emergence a semitone lower of the fugue in inversion is magical since, though the instrument cannot fully sing, it can in *una corda* exquisitely evoke the ghost of a song. The transition back from the ghost of the Hidden Song, by way of the jazzy syncopations and cross-accents (bars 146–67), to the final statement of the Song untrammelled, accompanied by searing semiquavers and thunderous bass, is as revelatory as the final variation of opus 109. A modern instrument must emasculate this conclusion, for the bass, though louder, sounds less cataclysmic and the right hand's arpeggios less bravely brazen. Demus's performance is as magnificent as the music.

Badura-Skoda's version of opus 110 is scarcely less distinguished, and profits from the fact that his 1824 Graf is more limpid than the Bonn instrument. Thus the early-Mozartian Rococo figuration in the first subject sounds luminously Edenic, and the 'soft drum' beneath the dust-motes passage darkens the texture without destroying radiance. In the transition to the second subject, on the other hand, the contrast between the right hand's aspiration and the growling trills in the bass is sharply pointed, the two sonorities being so disparate that they indeed seem to segregate celestial sparkle from earthy mire. Badura-Skoda handles the simple but sublime shift into the development exquisitely; plays the development itself neutrally, which (as we saw) is a possible response; lights up the dominant approach to the coda; and plays the haltingly displaced chords in bars 101–5 with an effectively glassy transparency. Tempi throughout seem to me on the mark, relaxed but not lingering; and if his scherzo is less bucolically fierce than Demus's it perhaps accords better with the temper of the work as a whole. The crazy trio is less precipitately scary than Demus's, but its cross-accents and metrical dislocations are more precise, and for that reason more telling. In the adagio recitative the sonority 'speaks' even more heart-rendingly than on Demus's fiercer instrument. The tempo is beautifully judged, and the fugue subject, as it emerges from the chiming octaves that conclude the arioso, almost persuades us that we are listening to human voices. In this instance the early piano is thus by no means inferior to the modern instrument, nor is it in the fugue's ghostly inversion; in the coda, in Badura-Skoda's performance no less than in Demus's, the contrast between the blaze of the right hand melody and the murky terror of the left hand semiquavers is cataclysmic, truer to the music than any modern piano can hope to be.

Badura-Skoda has recorded opus 111 on the same instrument. Not surprisingly the maestoso introduction and the allegro are effective in much the same way as is this pianist's performance of the Hammer-klavier fugue on this Graf piano. The music's waywardness and fury find a ready response in the instrument's agile action and multifarious sonorities. The 'two-part invention' section crackles and the octave semiquavers scintillate, though Badura-Skoda's rapid tempo hardly allows the (however frustratedly) lyrical second subject to sing. For the same reason, perhaps, the fugato at the beginning of the develop-ment lacks its mysterious expectancy; at the pounding diminished sevenths over a semiquaver-decorated dominant pedal the tempo works powerfully, leading irresistibly into the recapitulation. No modern piano could create this impression of fire and brimstone. In the wonderfully spaced coda Badura-Skoda's tempo again seems to me a shade too fast to allow the top line lyrically to flower; but the final ritardando.is perfectly graded, both temporally and texturally. The instrument's wide range of colour helps: the left hand's tenth creeps into the semiquaver accompaniment with unobtrusive assuagement; the final low C opens unfathomable depths.

The opening statement of the Arietta does not convince: being the most 'ideal' of Beethoven's consummated songs, it calls for, but cannot receive, unremittent sostenuto and complete evenness of tone throughout its concordant texture. The variations do not effect a continuous, unbroken flowing of the waters, though here there are minor compensations: for instance the inner voices and displaced bass of variation 1 which, clearly delineated on separate planes, reveal the music's rhythmic and harmonic subtleties; or the 'dark dove with the flickering tongue' of variation 3, wherein the licking flames sting, as they cannot on the more mellifluous modern grand. In variation 4 the sepulchrally turning earth of the first statement of each half is im-pressive; the ice-glinting repeats bring both profit (in that the demi-semiquavers are impeccably lucid) and loss (in that their clarity tends to deprive them of their aura of the supernatural). The chiming bells in the repeat of the second half are, however, astonishingly evocative, as is the famous chain of trills in the retrospective modulatory middle section. Again it is easier, on the Graf, to control the metrical ambiguities of this passage; and again discipline adversely affects the phantasmagoric quality which seems to us its essence. In the epilogue the left hand's demisemiquaver triplets generate awe as well as excite-ment, for the noise is not merely massively reverberant, but also a bit horrendous. The Graf articulates the two notes of the final, apparently endless, halo of trills far more distinctly than can a modern piano, and this matters, because in Beethoven's paradisal trills motion seems to become immobility and duality to become unity; for this to happen one needs to be aware of duality as a starting point. One has to admit, however, that the more amorphous sonority of the trills on a Steinway makes them sound dreamier, and perhaps therefore to our ears more seraphic. I am not sure whether Beethoven would have thought this more appropriate to his 'ideal' sonority, could he have heard it. In any case historical Ifs are meaningless; we may be romanticizing in preferring our trills to his, but we cannot know what the trills sounded like to him and his contemporaries as they listened to them in *their* historical context.

Demus does not seem to have recorded opus 111. He has, however, recorded on Beethoven's Graf the last set of Bagatelles opus 126; and, as with the sonatas, the lyrical contours of Beethoven's rediscovered, almost folk-like songs are not sustained, and so do not adequately speak, let alone caress. On the other hand the mellowly hymnic sonorities that often accompany these tunes in middle register are deeply affecting. In no. 1 the delicate passage work, interweaving inner parts and miniature cadenzas are beautifully integrated into the whole; in no. 3 the repeated notes of the dominant pedal, beneath the arching tune, acquire a gentle urgency which needs to explode in the little cadenza, exquisitely played *una corda*, after which the tune rings offbeat through the left hand's figuration, beneath the right hand's continuous trill. In no. 4 the scherzo's tight-lipped rhythmic and modulatory surprises contrast sharply with the trio's dreamily droning bagpipes; the other quick piece, no. 2 in G minor, acquires on the Graf an incisive venom, emerging as a piece far more alarming than one had suspected. More subtly, the contrasts of mood as well as of texture in the last piece (no. 6) sound more startling than they do on a modern instrument. The deep rocking triplets in the bass of the A flat section more disturbingly recall the muffled, 'turning earth' sonority in the fourth variation of opus 111's Arietta; and this recollection of sublimity makes the trivial racket of the prelude and postlude seem the more outrageous. It becomes an iconoclastic gesture, comparable in its small way with the cataclysmic coda to the Gloria of the Missa Solemnis: except that its empty-headedness and stony-heartedness are presumably ironic in reflecting the folly of man rather than the foolishness of God.

If, after hearing Demus play the Bagatelles on the 1825 Graf, one listens to Jacob Lateiner's exquisite performance of them on a modern concert grand, or if, after hearing Badura-Skoda's performances of the last five sonatas, one listens to Pollini's justly celebrated recordings, one has to admit that the players of the modern instruments achieve a continuity of line and a *gradation* of tone-colour which seems entirely under their control. The movements are individually shaped and interrelated, so that the ultimate summation in song sounds inevitable. This is a considerable asset, especially in the Arietta of opus 111, where the Song finally sings with a dulcet lucidity approaching that which echoed, we may hazard, in Beethoven's inner ear. Against this one has also to admit that, hearing the 'ancient and modern' performances in proximity, the twentieth-century piano sounds incorrigibly bland. The early nineteenth-century instrument responds to the intensities of Beethoven's experience: which is what one would expect, since it is a product of the Zeitgeist he represents. The modern piano denatures that urgent reality; and even if it offers something resembling the ideality that Beethoven prophetically imagined for his Hidden Song, it misrepresents him in effacing the purgatorial rigours and shocking subversions whereby that ideality was approached.

Taking it all round, one may say that while Beethoven will and should continue to be played on modern instruments, today's pianists can and should learn much from listening to discs such as those of Demus and Badura-Skoda, and still more from themselves exploring the potentialities of adequately restored and newly created forte-pianos. One knows in a general way that Beethoven is a wild composer, with a discipline equal to his audacity. Hearing his music on the pianos for which it was intended makes clear how damagingly his sound has been tamed by modern mechanical techniques, and possibly also by the machine-like dexterity of our performing skills. Having listened to these discs, one hears Beethoven's piano music with new-old ears. This cannot but affect one's modes of performance.

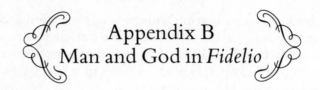

Appendix B
Man and God in *Fidelio*

Opera, being an on-stage imitation of human action, is the most directly social of musical conventions. Since this book is concerned with Beethoven as a religious composer, opera would not seem to be directly relevant to it; and Beethoven completed only one opera, in the middle years of his life, when he was most occupied with the impact of his art on social and political change. None the less *Fidelio* doesn't fit readily into any preordained category of the social arts; it is unlike any other opera, and remains central to Beethoven's experience, profoundly revealing the interrelationships, within his music, between the private and the public life. There is even a sense in which it might be called a religious opera; to explore this sense seems pertinent to our purpose, especially since this book has made several references to *Fidelio*, and to the first act's canonic quartet in particular.

On the surface it is patent that *Fidelio* is a political opera; Beethoven took over Bouilly's stock torment-and-rescue libretto because he knew that it would be recognized by his public as having political implications. None the less, although he was still passionately convinced that the spiritual revolution of his music could and should have social consequences, he also knew that these effects would not be seriously consequential unless they were rooted in transformations of the individual psyche. This is manifest in the fact that the core of the conflict in *Fidelio* is contained in the overtures, especially *Leonora no. 3*, which concerns imprisonment, freedom and enlightenment within the mind and senses; and in the fact that this theme is enriched, not effaced, by Beethoven's relation of the inner struggle to the external world by way of theatrical projection. Admittedly, he found the undertaking arduous; laboured on it long and hard, even by his standards of assiduity; revised and recast it. Given Beethoven's genius, which is a lot to ask for, he none the less emerged victorious, as was his wont. An unsatisfactory medium, that of *opéra comique*, which seems to destroy itself in juxtaposing the naturalism of spoken dialogue with the sublimation of song, becomes revelatory; common life and everyday routine are not obliterated, though Beethoven's music endows them with uncommon grandeur.

In brilliant paradox Beethoven makes the *conventionally* operatic features of his score conformable with the demotic gestures of relatively low types who might be expected to speak rather than sing: so that when they shift gear from one medium to the other there is no disturbing hiatus. Marzelline's lyrical amiability tends to be arch, Rocco's buffo bluffness to be bovine, because arch and bovine is what, in their conforming commonness, they are. It does not follow that they are puppets; they are human beings moulded, and also limited as we all are, by the social prejudices they try to live by. Nor is Pizarro a stock tyrant; it is significant that, although his prisoners, including Florestan, are political, the impetus behind his fury is not political nor even public, but is a consequence of private spite, animated by personal terror: he dare not face the destruction of his public image. As a prose drama the sometimes reviled libretto has much to say about the mesh of public and private motivations, and it strikes home forcefully today. We have met many Roccos, torn between timidity, cupidity, stupidity, and conscience; we may even have been one, pleading that our baser actions were only at the behest of others more highly placed. And although not many of us are as near-psychotic as Pizarro, we have all felt twinges of venom about people whose truthfulness threatens our self-esteem. Even gentle Marzelline, wavering between her 'steady' boy-friend and her unsteady infatuation with the pseudo-boy Fidelio, teeters like most of us between the social role she expects and is expected to play, and wilder feelings she cannot understand and is therefore scared of. So it is not surprising that the opera's action should be inaugurated by that sublime musical wonder: the canonic quartet wherein Marzelline, her father, her ordinary lover and her potentially ideal lover sing an Ensemble of Perplexity, not for risible effect, as in Rossini, but to reveal the soul's solitariness and the human need for love. The softly padding gait, the dove-tailed perfection of the counterpoint, induce a trance that, carrying the protagonists outside Time, hints that there are realms of truth beyond the masks they pathetically or comically present to the world. The deeper irony lies in the fact that at this stage Leonore-Fidelio is literally masked in disguise; the common folk cannot see her for what she is, though it is her truth, and to a lesser degree that of her husband, that is creating through Beethoven's music a world for heroes, or rather for men and women common or uncommon, to live in.

For the tragic characters, Leonore and Florestan, are common only in being without hereditary rights, uncommon in their ability to love and suffer and, like Beethoven, to triumph through their suffering; this makes them *truly* heroic, not in the spirit of High Baroque Glory, but in that of Beethoven's more or less contemporary Fifth Symphony. For these characters Beethoven evolves a new kind of dramatic arioso, incorporating what might have been formal aria into a large-scale symphonic organization. A marvellous example is the duet to which Leonora-Fidelio helps Rocco to dig Florestan's grave. It recalls the first act's Ensemble of Perplexity in that, built over an ostinato figure suggested by the hammering of picks and shovels, it is time-destroying and trance-inducing: out of apparent death, life burgeons. The key, A minor, is significantly the *relative* of the C major in which the opera (like the Fifth Symphony) will blazingly end; both psychologically and musically, rebirth is already in process, through the agency of Fidelio's faith. There is point in the fact that Beethoven's supreme protagonist should be a woman, blessed with the heavenly gift of intuition, as opposed to the patriarchally dominating Will which Beethoven himself so nobly represents yet also transcends, since he knew how, throughout the centuries, it had fashioned the social masks by which we have been simultaneously protected and perverted.

Through the *un*masking of Fidelio's fidelity, Florestan flowers, as his name signifies, from the dungeon's traditionally lugubrious F minor to the resigned acceptance of its A flat major relative, and so to the traditional F major of pastoral sunlight: a long-range tonal effect that would have been inconceivable to a Baroque composer, though not to the Mozart of *The Magic Flute*, a trial-and-rescue opera much admired by Beethoven, with a story similar to that of *Fidelio*, but less realistically presented. The realism of Beethoven's opera should not, however, be overstressed; we accept the Governor's nick-of-time reprieve as allegorically convincing, because regeneration has already happened in the music. His trumpet heralds the dawn of *true* judgement; having the yardstick of convention to measure Leonore and Florestan against, we recognize that their failure to conform is the essence of their (godly) heroism which we, shedding the perfunctory piety, malice or crassness of the minor characters, might hope to emulate. Such is the burden of the prisoners' choruses which, anti-cipating the choral writing of the Ninth Symphony or even of the Missa Solemnis, ultimately irradiates the oppressed homophony of (in their case unwonted and unwanted) conformity with exaltation. The manner is complementary to the wondrously tipsy duet of the liberated and heroically reborn lovers; just as Pizarro's private spleen had been the force driving his public oppression, so at the end the fulfilment of private love transforms and validates the public world. A common-weal(th) is attained, within the mind and potentially within the community of which the chorus, and you and I, are part.

There are three main and tremendous difficulties in achieving an adequate, let alone worthy, performance of *Fidelio*. The first is the hybrid nature of the convention, whereby Beethoven naturalistically tells a tale, while allegorically uttering profound truths about human nature and destiny; the second, related to the first, is the necessity for musical and dramatic command over extremely complex, often contradictory, material developed with the formidable imaginative logic of the mature symphonic Beethoven; the third is the simultaneously vocal and psychological demands made on the singers, and in particular on Leonore, whose role might claim to be the most emotionally, if not vocally, exhausting in the entire operatic repertory. Experience suggests that the opera works if the performers trust Beethoven. The minor characters convince if we admit that their song lives in the same dimension as their speech. Marzelline, when she sings, seems bemused but not broken by the dreadful events she uncomprehendingly lives through; her song may not be sublimatory, but it enables her to go on living. Her father cannot assay her youthfully unlicked lyricism; speaking or singing, he remains fuddled in wary self-interest, his parlando lines and pawky tunes being an inspired re-creation of *buffo* convention. Only Pizarro, among the minor characters, is carried away by a frenzy that, in the spitting virtuosity of his aria of hate, springs irresistibly from the scary words that, in speech, he hisses. Song and the discipline of form are obligatory if his personality is not to disintegrate before our eyes and ears; there is a savage irony in the fact that he, fanatically obsessed with his public image, should channel his aria of destruction into a Baroquely heroic mould. The minor characters' normal mode is speech, which their song does not contradict; Pizarro, a lordly though perverted leader, makes a fallacious pretence of heroism, so his formalized song becomes an ironic gloss on his spoken words. We recognize the nasty veracity of his aria's pyrotechnics, which sound like distinctive human attributes mildewed into inhumanity by the jittery rhythms and flickering diminished fourths. Against his cankered grandeur is poised that of

Leonore and Florestan, genuinely heroic beings, whose normal mode
is therefore song, to which speech is an undercurrent they resort to
when song fails them as they blench at some human's inhumane
depravity. The transitions are as powerful musically as they are
dramatically thrilling; Leonore's speech becomes a kind of recitative, a
further extension of the vocal demands made on her.

It should now be evident that *Fidelio* accords with the theme of this
book, which equates Beethoven's 'religious' experience with a search
for a Song that has been lost or forgotten. In this context the relation
between *Fidelio*'s heroes and villains is subtle. Pizarro does sing, in the
conventionally heroic mode; yet his song is 'placed' by the march that
grotesquely precedes his approach. For the metrical symmetry of the
march's tootlingly footling military arpeggios is oddly displaced,
generating a bizarre glee that, despite the ostensible comedy, embraces
the menace that will explode in Pizarro's aria. He is thereby cut down
to size, but not deflated: which is right, since destruction is never
heroic, but may, as in this case, be awe-ful. Such psychological and
musical depth is the hallmark of Beethoven's genius, at which here, as
at the Missa Solemnis' comparable identification of the forces of light
and darkness, our minds increasingly boggle. What Beethoven does
negatively in the case of villainous Pizarro, he does positively in the
cases of Leonore and Florestan. The public march that introduces
Pizarro's private aria demonstrates the roots of his sadism in an
authoritarianism turned sour and even (since his motivation is mad)
silly. Complementarily, Leonore's intimately fraught speech-
inflexions, her ringing bel canto and her exuberantly whirling color-
atura carry us, through arioso of despair and aria of liberated joy, into
the jubilation of the *O namelose Freude* duet: the private ecstasis of
which leads into the public fulfilment of the corybantic choral finale.
Leonore's vocal quality in the duet should sound superhuman in its
very assertion of humanity, for this metamorphosis is the theme of the
opera. There is even point in the fact that Florestan, both vocally and
musically, finds it hard to compete with her, for this bears on Beethoven's miraculous equilibrium between psychological truth and
material reality. As the patriarchal male Florestan has his nobility:
which must none the less be subservient to Leonore's female, god-
given intuition; and the spiritual dimension is complemented by practical circumstances, for we would hardly expect Florestan, after
months of near-starvation in a fetid dungeon, to emerge with Leonore's pristine fervour! Beethoven's balance between material and

spiritual truth is always exact: as is evident too in the final appearance of the ministerial *deus ex machina*. His line sounds grand enough to act as supernatural angel as well as political agent, yet not so grand as to sully the lustre of Leonore, whose superhuman majesty is the crown of her humanity, as Pizarro's violence is the paradoxical apex of his. Though Leonore's voice is not quite the Voice of God that Beethoven is to hear in the Missa Solemnis and, more intimately, in the last sonatas and quartets, she does herald it. In this sense *Fidelio* is a religious opera, pivotal at the heart of Beethoven's experience.

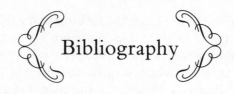

Bibliography

This is not a comprehensive bibliography of books relevant
to Beethoven studies, but a list acknowledging works I have
referred to or quoted from in the text.

Anderson, Emily, ed. and trans., *The Letters of Beethoven* (3 volumes)
(London, 1961)

Breuning, Gerhard von, *Aus dem Schwarzpanierhaus* (Vienna, 1874)

Czerny, Carl, *Über den richtigen Vortrag der sämtlichen Beethoven*
(Vienna, 1963)

Kerst, Friedrich, and Krehbiel, Edward, eds. and trans., *Beethoven the
man and the artist, as revealed in his own words* (Berlin, 1904; New
York, 1964)

Nohl, Walter, ed., *Beethoven: Konversationshefte*, Vol. 1 (Munich, 1924)

Schünemann, Georg, ed., *Beethoven: Konversationshefte*, Vol. 2 (Berlin,
1942)

Schünemann, Georg, *Musiker-Handschriften von Bach bis Schumann*
(Berlin, 1936)

Schindler, Anton, *Ludwig van Beethoven* (Munster, 1927)

Thayer, Alexander, *The Life of Ludwig van Beethoven* (3 volumes)
(Berlin, 1866–79; New York, 1921)

Wegeler, F. G., and Ries, Ferdinand, *Biographische Notizen über Beethoven* (Coblenz, 1838)

Arnold, Denis, and Fortune, Nigel, eds., *The Beethoven Companion*
(London, 1971)

Ballantine, Christopher, 'Beethoven, Hegel and Marx': *Music Review*,
Vol. 33 no. 1 (London, 1972)

Cooper, Martin, *Beethoven: the Last Decade* (London, 1974)

Hamburger, Michael, ed., *Beethoven: Letters, Journals and Conversations*
(London, 1951)

Robbins Landon, H. C., *Beethoven: a Documentary Study* (London,
1970)

Réti, Rudolf, *The Thematic Process in Music* (New York, 1951)

Réti, Rudolf, *Thematic Patterns in Beethoven's Piano Sonatas* (London, 1967)

Rosen, Charles, *The Classical Style* (London, 1971)

Tovey, Donald Francis, *Beethoven* (London, 1944)

Sullivan, J. W. N., *Beethoven* (London, 1927)

Zuckerkandl, Victor, *Sound and Symbol* (New York, 1956)

Zuckerkandl, Victor, *Man the Musician* (2 volumes) (New York, 1973)

Armstrong, John, *The Paradise Myth* (London, 1969)

d'Arcy, M. C., *The Mind and the Heart of Love* (London, 1945)

Austin Baker, John, *The Foolishness of God* (London, 1970)

Boehme, Jacob, trans. J. R. Earle, *On the Election of Grace and Theosophical Questions* (London, 1930)

Bonhoeffer, Dietrich, *Ethics* (London, 1955)

Bosman, Leonard, *The Meaning and Philosophy of Numbers* (London, 1932)

Brophy, Brigid, *Mozart the Dramatist* (London, 1964)

Buber, Martin, *The Eclipse of God* (New York, 1952)

Buber, Martin, ed. and trans. Walter Kaufmann, *I and Thou* (New York, 1970)

Dodds, E. R., *The Greeks and the Irrational* (Berkeley, 1964)

Eliade, Mircea, trans. W. R. Trask, *The Myth of the Eternal Return* (New York, 1955)

Eliade, Mircea, *Images and Symbols* (London, 1961)

Fromm, Erich, *The Anatomy of Human Destructiveness* (London, 1973)

Fromm, Erich, *The Art of Loving* (London, 1957)

Frye, Northrop, *Fearful Symmetry* (Princeton, 1947)

Frye, Northrop, *The Stubborn Structure* (London, 1970)

Jaspers, Karl, *Reason and Existenz* (New York, 1955)

Jaspers, Karl, *Truth and Symbol* (London, 1959)

Jung, Carl Gustav, ed. Herbert Read, trans. R. F. C. Hull, *Aion: Researches into the Phenomenology of Self* (London, 1956)

    Answer to Job (London, 1954)

    Symbols of Transformation (London, 1959)

Jung, C. G., and Kerényi, C., *The Myth of the Divine Child and the Mysteries at Eleusis* (London, 1960)

Laing, R. D., *The Divided Self* (London, 1960)

Lukács, Georg, *Art and Objective Truth* (London, 1970)

May, Rollo, *Love and Will* (New York, 1969)

Miller, E., ed., *God and Reason* (New York, 1970)

Otto, Rudolf, *The Idea of the Holy* (London, 1923)

Rahner, Hugo, *Man at Play* (New York, 1972)

Raine, Kathleen, *Blake and Tradition* (2 volumes) (New York, 1968)

Storr, Anthony, *The Integrity of the Personality* (London, 1960)

Taylor, Thomas, ed. K. Raine and G. M. Harper, *Selected Writings* (London, 1969)

Thomson, Katharine, *The Masonic Thread in Mozart* (London, 1977)

Tillich, Paul, *Dynamics of Faith* (New York, 1957)

Vann, Gerald, *The Water and the Fire* (London, 1953)

Watts, Alan W., *Myth and Ritual in Christianity* (London, 1953)

Wilkins, Eithne, *The Rose-Garden Game: The Symbolic Background to the European Prayer Beads* (London, 1969)

Whone, Herbert, *The Hidden Face of Music* (London, 1974)

Index